Injustice

Injustice

How Politics and Fear

Vanquished America's

Justice Department

Carol Leonnig and Aaron C. Davis

Penguin Press · New York · 2025

PENGUIN PRESS
An imprint of Penguin Random House LLC
1745 Broadway, New York, NY 10019
penguinrandomhouse.com

Designed by Claire Naylon Vaccaro

ISBN 9780593831373 (hardcover)
ISBN 9780593831380 (ebook)

Printed in the United States of America
1st Printing

The authorized representative in the EU for product safety and compliance is Penguin Random House Ireland, Morrison Chambers, 32 Nassau Street, Dublin D02 YH68, Ireland, https://eu-contact.penguin.ie.

For John, Elise, and Molly

For Nicole, Alex, and Emilia

No free government can survive that is not based on the supremacy of law

—Inscription chiseled on the Justice Department building in Washington, D.C.

CONTENTS

Authors' Note *xiii*

Introduction *xvii*

Part One

[1] A Righteous Prosecution? *3*

[2] Was Trump Beholden to Egypt? *13*

[3] A Trusting Mueller and a Failure to See the Endgame *21*

[4] Where Did the $10 Million Go? *33*

[5] "I'm Pretty Sure I'm Getting Indicted Today" *39*

[6] Forced Out *48*

[7] A "Very Unfair Situation" *55*

[8] "Truth Still Matters, OK?" *63*

[9] Winners Write the History *66*

[10] Sowing Chaos *73*

[11] "He's Asking You to Be Wild" *81*

[12] "A Hot Mess"   *89*

[13] January 6   *101*

Part Two

[14] An Early Distraction for Investigators   *119*

[15] A Prosecutor's Plan Is Batted Down   *135*

[16] Family Feud   *143*

[17] Unmoved by Trump   *161*

[18] Hill Investigators Find "the Scheme"   *171*

[19] The Lone Prosecutor   *183*

[20] "I'm Not Subpoenaing the Friggin' Willard"   *189*

[21] One Year Later   *197*

[22] "Weapon Left at the Crime Scene"   *203*

[23] A New Matter   *211*

[24] Operation "Arctic Frost"   *220*

[25] "I Don't Want Anybody Looking Through My Boxes"   *232*

[26] House Investigation Blindsides DOJ   *248*

[27] Family Feud—Part II   *261*

[28] No Choice   *279*

Part Three

[29] Existential Threat   *293*

[30] Great Story, Not a Great Case   *314*

[31] "The President Is Now a King"   *327*

[32] "The Judiciary Failed"   *346*

[33] Servare Vitas   *360*

[34] Sign, Quit, or Get Fired   *385*

[35] "At the Directive of Donald Trump"   *402*

Acknowledgments   *419*

Notes   *423*

Index   *457*

AUTHORS' NOTE

Displayed on a wall in the center of *The Washington Post* newsroom are six gold medals, one from each time its reporters have won the highest honor bestowed in American journalism, the Pulitzer Prize for Public Service. The first, awarded in 1973, honored the newspaper's investigation of Watergate and a president's corrupt use of his office. It now hearkens back to a fixed point in American history, when the country collectively endured and processed a profound scandal, with the vast majority of Americans agreeing this marked a distressing low point for the nation.

The Pulitzer board granted us and our colleagues the most recent medal for coverage of the attack on the U.S. Capitol on January 6, 2021. Their announcement said our reporting had provided the public with "a thorough and unflinching understanding of one of the nation's darkest days." But in the few short years that have elapsed, it's grown hard to walk by the wall of medals without questioning how the country's memories splintered so sharply, and why, unlike so many historic events methodically reported by our newsroom, many Americans had rejected the reality of January 6.

We set out to write this book in the summer of 2023, intent on building on our *Post* reporting about how the Justice Department was a central character—and punching bag—in the country's growing division. We had uncovered new and gripping details about how several actors and forces had manipulated, outmaneuvered, and weakened the department, an anchor of American democracy. We learned the Justice Department had hesitated to formally begin investigating if then former President

Trump and those around him had been criminally culpable for setting the day's violence in motion. Trump, meanwhile, filled the vacuum and began to rewrite the history of that day with his diehard supporters eagerly following suit.

We saw January 6 as neither a starting point nor an ending point, but the middle of a much bigger story. We needed to understand how the people of the vaunted U.S. Justice Department had come to seemingly quake at investigating Donald Trump, even after he had fomented a crowd to march on the Capitol. We found that Trump's previous assaults on the rule of law and attempts to make the Justice Department a tool for his political benefit shaped so much of what came after. Today, Donald Trump is president again and the state of the country has arrived at this contentious moment because of the events recounted in this book. Our reporting on his new administration's rejection of the rule of law and other sacred norms offers a signpost of where the United States is likely heading. Whether you like or dislike what the Justice Department is doing under Trump in his second term, many inside the department fear a cycle has begun of mixing politics and prosecutions that will fundamentally change justice in America for decades to come.

This book is the product of rigorous, careful reporting and interviews with more than two hundred and fifty people, including senior officials in the Trump and Biden administrations, government prosecutors, and federal agents as well as outside advisers who were firsthand witnesses to one of the most devastating and challenging periods the Justice Department has faced in its history. Many of the people who spoke to us agreed to share their full accounts only on the condition that we not name them because they feared damage to their careers or retribution from those angered by their candor.

But we never took just one person's word for it. We are objective journalists who seek to determine the truth and to report it to the public as closely as we can ascertain. We reconstructed scenes in this book based on multiple independent accounts of participants, principals, or others who had been made aware of the events. Whenever possible, we corroborated accounts with government records, reports, court transcripts, contemporaneous notes, or other documentation, including texts, emails, screenshots, and slideshows.

People do not generally record their conversations in daily life, so dialogue cannot always be exact. But the dialogue we reconstruct here is largely based on the memories of participants and efforts to corroborate with others who were present.

To reconstruct events that played out in public, we relied upon video, as well as news reports, books, and government records. We credit those prior works in our endnotes. Building on the work of so many great journalists, we offer this new, rich history hidden behind the headlines and stories you thought you knew. Thank you for reading.

INTRODUCTION

For more than seventy years, the U.S. Department of Justice has each fall chosen a crop of outstanding law school graduates to join its ranks through a recruitment effort called the Attorney General's Honors Program. The competition has long been intense, with the department recently welcoming only about one hundred of the several thousand who applied. Since the administration of President Dwight D. Eisenhower, the program has successfully mentored the next generation of lawyers to faithfully execute the department's mission and come to personify its core values. That righteous mission is threefold: to enforce the laws of the country fairly and impartially, to keep the country safe from domestic or foreign threats, and to protect Americans' rights as citizens, even from the actions of the government and the department itself. No federal agency more fully embodies the principles of American freedom and fairness. And no employees within the executive branch carry more responsibility than those of the Justice Department to uphold and defend the founding principles enshrined in the U.S. Constitution.

The newly deployed recruits have often found their employer's expectations inspiring—and daunting. They learn DOJ lawyers and agents have a duty to be fair and consistent in using the department's immense powers to investigate and punish crimes, without regard for the wealth or clout of the suspect. They also must be painstakingly truthful, admitting any mistake and candidly sharing key facts they have gathered, including those that weaken their case and aid a suspect's defense.

Department veterans warn the prosecutors-in-training of Justice's past failures to be transparent and impartial. Such violations risk undermining public confidence in the justice system, leading witnesses to refuse to cooperate, the guilty to escape consequences, and crime to rise. Supreme Court Justice George Sutherland captured that lofty charge in a 1935 opinion when he admonished an assistant U.S. attorney for misleading a jury to secure a conviction. Every federal prosecutor, he wrote, "is the representative not of an ordinary party to a controversy, but of a sovereignty whose obligation to govern impartially is as compelling as its obligation to govern at all; and whose interest, therefore, in a criminal prosecution is not that it shall win a case, but that justice shall be done."

Through the passage of decades, Justice has become a living, breathing organism of dedicated public servants yoked together to uphold these shared values in Republican and Democratic administrations. They pledged to keep Justice blind and impartial—and independent from political influence. They agreed that the facts and the law would guide their decisions on whether to charge a suspect or drop a prosecution when the evidence warranted.

The department's political independence, however, was never protected under law, but instead flourished through American presidents' shared respect for this core precept. Each president chose their attorney general and other top leaders as political appointees who ultimately answered to him. But since the department's founding amid the ashes of the U.S. Civil War, each president historically honored Justice Department leaders' autonomy to enforce the laws free from his, or his political party's, meddling.

But as America neared its 250th birthday, that all changed when the Department of Justice collided violently with Donald Trump in his rise to power, and for the first time in history, our nation's rule of law was brought to the precipice of collapse.

This is the epic story of how the public servants and top leaders of the Department of Justice were tested and battered by a president who manipulated facts, fanned conspiracy theories, and flouted the law. It shows for the first time how their actions and inactions, often well-intentioned, helped pave a path for Trump's reascendance, and his eventual unraveling of the department's core mission.

It is a story of gutter politics and honor, hubris and bravery, intransigence and naivete, and of a battle waged over the Founders' promise of fair treatment under the law. It is a tragedy in three acts, told from the rooms where it happened.

In the first, a novice President Trump tries to manhandle the power of the Department of Justice for his own political gain, to shield himself and his allies and then to punish and harass his political enemies.

In the second act, new leaders installed by President Joe Biden atop the Department of Justice arrive to wrestle with one of the greatest crimes against democracy in American history: an attempted coup fomented by Trump as he sought to overturn Biden's victory. This is also the fullest account to date of how the department launched a belated and ill-fated election-interference investigation under pressure from an aggressive congressional probe, and that investigation's stunning discoveries. At the same time, the department juggled undeniable evidence it uncovered that the former president hoarded and likely tried to conceal top-secret documents, crimes for which others had been court-martialed and imprisoned.

The third act provides the first authoritative reporting on the secret inner workings of Special Counsel Jack Smith's probe, and how his team raced to complete their unprecedented and high-stakes assignment. Through delays and miscalculations, and the foot-dragging of the Supreme Court, the country's justice system failed the American people by denying a jury the chance to decide if Trump was guilty of his alleged crimes before he won back the White House. In the final chapters, we show the wholesale overthrow of the Justice Department as Trump inserts his dutiful former defense attorneys and 2020 election deniers atop the department. We take readers into the meetings where those loyal Trump lieutenants set about disemboweling the department that just months before had assembled what investigators considered ample evidence to send Trump to prison. Disregarding the department's careful system of using a high threshold of evidence to determine when to pursue a possible crime, Trump signed executive orders directing his DOJ to investigate his first-term critics; to blacklist law firms who employed attorneys who challenged him; to investigate Democrats' online fundraising; and then, to investigate whether Biden himself was mentally competent, a potential first step to nullifying thousands of pardons and other actions his predecessor took while in office. Trump's DOJ appointees, meanwhile, scoffed at calls to investigate Trump's defense secretary when he mistakenly shared classified U.S. war plans with a reporter on an unsecure messaging app. They defended handcuffing a Democratic U.S. senator for interrupting a news conference, and federal immigration officers for arresting a Democratic member of congress and local lawmakers in New York and New Jersey, claiming they interfered with arrests. Trump's DOJ also defended the president federalizing thousands of National Guard soldiers as military backup for immigration raids in Los Angeles. In July, amid Trump's efforts to quash news coverage about his long connection to Jeffrey Epstein, his intelligence director made unsubstantiated claims that former President Barack Obama sought to undermine Trump's first presidency; the Justice Department promptly announced an investigation. Weeks later his administration seized control of the D.C. police department, with Trump claiming a crime emergency in the nation's capital. His appointees ordered hundreds of Guard troops and federal agents into the streets, where they set up nightly checkpoints and made arrests.

As investigative journalists for *The Washington Post*, we began the reporting that would form the basis for this book three years ago. We had each previously covered aspects of Trump's first term, after he won the White House in an upset and then proceeded to shatter almost every norm of the presidency, up to and including the ending of America's two-century-long streak of peaceful transfers of executive power. By 2022, we had spent months extensively reporting on the causes and costs of the January 6 attack and were following a tip that would lead to a significant revelation about how the Justice Department had hesitated to investigate Trump. The information panned out, as we found that most of a year had elapsed after the attack before a lone federal prosecutor in D.C. was assigned to open a fledgling probe. Several more months passed, we found, before FBI agents later agreed to join the effort.

As we dug in to understand the delays, we found an FBI workforce still shell-shocked from its run-ins with Trump during the investigation into Russian meddling from his first campaign for president. For them, the story of the Justice Department's disastrous entanglement with presidential politics had begun earlier, four months before the 2016 election. That was when FBI Director James B. Comey had called a surprise news conference to announce—without the attorney general or DOJ prosecutors—the Bureau's findings from a federal criminal investigation into a private email server kept at the home of Democratic presidential candidate Hillary Clinton during her time as secretary of state. Though Comey said he broke protocol to preserve public trust that the department made its decision free from politics, many inside and outside the department felt his comments likely swayed the election, something DOJ had a core duty to avoid.

Over the next four years, Trump attacked and belittled the Justice Department to minimize the political fallout he faced from the Russia investigation. He cast the case as a sneak attack by liberals and the "deep state" to thwart his presidency. He pushed Justice into uncharted territory, firing Comey for refusing to publicly clear him of wrongdoing, and then threatened to fire Special Counsel Robert S. Mueller III after he was appointed to take over the investigation. Trump convinced millions of Americans that the Republican former head of the FBI was leading a "witch hunt" with a band of "angry Democrats" to get him. He pressured "his" DOJ to target and prosecute his political foes.

Cumulatively, Trump's actions amounted to an assault on the rule of law by the nation's chief executive unlike any the country had experienced since President Nixon in the 1970s. At the Justice Department, the barrage landed like waves of a storm eroding a beach. Line prosecutors and agents despaired, watching somewhat helplessly as Trump tried to wield the department as his cudgel and publicly attacked them and their colleagues by name, battering reputations and careers.

Enter Attorney General Merrick Garland. The careful and thoughtful appellate court judge with impeccable ethics arrived to lead the Justice Department with a noble goal: restore trust in the department.

Under Garland, the U.S. Department of Justice would soon cede to local prosecutors in Georgia an investigation into Trump's effort to overturn the state's election results, despite public evidence that included a tape-recorded call in which the sitting president threatened a Georgia election official that he had to "find" Trump enough votes to win the state. The department also passed initially on investigating fake elector documents that public reporting had linked to the Trump campaign's effort to block the certification of Biden's victory on January 6. Garland, who had not worked as a prosecutor since Bill Clinton was president, methodically considered decisions, much as he had over nearly a quarter century on the bench. He insisted that prosecutors and agents mostly work upward and outward from the violence caught on camera at the Capitol. Doing so, he said, would prove to be the most defensible path for any investigation should one lead to politicians or even the White House.

With limited hindsight, it's clear that Garland's approach failed to meet the moment. Garland was fond of another maxim—"The essence of the rule of law," he would say, "is that like cases are treated alike." But when it came to January 6, there was no *like* case to weigh against. That Trump had sought to blot out the result of a democratic election and set the stage for a riot was unprecedented. Garland and others erred in thinking Trump's political career had ended with the riot and he could never convince voters to return him to power. It turned out Garland and the Justice Department had but a fleeting moment to try to hold Trump accountable for his assault on democratic norms before the organization would be forever changed.

On the campaign path, Trump successfully converted dozens of criminal charges eventually levied against him into his most powerful argument for his reelection in 2024. After the Special Counsel's Office indicted Trump in the summer of 2023 for election interference and concealing classified records, Trump told a right-wing evangelical audience he was the victim of Biden's "weaponized law enforcement" and considered the charges a "great badge of courage."

"I'm being indicted for you," he said.

Polls showed that Trump successfully cast himself as a martyr for conservative America. Republican support for his return to the White House rose markedly after he was criminally charged, from 55 percent of party voters endorsing his reelection in the spring to 63 percent that August. In a cynical twist, Trump falsely accused Democrats of intentionally waiting to investigate until he was a candidate so as to torpedo his reelection chances.

The story of Donald Trump's rise, his fall, his resurrection, and now his unprecedented consolidation of power over the country in his second term cannot be told without understanding the pressures, both internal and external, that have buffeted the Department of Justice. Almost every step of Trump's march included him falsely and repeatedly accusing his political enemies of wielding the department as a "rigged" and corrupt political tool. He has helped create a self-fulfilling prophecy. Instead of a nation of laws, in which all expect to be treated equally, Trump's America is well on its way to becoming a nation where might makes right.

Amid Trump's purge of so many experienced career prosecutors and agents immediately after he retook the White House, his appointees also rescinded offers for the entire incoming class of Honors Program students. Days later, they canceled all two thousand Justice internships for the coming year, choking off the department from its well of bright minds and renewal among its ranks. Instead, new hires and political appointees for top Justice jobs faced a new, jarring test: They were asked if they had voted for Trump and would be loyal to him.

As Trump neared one hundred days back in office, Judge Harvie Wilkinson, a stalwart conservative judge serving for four decades on the

United States Court of Appeals for the Fourth Circuit, scolded the Trump administration, writing that it had flouted the country's sacred due process protections in sending immigrants to foreign prisons. Wilkinson sounded a pleading note, asking Trump and his aides to take heed of the danger he was courting with this rejection of the law. If his administration continued on this path, the public would begin to rightly see the government as lawless and the "law in time will sign its epitaph."

"We yet cling to the hope that it is not naive to believe our good brethren in the Executive Branch perceive the rule of law as vital to the American ethos," Wilkinson wrote. "This case presents their unique chance to vindicate that value and to summon the best that is within us while there is still time."

Part One

[1]

A Righteous Prosecution?

In 2018, a week before Thanksgiving, Kamil Shields and David Kent—two federal prosecutors who worked in the U.S. Attorney's Office for the District of Columbia—were losing sleep over high-level interference in their criminal case. It was shocking to them, they confided to colleagues, but the person imperiling a fair prosecution was their ultimate boss, the president of the United States.

Outside the legal community, the work of federal prosecutors such as Kent and Shields has often not been well understood. They were cogs in a network of ninety-three U.S. Attorney's Offices, which fan out across the country from the Department of Justice's main headquarters in Washington, D.C. Together, the attorneys in those offices form a field army that, since President George Washington's first appointments to such posts, has been charged with carefully investigating crimes and pursuing justice on behalf of the U.S. government. Shields and Kent were on the front lines, and their assignment was among the department's most sensitive. Secretly, they were probing one of the government's highest-ranking law enforcement chiefs, Andrew McCabe, who had recently departed as second-in-command at the Federal Bureau of Investigation.

As if the case wasn't fraught enough, the occupant of the Oval Office was ratcheting up the stakes, and the stress level, for the prosecutorial team. Since his surprise victory in the 2016 presidential election, Donald Trump had become locked in an increasingly tense standoff with leaders of the Justice Department, the traditionally rigorous executive branch agency. The FBI, the investigative arm of the department, was the lead federal agency responsible for identifying and interrupting threats to national security. In fulfilling that role, its agents had been probing unusual contacts between Trump's campaign advisers and the Russian government before the election, but the new president had abruptly fired James B. Comey when the FBI director refused to bend to Trump's pressure to either shutter the probe or publicly exonerate him. The dramatic removal, less than four months into Trump's arrival in the White House—and six years before Comey's ten-year term was set to expire—prompted McCabe to open an investigation of the president. It also compelled DOJ leaders to appoint an independent special counsel to take over the Russia investigation and to determine if, by removing Comey, the president had intended to obstruct that probe. In social media posts, Trump had repeatedly blasted the ongoing investigation led by Special Counsel Robert S. Mueller III, the widely respected former FBI director. Trump questioned why Democrats and their sympathizers should not also be subject to federal investigations, and McCabe was one of the president's top targets. In Trump's view, McCabe sat alongside the ranks of Hillary Clinton, Comey, and others whom Trump labeled as criminals.

McCabe had, in fact, erred. He had initially given investigators a false account of his role in leaking information to the press. That was why he was no longer the current FBI deputy director. But the president wasn't supposed to decide if that wrongdoing rose to the level that it should be prosecuted criminally. In fact, he should have steered far clear.

Under a system of guidelines and case reviews honed over more than a century—and then tightened significantly following the Watergate scandal—the Justice Department had a tried-and-true method for deciding whether to criminally prosecute a U.S. citizen. That careful review process had made the Justice Department a beacon for democracy worldwide. And that was in no small part because every time, deep in the bureaucracy, the real work of evaluating a case began with attorneys like Shields and Kent. They were among a class of career attorneys who did their jobs year in and year out, under Republican presidents and Democratic ones, insulated from politics and expected to focus on the facts of a case and how the law applied given each particular set of circumstances. Often, attorneys drew cases based solely on merit and the track record they had amassed in successfully representing the government. Kent, forty-six, had spent most of his legal career in the D.C. office, investigating and indicting the architects of complex crimes and frauds. Peers viewed him as having a thoughtful legal mind. A Stanford Law graduate, he pored over the details and precedent of his cases. His coworkers in the esteemed Fraud and Public Corruption Section, which handled some of the office's toughest cases, considered him a mensch and "a good soldier." In other words, he didn't shy away from problem cases.

Shields, forty, had been on the government staff for nearly five years, primarily prosecuting cybercriminals who had stolen money or secrets by hacking. A Harvard undergrad and Yale Law School graduate, she had been rated a rising star at the prestigious New York firm Sullivan & Cromwell but left before making partner. Not long after becoming a prosecutor, she and her husband had welcomed their first child, a boy.

The two were what are known as line attorneys, due to their position on the front lines in upholding the nation's laws. They partnered with FBI agents to gather the facts of a case, and when they found evidence of serious crimes, they presented it to a grand jury that met in secret. When a jury agreed with the prosecutors that a suspect's acts merited criminal charges, it handed down an indictment, and the line attorneys proceeded to argue for conviction in court. At key steps along the way, they had to answer to layers of supervisors and section chiefs above them. Those checks repeatedly stress-tested the facts of a case and allowed for healthy second-guessing as to whether prosecutors had properly applied the law. Shields, Kent, and their colleagues in the D.C. office—one of the largest and most prestigious in the country—paused before bringing major charges, gathering in a conference room stuffed with well-worn chairs to "murder" one another's draft prosecution memos. Fellow prosecutors would sit around for hours, attempting to attack a proposed argument as a defense attorney or a judge might in hopes of preemptively identifying flaws that could doom the government's quest for justice.

Like so many of their colleagues, Shields and Kent took pride in not just winning convictions but hewing closely to the Justice Department's strict guidelines for impartial decision-making. Both accepted a fraction of the compensation available at private law firms because of the sense of mission and, candidly, the excitement that came with defending the rule of law. Countless federal prosecutors over the years had eventually moved on to jobs in politics, policy, or even plum gigs in private practice, only to wistfully recall their days on the line for the government. There was nothing quite like running a federal investigation, protecting the public, and having the license to go after bad guys no matter how powerful. The work was a calling.

Nine months earlier, in February 2018, Shields had been a little surprised when her supervisors had assigned her and Kent to investigate McCabe, who for a time after Comey's firing had risen to acting director of the FBI. The prosecutors were tasked with reviewing evidence that he had lied to federal agents about the leak of investigative information to a newspaper. A criminal probe of such a senior public official would normally be handled exclusively by the Fraud and Public Corruption Section. A supervisor in that division had decided Shields would be a good fit for the assignment, but she wondered aloud if he had pulled her into the McCabe investigation because no one else was willing to take it on. For much of 2018, Trump had roared that his Justice Department must fire McCabe. His demand had laid bare that the independence and integrity of the Justice Department, foundational goals when Congress created the executive branch agency in 1870, rested almost entirely on whether the elected occupant of the White House faithfully executed their oath of office to preserve and protect the Constitution.

In the five decades since Watergate, the notion of a president pushing the department to prosecute an individual American had become implausible, laughable even, to federal prosecutors. The department's informal motto was to pursue justice "without fear or favor." After President Nixon had resigned in disgrace, Congress had enacted reforms, and Justice had strengthened its code of conduct to try to prevent another president from misusing the immense power of the department. But Trump spoke of the Justice Department as an impediment to his agenda, and as lacking a key ingredient to his liking: loyalty to him. That summer, Trump's adviser Steve Bannon was explicit in a closed-door meeting with special counsel attorneys and FBI agents. Trump, he said, viewed a good attorney general and Justice Department attorneys as "people who really protected their president."

Since early summer, Shields and Kent had been trying to ignore the president's comments about McCabe, they told colleagues. They just wanted to follow the normal painstaking steps in making a case, calling witnesses to testify before a grand jury that was meeting at a federal courthouse near the U.S. Capitol. Bit by bit, they had assembled evidence indicating that McCabe had withheld information from federal agents. Still, the two prosecutors told colleagues they had serious doubts about whether the Justice Department should proceed. It wasn't clear the U.S. government could win in court, and primarily for one unusual reason: Trump's public statements and potentially other actions by the White House could backfire and kill the case. The president's cries that McCabe had "committed many crimes!," as well as his all-caps tweets demanding McCabe's imprisonment, could lead a jury to see the prosecution as politically motivated. They also had reason to fear a potential "ticking time bomb" of broader White House interference that could upend the case in embarrassing fashion.

Heading into the Thanksgiving holiday, however, they faced a deadline.

J. P. Cooney, an aggressive prosecutor who had recently been promoted to chief of the Fraud and Public Corruption Section, told Shields and Kent that it was time to give him a "CIM," a case impression memo, summarizing the strengths and weaknesses of charging McCabe. The two were fast approaching the line in the American criminal justice system that every prosecutor must decide whether to cross—and then live with afterward—to prosecute or not?

Federal prosecutors are trained to wield their enormous power—to poke into a person's bank accounts or survey their phone contacts—with care. Long before any charge, a single subpoena for information can forever tarnish an innocent person's reputation. And then, when prosecutors know they have the goods to prove the elements of a crime, they must weigh whether the costs of bringing the charges are worthy and will serve the greater cause of justice and the rule of law. So fraught is the decision that the Justice Department maintains a twenty-three-thousand-word *Principles of Federal Prosecution*—a bible of sorts for its attorneys to consult about when to prosecute or not.

Shields and Kent believed that McCabe had initially withheld the full truth about his role two years earlier in directing information to *The Wall Street Journal,* they told their colleagues. They had established that McCabe had instructed Lisa Page, an FBI attorney and his legal adviser, to confirm to a reporter the existence of an investigation into then presidential candidate Hillary Clinton's family foundation—and in a way that described McCabe as supporting several field offices pressing forward on this politically sensitive probe. The story stood to benefit McCabe, an internal watchdog found, by countering complaints from some right-wing pundits and conservative FBI agents that McCabe was conflicted because of his wife's ties to a Democratic donor close to Clinton who had supported her failed run for a state senate seat. After the story ran, however, investigators said McCabe had given his boss, Comey, as well as others, the impression that he didn't know the source of the leak. Initially, McCabe also gave an inaccurate account to investigators, but days later called them to say he had been distracted when they first spoke and now thought he might have authorized a deputy to talk to a reporter.

Making a false statement to an investigator is a federal offense—a 1001, as it's known. The FBI academy drills into agents that, if the government is going to hold anyone to account for mistruths, a sin that can upend the work of solving a crime, it will be them. Yet Kent and Shields felt intense unease about seeking an indictment.

Over that sleep-deprived Thanksgiving weekend, the two wrote and rewrote the CIM, spelling out the challenges of indicting McCabe amid Trump's white-hot pressure campaign, in which he often conflated the McCabe probe with Mueller's Russia investigation. "Universities will someday study what highly conflicted (and NOT Senate approved) Bob Mueller and his gang of Democrat thugs have done to destroy people. Why is he protecting Crooked Hillary, Comey, McCabe . . . and all of his friends on the other side," Trump ranted on November 15, the Thursday before Thanksgiving. Upon returning to work, Shields and Kent shared their memo—and their reservations—with Cooney, their new boss.

Shields and Kent had closely studied the reactions of the grand jury hearing the McCabe case, something prosecutors do to "read" the jurors for doubts or concerns to better tweak or hone their arguments. Prosecutors are legally prohibited from publicly discussing what happens in a grand jury, but word of their CIM and briefings with supervisors circulated in the office. Shields told Cooney the jurors had had very strong and sympathetic reactions to key FBI witnesses who worked with McCabe. Lisa Page, the lawyer and former counselor to McCabe, had laid bare to the grand jury critical weaknesses in a potential prosecution of the FBI leader. She explained that McCabe had a terrible memory for the high volume of cases and decisions that crossed his desk, and frequently had to be reminded by his notes or aides. Importantly, Page also shared that McCabe had no practical reason to lie about or hide what he had done; he was one of the few FBI officials explicitly authorized to communicate with the press. What's more, the FBI's chief press officer had also forgotten McCabe's instructions to share probe information with a reporter when he was questioned. Yet the press officer wasn't being eyed for charges of lying to investigators. The jury clearly liked Page, Shields explained, and watched her with pathos and rapt attention as she recounted the personal toll of Trump's attacks. Page had broken down in tears describing how she felt she had let McCabe down when her internal texts were collected and revealed she had been having an affair with another FBI official, Peter Strzok. Page and Strzok were public figures by this point, after disparaging remarks they had privately shared about Trump being an "idiot" and other personal messages were turned over to Congress and reported on nationally. Trump had subsequently crusaded against them, often vilifying the two as liberals who had helped launch a "Rigged Witch Hunt" to hobble his presidency. He repeatedly called on Congress and other authorities to "Investigate the Investigators."

Shields and Kent stressed to Cooney that they couldn't undo Trump's relentless campaign to disparage McCabe—which by then tallied more than fifty public statements. Shields concluded that Trump's pressure campaign on the department to prosecute McCabe had, ironically, likely wrecked their chance to win a conviction. Shields also noted that the department's manual encouraged government attorneys to go forward with charges only if they believed a "person will more likely than not be found guilty . . . by an unbiased trier of fact."

But Cooney wanted to come out swinging at McCabe and told the prosecutors they had strong evidence of a top law enforcement official lying. Cooney had personally assigned a trusted, favorite prosecutor, Molly Gaston, to join Shields and Kent on the high-profile case, and his natural inclination to charge came as no surprise. Anyone who had known Cooney since his law school days at the University of Virginia in the early 2000s—staying up late to prep for moot court, then, in his booming voice, crushing opponents—knew he could be quick to flash a warm smile but was zealous in applying the law. To many admiring classmates and colleagues, Cooney had in his first decade out of college at the Department of Justice come to exemplify much of what Attorney General Robert H. Jackson had once famously articulated in a 1940 speech as the traits of an ethical prosecutor: Cooney was aware of the power that came with his post and didn't mind wielding it to right society's wrongs. "The prosecutor," according to Jackson's speech, which is taught in law schools nationwide, "has more control over life, liberty, and reputation than any other person in America. . . . At his best [he] is one of the most beneficent forces in our society, when he acts from malice or other base motives, he is one of the worst." If there was an area where Cooney was still maturing, however, it was learning how to apply another of Jackson's virtues: temperance. "What every prosecutor is practically required to do is to select the cases for prosecution and to select those in which the offense is the most flagrant, the public harm is the greatest, and the proof the most certain. . . . The citizen's safety lies in the prosecutor who tempers zeal with human kindness." If Cooney had a bias, some would say, it was to indict. He didn't care whose political ox was being gored. He went for the throat when he thought there was a solid criminal case to be made. It was the model he wanted to emulate, from another no-nonsense prosecutor, for whom he'd worked early in his career in Justice's Public Integrity Section, Jack Smith.

"I love him, but J. P. would indict his mother for a '1001'—in a heartbeat," a colleague said of the false statement charge.

When it came to McCabe, Cooney wasn't convinced they would lose. And even if the odds of winning were low, he reminded Shields and Kent of the righteousness of this potential prosecution.

In the parlance of Justice Department attorneys, a righteous case was one that prosecutors felt compelled to bring because the charges were just and fair. Leveling the accusation was considered worthwhile to signal that such illegal conduct would not go unanswered. "Something can be a righteous prosecution even if" you face significant hurdles, Cooney told the prosecutors.

But Shields and Kent had another important reason to worry whether this *was* a righteous case. The U.S. Attorney's Office had received credible information that political appointees within the executive branch had been working to smear McCabe, which, if true, could blow up the case at trial. Specifically, senior DOJ attorneys had information that White House officials had sought to plant negative stories about McCabe. Kent argued that the prosecutors needed to pursue that lead by interviewing department leaders, and possibly query the White House. Any coordinated campaign against the former FBI's number 2 would smack of selective prosecution and have to be disclosed to McCabe's side if they went to trial. Shields also wondered if McCabe had already been punished enough. He had been fired and stripped of his ability to claim his pension. Was it worth criminally prosecuting a man who had worked for decades as a public servant for lying about something he voluntarily corrected? Another tenet in the prosecutors' DOJ handbook stated that a prosecution must serve a "substantial federal interest." This case would drag McCabe, and by extension the entire FBI, through the meat grinder of a public trial.

"The conduct isn't worth the consequence," Shields told Cooney.

Cooney ultimately told Shields he remained in favor of indicting McCabe. Gaston, a Cooney confidante who had shown a similar streak of being willing to go for tough cases that she couldn't always win, agreed with him.

Cooney instructed Shields and Kent to take the Christmas holiday and make their final decision. He wasn't angry or threatening, just matter-of-fact: "Look, if you guys aren't comfortable moving forward with the case, we can find others who can take it over."

Shields and Kent said they would get back to Cooney, but Shields soon shared with colleagues she was concerned. The decision seemed like a proxy for something else—a much larger threat to the department's independence. If Trump got his way and the Justice Department prosecuted McCabe, what might he demand next?

[2]

Was Trump Beholden to Egypt?

I n mid-December, in the same federal courthouse where Shields and Kent had been secretly presenting evidence in the McCabe case, the extraordinary first hints of another, more sensitive investigation appeared. The U.S. Marshals and court staff were instructed to seal off an entire floor of the building to shield the identities of those coming and going.

December 14, 2018, was a Friday, the day when Mueller's Special Counsel's Office typically filed motions or asked juries to vote on indictments, so news cameras were already stationed at entranceways, and the building was teeming with reporters, all of whom immediately speculated about the lockdown. Was this the work of Mueller's team? In keeping with the way he had run the FBI, Mueller had insisted he and his team wouldn't speak a word about their investigation other than in court filings. But the evidence that his team had repeatedly served up revealed a disturbing picture of the Russian government's efforts to help Trump win the White House—as well as some of his aides' attempts to lie about and conceal their communications with Russians before Trump took office.

The party entering the courtroom under a cloak of secrecy was indeed a group of attorneys from Mueller's team. But the topic was far removed from Russia. In fact, it had to do with an entirely different continent, and whether or not a second foreign country—Egypt—had also helped Trump get elected president. The Egypt allegations were, if true, far more direct and explicitly illegal than some of the ways Russia had boosted Trump. Unbeknownst to the public, Mueller's team had from its very first days been probing credible U.S. intelligence that Egyptian President Abdel Fatah El-Sisi had directed aides to funnel $10 million to Trump in the final stretch of his campaign.

Unlike the many widely reported developments of Mueller's investigation regarding Russia, the mere existence of this Egypt probe remained hidden for years. When the case mysteriously surfaced in court that day, clerks, judges, lawyers, and reporters witnessing the scramble all knew something big was up. Just before 11:00 a.m., a panel of judges on the circuit court—often the last stop for cases before the Supreme Court—announced a brief recess. Soon after, the U.S. Marshals began clearing visitors from the fifth-floor courtroom and its hallways. Reporters quickly recognized this was no ordinary security sweep. Marshals locked doors to side rooms, searched coat closets, and began herding anyone remaining toward elevators. When the public was safely sequestered, a three-judge panel convened to consider an extremely rare request: Mueller's team wanted to compel the state-run National Bank of Egypt to turn over account information from a bank branch in Cairo. U.S. prosecutors had a jarring goal: They wanted to determine if an illegal campaign contribution flowed from the account to Donald Trump. The Bank of Egypt had been resisting the Mueller team's subpoena for almost six months. In similarly secret hearings, the chief judge of a lower trial court had ordered the bank to comply. Still, the bank had continued to appeal.

Prosecutors before the appeals judges noted that classified U.S. intelligence supported their case, and pointed them specifically to this bank and this account. In fact, a longtime CIA source had relayed to agency handlers that El-Sisi instructed his aides to get $10 million to Trump, and that they then used the Egyptian government–linked bank account in Cairo to move the money. In trying to vet that explosive intelligence, FBI agents had tapped into the U.S. government's trove of routinely intercepted conversations between foreign diplomatic officials and, given the CIA source's tip, found something highly intriguing. Officials at the Egyptian embassy in Washington had discussed, albeit in veiled terms, a special task that needed to be taken care of at roughly the same time that the CIA asset said Sisi had given his order. The officials also discussed possibly contacting someone connected to the Trump campaign regarding the task.

The information was, in the words of one official, "stunning." National security prosecutors elevated the matter to Rod Rosenstein, a longtime U.S. attorney in Maryland whom Trump had named his deputy attorney general. Following the recusal of Attorney General Jeff Sessions for his own undisclosed contacts with Russians, it had been Rosenstein who was thrust into the powerful position of overseeing the Russia probe and who had chosen Mueller as special counsel.

Rosenstein and his aides reviewed the CIA source intelligence and decided the Egypt matter should be folded into Mueller's assignment. From Rosenstein's thirty-thousand-foot perspective, the intelligence aligned with the Russia investigation, raising similar concerns of possible foreign interference in the election.

Mueller decided that one of the rising stars on his team—Zainab Ahmad—was a natural choice to head up the Egypt probe. A federal prosecutor from the Eastern District of New York, Ahmad had over the previous decade successfully prosecuted a string of thirteen major terrorist suspects. An Arabic speaker, she had traveled repeatedly to the Middle East and elsewhere, leading sensitive discussions with foreign law enforcement.

Mueller had organized his staff into three primary teams. One was code-named Team R, focusing mostly on Russian interference. A second,

Team M, had zeroed in on Trump campaign manager Paul Manafort's shady financial transactions. Team 600, named after the statute authorizing special counsel work, was investigating whether Trump had committed obstruction. A smaller fourth team came to be known as Team 10—as in $10 million—and focused on the Egypt case. Because the intelligence about a possible bribe came from a confidential human source, the team had to operate in secret, rarely even interacting with other Mueller prosecutors. Ahmad and a handful of FBI agents began examining a September 2016 meeting between Trump and El-Sisi in the closing months of the presidential campaign.

El-Sisi, a longtime military general, had seized power in 2013 amid the collapse of the government formed in the wake of the Arab Spring uprising two years before. Trump unexpectedly turned up on the sidelines of the United Nations General Assembly in New York on September 19, 2016, and, following Hillary Clinton's announced meeting with El-Sisi, sought a tête-à-tête with the Egyptian strongman.

Trump's senior advisers at the time were concerned his campaign was running low on funds and had lobbied him to contribute more of his own money for the final push. More than a month after the El-Sisi meeting, and with Election Day a little more than a week away, Trump's campaign had less than a quarter of the cash that Clinton had on hand, and the Republican nominee was quickly burning through what little was left, according to campaign finance reports that Ahmad's team studied.

The New York real estate tycoon had early on pledged to put $100 million of his own money into his campaign but had contributed barely half that. News reports showed that the campaign might be unable to fund final rounds of television and online ads, and Trump was increasingly reluctant to continue writing personal checks, especially since he was trailing in polls. Then, on October 28, to the delight of his son-in-law Jared Kushner and adviser Steve Mnuchin, Trump relented, writing a check for $10 million, his single largest contribution to the campaign. The intelligence in Team 10's hands raised the question of whether

Trump's meeting with El-Sisi might be linked to that final campaign contribution.

There was something else that Team 10 found striking. Almost immediately after his inauguration, Trump did an about-face on U.S. policy toward Egypt, publicly embracing El-Sisi. President Obama had refused the dictator's requests to come to Washington and had instead pressed El-Sisi to first show that he would curb government human rights abuses.

In April 2017, however, Trump welcomed the Egyptian leader as one of the first foreign leaders to visit him in the Oval Office, and the exchange left no question that the Trump administration now fully supported El-Sisi's increasingly authoritarian regime. "I just want to let everybody know in case there was any doubt that we are very much behind President El-Sisi. He's done a fantastic job in a very difficult situation," Trump said. "We are very much behind Egypt and the people of Egypt. The United States has, believe me, backing, and we have strong backing."

By that fall, Mueller investigators were interviewing key Trump advisers and campaign staffers about Russian contacts. Ahmad and FBI agents pursuing the Egypt probe sat in to ask their own questions. The team pressed Steve Bannon, Michael Flynn, and others: Did they know how the meeting between Trump and El-Sisi in New York came about in the fall of 2016? What about the $10 million contribution Trump made to his campaign weeks later?

In 2018, Bannon told Mueller's team he had little insight into the meeting. But he remembered quite a bit about Trump's reluctance to spend any more on the campaign. Mnuchin and others thought they needed $50 million from Trump for the final six weeks of the race. Kushner said his father-in-law was unlikely to agree to even $25 million: "Not going to happen," an agent wrote, summarizing Bannon's recollection.

Less than two weeks before Election Day, Mnuchin sprung documents on Trump proposing he chip in $10 million as a critical last-minute infusion but as a loan for which Trump could be repaid. Trump looked up, seeming to frown at the talk of parting with his millions under any condition. They left Trump Tower and continued the pleading as they boarded Trump's jet, explaining how donations arriving right before or after the election could be used to repay the money. Finally, Trump seemed convinced and he signed the papers.

The interviews were only getting Team 10 so far. As they would in almost any money-laundering or bribery case, investigators next needed to look at bank records to see if Trump had received a windfall that could be traced back to Egypt.

In complex financial cases, FBI agents as a matter of course frequently obtained several years of tax returns and financial records of a person they were investigating to understand their debts, alliances, and conflicts. But Trump had warned that probing his and his company's finances would constitute a red line that could not be crossed. He threatened he would fire Mueller and his team for doing so. Since then, Trump had unleashed an almost daily barrage of insults on the special counsel team—more than a thousand in all—with many seeking to brand Mueller's deputies as a band of "angry Democrats" bent on pursuing him.

Mueller and his deputies, including Chief of Staff Aaron Zebley, had initially told colleagues they believed the American public would see through Trump's attacks and rally behind the team as they worked to expose Russian meddling in an American election. But the team soon had reason to worry they would be fired before they could make real headway. Some in the office saw Mueller's deputies pulling back to not provoke such a confrontation. Six months into the investigation's first year, some managers were told they could not hire additional attorneys over concerns that it would look like the office was spending too much taxpayer money. Later, Mueller and his deputies decided the team did not have a basis to conduct a deep analysis of Trump's tax records, nor the time or support necessary for a lengthy court battle to secure an in-person interview with the president about how much he knew of Russian support for his campaign and his intent in firing Comey. Several concerned investigators found Mueller's and Zebley's choices troubling.

They saw ample evidence to investigate Trump more aggressively. For starters, Mueller and his team had learned that Trump had sought to shutter their probe by ordering Donald F. McGahn II, his White House counsel, to fire Mueller. McGahn told investigators he simply ignored the order. But Mueller had only tiptoed in the direction that the Egypt team wanted: to examine several years of records from Capital One, where Trump and his company held more than two hundred accounts.

Mueller would agree to subpoena transactions from only a couple of dozen of those, and only across a relatively short window of time when Trump was actively campaigning. Mueller and his deputies drew a hard cutoff at November 2016. They would not allow the team to peer into Trump's accounts after he became president-elect.

Mueller's inner circle feared a leak about obtaining some of the president's bank records might spell the end of the Special Counsel's Office. So they worked discreetly, only making their requests by account number and insisting that only one officer at Capital One handle their requests. As Team 10 investigators expected, the limited bank data did not reveal a single obvious deposit to Trump's account that likely came from the Bank of Egypt. Investigators figured that if the intelligence was correct, the Egyptian money would have taken a complicated path through Trump businesses. Ahmad and Team 10 decided instead to try another, trickier route: They would seek to track the $10 million from the source, as it left Egypt.

On July 11, 2018, without mentioning Trump, Mueller's team subpoenaed the Bank of Egypt to turn over records for the suspected Egyptian spy agency account the CIA informant had flagged. It was a move they knew risked drawing the attention of El-Sisi's regime in Cairo. But Mueller's team thought they had a good case. The Egyptian bank maintained a branch in New York City, a toehold on U.S. soil that gave the government standing to seek its records. Attorneys for the bank quickly claimed that, as an entity controlled by a sovereign foreign government, the bank was immune from such a subpoena in a U.S. criminal investigation. Judge Beryl A. Howell, the chief of the United States District Court for the District of Columbia, said such broad immunity was implausible and ruled that Mueller was entitled to the records.

"Foreign governments can send their instrumentalities and agents over here, just run amuck and, if caught, can just escape with impunity?" she asked the bank's lawyers incredulously. "Wow. That's pretty extraordinary."

The bank's lawyers appealed, leading to the mystery hearing before the appellate panel on December 14, 2018. Inside the sealed courtroom, Ahmad and Adam Jed, another Mueller team prosecutor, faced questions about why such a step was necessary. Finally, asked by Judge David Tatel how quickly the panel needed to rule, Jed said that time was of the essence. "Any Grand Jury investigation is a time sensitive investigation," Jed said. "But this is particularly time sensitive."

Jed didn't reveal just how little time they actually had; Mueller's team had by then told a select group of DOJ officials the office would be closing up shop in early 2019. Four days later, the appeals court panel upheld Judge Howell's ruling that the bank had to turn over its records. But its attorneys appealed again, asking the U.S. Supreme Court to intervene. They warned U.S. courts were for the first time in history about to exercise "criminal jurisdiction over a foreign state." On Sunday, December 23, Chief Justice John Roberts temporarily stayed the appeals court ruling to consider the bank's request.

[3]

A Trusting Mueller and
a Failure to See the Endgame

During the same Christmas break, as Chief Justice Roberts reviewed the Egyptian bank case, Shields and Kent pored over the McCabe investigation. The two had become close; they talked on the phone about the case, debating their options and second-guessing themselves. Kent said he worried about bringing a case without knowing all the facts, and whether the White House had tried to slime McCabe. Shields wondered if she was being timid in not wanting to charge McCabe with lying. When the two returned to work, Kent delivered his conclusion: He couldn't get behind a prosecution unless the U.S. Attorney's Office would fully investigate possible White House interference.

Shields arrived at an even bigger decision. The behavior of the president, his bullying of the Department of Justice, had sickened her. Every day that Trump pushed for a specific outcome in their case, she saw the department she loved weakened and diminished. Shields thought it was time to get out. The firm where she had worked after law school had made her an attractive offer, if she was interested. She began making exit plans.

Shields was far from the only one growing disillusioned. The first days of 2019 were no less fraught for prosecutors and FBI agents detailed to the Special Counsel's Office. They had labored for more than a year and a half to investigate Russian efforts to influence the U.S. presidential election. Still, time was running out. Mueller was moving to close down the office, and with a major question still hanging over the probe: For all the indictments of Trump aides and Russians working to elect him, was there convincing evidence Trump had committed a crime?

Mueller's team had all but exhausted its investigation into the president—at least, within the confines that the former FBI director had imposed, as well as the roadblocks that DOJ leaders above him had thrown up. Several prosecutors in the office thought one lost opportunity towered over others: not getting to question the president under oath.

Mueller had wanted to do so. He had pressed Trump's attorneys for an in-person interview and held out the threat of a subpoena and court fight for one if Trump didn't acquiesce. But Mueller's bosses backed away from the threat, resulting in significant delays.

The about-face meant that Mueller and his senior advisers were stuck sending Trump's attorneys a series of letters, requesting the president voluntarily answer written questions about his actions. For twelve months, little had come from the negotiations.

In the fall of 2018, during a meeting of Mueller team supervisors, Andrew Weissmann, the head of Team M, which indicted Trump campaign manager Paul Manafort, vented the frustration over what he and others felt were the timorous negotiations.

"If we do not subpoena the president in this investigation, how can others justify the need to do so? The facts warrant it," Weissmann said. "If we don't pull the trigger, it will be on us."

Mueller late that year considered one last time whether he should launch a legal battle to demand an interview, which could stretch out the special counsel's work another year or more. He decided against it and set his sights on closing down the office. From the investigation's first days, Mueller had told his inner circle that one of his top priorities was to avoid the mistakes of Ken Starr, who in 1994 had investigated President Bill Clinton's and then First Lady Hillary Clinton's real estate deals and let the probe drag on and expand. He ended up issuing a report to Congress four years later, in 1998, that became infamous for shifting to focus on Clinton's lies about an affair with a White House intern.

As the Special Counsel's Office was wrapping up its work at the start of 2019, however, Team 10 finally received good news. On January 8, the Supreme Court concluded it would not intervene in the Egypt case. The Bank of Egypt would finally be held in contempt for failing to comply with the subpoena issued six months earlier and, if it continued to resist producing records, face fines of $50,000 a day.

At the same time, Mueller's Team R was preparing one final Russia-related indictment, which they hoped against odds might finally shake loose what President Trump knew of Russia's efforts to help him win. They expected it to be heavily scrutinized. Team R's leader, Jeannie Rhee, had an exacting process to catch mistakes, ensuring every sentence was clear. She summoned her team and others from Mueller's office—fourteen prosecutors, supervisors, and agents in all—to a conference room. With the proposed indictment on an overhead screen, they took turns, reading every word of the twenty-three-page draft aloud.

On the unusually warm winter morning of January 24, 2019, Rhee's Team R entered the federal courthouse near the Capitol and spent the day going over evidence that Trump's longtime adviser Roger Stone had lied to Congress and investigators about his contacts with WikiLeaks. Mueller's team showed that Stone had advance knowledge that WikiLeaks, working with Russian operatives, planned to publish emails hacked from the Democratic National Committee that embarrassed Clinton's campaign. By sunset, the grand jury returned a sealed seven-count indictment, and a judge signed an arrest warrant for Stone.

More than six hundred days had elapsed since Trump fired FBI

Director James Comey and Stone became the thirty-fourth and final person indicted by the Special Counsel's Office. The next day, federal agents arrested Stone and seized his cell phones, computers, and hard drives. But when it came to determining what Stone knew about Trump's culpability, his longtime adviser stayed mum.

That very same day, several attorneys in the office were packing up and handing off a dozen of their unfinished investigations to prosecutors in U.S. Attorney's Offices around the country. The most significant baton to pass was that of the Egypt investigation. Meeting with prosecutors from the U.S. Attorney's Office in D.C., Mueller's team laid out the evidence gathered so far and the recent developments in court. It was the most promising moment in the investigation in many months, and some investigators who had been frustrated by not being allowed to subpoena a larger set of Trump bank records under Mueller hoped a fresh start and new boss could breathe new life into the investigation.

Meanwhile, several attorneys in the office were also busy writing the special counsel's final report to the attorney general, concluding delicately that, while they found Trump and his team were aware of and receptive to Russian help, they did not establish that Trump had actively coordinated with Russia. On the obstruction side, Mueller's team identified four episodes in which there was "substantial evidence" Trump had sought to obstruct the special counsel's investigation. That was prosecutorial code for saying they could probably have indicted based on the facts. But in part because they had never questioned the president, they hadn't learned Trump's true intent. Mueller pressed his team to finish their respective drafts in order to deliver the final report.

On Thursday, February 14, 2019, Chief Justice Roberts swore in William P. Barr as Trump's new attorney general. The brief ceremony was held in the Oval Office, with Trump staring straight ahead at Barr. Immediately, the president and his new attorney general shared a hearty handshake. It was the beginning of a political marriage, and in the very room that both men viewed as the epicenter of unequaled power in the U.S. government.

Barr had for decades subscribed to the legal theory that the Constitution grants the president ultimate power over the executive branch, up to and including taking many actions without approval from Congress or the courts. It was a controversial theory he had put into practice as a much younger Justice Department attorney in 1989, writing a memo for the White House supporting the idea that the FBI could abduct people abroad without legal consent from the other country. Barr's memo helped form the basis for the justification of the invasion of Panama and the arrest of Manuel Noriega for extradition to the United States. Barr's views on executive power had only grown stronger over the years. In an unsolicited memo to the Justice Department in June 2018, Barr had claimed it was legally impossible for the special counsel to find the president guilty of obstruction of justice. The president, he stated, was the very instrument of justice. "The authority to decide whether or not to bring prosecutions, as well as the authority to appoint and remove principal Executive officers . . . are quintessentially Executive in character and among the discretionary powers vested exclusively in the President," Barr had written of Trump's firing of the FBI director. "When the President exercises these discretionary powers, it is presumed he does so lawfully, and his decisions are generally non-reviewable."

The next morning, on February 15, 2019, Barr strode into the stately Robert F. Kennedy Department of Justice building. Before long, dozens of his deputies assembled under the murals in the attorney general's wood-paneled conference room to welcome him. Barr wanted to be brought up to speed, and one of the first topics on his list was the special counsel's investigation.

Early the following week, Rosenstein, who was officially in charge of overseeing Mueller's work, and his top deputy, Ed O'Callaghan, who had been keeping tabs on Mueller's team, had outlined for Barr the status of its several investigations.

In 2018, O'Callaghan had had mild worries about returning to the department at a time when it was taking political fire from the president and both parties in Congress, but Rosenstein had convinced him. Ironically, O'Callaghan ended up being the department's point person on the contentious special counsel investigation. Every two weeks, O'Callaghan met in the department's sixth-floor SCIF, or sensitive compartmented information facility, with Aaron Zebley, who ran the day-to-day operations of the office, and Jim Quarles, a former Watergate investigator, who was Mueller's chief liaison with the White House and Trump's lawyers. On Mueller's orders, the pair played no games of hiding the ball to stay on good terms with the bosses at Main Justice. It helped, at least initially, that the two sides also had an old bond. O'Callaghan and Zebley had worked together in the aftermath of the September 11, 2001, attacks, when O'Callaghan was a prosecutor in the Southern District of New York and Zebley was an FBI agent. The result was O'Callaghan had a pretty clear window into what Mueller's team had found and had guided them in some key steps they considered taking.

He now outlined for Barr that Team R had found insufficient evidence to charge Trump campaign officials with conspiring with the Russians for their help. Barr was more interested to know where Mueller was landing on Team 600's probe. In firing Comey or taking other actions, would Mueller find the president had obstructed the investigation of himself and his campaign? Barr had already in his earlier memo dubbed such a theory "fatally misconceived." O'Callaghan said he couldn't say for sure. He knew Mueller took seriously a twenty-year-old opinion of the department's Office of Legal Counsel that barred indicting a sitting president. O'Callaghan had asked Zebley point-blank if Mueller would ultimately say that he would indict Trump except for that policy.

"No. We have determined not to make a decision about whether the president's conduct amounted to a crime," Zebley had answered. But Barr said he wanted to hear Mueller say it himself.

A few weeks later, on March 5, Zebley, Quarles, and Mueller traveled to the attorney general's conference room. To keep the meeting a secret, Mueller had his security detail bring him up through the basement and in a private elevator. Barr and Mueller, friends from their work together in the Bush administration, greeted each other warmly. Mueller then opened the briefing by giving an overview of the team's work. But Barr and Deputy Attorney General Rod Rosenstein were surprised at Mueller's manner. He read briefly from notes on a piece of paper, his hands appearing to tremble, then turned over the meeting to his team. Barr had a sinking feeling that Mueller was not himself, not the commanding and razor-sharp G-man from only a few years back. After the meeting Rosenstein shared his concern: "That is not the Bob I know. I wonder if he is ill." In fact, Mueller, then seventy-five, had been slowing down physically and in his speech. Deputies in the Special Counsel's Office, including some of those critical of his choices, found his decision-making throughout the probe unimpeachable. But in another two years, the stoic leader who had devoted his life to keeping the nation safe would retire from private practice, sell his Georgetown home, and move to a senior living facility near his daughter. There, unbeknownst to the public, he would come to struggle with symptoms of Parkinson's and cognitive decline. While this book was being written, his family would ask for privacy, as this great American patriot's health had severely deteriorated.

As the special counsel's meeting with Barr continued that March afternoon, Zebley reviewed the team's findings of Russian interference and Quarles outlined Trump's repeated attempts to pressure his aides to fire Mueller and either shut down or limit the investigation. Quarles stressed that Mueller and his senior advisers had chosen not to publicly state whether their evidence showed that Trump had committed a crime. Barr remained surprised and confused; Mueller had been appointed to investigate Trump's actions and make charging decisions. But he was deciding *not* to decide. Reaching a conclusion struck Barr as key to Mueller's assignment. Even some of Mueller's lawyers were uncomfortable with this choice, which Mueller's inner circle had reached months before.

Barr and his deputies kept asking questions.

Mueller tried to explain his team's reasoning: Department policy prohibited indicting a sitting president. So it would be just as inappropriate for them to accuse President Trump of a crime and give him no route to clear his name in court. Mueller said they gathered the evidence while recollections were fresh, and the department might reconsider their findings later when Trump was no longer in office.

"It would be possible for somebody else later on to decide," Mueller said.

As the meeting ended, Barr wore a wide smile and walked out with Mueller. Trailing behind, Zebley heard Barr ask: "Will the report have an executive summary?"

In early March, the leaders of each of Mueller's three main investigative teams were focused on finishing what would become the team's 448-page report

Rhee, the head of Team R, hustled for weeks to meet the deadline for her portion of the report, and at times found herself locked in a tussle with Zebley over key takeaways in both the report and executive summary. She recognized the latter was more important.

"Let's be honest," Rhee said to a member of her team. "Nobody reads the chapters. It's the introduction and the executive summary that matter."

Rhee worried Zebley's suggestions watered down her team's more declarative findings about Putin's interference operation and Trump campaign contacts with Russian operatives, she told colleagues. He wanted to avoid extra details that didn't prove a crime.

It seemed like a replay of the pair's earlier battle the previous year, one in which, Rhee now confided to her team, she regretted relenting.

In January 2018, Zebley had agreed with O'Callaghan's recommendation to delete a telling detail from Rhee's draft indictment of Russians who had been manipulating American social media to interfere in the 2016 presidential election. Rhee's team had discovered these Russian troll farm workers, part of a multimillion-dollar influence operation funded by a Putin-allied oligarch, broke into celebration when they learned Trump had won the election.

"And when around eight a.m. the most important result of our work arrived, we uncorked a tiny bottle of champagne . . . took one gulp each and looked into each other's eyes," a member of the Russian operation said. "We uttered almost in unison: 'We made America great.'"

Zebley cut it, wanting to avoid appearing to take a cheap shot. The Mueller team didn't share this distillation of the Kremlin's goals with the American public in its 2018 indictment.

At the time, Rhee was willing to accept this small sacrifice, giving up a pawn here or there as they developed the board and focused on the endgame to finish the investigation. For his part, Zebley endorsed O'Callaghan's cut because it fit Mueller's directive: pare back that which is not essential to the legal argument.

In hindsight, Rhee concluded political appointees atop Trump's Justice Department had succeeded in deleting a fact to avoid embarrassing the president.

Now the danger of the special counsel being fired had passed. Still, Zebley pressed Rhee to consider writing a summary section explaining what the Special Counsel's Office had *not* found, expounding on the lack of evidence to prove a conspiracy between the Trump campaign and Russia.

Rhee grew incensed. It sounded like he wanted to say the special counsel team had found no connection between Putin's operatives and Trump's advisers and family. "What?" she shot back. "You can't say that?"

Zebley gave up on trying to say what the office did not find. But he took the pen himself and rewrote the first two pages of the executive summary.

On Thursday, March 21, the night she was to leave for a family vacation, Rhee remained in the Special Counsel's Office late into the evening, sending back and forth suggested tweaks to the final draft. She left just in time to catch a cab, race through security at Dulles, and meet her family in the terminal for their 11:00 p.m. international flight.

Three days later, on Sunday, March 24, big news was breaking. Reporters had gotten hold of a letter that Barr had written to Congress, in which he summarized what the mighty and mysterious Mueller team had found out about Trump and his campaign. This was a moment Washington had been waiting for.

Barr's letter gave his own summary: It concluded that no one in the Trump campaign or anyone associated with it had conspired with Russia. On the big question of whether Trump had committed the crime of obstruction, Barr noted that Mueller's team had declined to make a "traditional prosecutorial judgment," and so he decided to make one for them. Barr said he had reviewed the evidence, and it was not sufficient for a charge.

Reporters began writing the simple takeaway. The news of how Barr described the investigation—no collusion, no obstruction—reached some team members who were still finishing up last chores in the office, and others in more remote locations. Weissmann, the head of Team M, heard the news on his car radio while driving to Washington on the New Jersey Turnpike. He was sure the CNN reporters had misunderstood Barr's summary; those conclusions weren't right. The news came to Rhee in Europe as a breaking news headline on her mobile phone. For so many team members, it felt like a kick in the stomach.

Rhee set aside her feelings of fury. She wanted to talk to her team and make sure they were doing OK. But she was in a foreign country, so she couldn't say anything specific over the phone.

She called the office, where she reached a few of her teammates.

"Obviously, I read the news," Rhee said. "I am with you in spirit."

Her team explained that the mood at their offices in Patriot's Plaza in Southwest Washington was grim. A few members of the team were going out drinking, then bowling at Lucky Strike in Chinatown, they said. They needed to give themselves something else to think about, but also to be together.

Michelle Taylor, the type A agent on the team who had helped carry out almost all the major interviews on the obstruction case, had never held back when Mueller or other prosecutors asked for her opinion. A competitive runner, mother of two, and Army vet, she found the FBI's rigid rules familiar, even comfortable, and took pride in the righteousness of the Justice Department. The special counsel work had made her more jaundiced.

In interviewing some Trump administration leaders, she'd been taken aback by their lack of rigor and seeming cluelessness about Russia's goals to weaken America. She greatly admired Mueller, but also had disagreed with him, especially over his not demanding the DOJ back a court fight to ensure Trump answered questions under oath. Mueller had told his team he had not wanted to put the department and Barr in the "awkward" position of refusing him. Taylor told colleagues that Mueller's stubborn faith in the institution had been honorable but naive. He, Zebley, and Quarles had hunkered down, ignoring the political winds blowing from Trump appointees atop the DOJ. Because of their inability to sense this coming, the whole team had been played.

Mueller's deputies soon had regrets too. They had long assumed the report's release would usher in a period of new public accountability, with congressional hearings and Americans learning of the severity and danger of the Kremlin's interference in the 2016 election. That Monday morning, Zebley called O'Callaghan requesting that the department release the team summaries that Mueller had provided to Barr, because those would be a fuller representation of the special counsel's findings. O'Callaghan didn't commit, but said Barr, Rosenstein, and he would consider it. He asked Zebley to have his team remove any sensitive grand jury material from the summaries. Later that day they were delivered and Zebley called O'Callaghan again, channeling the team's growing anger: Barr's letter was leading to confusion about what the team had actually found.

The next day, Mueller called the team together at the Special Counsel's Office and was uncharacteristically raw. "I know you are pissed," he began, explaining their pressing to get Barr to release the team's top-line findings. Even now, as Barr had shaded the team's findings, Mueller was taking the high road, trusting he could navigate within the institution to put things right. Two years of work seemed to hang in the balance. After another day or two with no movement, Rhee told Weissmann and her teammates that releasing the summaries would make little difference. They could not undo the first impression the public had absorbed via headlines and chyrons.

"No matter what we do, we can't fix this," she told her team. "We can work for the next thousand hours on this. But we've lost."

Rhee liked to play chess. She had come to the game late in life but particularly liked endgame puzzles. Those final moves sorted very good players from the merely competent. Anyone could memorize an opening, but endgame brilliance called for creativity as well as deep study.

As the probe evolved, Rhee and many in the office had openly debated what they would do if the attorney general didn't release their report or findings to the public. How would they communicate and preserve their work? What was their endgame?

Conversely, Barr's endgame seemed clear: to protect the president from what he considered an unfair—and politically damaging— investigation. Rhee told colleagues that Mueller had reasonably assumed that laying out the impartial facts in DOJ tradition would be enough. Old-school to the end, Mueller played into a trap set on the board by the leaders of his own Justice Department.

[4]

Where Did the $10 Million Go?

Three days after Barr sent Congress his summary of the Mueller report, Team 10 prosecutors were once again in the federal courthouse in D.C., seeking more Egyptian banking records. But first Judge Howell had a question.

"What are we doing here?" she asked near the start of the March 27 hearing. "Why isn't this whole matter over as of . . . when Mr. Mueller delivered his report" to the attorney general?

Again, the hearing was hidden from the public. U.S. Marshals stood outside the door. But Assistant U.S. Attorneys Zia Faruqui, Peter Lallas, and David Goodhand had replaced Mueller's team. The handoff of the Egypt investigation to the D.C. office under U.S. Attorney Jessie Liu was complete. A daughter of Taiwanese immigrants, Liu had from an early age dedicated herself to excellence in the law and built a résumé to match: Harvard undergrad; Yale Law; a clerkship in the Fifth Circuit; a line prosecutor; a founding member of the Justice Department's National Security Division, created after September 11; and later, a deputy assistant attorney general in the Civil Division, defending the federal government's policies across the nation.

Liu's distinguished career had made her a standout to lead the D.C. office. Her leadership had comforted the office's rank and file amid Trump's assaults on the department. Liu had walked in their shoes. She was confirmed by the Senate in September 2017 and quickly earned high marks from her troops, most of whom viewed her as rigorous and impartial. In early February, just before Liu's office took over the Egypt case, the Bank of Egypt had relented after running up nearly $1 million in contempt fines and turned over to Mueller's team almost a thousand pages of records. Liu's attorneys had found some tantalizing new evidence in the records, and now they were coming out charging to get more.

Addressing Judge Howell, Faruqi, one of Liu's prosecutors, said the government was asking the court to compel Egypt to produce more documents and, if they refused, to impose a whopping $300,000-a-day fine.

The Bank of Egypt records, Faruqi told the judge, "involve issues that have not or are in any way close to being resolved and . . . [require] I think, a great deal of resources, time and attention, by the Government."

What the bank had turned over shed new light on some highly suspicious transactions for an account linked to Egypt's version of the CIA, the General Intelligence Service. Five days before Trump's inauguration as president, on January 15, 2017, four people, including two with ties to El-Sisi's intelligence service, walked into a Bank of Egypt branch near Cairo International Airport and, according to a bank employee, walked out with two large bags containing almost $10 million. Strikingly for a country then believed to have limited reserves of U.S. currency, the withdrawal was delivered not in Egyptian pounds but in U.S. $100 bills. Incredibly, the line prosecutors contended, the state-controlled bank reported it had not one email and scant internal records to formally document the withdrawal. In apparent violation of its own written policies, the bank had also not photocopied the ID of one of those who requested the money, or asked him to sign a standard withdrawal slip for the millions in cash.

Faruqi explained to the judge the importance of pursuing this money trail, and said prosecutors and agents joining them from Mueller's team would be taking new investigative steps.

With Liu's backing, the line attorneys argued to Howell that it was implausible the bank had so few records regarding such a large withdrawal. They asked Howell to force the bank to produce a records officer who could be questioned. In one filing, prosecutors urged Howell to consider the spectacle of someone having walked out of a bank in Cairo with $10 million in cash. Liu's office had done the math: The $10 million in $100 bills would have weighed about 220 pounds. These would have been large—*and heavy*—bags. Howell declined the prosecutors' request, however, saying she couldn't leap to assume the bank was lying about a lack of records.

Liu was fast approaching the same uncomfortable choice that Mueller had faced. The only way to determine if this money had ended up with Trump, as U.S. intelligence agents feared, might very well be to subpoena more of Trump's bank records—including those from after he had moved into the White House.

A contingent of Liu's team also pushed for the U.S. to take another step: press the Bank of Egypt and other connected financial institutions around the world to look for records that could help track where the cash was later deposited. Investigators surmised any number of Trump's dozens of foreign investments could have been used to siphon money back to him. Had $10 million been sprinkled into Trump's golf course in Scotland as sales or to a commercial property elsewhere?

For the FBI, the transfer of the case to Liu's office also changed an important dynamic. For almost two years, the agents had been on an island of sorts, answering exclusively to Mueller's prosecutors. Suddenly, they were back under their own supervisors and reporting important developments up their own chain of command about the Egypt investigation—or, as the FBI had code-named the case: Red Massari.

By June, increasing numbers of senior FBI officials were aware of Liu's looming decisions on subpoenas. Contingents of agents and supervisors were briefing her, with many urging her to go forward. Liu at one point told a colleague that she was "impressed" with the U.S. intelligence that had sparked the investigation. But the Central Intelligence Agency registered concerns with her that additional subpoenas to foreign institutions could risk exposing how the U.S. first received the intelligence.

The CIA also was worried about Justice seeking out foreign cooperation that could widen the circle of people capable of piecing together the nature of the Egypt investigation and potentially compromise the president on the world stage.

In a meeting with FBI officials in mid-June, Liu said she was inclined to support a subpoena for a limited set of Trump's bank records from the time around the suspicious cash withdrawal in Cairo. As the meeting broke up, however, Liu mentioned almost in passing that she would run the plan by Attorney General Barr.

News of Liu's decision quickly spread through the office. No U.S. attorney would have bothered the attorney general about a fairly standard subpoena for bank records. But this one was not normal. It involved the president, and investigators feared Barr would instinctively oppose prying into Trump's accounts.

"Oh, it's over now," one investigator privately joked to another.

At her next scheduled meeting at Justice, Liu arranged to talk with the attorney general in his office for a few minutes and explained what was, to him, spanking new information. She told Barr the investigators on the Egypt case wanted to look and see if the money went to Trump after the January 2017 time period in which they now knew it had left the bank in Cairo. Given that there had been one subpoena for bank records under Mueller, Liu called this next batch a "second bite at the apple."

Barr told Liu that obviously the DOJ had to meet a high bar in seeking the personal bank records of the president, but even if Trump wasn't president, he said, there had to be a predicate for digging deeper.

"Is that really justified at this point?" he asked.

Barr, who would later say he never told the White House about the investigation while it was underway, urged Liu to go to CIA headquarters to eyeball the underlying intelligence that had launched the probe two years earlier. He said Liu had to know the facts herself to decide.

A week passed with no news. Inside the FBI, officials were beginning to wonder: Why had the subpoenas for the president's bank accounts not yet gone out?

The following week, still no news. In a meeting, an FBI official reiterated to Liu that the plan for the subpoenas had been briefed all the way up to Director Christopher A. Wray, and Bureau leadership was "fully supportive of the investigation and specifically for subpoenaing Trump's bank records."

Liu had spent hours reviewing the raw intelligence. It was a highly unusual step for the top political appointee in an office of hundreds of career prosecutors. Even line attorneys typically left the work of looking at the raw data to the good judgment of FBI agents with years of experience analyzing this kind of information. After her CIA visit, Liu briefed Barr that she shared the CIA's confidence in the reliability of the informant. But she was concerned about the discrepancy in the timing between when the informant said the money was supposed to go to Trump, during his campaign, and when $10 million was actually withdrawn, following the election. Liu said investigators were pressing her to approve a subpoena for additional Trump bank records and might suspect political motives if she turned them down.

Barr believed Liu was worried about being sandbagged by angry quarters of her office, he later told aides. To Barr, she seemed like she was dancing to avoid making the call herself, hoping he would make it for her.

After Liu departed, Barr began to worry more about the motives of the FBI line agents involved in the Egypt probe; some had just rolled off the Mueller probe and, he suspected, likely tilted heavily against Trump. Some Barr advisers already thought agents in the Bureau's Washington Field Office generally leaned to the left and had dubbed it "the DNC of the FBI."

Barr thought that if Liu deferred to agents on the case, the Egypt probe could leap forward based on a vacuum of high-level decision-making. He arranged a private session with FBI Director Chris Wray and Deputy Director Dave Bowdich, in which he told the two top FBI leaders he had doubts there was a predicate to dig further into the president's bank records. He said Liu felt "jammed" by agents. The attorney general told Wray and Bowdich that he needed them to step in and exercise some "adult supervision" over their agents.

"I have a U.S. Attorney who is frozen; she's not comfortable with what's being pressed on her, but she can't make a decision," Barr said. "I want to be sure the judgments reflect the best judgment at the FBI, not the most junior people."

Barr said he wanted to be clear: He wasn't telling the FBI what to do.

"It's a big case, let's be honest. People are going to scrutinize it . . . no matter what happens here," Barr told them, given everything that had happened "with Russia and everything else."

"This is not the time for short-circuiting," he said. "The predication has to be there."

Afterward, FBI leaders told supervisors in the Washington Field Office that they needed Liu's support for the subpoena of Trump's bank records. Without it, there was little the FBI could do to counter Barr's resistance. Agents began preparing for their last pitch.

[5]

"I'm Pretty Sure
I'm Getting Indicted Today"

On September 11, 2019, Andy McCabe remained a man under active criminal investigation. It had been eighteen months since the FBI had begun its probe into whether McCabe, the Bureau's former deputy director, had lied to federal investigators. But on this bluebird day, McCabe was enjoying a midmorning run along the Hudson River in New York. It was familiar territory for McCabe. He had been born in Flushing, Queens, and in 1996, his Bureau career started at the FBI's massive New York Field Office, where he specialized in investigating organized crime and, later, terrorism cases. Then came a big promotion to Washington, where he and his wife had raised two kids as he climbed to deputy director and, for a time, to acting director. It had all come to a crashing halt when, at Trump's urging, he was fired a day before his planned retirement.

At fifty-one, McCabe was back in New York to meet colleagues at CNN, where he had just been hired as an on-air contributor. He would help the cable channel's audience make sense of the special counsel cases still swirling around Trump. McCabe, after all, had been the one who started the biggest probe of all, deciding as acting director that the FBI must open a criminal investigation into whether Trump had fired Director James Comey to thwart an investigation into his campaign's contacts with Russians.

As he ran, McCabe was listening to a podcast hosted by his good friend Chuck Rosenberg, who had been Mueller's counsel at the FBI. Rosenberg's guest was recounting how he rushed to the Pentagon while it was still on fire on September 11, 2001. Suddenly, it dawned on McCabe: It was the eighteenth anniversary of the attack, when he had driven alone across a closed Triborough Bridge, the lights on his black FBI Suburban flashing, racing toward the smoke billowing out of lower Manhattan. As he ran, McCabe looked up to see the FBI's Twenty-Sixth Street garage, which the Bureau had turned into its investigative command center following the attack. For months, his mornings had begun right there. His emotions welled up. He dialed his wife, Jill, and, after a few minutes of describing his flood of memories, asked about her.

"So what's going on at home?" McCabe asked. His wife hesitated.

"Um, I don't know what's going on but there's a ton of media on our front lawn," she said.

McCabe inhaled deeply, and quickly told his wife he would call her back. He suspected the reason. He called his lawyer, Michael Bromwich, and Melissa Schwartz, a public relations veteran helping McCabe's lawyers. They told McCabe they had heard through reporters and others that the grand jury, which prosecutors were using to investigate McCabe, had been called back to the federal courthouse after a long hiatus. McCabe and his lawyers knew this was ominous.

"The only reason they do that is to vote the case," his lawyer warned him. The standard for returning an indictment was low; normally, a majority of a twenty-three-member jury must agree there is strong suspicion or probable cause to believe that a crime occurred. Grand juries also only hear the prosecutors' arguments for charging someone and not the suspect's defense. For these reasons, in the overwhelming majority of cases, juries vote to indict.

"Oh my God," McCabe said to himself. "I'm going to get indicted on my first day at CNN."

In the early afternoon, Bromwich called McCabe back with an update. The grand jury had left without an indictment. He had heard one rumor: Prosecutors didn't want to ask the grand jury to vote on September 11, when so many families grieve for fallen officers.

Later that evening he called his shaken son and daughter at their respective schools to prepare them. They might soon see in the news that he had been charged with a crime. It was the worst moment for him of the entire saga.

Behind the curtain, intense hand-wringing had continued over whether to charge McCabe. The departures of Assistant U.S. Attorneys David Kent and Kamil Shields had slowed the case but not stopped it. At one point, a room full of prosecutors were called in to murder the draft prosecution, and many of the office's most experienced career attorneys had panned it, saying the evidence was thin. The case, in fact, had become one of the most difficult in recent memory for prosecutors in the D.C. office.

Liu confided to her leadership team that she didn't doubt McCabe had misled federal agents, but the case had grown increasingly fraught because of Trump pressing for a specific outcome.

Barr told aides he believed McCabe had intentionally lied. At the same time, however, Barr had doubts there was a good justification for charging Trump's former national security adviser, Michael Flynn, for a similar offense. Flynn had pleaded guilty to lying to the FBI about conversations he'd had with a Russian ambassador, but Barr saw Flynn as a public servant whose misstatement was of no legal consequence. Barr later complained the agents had rushed over to the White House to interview Flynn without alerting any White House officials and appeared to be trying to "gin up" a false statement charge, given his conversation with the ambassador wasn't a crime. Yet inspector general agents had summoned McCabe to ask him about one matter, then switched to the topic of the newspaper leak.

Liu told her prosecutors that she saw the McCabe and Flynn cases as near mirror images with one key difference: Flynn was a devoted Trump ally, while McCabe had called out Trump as a pox on democracy.

In the late summer, Bromwich and co-counsel Dave Schertler had also made a final appeal to both Liu and Jeffrey Rosen, the new deputy attorney general who replaced Rosenstein, arguing the department should drop the case.

"You have the president of the United States bashing our client," Bromwich said in one meeting. "You're going to have a very hard time avoiding a motion to dismiss."

Barr hadn't attended, but in August Ed O'Callaghan, fresh from managing the department's response to the Mueller report, delivered the DOJ's decision. Coming from O'Callaghan—or "Eddie O'C," as McCabe knew his old partner from his days in the New York City office—the news cut like a dagger. The department was authorizing the D.C. prosecutors to pursue an indictment.

The next morning, on September 12, McCabe was meeting with CNN chief executive officer Jeff Zucker. Shortly beforehand, Bromwich had called McCabe. The grand jury was coming back that morning. Bromwich said they needed to prepare for an indictment.

McCabe hung up and was soon ushered into Zucker's seventeenth-floor suite. He came in with a pit in his stomach.

After some pleasantries, McCabe told Zucker: "Look, I need to tell you something. I'm pretty sure I'm getting indicted today."

Zucker looked down his nose through his glasses and frowned.

"Fuck it," Zucker said after a short pause. "I think it's all bullshit anyway. It's garbage. Don't worry about it, man."

Later McCabe explained that if he was indicted, he might have to appear in court in D.C. the next day.

"I've got to get a flight back," McCabe said.

"You don't want to fly," Zucker said, warning McCabe it could be uncomfortable and fodder for social media if he was on a commercial plane or in a busy airport when news broke of charges.

Zucker mashed a few buttons on his phone and had a driver ready to take McCabe back to Washington, D.C., a four-hour journey.

On the car trip, McCabe recalled his final twenty-four hours at the J. Edgar Hoover Building over eighteen months earlier. The events of that day still felt like a shock. In the cafeteria of the FBI headquarters building, he had attended countless afternoon send-offs filled with speeches, cupcakes, commemorative coins, and gag gifts for retiring agents. With his own planned retirement date then approaching, McCabe had begun to imagine his own happy farewell.

Instead, late on the Sunday afternoon of January 28, 2018, McCabe received a surprising message on his phone from FBI Director Chris Wray, whom Trump had appointed to replace Comey five months earlier. McCabe was then driving home on the Jersey Turnpike with his wife after a weekend visiting their son at college in Connecticut, and expecting to celebrate their eighth-grade daughter's birthday that night in Virginia. But Wray made an unusual request: He wanted McCabe to meet him at the office as soon as he reached D.C.

Wray had led the Justice Department's Criminal Division under President George W. Bush, and spent the last decade as one of the country's highest-paid corporate defense attorneys at the global powerhouse firm King & Spalding, representing clients facing government investigations.

Friends had cautioned Wray against taking the FBI job, noting how good he had it. Wray was living in his beloved Georgia with his doting family. Working for a mercurial president would inevitably lead to trouble, they warned. But Wray received encouraging calls from former FBI agents and was motivated to take the helm if for nothing else than to be the anti-Comey. He felt his predecessor, and former boss in the Bush-era

DOJ, had done the FBI and the Justice Department a huge disservice by talking too much. Friends and colleagues who had known Wray for a decade or more struggled to recall more than a couple of times they had seen him display raw emotion. But one had been in 2016, when Comey took it upon himself to hold a press conference during the campaign to divulge details of an investigation into Democratic presidential candidate Hillary Clinton.

While no one on Comey's senior staff ever had to guess what he was thinking, Wray was rigid in his bearing. He asked plenty of questions but maintained a poker face, not wanting agents and supervisors to react to or shape their investigations based on what they thought he wanted.

Wray's idea of a joke was talking about how boring his teenage kids thought he was, and he tried to pull the Bureau in his direction. After his confirmation, he had mandated that all senior staff travel to the FBI academy for training on ethics and on keeping personal and political opinions separate from work. He also ordered an audit of all investigations being run out of FBI headquarters, resulting in many being closed and the remainder being shipped to field offices where they would be under the direction of career agents, often far from Washington.

Wray and McCabe had logged some important time together in Wray's first months. That past winter, amid a fight with Republicans in Congress to turn over documents related to Clinton's email investigation, Wray called McCabe for advice at a key moment. It was late one evening and McCabe answered his cell phone as he left a haircut at a strip mall barber shop. Wray explained that Trump's White House Chief of Staff John Kelly was no longer going to help the agency withhold investigative files that could divulge a Bureau source. Wray had been a criminal prosecutor, but never a field agent, as McCabe had been, in charge of navigating the tricky work of protecting confidential informants. For the FBI and counterintelligence prosecutors, promises to protect the identities of such sources were sacred.

"We've played all of our cards here, the last option is for me to quit,"

Wray said, seeming to let down his guard, if briefly. "If you think this is the red line I should quit over, I want to know."

McCabe replied that he didn't think so, but with Trump's track record, "it might be right around the corner."

Months later, on the Sunday night of Wray's unexpected call, McCabe arrived at the J. Edgar Hoover Building after dark. Reaching Wray's seventh-floor office, where the windows were perpetually covered for security, McCabe took his usual seat to the right, in front of the director's desk. Wray got to the point. He had received a briefing on the draft IG report about the leak, and Wray said it was "devastating" for McCabe, perhaps "the worst thing ever written about a DOJ employee." Wray told McCabe he couldn't let him stay as deputy director, not even for a day. McCabe repeatedly asked Wray to tell him what it said. Wray said the report found McCabe had authorized the release of Bureau information out of personal interest and "lacked candor" with superiors and then again with investigators when they asked him about it.

Wray gave McCabe an ultimatum: The deputy could announce the next morning to all the senior staff that he was stepping down voluntarily. Then he could work to get the Bureau's third-in-command, David Bowdich, up to speed to take over his duties and ride out the final weeks before he qualified for retirement. If he refused, he'd be stripped of his responsibilities, and forced to leave in disgrace.

The two men argued, and McCabe refused to give an answer, saying he had to talk this over with his wife. On the drive home across the bridge into Virginia, he couldn't help but see this as the consequence of his choice to launch a probe of Trump for possible obstruction.

"I knew when I opened a case against Trump that it wasn't going to end well," he told his wife.

McCabe didn't know how hard this had also been for the director. In fact, Wray and a small group of DOJ officials would keep secret for Wray's entire tenure the extent to which Trump and his appointees had pressured Wray—beginning in part with orders to fire McCabe. Trump's

Justice Department appointees repeatedly pressed him to oust McCabe, and then did the same with an expanding list of Bureau executives whom Trump wanted gone. The White House demands didn't let up. Less than two months earlier, Matthew G. Whitaker, then Sessions's chief of staff, had come to Wray's office demanding that Wray remove one of the officials that day. The FBI director listened and, as Whitaker kept talking, pulled a piece of paper from his desk and began moving his arm as if to begin scribbling. "What are you doing?" Whitaker demanded to know. "Writing my resignation letter," Wray said. "Because if that's an order, I'm done." Whitaker appeared surprised and backed off. Wray repeatedly stiff-armed those channeling Trump's orders to boot McCabe, saying he would let the inspector general's investigation play out and then make his decision based on the facts. With the finished report accusing McCabe of lying, Wray had no choice.

On January 29, the morning after their Sunday night meeting, McCabe gave Wray his own ultimatum: He would not voluntarily step down. He would retire as deputy director in the next few weeks, and until then take whatever leave was owed to him. It was an emotionally strained moment. Wray, palpably frustrated, turned away, saying, "I can't believe you're doing this." McCabe swallowed and replied: "I can't believe *you* are."

McCabe arrived from New York at his lawyer's firm in Dupont Circle late that Thursday afternoon of September 12, 2019. He found his wife waiting in a dress, ready to stand by his side whatever came. Within twenty minutes, though, Bromwich and Schertler had a new update. The grand jury had left the courthouse—again—without returning an indictment. The lawyers had reached Cooney, who was now supervising the case, by phone and asked him what had happened. Cooney gave a terse reply that didn't explain much.

"In the event your client is ever indicted, we will let you know," Cooney said.

McCabe felt a mix of emotions. First, relief that the worst had not come. Later, anger that Justice officials had tipped off reporters to be ready that afternoon for his possible indictment. Department officials too were barred from discussing the workings of a grand jury. McCabe ended that night with a muddy feeling of resignation. Both he and the department had been stained by Trump's hand.

Reporters covering the case scrambled for days after, making calls and buttonholing sources to find out what in the world had happened. Was it possible the grand jury had refused to indict? Prosecutors only had to show jurors there was "probable cause"—a reasonable belief that a crime had occurred—for them to justify charges. It was a threshold so low that, in the 1980s, a New York judge urging reforms had once famously said prosecutors could get jurors to indict a "ham sandwich." A grand jury concluding the government lacked cause to bring charges was a rare and highly embarrassing event for any federal prosecutor's office. Word spread through the U.S. Attorney's Office and Main Justice, with multiple people hearing that the grand jury had decided not to indict.

Later, prosecutors walking the hall near Cooney's office noticed a table set up with stacks of copies of court transcripts. When they asked what was up, they heard it was at the request of the attorney general. Barr was assigning someone to review what had happened in the McCabe grand jury and if they could still pursue this prosecution.

[6]

Forced Out

I n August 2019, Jessie Liu had her eyes on a sweet promotion and a graceful exit. It had been only seven months since Barr had become attorney general, but she could already tell their decision-making clashed. Liu's style was pensive and Socratic. Barr wrinkled his nose at long discussions. He preferred snap decisions and gut instinct. Liu and an attorney from another Justice Department office had recently briefed Barr on a complex case with a set of difficult choices. After just ten minutes, Barr was annoyed they were still talking about it. Though the two tackled problems differently, Liu felt she could work with Barr. But she knew more cases were looming that would require her office to make decisions involving Trump allies that would hit close to the White House.

That August, when a good friend had asked Liu if she would be interested in a big, new job, replacing her as a Treasury undersecretary for terrorism and financial crimes, the U.S. attorney said yes.

A few weeks later, Liu met with Treasury Secretary Steve Mnuchin, who then asked the White House to nominate her for the open post. Liu alerted Barr through his aides, and was assured Barr was sorry to see her go, but happy she would still be of service to the country. On December

10, the White House announced that President Trump would nominate Liu for the job.

Within half an hour of the news release, Barr's assistant called Liu to set up a private chat with the boss in a week's time. Liu surmised he wanted an overview of major outstanding cases in her office. Barr ended up having a conflict at the appointed time on December 19, so his chief of staff, Brian Rabbitt, met Liu instead.

Rabbitt got right to the point: What did she think about her timing for transitioning out of the office? Liu explained she was planning to follow the standard path for most political appointees and continue working in her current post as U.S. attorney until she was confirmed for the Treasury spot. That wasn't what Barr had in mind.

Rabbitt said that the AG wanted her to leave as early as possible, in January preferably, because he didn't want uncertainty in this prominent prosecutors' office for the rest of the year.

Liu was floored. She'd previously had to withdraw from a DOJ nomination in 2017, so she knew confirmation was never guaranteed. Liu told Rabbitt she generally opposed the idea and couldn't make that decision without a lot of thought. He told her to get back to him with an answer soon. Liu wasn't looking to antagonize Barr, but didn't want to step down without the new position being finalized.

As Liu wrestled with how to proceed, her office was facing a January 2020 deadline from a judge to recommend punishment for Trump's former national security adviser, Michael Flynn. Mueller's team had agreed as part of Flynn's guilty plea to give him what was called a 5K letter, named after Section 5K1.1 of the federal sentencing guidelines, which would ask the court to consider reducing Flynn's punishment. Flynn had admitted not only to lying about contacts with Russians but also to concealing lucrative work for the Turkish government without registering as a lobbyist for a foreign government. Flynn had promised to testify for the government in an illegal lobbying case against Flynn's Turkish business partner. But over the summer of 2019, Flynn had retreated from his pledge and claimed he had never lied about his work with Turkey—or anything else.

Flynn's about-face left a huge hole in the government's case against his partner and forced prosecutors to eventually drop those charges.

Brandon Van Grack, a national security prosecutor at Main Justice who had led the Flynn investigation on the Mueller team, had taken a special detail to the U.S. Attorney's Office to finish Flynn's sentencing. A dark-haired and fit native of Montgomery County, Maryland, just over the D.C. border, Van Grack hailed from a family of lawyers and had worked for ten years at Justice, mostly as a counterterrorism prosecutor in the National Security Division. Around Christmas, he and another attorney on Liu's staff, Jocelyn Ballantine, had argued they had to withdraw the 5K letter now that Flynn had reneged on his pledge to cooperate. Van Grack and Ballantine made clear to Liu that they had to treat Flynn as they would anyone else who had broken a plea agreement. But that move was certain to infuriate the president and agitate the attorney general.

Liu opposed rescinding the 5K letter, saying it wasn't worth the waves it would make. The sentence would fall somewhere between zero and six months in prison either way, she said, so why not let the judge decide?

Van Grack insisted it was a matter of principle. Guilty defendants shouldn't benefit from promising cooperation that they later refused to give. He and Ballantine tried to make their case to the senior leadership of Main Justice, but word spread that Deputy Attorney General Jeff Rosen and his lawyers wouldn't meet or talk with them about the facts. Instead, Seth DuCharme, Rosen's new principal deputy, tried to resolve the dispute and heard out Van Grack's key points.

The day before the January 7 deadline, Van Grack and Ballentine learned Rosen's office had green-lit their plan to withdraw the 5K letter. DuCharme had agreed with Van Grack, but stressed they write a memo to the court laying out dispassionate facts so the judge could decide on punishment. The two prosecutors filed a thirty-three-page sentencing memorandum explaining how Flynn had broken the law and his promises and should go to prison for up to six months. The two emphasized the gravity of someone in Flynn's position breaching his oath to his country.

"The defendant's conduct was more than just a series of lies; it was an abuse of trust," the memo said. "During the defendant's pattern of criminal conduct, he was the National Security Adviser to the President of the United States, the former Director of the Defense Intelligence Agency, and a retired U.S. Army Lieutenant General."

The memo noted that the Russians and Turks likely sought out Flynn because of the future sway he would have in Trump's administration, and the Turkish government had even paid Flynn's company $500,000, through an intermediary, for this special access.

"The defendant monetized his power and influence over our government, and lied to mask it," the prosecutors' memo read.

Their recommendation of prison time became the subject of breaking news stories that afternoon. Within about an hour, Liu's office got a call from DuCharme.

A frustrated DuCharme said the memo was gratuitously harsh.

"You were too hard on him," DuCharme said of the memo. "You didn't give credit for all his service."

It was certainly not the dispassionate approach that they'd agreed upon, he said. Worse, "this is not what Barr expected," he added. "Now I'm going to have to manage this upstairs."

The next day, on January 8, Liu went to Rosen's office for a meeting on a different matter. Barr did not attend, but Rabbitt asked Liu to stay behind after the group left. When the door closed, he reminded her that he and Barr wanted her commitment to leave the office, stat. In an email to Rabbitt the same day, Barr had indicated he wanted his adviser, Tim Shea, to replace Liu: "I want Tim in place by the time I leave for Mexico. ASAP."

Liu suggested she just stay on as U.S. attorney instead of pursuing the Treasury job. "Let me go back," she said.

No, Rabbitt said, that wasn't possible, and he explained they had set up interviews for potential replacements. He proposed she consider another job at Main Justice. She declined. Rabbitt said he would follow up with her the next day. When they reconvened, Rabbitt was even more insistent that the AG wanted a date that was her last day.

Liu said she wanted to talk to Barr before she decided what to do. She was summoned to Barr's office that afternoon. Rosen joined them. Barr seemed calm, but also unwavering. He repeated many of the arguments Rabbitt had already conveyed. The office needed a new leader for the final year of the president's term.

"We can't have this uncertainty," Barr said. He said they should set a date for her departure and asked her thoughts.

"I would very much like to stay until I'm voted out of committee so I won't have to make this move and answer questions in the hearing about why," Liu said. "I think it would be better for everybody."

"No," Barr said flatly. "I want it to be February 1."

It was done. Barr proceeded to explain how he'd help seal her Treasury confirmation. Liu stopped debating. An independent, vetted, and Senate-confirmed U.S. attorney had been removed.

On the next day, January 9, Liu sent out an office-wide email telling her staff she had decided to leave her position earlier than planned. She didn't say who was rushing her to the exit. Then, on January 30, hours before her own departure, a Rosen deputy called to tell her that Shea, the fifty-nine-year-old senior counselor to Barr, would now run the office.

But the news had already leaked to the Associated Press. Liu didn't get to prepare her staff, many of whom were upset. Nobody had ever heard of Shea; their online searching showed he had mostly been a lobbyist and lawyer at a little-known firm. He hadn't been a prosecutor since a brief stint in the 1990s. Rosen's office asked Liu and her first assistant to brief Shea the next day, January 31. They would spend three hours together, going over how the office operated and reviewing a list of cases coming up in the first two weeks of February, things Shea had to get on top of right away. Lastly, they flagged the fast-approaching deadline for the sentencing recommendation for one of Trump's oldest and closest confidants, Roger Stone. Liu and her principal deputy also arranged to meet Shea later to show him around the office and court operations. He had one question: What was the address of the U.S. Attorney's Office again?

Before she walked out of her office for the last time, on Friday, January 31, Liu left some late-night sustenance and a note on the desk of Jonathan Kravis, one of the Stone prosecutors she had a kinship with—a large bag of Doritos and another of potato chips.

"I have a feeling you'll need this when I'm gone," she wrote. "Love, Jessie."

In Shea's first full week on the job, the incoming top federal prosecutor in the nation's capital gathered with his deputies, including chiefs of the Fraud and Public Corruption Section. It was time to bring Shea up to speed on the office's most sensitive ongoing investigations.

Prosecutors eventually turned to describing the Egypt case, its bags of $100 bills, and the credible intel that the foreign cash had been intended for Trump. Shea, Barr's new handpicked chief, looked up and asked only one question:

"Who else knows about this case?"

Some of those around the table exchanged glances. Shea would later say he was concerned whether Main Justice had been alerted. But to several others, Shea seemed worried about only one thing: How many people outside of that room knew about a suspected bribe flowing from Egypt to Trump? Shea added that he didn't want any further investigative steps taken on this case until he got up to speed. No one in the room challenged Shea or advocated strongly for the case to go forward, and the meeting ended.

Afterward, one person involved in the case headed for the office of a trusted supervisor.

"Are we about to get hit?" he said, stunned. "Because that felt like a mob hit in preparation."

The supervisor's eyes widened when told of Shea's apparent lack of curiosity about any details of the case. The two career Justice Department employees joked that if they turned up missing, this case was probably why.

"We should have said a lot more people knew about this than just us," the one said to his supervisor.

Cooney, the fraud chief, sounded resigned as he left the same meeting.

"Well, that's that," he said to a fellow prosecutor. The one-liner by the man who always went to the mat for a righteous prosecution made it around the office. The case file might have still been technically open, but the Egypt investigation was all but dead. A draft subpoena for more Trump bank records would gather dust at the U.S. Attorney's Office in D.C. for eighteen more months before another Barr appointee would write to FBI officials in June 2020, saying he was closing the probe for "a lack of sufficient evidence to prove this case beyond a reasonable doubt." Normally, federal prosecutors closed a case with a detailed memo explaining what dead end they hit and why they couldn't continue. It was common practice in the office even for street crimes. Yet for all the years of work on whether a U.S. presidential candidate had won the White House with the help of a secret contribution from a foreign government, despite the involvement of a Special Counsel's Office, the Supreme Court, the attorney general, the FBI director, and the CIA and a concrete investigative step left on the table, no one wrote the standard memo to memorialize the decision to end the Egypt probe. When two *Washington Post* reporters later pieced together that the case had been dropped without the DOJ subpoenaing Trump bank records for any period after the money was found to have left Egypt, a spokesman for Trump issued a statement saying the investigation had found no wrongdoing and the allegations had no basis in fact. The paper and its reporters, he said, were "consistently played for suckers by Deep State Trump-haters and bad faith actors peddling hoaxes and shams."

[7]

A "Very Unfair Situation"

On February 5, 2020, four federal prosecutors in the D.C. office who had successfully convicted Roger Stone in a trial that November received the hoped-for news that superiors had endorsed their recommended prison term. The team had been holding their breath, concerned that Shea, their newly arrived boss, might undo the last step in a carefully argued prosecution. It was time for Stone's sentencing, and the presiding judge had set a deadline for the government to file its recommendation in five days, by February 10.

The prosecutors—Jonathan Kravis, Aaron Zelinsky, Adam Jed, and Michael Marando—were a picture of the Justice Department's emerging next generation of leaders. Zelinsky, thirty-six, had been a *Yale Law Journal* editor and had clerked for two Supreme Court justices on his way to becoming a top national security prosecutor in the Maryland U.S. Attorney's Office. Jed, thirty-eight, had won top honors at Harvard Law and clerked at the Supreme Court before going on to argue more than thirty cases for the DOJ as a civil appellate attorney. The two had decided to stay with the Stone case after Mueller's office shut down in the spring of 2019. There they joined D.C. office prosecutors Marando and Kravis. Marando, forty-two, who had come to the DOJ after Cornell Law School, had gained a reputation for successfully prosecuting complex money-laundering and bribery cases and displaying the grit and street smarts of a city district attorney. Kravis, forty-two, was arguably the most decorated, a Yale Law grad who had clerked for Federal Appeals Court Judge Merrick Garland and Supreme Court Justice Stephen G. Breyer. He'd worked in private practice, as associate White House counsel to President Barack Obama, and then under Jack Smith and alongside Cooney in the Justice Department's revered Public Integrity Section. Kravis was now the most senior of the four on the Stone case, serving as Cooney's deputy chief of the Fraud and Public Corruption Section.

The four had reason to feel their Stone prosecution was righteous. A jury had convicted him of all seven felony counts they had charged—obstructing a congressional investigation, making false statements to Congress in five instances, and tampering with a witness. They planned to recommend that a federal judge sentence Stone to up to nine years in prison.

Stone was a unique felon. Having been a campaign aide to President Nixon as a teenager, he had become one of the highest-paid political consultants in the country, often sporting suits worth thousands of dollars and flashy jewelry as he employed his self-described "dirty trickster" tactics to gain an edge for his candidate. Over the years, Stone had also grown extremely close to Donald Trump, who brought him on as a trusted adviser for his run for the White House. Inside the campaign, Stone boasted about his access to WikiLeaks publisher Julian Assange, and months in advance had informed aides that the website would leak information damaging to Hillary Clinton's campaign.

Mueller's team could never tell if Stone really had any pull with Assange, finding that at the same time he bragged about their connection, he also urged contacts to put the two in touch. But they learned Stone had lied under oath to Congress. They also learned he pulled some mobster-like moves when under investigation; he threatened Randy Credico, a

New York comedian and radio personality, to back up the story Stone had given Congress, writing at one point: "You are a rat. A stoolie . . . I am so ready. Let's get it on. Prepare to die."

The nine-year sentence was at the low end of what prosecutors could have recommended under federal guidelines, due to the conviction for witness tampering. Stone had also shared on social media an image of the judge presiding over his trial, Judge Amy Berman Jackson, with gun crosshairs next to her face.

On February 4, Kravis, the lead prosecutor, briefed Shea on the recommended punishment for Stone. It was Shea's second full day on the job. He said he'd "like to take a closer look," and they could discuss it again. But privately, Shea was taken aback, thinking of violent criminals who get lower sentences. Shea complained later that day to the office's second-in-command, Principal Assistant Alessio Evangelista, that the suggested punishment was "surprisingly high" and "out of whack" with comparable cases. Shea's concern sparked a series of conversations among Evangelista, Kravis, and his boss, Cooney, about whether it would be appropriate to soften the recommendation, including the consideration that Credico had recently written to the judge urging leniency for Stone. Both prosecutors opposed any change, with Kravis saying it was inappropriate to diverge from sentencing guidelines their section always followed. Cooney couldn't help wondering if Stone's close ties to Trump motivated DOJ higher-ups to intervene at this late stage in the case. Cooney privately told Evangelista that he doubted they would be discussing how to soften Stone's sentencing memo "if he wasn't the friend of the president." So, on February 5, it came as a relief when Cooney told the prosecutors that their draft sentencing memorandum for Stone was good to go. In an email, Cooney applauded their work and said Stone "deserves every day of the 87 months" in prison that they recommended.

But two days later, Cooney reported that their proposal was suddenly in serious trouble. Shea had consulted with a senior aide to Barr, who urged Shea, as the final authority in the office, to recommend something lower than the sentencing guidelines.

In a meeting that Friday afternoon, Kravis felt sickened listening as Shea urged the prosecutors to delete descriptions of Stone's threats to a witness and other conduct he'd been convicted of to reduce the proposed punishment. In a Saturday night call with the prosecutors, Cooney sought to broker a compromise. He confided to the prosecutors that the softening of the sentencing recommendation appeared unethical and brazenly political. He said Shea was afraid of getting heat from President Trump and his allies on the right. But some on the call sensed Cooney was wavering. His post as a senior supervisor over the office's fraud and corruption cases was also potentially at risk.

"People's jobs are on the line," several recalled Cooney saying, unsure if he had meant theirs, his, Shea's, or everyone's. Cooney would later tell investigators seeking to reconstruct the call that he was exasperated and worried that all of them were heading toward a dangerous impasse over a few sentences in the recommendation. "This is not the hill to die on," he told them.

The team was disgusted by the whole situation. While it was normal practice for the Justice Department's top political appointees to review key decisions in high-profile matters, sentencing recommendations were pro forma calculations based on federal guidelines. Shea felt prosecutors had tunnel vision in pushing a draconian punishment; they thought he was determined to deviate from the guidelines. Some on the team feared a ripple effect if an aggressive supervisor like Cooney seemed susceptible to that pressure. The prosecutors searched for and could not find another example of when the Fraud Section had ignored some of the most egregious aspects of a defendant's bad conduct in recommending a sentence.

The four prosecutors refused to make the modifications Shea sought. On Sunday night, Cooney emailed the prosecutors a revised draft recommendation, removing Stone's threats and other violations. During a call with Cooney that night, the prosecutors privately texted each other in frustration as Cooney acknowledged how this case diverged from the office's long-standing practices.

"We are going to treat Roger Stone differently than every other defendant," some of the four later recalled Cooney telling them.

Three of the four prosecutors, Kravis, Zelinsky, and Jed, explained they planned to resign from the case if pressured to sign any document that ignored Stone's repeated attacks on the justice system.

A resignation from the case at this late stage would threaten what lawyers called a "noisy withdrawal"—an embarrassing red flag alerting the court and the media that the departing attorney had a profound disagreement with how the case was being handled, likely one based on principle. Such disputes were almost always settled privately. Cooney asked the team to hold off on resigning. He thought they could possibly work this out the next morning, the day of the Monday deadline.

Zelinsky, on loan to the D.C. office, went ahead that night and drafted his notice of resignation, just in case. On Monday morning, he called his trusted boss back in Maryland, Acting U.S. Attorney Jonathan Lenzner, explaining the pressure to shield Trump's friend and asking if he could return to Maryland if he needed to resign from the Stone case. Lenzner said yes.

That morning, Cooney alerted Shea that several of his prosecutors were threatening to leave the case. Cooney pushed for Shea to consider reverting to the tougher recommendation, given that the deadline for filing was only hours away. But Shea said he wanted to discuss it with Barr first.

That seemed to spook Cooney, who then told Kravis that their acting U.S. attorney "is getting pressure from Main Justice about the Stone sentencing recommendation and Tim Shea is terrified of the president."

A little after 11:45 a.m., a *Washington Post* courts reporter, Spencer Hsu, called a top supervisor in the D.C. office saying he had heard there was a dispute over a recommendation to sentence Stone for eighty-seven months and prosecutors had been told to go easier on Stone because he was the president's friend. Someone had leaked.

Over at the attorney general's office, Shea didn't know about the leak. As an 11:00 a.m. meeting with Barr ended, he asked to speak with Barr privately.

They chatted in the attorney general's office for five or ten minutes and left with utterly different takeaways. Barr heard Shea lay out two options. They could stick with the nine-year guideline recommendation and rely on the court to decide what was best, *or* spell out that the guidelines were more appropriate for a mafia boss tied to violence and urge something lower but defer to the court to decide the number.

"Well, that sounds very reasonable to me," Barr said, focusing on the second option. "Let's try to do that."

Shea only heard Barr's instruction to "defer to the court," and believed Barr meant he could use his discretion on the recommendation.

When Shea got back to the office, his deputies alerted him to calls from the reporter who had gotten wind of the dispute. Shea was angry, accusing someone in the office of leaking to intimidate him. Shea then met with Cooney and told him his understanding of the meeting with Barr: The attorney general had signed off on a sentencing recommendation aligned with the guidelines. At Shea's instruction, Cooney found Kravis, his deputy, who had become the go-between for the four.

"Tim wants to talk to you," he said. "Just you."

When Kravis was inside the U.S. attorney's private office at the end of the hall, Shea began asking questions that came off as shockingly elementary.

"Explain to me: What's the problem with the sentencing recommendation?" Shea asked. "What's going on here?"

Kravis laid out the basics and how sentencing guidelines called for a specific range of time in prison, seven to nine years.

"It's your call. You're the U.S. attorney," Kravis said. "If you want to make another recommendation, do it. I'm just not going to sign it."

"What is it that you want?" Shea asked.

"That we just write a sentencing recommendation that complies with the guidelines," Kravis answered.

To Kravis's shock, Shea seemed to back down: "OK. Let's do that."

"OK. That's great," Kravis said.

Shea let Barr's office know he had struck a compromise to move forward. A short time later, Cooney wrote to all four prosecutors to say they could stick with the nine-year recommendation. He said there was one condition: The bosses didn't want the team to bring up Stone's egregious conduct in the written memo, but they could mention it in the sentencing hearing. The four prosecutors conferred and agreed.

At 2:00 p.m., Zelinsky emailed Lenzner an update: "It looks like they are blinking."

By 4:00 p.m., Kravis had sent his fellow prosecutors and Cooney a new draft sentencing memorandum.

A few minutes after 6:00 p.m., Cooney emailed the four prosecutors the go-ahead to send it to the judge. They hit the button and the sentencing recommendation appeared on the court's public filing system at virtually the same moment.

They all—either in email or in person—thanked Cooney for his help in avoiding disaster.

Just before 8:00 p.m., Barr was at home and got a call from the DOJ's chief spokeswoman alerting him to news reports about a high prison sentence prosecutors had recommended for Stone. Barr immediately called Rabbitt, his chief of staff.

"Why is the media reporting DOJ recommended seven to nine years for Stone?" Barr asked. "This isn't what I had decided."

If it was true, Barr said, "we're going to have to fix it first thing in the morning."

Kravis had a full plate that day: an early morning dentist appointment, followed by a 10:00 a.m. court hearing. Waiting at the dentist's office, Kravis saw an incoming email from his mother: a link to a news story about President Trump ragefully tweeting at 1:48 a.m. about the government's treatment of his friend Roger Stone.

"This is a horrible and very unfair situation," Trump's tweet read.

"The real crimes were on the other side, as nothing happens to them. Cannot allow this miscarriage of justice!"

Once upon a time, a president publicly ripping into federal prosecutors would cause panic. But Trump's tweets were old hat. Besides, Kravis thought the battle was over. Stone's fate was now up to a judge to decide. After the dentist, Kravis quickly drove home, then hopped the Metro and hustled back to the E. Barrett Prettyman federal courthouse. Following standard procedure, Kravis turned off his phone for the duration of his hearing, clueless to anything happening outside the wood-paneled walls of Courtroom 14.

Exiting the courtroom hours later, Kravis noticed *The Washington Post*'s Spencer Hsu, who had reported on the sentencing dispute, waiting just outside. Hsu observed the courthouse prohibition on conducting interviews in the courthouse's halls. But he silently followed Kravis to the court's main elevator banks. As Kravis stepped into the elevator to depart, Hsu held up his cell phone in front of Kravis's face. Kravis leaned forward, trying to make out the details as the elevator doors began to close. The screen showed a Fox News breaking-news alert, and the headline was all he needed to see: "DOJ Expected to Scale Back Roger Stone's 'Extreme' Sentencing Recommendation."

[8]

"Truth Still Matters, OK?"

Kravis pulled up the article as he beat a rapid retreat to the U.S. Attorney's Office, four blocks to the north of the courthouse. The news flash said Justice Department brass had been "shocked" by the sentence and planned to shorten it. By the time he reached his desk, Kravis found an already long email thread among his fellow prosecutors and Cooney expressing disbelief and agitation.

Just after noon, fellow prosecutor Mike Marando, who had also been stuck in a sentencing hearing all morning and unaware of the chaos, forwarded to Cooney an email from a reporter at *The Hill* newspaper. The reporter was seeking comment about the Fox report of a scaled-back sentence.

Cooney instantly replied with one word: "False." But he was unaware of what bosses at Main Justice were planning.

Zelinsky then shared a CNN reporter's tweet saying his network had confirmed the Fox report.

"This is not what had been briefed to the department," CNN quoted an unnamed senior DOJ official as saying. "The department believes the recommendation is extreme and excessive and is grossly disproportionate to Stone's offenses."

An outraged Zelinsky told his teammates that favoring a presidential ally with a reduced sentence would violate his oath as a prosecutor.

By 1:00 p.m., he emailed Lenzner. "Sorry to bug you with an urgent request," Zelinsky wrote, but he needed to confirm he could resign from the Stone case and return to his old job. Yes, he had their support.

Within a half hour, Zelinsky drafted a motion to notify the court of his withdrawal. All four talked on the phone over the next hour about whether each would follow suit.

Just before 3:00 p.m., Zelinsky sent Cooney his withdrawal notice from the Stone case and explained he was now leaving the D.C. office. Cooney wrote back a minute later: "I am not approving of you withdrawing from this case right now."

But it was too late. Over the next two and a half hours, Jed, Marando, and Kravis would all withdraw from the case.

Kravis took an even more dramatic step. After ten years as a federal prosecutor, and with a résumé that could have taken him to the highest levels at DOJ, Kravis instead chose to resign from the department.

In her temporary digs at Treasury, Jessie Liu, the team's former boss, was stunned by the texts and calls coming from inside her old office. She felt a tinge of relief she wasn't there in the maelstrom, she later told friends, but also second-guessed her decision to leave. She had been confirmed by the U.S. Senate and would have had more leverage to stand up for her old staff. Liu tried to comfort herself, thinking she could make a difference in the Treasury job, she told colleagues. Her nomination hearing was set for February 13, just two days later. But out of the blue, Secretary Mnuchin's office called that afternoon, asking her to come over for a meeting. Surprised, she asked the young aide what the meeting was about.

"It's about this stuff that's in the news today," she explained.

After a hasty greeting, Mnuchin was matter-of-fact.

"I know you only wanted this job if you could be Senate confirmed. And you can't be Senate confirmed."

Stunned, Liu asked: "Why?"

"I have to call over and withdraw your nomination," Mnuchin said.

She wanted to know why. He said he could not tell her. Mnuchin asked a reeling Liu if there was anything else she might want to do at Treasury. They parted with her saying she would think about it.

When she returned to her temporary Treasury office, she saw texts from Kravis, who said he was quitting the department. She also soon received a stream of colleagues dropping by to share their regrets over her nomination being yanked by the president. As Liu drove home, she heard blaring radio reports about the mass resignation of prosecutors from the Stone case. The news was like the aftershock of an earthquake, another discombobulating episode coming before anyone had time to recover from the first.

That evening, at the Carving Room—a favorite venue among prosecutors a few blocks from the U.S. Attorney's office—news of the resignations scrolled across a large TV screen behind the bar. It was an unusual sight. The television there was typically tuned to sports highlights or the big game of the day. Fellow prosecutor Molly Gaston had taken Kravis for drinks to mark the occasion of his sudden last day.

Soon, Marando and other lawyers trickled in to join the gathering—part wake, part group-therapy session. As they sat together lamenting how Barr had forced the office to flout its standards, CNN recounted part of Marando's closing argument from Stone's trial back in November: "Truth still matters, OK?" the cable news host said, quoting Marando's summation. "In our institutions of self-governance, committee hearings, courts of law . . . truth still matters."

Kravis and Marando happened to sidle up to the bar at that moment. As the segment ended, Kravis lifted his glass to Marando:

"Truth still matters!"

[9]

Winners Write the History

On Wednesday, the day after the Stone debacle, prosecutor Brandon Van Grack was in court to talk about another sentencing. This time, for Michael Flynn.

Van Grack had endured rounds of fierce criticism from Trump and his allies in recent months after recommending up to six months in prison for Trump's former national security adviser. In court, he had defended the prison time as "warranted" but also said that if the judge recommended probation, that would be a "reasonable sentence." In 2017, Flynn had fabricated for FBI agents a conversation he had with Russian Ambassador Sergey Kislyak, claiming he simply conveyed his holiday greetings. But U.S. intelligence had recorded Flynn's actual conversation. When confronted with the intercepts, Flynn twice swore under oath to a federal judge that he took full responsibility for lying to the agents.

But since the summer of 2019, Flynn's new lawyer, Trump ally Sidney Powell, had been insisting that Mueller and Van Grack withheld damning evidence of an FBI plot to entrap Flynn. Far-right podcasters and Flynn supporters quickly picked up on the baseless conspiracy, giving it life on the internet.

Prosecutors considered it a solemn duty to turn over to defendants any evidence that would help their defense, under what is known as the Brady rule. Violations are considered career-ending. A young prosecutor implicated for withholding evidence in the prosecution of Sen. Ted Stevens had committed suicide.

After the allegations were lodged, one former Mueller teammate who had left government checked in with Van Grack to ask if it might be time for Van Grack to get out too. A small group knew that he felt falsely accused and had already written a draft resignation letter and kept it handy. He told his former colleague that he wanted to stick with the case, fearing political supervisors might echo those accusations in his absence.

Asked about how things were really going, Van Grack replied, "You have no idea."

Facing the continued allegations from Powell, Van Grack was adamant in court that he'd done nothing wrong. In December, U.S. District Court Judge Emmet G. Sullivan agreed, concluding that Van Grack's work was above reproach. Despite making fifty allegations, Flynn's attorney had "failed to establish a single *Brady* violation."

Still, the episode had been scarring, Van Grack told colleagues. He could feel his department wavering on the rock-solid case, and he dated the shift to when Barr had complained in January about him and Ballantine being too "harsh" in describing Flynn's lies. Van Grack's trepidation soon proved prescient. In late January, Barr had quietly asked Jeff Jensen, the U.S. attorney in St. Louis, to review the handling of the Flynn case.

Weeks later, on February 12, Powell made what seemed like another Hail Mary attempt to dismiss the Flynn case, this time with a new rationale. She claimed a government watchdog report had raised questions about whether the government ever had a right to investigate Flynn. Van Grack and Ballantine responded that that wasn't true; the inspector general himself had said the FBI had "sufficient predication" to open the case against Flynn.

As the COVID-19 pandemic began and prosecutors started working mostly from home, however, the U.S. Attorney's Office began responding to Powell's allegations in an unusual manner. Shea's deputies began to release documents in response to Powell's allegations, not to her directly, but on the court's public website, with some of the releases seemingly aimed at stirring doubt about the justification for the Flynn case.

Van Grack refused to sign one of the filings, revealing clear disagreement about the strange new approach to the case. Shea told colleagues the office had a duty to share discovery, and among the government's voluntary disclosures were senior FBI officials' notes about the Flynn interview. Shea also released a memo the FBI prepared in anticipation of closing the counterintelligence investigation of Flynn's contacts with Russia. It was never acted on because the FBI had soon learned about Flynn's call with Kislyak and that he had lied about it to the vice president. But Sidney Powell hailed it as a smoking gun that FBI agents set out to frame Flynn.

"It's like there's this result they want to get to but nobody is saying anything," Van Grack would later tell an associate about the filings.

On the weekend of May 2, Van Grack, Ballantine, and others in the office were notified by a supervisor that the Attorney General's Office was considering dropping the Flynn case. No prosecutor could recall it ever happening before—a case being dropped when the defendant had pleaded guilty to the crime and there were no fouls on the government's part.

Van Grack wouldn't be part of it. On Thursday, May 7, he formally resigned from the case, knowing what his bosses intended to do that day. An hour later, Barr's DOJ claimed that there had never been a good reason to consider or pursue criminal charges against Flynn. Any false statements Flynn made to FBI agents were "untethered" to any material probe, the filing stated. "The Government is not persuaded that the January 24, 2017, interview was conducted with a legitimate investigative basis and therefore does not believe Mr. Flynn's statements were material even if untrue," the filing read. The language was largely conceived and planned at Main Justice, but Shea, Barr's acting U.S. attorney, signed it. As the day unfolded, the full drama of what had transpired began to trickle out in conversations around the office. Shea had told both Van Grack and Ballantine they needed to sign the motion alleging the government's entire prosecution had been flawed unless they could identify that it contained something inaccurate. But in an apparent carrot for them to get on board, the draft filing stated the prosecutors assigned to the case had done nothing wrong. It was a blanket statement of U.S. government support that would shield them from future investigations seeking to exonerate Flynn and potentially blame them. Van Grack and Ballantine, however, still wouldn't budge and gave their final answer: They would not sign. Hours later, the final version that Shea's office filed in court contained a key material difference from earlier drafts. His office had deleted the line vouching for the career prosecutors' honorable work.

Trump celebrated the dismissal, calling Flynn "an innocent man" unfairly targeted by the Obama administration's Justice Department, despite Flynn's plea agreement having been negotiated in 2017, when Trump himself was president. Talking to reporters that same day, the president ominously hoped aloud for the Justice Department investigators involved in the Flynn and larger Russia investigation to face some pain.

"I hope a lot of people are going to pay a big price because they're dishonest, crooked people," Trump said. "They're scum—and I say it a lot, they're scum, they're human scum. This should never have happened in this country."

Four days after the Flynn case was withdrawn, nearly two thousand alumni of the Department of Justice jointly published a public letter asking Barr to resign. The group, which had served under both Republican and Democratic administrations dating back to President Eisenhower's administration, said Bill Barr had assaulted the rule of law. They also called on Congress to censure Barr publicly and on Judge Sullivan to independently assess how to proceed with the Flynn case.

"Our democracy depends on a Department of Justice that acts as an independent arbiter of equal justice, not as an arm of the president's political apparatus," the group said in its letter.

That same morning, on May 7, Barr had appeared in an interview with *CBS This Morning* to defend his decision in the Flynn case. He said he wasn't doing the president's bidding.

"I'm doing my duty under the law as I see it," Barr said.

Asked by his interviewer how his decision would go down in history, Barr grinned.

"History is written by the winners, so it largely depends," he said, breaking into a chuckle, "on who's writing the history."

Behind Barr's public nonchalance, however, the mounting criticism was getting to him. After back-to-back revolts inside the U.S. Attorney's Office over the Stone and Flynn cases, Barr told his aides that he needed someone more skilled running point. He also had no choice.

Shea had angered another critical constituency. Several federal judges in the U.S. District Court in D.C. were repulsed by his backpedaling role in the Stone and Flynn prosecutions. In a call in early May, Chief Judge Howell alerted Shea that she and likely her entire bench of judges in D.C. would refuse to vote in favor of extending him in his interim role. After an acting U.S. attorney had been in the job 120 days, the law required the presiding court to either reappoint that person or choose another.

"I'm sorry. But I cannot support you now," Howell told Shea. "You have to take this to your department and take this into consideration as you decide what to do."

Shea did so, alerting Barr's aides and feeling the judges were acting political and unfair.

It gave Barr an opening to bring in new blood. He had already inserted Mike Sherwin, a scrappy, fast-talking, longtime assistant U.S. attorney from Miami, as a deputy in the D.C. office, and he was pleased with the test run. Barr had first taken a liking to Sherwin when the prosecutor briefed him on the case of a Chinese national caught trespassing at Trump's Mar-a-Lago resort in September 2019. Barr had asked Sherwin to come work at headquarters, tapping him to review national security matters. Sherwin reinforced Barr's favorable impression with his no-

nonsense help on the investigation into a shooting at the Pensacola Naval Air Station. Barr opted for Sherwin to replace Shea. In describing Sherwin to his deputies, Barr had bestowed one of his highest compliments: "You give the guy a job and he just goes and gets it done."

For all of Barr's efforts to shape prosecutorial decisions to Trump's liking, there was seemingly no end to the president's displeasure with the department, especially its investigative arm.

On May 8, the morning after the Flynn decision, Trump dialed into *Fox & Friends*, adding a new concern for the FBI director and his team.

What about Wray? a Fox host asked the president. Should his appointed FBI director have done more to halt the Flynn case? "Let's see what happens with him," Trump said. "The jury is still out."

The president kept talking, as if working through a decision about Wray's fate on live television. He had every right to fire the FBI chief again, Trump said, though doing so might not help him politically. Trump recounted how messy that had gotten three years earlier: "When I fired Comey, you-know-what hit the fan, and it was big, it was big, it was a monster."

Three days later, the president kept up the attack on his appointed FBI director and the Bureau, beginning with seven late-night tweets or retweets. In several, Trump repeated conspiracy theories that the Bureau had "gone rogue" and had fabricated the basis for the Russia investigation.

The president was openly leaning on the FBI director to help lift the continued cloud of suspicion around his campaign's dealings with Russia. But Wray wouldn't comply, which made it all the more surprising to Trump that Attorney General Bill Barr was still defending Wray. There was a reason for that. "He knew how to read an org chart," said a person who watched the dynamic. Barr felt Wray generally deferred to him, and they worked well together. In private, Barr tried to explain to Trump that the FBI director was an apolitical position, and could not actively support Trump the way Barr could. He warned that firing Wray could be a devastating misstep in an election year. Barr joked to aides he was Wray's "heat shield."

Unbeknownst to the public, Barr knew Trump was considering replacing Wray and hiring as deputy director Kash Patel, a former aide to Rep. Devin Nunes, who together had put on hearings to undercut the Mueller investigation. Now it was Barr's turn to threaten to resign. Barr had been willing to do a lot that no predecessor had done for a president. But the FBI's number 2 position had always been for the senior-most career FBI agent, someone who had worked their way up through details on SWAT or hostage rescue, investigated complex criminal cases, or run field offices. Barr warned Trump's chief of staff he would resign as AG if the president installed the inexperienced nonagent Patel: "Over my dead body."

[10]

Sowing Chaos

That July, Richard Pilger was marking his tenth year as the director of what he acknowledged was a slightly nerdy, though still important, back bench in the Department of Justice: the Election Crimes Branch, which operated as a kind of national hotline response team to guide FBI agents and federal prosecutors around the country on how to handle allegations of election crimes and voting irregularities. A devotee of U.S. history and a three-decade veteran of the department, Pilger, fifty-five, was known for being able to quote the arcanely worded statutes of U.S. federal election law by heart. He also knew that confirmed instances of election tampering—destroying ballots, buying votes, or stuffing ballot boxes—were rare.

His office had announced an indictment against a former Philadelphia-area congressman for bribing local officials there to inflate vote counts from 2014 to 2016, but such cases were infrequent. Most often, Pilger's department consulted in the background as local, state, and federal prosecutors wrestled with one-off cases like a resident casting a vote in two states where they owned homes, sending in a ballot for a dying or deceased relative, or voting in the wrong jurisdiction or by absentee and then again in person.

Still, allegations of more systemic voter fraud, sometimes the product of misunderstandings, always spiked during an election season. The Election Crimes Branch had been created in 1980, not long after a somewhat sensational federal investigation of a vote-buying scheme in Louisiana, but now generally offered its expertise so that investigators handled such allegations confidentially and consistently. Its goal was to figure out quickly in real time if there was a problem that threatened to undermine the integrity of an election and, if not, deal with prosecuting any individual criminal offenses afterward. The often behind-the-scenes work of Pilger's branch was easily overshadowed by its larger DOJ parent organization, the Public Integrity Section, best known for its comparatively swashbuckling team of prosecutors who regularly made front-page news by indicting public officials for bribery, fraud, and other forms of corruption. For nearly all three decades that Pilger led the elections branch, the public, the press, and even the senior leaders of the department generally had paid scant attention to his work. His colleagues knew Pilger took immense pride in his team's role in ensuring the smooth operation of elections and maintaining public faith in their results.

But the election of 2020 was already shaping up as unique. Nearly every state was in varying degrees of lockdown due to the coronavirus pandemic. Legislatures coast-to-coast had expanded voting by mail to conduct primary contests. Election officials in some states had already preemptively decided to send absentee ballots to all registered voters for the general election, in anticipation of COVID cases spiking with the onset of winter. Pilger decided to institute a zero-tolerance policy for postal carriers mishandling election material. If there was any problem, the branch would investigate. What the country needed most, Pilger thought, was reassurance and close monitoring to ensure the system would work.

Instead, in an interview with Fox News's Chris Wallace in July, Trump cast doubt on the integrity of the upcoming vote. Trump refused to say if he would accept the results of the election. In a tweet later that month, he blasted universal mail-in voting: "2020 will be the most IN-ACCURATE & FRAUDULENT Election in history," he wrote. In August, he continued, telling Axios mail-in voting inherently would bring "massive cheating." And in accepting the Republican nomination at the party's nationally televised convention, Trump posited that the only way he would lose was "if this is a rigged election." Pilger, perhaps more than anyone else in the country, knew the president was wildly exaggerating the risks of ballot fraud, but he assumed Trump's aim was simply to save face should he lose. Pilger took comfort in the Department of Justice's time-honored rules to ensure the vote results were above reproach.

On August 26, two days after Trump's acceptance speech, he was heartened when officials from the FBI, the Department of Homeland Security, and the Office of the Director of National Intelligence held a background conference call with reporters to make sure the public heard a more stable and sane message about the election.

There was no evidence of vote tampering, the officials told reporters—none at all. Intelligence officials had privately briefed Trump months earlier in the Oval Office that the risk was exceptionally low, but he ignored that assurance after the pandemic tanked the economy and imperiled his chances for reelection. Still, Pilger was pleased by the united front taking shape among government agencies. No matter what Trump—or for that matter, Pilger's boss, Barr—said about the integrity of mail-in ballots, election officials would do their jobs, and Pilger would be among the first to know if there was actually a problem with the election.

In the third week of September, Pilger was put on high alert when local officials in Luzerne County, in rural eastern Pennsylvania just south of Scranton, called his office with a problem. The county election office had discovered that a handful of ballots that military service members had mailed to their home county had ended up in the office trash. Pilger's office swung into action, giving advice on how to proceed. FBI agents based in Scranton, who reported to the Philadelphia Field Office, were dispatched on Monday, September 21, to interview county election officials on site. The agents even sorted through several days' worth of office trash. But investigators quickly concluded that the person who threw out the nine ballot envelopes was a mentally impaired member of a cleaning crew who likely wasn't aware of what he was tossing into a dumpster. It was almost certainly a mistake—not a criminal plot—and an insignificant one at that. Luzerne was not a highly competitive county. Trump had won the district by 20 points four years before and likely would again. The FBI field office and Pilger's team reported a summary of their findings up through his chain of command at the DOJ. Based on experience, Pilger figured it might amount to a sentence or two in a long briefing to the deputies of FBI Director Chris Wray and Attorney General Barr.

But a day or two later, Pilger learned something alarming that only a handful of people ever knew. Without talking to Pilger's office, Barr had seized on the internal report of discarded ballots in Luzerne County and called the U.S. attorney over that district, David Freed. Barr and his deputies urged Freed to go public and issue a press release stating that the federal prosecutor had an "ongoing" investigation and concerns about tossed ballots.

Pilger was stunned on multiple counts. First, the Justice Department had always worked triple-time to keep such investigations confidential, and it had drilled into its partners in U.S. Attorney's Offices and at FBI offices strict orders not to ever discuss them unless and until they filed charges. The department knew its public statements could have unwanted ripple effects, such as changing voter turnout based on unverified claims. Why would the AG want to push the federal prosecutor to breach the protocol in this way? Second, the attorney general, the highest law enforcement official in the land, would normally be focusing his time on making critical decisions to shield the country from terror plots and reviewing his staff's decisions on major criminal cases.

Finally, and perhaps most upsetting, several DOJ officials had already been alerted that the trashing of the ballots was likely a mistake, with no sign of a nefarious plot to worry about. Pilger questioned why Barr would exaggerate a nothingburger that seemed to help Trump fuel suspicion of election results. It didn't take long for Trump to grab ahold of that nothingburger with both hands.

In addition to encouraging Freed to make a public statement, Barr had also briefed Trump on the trashed Luzerne ballots on September 23, the day before Freed announced the investigation. On a Fox News radio interview on September 24, Trump presented the handful of Luzerne ballots as Exhibit 1.

"These ballots are a horror show," the president said. "They found six ballots in an office yesterday, in a garbage can. They were Trump ballots, eight ballots in an office yesterday, in a certain state. And they had Trump written on it, and they were thrown in a garbage can. This is what is going to happen, this is what is going to happen, and we are investigating that. It's a terrible thing that is going on with these ballots."

When reporters who had gathered for a midday White House briefing asked what the president was referring to, White House press secretary Kayleigh McEnany amped up the concern, saying mail-in ballots are a "system that's subject to fraud." She also teased to reporters that more information on the "cast aside" ballots would be coming soon.

That day, U.S. Attorney Freed released a press statement making his office's investigation public and providing some details of the FBI's review. Freed said the case remained open, but "based on the limited amount of time before the general election and the vital public importance of these issues, I will detail the investigators' initial findings."

Freed went on to explain in his statement, which was later corrected by the Justice Department on its website, that seven of the ballots had been cast for Trump and removed from their envelopes. The votes of two more were unknown, having been reinserted into their envelopes by staff.

"The preliminary findings of this inquiry are troubling," Freed's release read, "and the Luzerne County Bureau of Elections must comply with all applicable state and federal election laws and guidance to ensure that all votes—regardless of party—are counted to ensure an accurate election."

Left out of the press release and the president's bluster was any indication of the janitor's mistake, and that the case had already largely been solved. Instead, the president greeted reporters on the White House lawn later that day to reemphasize what he called the "big scam" of mail-in ballots.

"We want to make sure the election is honest," Trump said, "and I'm not sure that it can be."

Trump White House and campaign staffers amplified the message: "BREAKING: FBI finds military mail-in ballots discarded in Pennsylvania," Matt Wolking, a campaign spokesman, tweeted. "100% of them were cast for President Trump. Democrats are trying to steal the election."

The publicity blitz by the president and the Justice Department on September 24 surprised some FBI officials who'd been briefed on the facts in Luzerne. This would almost certainly have zero impact on the election outcome. Government investigators would later find Barr's actions had been troubling and Freed's had violated DOJ policy. But in real time Pilger confided to close colleagues that he wasn't sure he was going to make it through this election season with Barr at the helm.

When Election Day arrived on November 3, Pilger got word from his supervisors that Rich Donoghue, the principal associate to the deputy attorney general and a close ally of Barr's, was eyeing a way to allow armed military troops to be stationed at voting tabulation centers. That was contrary to years of DOJ policy, which specifically provided for the feds to criminally charge any military or civilian official who sent armed federal officers to polling places. The prohibition, dating from the time of the Civil War, was to prevent the military from ever seizing control of an election. Donoghue claimed troops could now go to tabulation centers—where the votes were counted—because that was different from polling places. Pilger and his team saw it as another phony way to undermine the vote and throw the results into doubt.

Barr and Donoghue had been concerned about the security of vote counting being conducted at Philadelphia's Convention Center. In the immediate aftermath of election night, Democratic-leaning Philadelphia and surrounding suburbs drew national attention because election officials still had mountains of mail-in votes to count, a process that might continue for days and was steadily eroding Trump's lead in the critical state of Pennsylvania. The Trump campaign made false claims that the Democratic-controlled city was illegally tampering with ballots to inflate Biden's count, and his supporters rallied outside the Convention Center and demanded that the vote counting be stopped.

Overnight, at 1:30 a.m. on November 4, Donoghue sent an email notifying all federal prosecutors in the field that armed troops could now be stationed outside vote tabulation centers around the country, both to secure those sites and to investigate or prevent potential voter fraud. At the Convention Center in Philadelphia, clashes between Trump and Biden supporters were growing tense.

Pilger told colleagues that involving the military was a violation of DOJ policy and wrote to his bosses insisting that his office would have to object to Donoghue's middle-of-the-night memo. That Pilger put his opposition in writing made some of his supervisors uncomfortable; Pilger was the resident expert, but what would be won by going to war with the attorney general?

A little after noon on Saturday, November 7, 2020, the vote counts of the last outstanding precincts in Pennsylvania showed Joe Biden had won the state, and with it the White House. Major news organizations declared the Democratic nominee the next president of the United States. Biden, learning the news as he huddled with his staff in Wilmington, issued a statement saying he was humbled by the victory.

Trump's statement from his golf course in Virginia shrugged off reality, claiming ballot fraud had swung the election: "We all know why Joe Biden is rushing to falsely pose as the winner, and why his media allies are trying so hard to help him: they don't want the truth to be exposed," Trump said in a statement. "This election is far from over."

That Monday, November 9, Trump's campaign filed lawsuits in federal court challenging the count. Barr moved the executive branch of the federal government in lockstep with the president's political campaign. The same day, he instructed all U.S. attorneys that they could ignore the long-standing prohibition on publicly investigating allegations of vote fraud before the election was certified, saying they could do so immediately. Barr told Donoghue privately that he believed the 2020 election presented a unique circumstance, because of mail-in ballots used in most swing states. He told Donoghue he didn't want the department "sitting on our hands." In his note to prosecutors, he called the existing policy a "passive and delayed enforcement approach." Donoghue explained to other Justice officials it was the attorney general's prerogative.

That was the last straw for Pilger. He read the memo in his office and then began alerting his bosses that he would be resigning his treasured role overseeing free and fair elections. He began typing up a letter to share with his colleagues.

He noted he was taking this extreme action in keeping with his most cherished award, the John C. Keeney Award for Exceptional Integrity and Professionalism. It was named after a revered DOJ lifer, "Jack" Keeney, who served the department for six decades and was considered its in-house ethicist.

"Having familiarized myself with the new policy and its ramifications . . . I must regretfully resign," Pilger wrote. "I have enjoyed very much working with you for over a decade to aggressively and diligently enforce federal criminal election law, policy, and practice without partisan fear or favor."

[11]

"He's Asking You to Be Wild"

On November 9, the same day that Trump's campaign filed a lawsuit over vote counting in Pennsylvania and Barr pressed the Justice Department to focus on voter fraud, another more radical Trump ally summoned his top deputies and field organizers to plot to keep Trump in the White House.

Stewart Rhodes, the founder of the Oath Keepers, gathered leaders of his far-right anti-government group from around the country on a conference call. He echoed Trump, insisting the election had been stolen, and said they couldn't allow Biden to become president.

According to Rhodes, the Oath Keepers had to prepare for a civil war and to fight in the streets. Rhodes suggested Oath Keepers could lure leftist protesters into skirmishes that would give Trump an excuse to invoke the Insurrection Act and, amid the chaos, allow militants like theirs to help Trump seize the office by force. He had been promoting the idea that Oath Keepers should replicate the Serbian revolutionaries who had stormed parliament to install their new president two decades earlier.

A new West Virginia member, Abdullah Rasheed, listened in with alarm. He was a former Marine and heavy equipment mechanic. He had joined the Oath Keepers after seeing a social media post inviting former military and law enforcement to convene with fellow patriots. But Rasheed had never envisioned it would involve armed rebellion. Hearing Rhodes map out a plan for "going to war against the United States government," Rasheed pushed the record button on his phone.

A little more than a week later, Rasheed called the FBI's national tipster hotline. Such calls are routed to the FBI's National Threat Operations Center in Clarksburg, West Virginia, where examiners are supposed to take callers' information, assess the urgency of the tip, and, if more investigation might be needed, pass them along to the right field office. On November 25, Rasheed's warning about Rhodes, along with his recording, was one of three thousand tips it fielded on average each day, and the tip died there. No agent followed up or called Rasheed to interview him.

On the same day as Rhodes's call, an FBI analyst assigned to a school for bomb technicians circulated an email with information from the SITE Intelligence Group, a private service that monitors online extremism. The email, which contained social media messages posted by people who identified as members of the Oath Keepers and other extremist groups, subsequently ping-ponged among state and local officials under the subject line: "Far-Right Chatter re Election Results." The writings clearly indicated that a vocal and potentially violent segment of the country believed that the election had been stolen from Trump. One analyst cited threats published on the alt-right message board TheDonald.win that were particularly alarming: "Death Threats: Militia groups are espousing increasingly violent rhetoric, declaring, 'The fight is now.' On a popular militia forum, users called to execute Biden, Democrats, tech company employees, journalists, and other 'rats.'"

Along with the Oath Keepers, some of the most violent rhetoric was emanating from members of the Proud Boys. In a debate six weeks before the election, Trump had infamously seemed to put the extremist group on alert. When asked about whether he would repudiate their violent clashes with Black Lives Matter protesters over the summer, Trump said only:

"Proud Boys, stand back and stand by." Several leaders of the Oath Keepers and the Proud Boys now saw this as the moment they had been waiting for. They discussed using violence and guns to keep Biden from becoming president. And they quickly began converging around plans for a "Million MAGA March" in Washington on November 14. In the days beforehand, Rhodes told supporters he was prepared to engage in violence on Trump's command. He also urged supporters to fight while Trump "is commander in chief and has a narrowing window" to retain power.

As planned, on the night of November 14, far-right groups and counterprotesters clashed violently in the streets between the Capitol and the Supreme Court. By the end of the night, one person was stabbed, four officers were injured, police took eight firearms from protesters, and more than twenty people had been arrested, many for inciting violence.

Four weeks later, on December 12, the groups returned to D.C. for another demonstration, and ahead of their arrival, several openly relished the prospect of more violence with counterprotesters. On the messaging app Telegram, the Philadelphia chapter of the Proud Boys shared an image of men in helmets and black tactical gear with assault rifles. A caption over the bottom half of the picture read "Shatter Their Teeth." As the crowd at the "Stop the Steal" rally swelled during the day, Michael Flynn took the stage to urge the president's supporters to remember the election wasn't over and that Trump needed them to keep fighting.

"There are still avenues" for a Trump win, he said ominously. "The courts aren't going to decide who the next president of the United States is going to be. We the people decide."

On the same stage, Ali Alexander, the leader of the Stop the Steal organization, which had promoted the rallies, alerted the group to another opportunity to keep Trump in office: January 6. He warned that if the Electoral College endorsed Biden's victory as expected, his group would turn its attention to pressuring Republican lawmakers to reject the result when Congress met to certify the election on January 6.

Later that night, some of the estimated seven hundred Proud Boys who joined the rally were marching through downtown streets, chasing counterprotesters and shouting "Move Out!" and "1776!" Skirmishes broke out between the two groups around an area then known as Black Lives Matter Plaza, and this time four people were stabbed. In the wake of a second round of violence between Trump supporters and foes, the FBI issued a tweet saying it was partnering with local police to identify suspects in the assaults.

Over the ensuing days, Proud Boys leaders exchanged dozens of messages lamenting injuries suffered by their ranks and making clear they saw lessons in the night's violence to plan for something bigger:

"This was a learning experience on how to march 1000 guys down a street," one Proud Boy organizer wrote to chapter presidents on December 17.

Inside the FBI, however, agents and supervisors in Washington were treating the ever-growing online chatter of extremist groups—often about overturning the election by force—as unrelated episodes and often too vague to act upon. Federal agents assumed that any future protests involving Trump supporters would follow the same script as the November 14 and December 12 events, with pro-Trump and anti-Trump protesters targeting one another. The FBI had still not followed up on the late November insider warning about Stewart Rhodes. Weeks later, in mid-December, the FBI similarly discounted a warning it received from a hotline about a jarringly ominous call for violence on the day of the certification.

"Please be in DC, armed, on the 6th," read an online post that a tipster pointed the FBI to on December 17. "You might have to kill the palace guards. Are you okay with [that]?" read one comment. Another post said: "Drop a handful, the rest will flee."

The FBI forwarded the December 17 post alluding to shooting cops to the U.S. Capitol Police, D.C. police, and other local law enforcement, but the Bureau reported that the post did not constitute a specific or credible threat.

Meanwhile, on the other end of Pennsylvania Avenue, Trump had run out of legal challenges to stay in office. The Electoral College had met earlier that week and affirmed Biden's victory. Federal judges, including several Trump-appointed ones, had rejected his claims of fraud as lacking even basic evidence. On the evening of Friday, December 18, Sidney Powell and Michael Flynn met with Trump in the Oval Office to brainstorm. The pair outlined a plan to have Trump deploy military troops to seize voting machines and block the peaceful transfer of power. Powell, mentioning an affidavit she said she obtained from an inside source, told the president that a series of voting machines had been rigged to flip votes for Trump to Biden. She described it as part of a communist plot, rooted in the Venezuelan government of Hugo Chávez, to help Democrats steal the election.

Flynn took out a diagram that supposedly showed internet addresses of people all over the world communicating with election machines, using connected devices he likened to Nest home thermostats. White House lawyers Pat Cipollone and Eric Herschmann looked on with a mixture of horror and incredulity. Cipollone, who had rushed to the meeting upon learning Powell and Flynn were with Trump, asked the pair to show the group their evidence for all these claims.

"Are you claiming the Democrats were working with Hugo Chávez, Venezuelans, and whomever else?" Herschmann asked mockingly, noting that the country's dictator had been dead for more than seven years.

The fighting got intense, with Powell and Flynn accusing the White House lawyers of being "quitters," and Trump asking Cipollone and Herschmann why they couldn't just try out Flynn's and Powell's ideas. Trump took a break in his dining room and resumed the conversation later from his residence. Shortly before midnight, Trump conceded the seizing of voting machines could not happen, and the meeting ended.

But Trump remained awake for hours. At 1:42 a.m. December 19, the president tweeted for his supporters to come to his aid:

"Statistically impossible to have lost the 2020 Election," he wrote. "Big protest in D.C. on January 6th. Be there, will be wild!"

Mary McCord had been monitoring the rise in extremist chatter for the last several months. After more than twenty years at DOJ, including serving in the highest national security jobs at Main Justice, McCord had resigned in April 2017, concluding that then Attorney General Jeff Sessions was incapable of properly leading the department.

What she and her partners at the Digital Forensic Research Lab had noticed was that Trump's call to fight election fraud had been met with an instantaneous, and frightening, response.

Just before the election, McCord had reached out to the Bureau to first warn them. They referred her to the office of Brian Gilhooly, who had become deputy assistant director for the FBI's Counterterrorism Division at headquarters. Like many leaders in that division, Gilhooly specialized in foreign terrorist threats, rather than the lower-priority teams tracking domestic threats.

On December 22, McCord again sent screenshots of online posts from members of the Oath Keepers. They were now pledging to go further and shoot people to keep Trump in office.

One extremist wrote: "There is only one way in. It is not signs. It's not rallies. It's fucking bullets!"

The parts that worried McCord the most were the members' references to being willing to die, to be the "sacrificial lamb," for the cause.

The FBI gave McCord the standard reply of the Bureau: information received. McCord knew the drill and didn't take offense. The FBI was often a one-way street when it came to information. Having become a civilian, all she could do was pass on her warnings. She didn't expect her FBI contact to share how the Bureau was proceeding. However, she had faith it would stay on top of it. But McCord later learned the warnings she shared were largely filed away without significant follow-up. The FBI concluded these comments were political speech, protected under the First Amendment, and so the FBI was barred from investigating.

McCord and her online researchers were not the only people growing very worried about what might happen on January 6. Rita Katz, who had founded the SITE group, had seen something categorically different from past chatter. Trump's supporters were openly plotting violence *and* had targeted a specific date and location for action.

Katz's group sent the FBI the most comprehensive catalogue of warnings yet about militia members and right-wing extremists interpreting Trump's December 19 tweet as a battle cry. In a new string of exchanges on the TheDonald.win, members encouraged one another to come to Washington on January 6 at Trump's request and to bring guns.

"He's asking you to be wild," wrote one poster. "*You've* always been the plan."

"He can't exactly openly tell you to revolt," another wrote. "This is the closest he'll ever get."

"Then bring the guns we shall," responded another.

"Armed and ready, Mr. President," one member posted.

"We have been waiting for Trump to say the word," another wrote. "There is not enough cops in DC to stop what is coming."

On Christmas Eve, staffers at the conservative social network site Parler went so far as to report their own users to the FBI for posting threats about January 6. One user had "called for the congregation of an armed force of 150,000 on the Virginia side of the Potomac River to 're-act to the congressional events of January 6th.'" It was one of more than fifty threats of violence Parler would forward to the FBI.

But the Bureau had, again, concluded that what SITE and Parler spotted was protected political speech and did not open an investigation.

On December 26, the FBI's National Threat Operations Center received another anonymous tip involving inside knowledge of planning by the Proud Boys.

"They think they will have a large enough group to march into DC armed and will outnumber the police so they can't be stopped," the tipster wrote. "Their plan is to literally kill people."

"Please, please take this tip seriously and investigate further," the person added.

"I think they will have large numbers with them and every single one of them is expecting and eager to use their weapons."

A day after this second insider warning, the FBI took a modest administrative step to keep track of the deluge. The Bureau had a central collection database for incoming tips from the public and law enforcement called Guardian, which it used to track all criminal and national security threats and to decide how to assign those tips for further investigation. The FBI began tagging all threats about violence involving the January 6 presidential certification vote in D.C. with the label: CERTUNREST.

The FBI logged and shared some of these threats with the U.S. Capitol Police and D.C. police, but mostly in the spirit of "FYI." In almost every case, FBI threat examiners had within a day or two stamped each one "Closed," judging the posts as protected political speech or lacking enough specificity to investigate further. Some of the passive posture was rooted in the modern FBI's eagerness to avoid the insidious overreach of the Bureau's past, when it investigated civil rights organizations for their peaceful protests in the 1960s. Other agents and FBI lawyers were more directly recoiling from having been criticized as Trump's authoritarian tools, after being deployed to crack down on racial justice protesters in cities around the country the previous summer.

Through a mix of self-restraint and disbelief that protesters could mean what they were saying, the FBI kept dismissing each Guardian tip in isolation, rather than as parts of a larger mosaic. On December 29, the FBI Washington Field Office emailed its Critical Incident Response Group that so far "we have not identified any specific threats" for January 6.

The warnings kept coming. On New Year's Day, Elliot Carter, a D.C. professional with no national security experience, reached out to the FBI. Carter had noticed a bizarre uptick in visits to "WashingtonTunnels .com," the obscure historical website the former Capitol Hill intern had created detailing underground tunnels in the nation's capital. But an unnatural flood of visitors was suddenly clicking onto the site's maps showing the U.S. Capitol's subterranean tunnel system. Carter speculated that people planning to protest the congressional certification in a few days' time were looking for covert ways to enter or exit the Capitol.

Carter emailed the FBI with his insight, but never heard back.

On January 2, Parler sent the FBI more posts by its users pledging violence on January 6.

"don't be surprised if we take the #capital [*sic*] building."

[12]

"A Hot Mess"

By Sunday, January 3, Jeff Rosen had been the acting attorney general for a total of nine days, and the veteran corporate lawyer's introduction to the role had been exceptionally bumpy.

Rosen, formerly the deputy attorney general, had agreed to Trump's request to take on the top job when the president had all but forced Barr to resign. In an Oval Office showdown on December 1, Trump had exploded at Barr for publicly declaring that day that the department had found no evidence of significant fraud that could conceivably swing the election his way. Trump was so spitting mad at their evening meeting that his limbs seemed to be twitching, and he angrily accused Barr of intentionally undercutting his plan to stay in office. "You must really hate Trump!" he roared, as White House Chief of Staff Mark Meadows and two senior White House lawyers looked on. An uncharacteristically subdued Barr offered that he could always resign if Trump wished. The president slapped his hand on the table and yelled: "Accepted!"

Trump hit the table once more: "Accepted. Go home. Don't go back to your office. Go home. You're done." Barr would later agree to resign and leave by the end of the month.

In the nine days since Barr had left, Trump had revisited a series of thoroughly debunked fraud claims as if they were new threads of gold. On Christmas Eve, he pressed Rosen and Richard Donoghue, who that day had moved into the department's number 2 position: Were they going to properly run these election crimes to ground?

At Trump's insistence, the department had already sent agents to check into unfounded claims that suitcases of ballots had been snuck into an Atlanta tabulation center; that a truck driver had driven thousands of ballots to Pennsylvania; that ten thousand votes had been illegally cast in Georgia using dead people's names; that an Italian aerospace company had coordinated with the CIA to switch Trump votes for Biden; and that Dominion voting machines had an error rate of more than 68 percent. Trump urged them to take a briefing from his campaign lawyer, Rudolph W. Giuliani, who was keeping close tabs on all this fraud for him. "Why aren't you doing more to look into this?" Trump asked.

But as Rosen and Donoghue tried to show Trump these allegations were often misunderstandings at best, and baseless conspiracies at worst, the president's mood grew bellicose.

In a December 27 call, Trump warned his new Justice Department leaders that they seemed to be failing at their job. He said his allies were urging him to change DOJ leadership.

"This election has been stolen out from under the American people," the president declared.

Rosen told Trump he could not "flip a switch and change the election." Trump explained he didn't need them to do that.

"Just say the election was corrupt and leave the rest to me and the [Republican] congressmen," Trump said. "Just have a press conference."

Donoghue couldn't believe what he'd just heard and grabbed a notepad from his wife's nightstand to jot down the president's words. The two senior Justice leaders told Trump the department could not claim game-changing fraud without evidence.

"We don't see that," Rosen told Trump. "We're not going to have a press conference."

Rosen and Donoghue were shocked that every day brought a new crisis. Next, Trump wanted them to name a special counsel to investigate election fraud and to file a complaint with the Supreme Court, where the department had no basis to sue.

As they resisted, Rosen and Donoghue learned Trump had another plan to get what he wanted: upend Justice leadership a second time in a matter of weeks and replace Rosen with yet another Justice appointee, conservative ideologue named Jeffrey Clark. To their shock, Trump had already met privately with Clark before Christmas to discuss how to pursue election fraud, at the urging of Republican Congressman Scott Perry. Clark had kept a low profile in the department, but in his private meeting with Trump, a fierce partisan side emerged. In meeting with Trump, Clark had violated reams of policy governing contacts between the DOJ and the White House. For starters, any discussion with the president related to ongoing or potential law enforcement matters had to go through the attorney general or deputy attorney general.

Clark, fifty-three, an anti-regulation Federalist Society member, had focused his private practice on defending corporations against environmental regulations. In 2018, Trump had chosen him to serve as an assistant attorney general for the enforcement of environmental laws. As more and more Justice Department leaders had departed the administration, Clark had moved up, temporarily filling in as the acting head of the entire Civil Division. Clark had no experience to investigate election matters, much less to run the entire department.

Clark had pressed Rosen and Donoghue to send a letter to Georgia's state legislative and election leaders falsely asserting that DOJ had serious concerns about fraud in the state's election results, and urging they call a special legislative session to investigate and consider rejecting the vote results.

Rosen and Donoghue, slack-jawed at the idea of the department citing unfounded claims to interfere in state elections, told Clark in a heated December 28 meeting that they would never agree. Donoghue called it "wildly inappropriate" for the department to recommend a state consider overriding certified election results.

"I think they are good ideas," a deflated Clark told his two bosses. "You don't like them. OK. Then I guess we won't do it."

Rosen and Donoghue believed they had batted down this idea, but not Trump's threats to remove Rosen. They briefed the department's third-in-line official, Steve Engel, to prepare him for the extraordinary possibility that Trump would fire them, and Engel would, by default, become the next acting attorney general. But the pair decided to tell no one else in the department's senior leadership, for now, not wanting to create a panic.

Trump refused to wake from the fever dream that "his" Justice Department would help him stay in office. Rosen sought gently to rein in the increasingly desperate president, but often let Donoghue, a close Barr ally who had served as the U.S. attorney for the rough-and-tumble Eastern District of New York, deliver the blunt reality.

"[T]hese allegations about ballots being smuggled in in a suitcase and run through the machine several times, it's not true," Donoghue told Trump.

Three days later, at roughly noon on Sunday, January 3, Clark called Rosen at home and asked to talk in person. When they met at 3:00 p.m. in Rosen's conference room, Clark surprised Rosen by informing him that Trump had offered him the job of attorney general, and he had accepted it. He said he planned to send the letter to Georgia officials shortly. Clark offered to keep Rosen on as deputy attorney general.

"There is no universe I can imagine in which that would ever happen," Rosen told Clark. He would discuss this with the president himself. Their meeting was over.

Rosen made a flurry of calls. He rang White House Chief of Staff Mark Meadows to arrange an in-person meeting at 6:15 p.m. with Trump at the Oval. He alerted White House Counsel Pat Cipollone to Trump's plan to fire him and asked him to join the Oval meeting that night. Cipollone agreed and suggested that others at the department should let it be known they were behind Rosen and Donoghue. Rosen told Donoghue to prepare for "AG Clark," and possibly to be fired.

"Are we going to find out in a tweet?" Donoghue asked. He went to his office and began taking plaques and personal items off his walls and putting them in boxes.

At 4:45 p.m., Donoghue and Rosen's chief deputy, Patrick Hovakimian, held a hastily arranged conference call to alert DOJ leadership to the Georgia letter and the crisis before them. Donoghue then asked who would resign if the president implemented his strategy.

All seven senior Justice officials—Engel, the number 3 official who oversaw the Office of Legal Counsel; the acting solicitor general, Jeff Wall; Donoghue's chief deputy; and four other assistant attorneys general who oversaw the department's core divisions said they would. That meant a total of ten Justice leaders would resign en masse.

Trump opened the meeting in the Oval, with Rosen, Meadows, Cipollone, Clark, and White House lawyers Pat Philbin and Eric Herschmann gathered near the Resolute Desk, with a salvo.

"One thing we know is you, Rosen, aren't going to do anything to overturn the election," he said.

Clark inaccurately claimed the department found "significant concerns" in the Georgia election, and called this the "last opportunity to sort of set things straight with this defective election."

"History is calling," Clark told the president. "This is our opportunity. We can get this done."

Over the next two hours, everyone except Clark tried to convince the president not to make Clark the attorney general and not to send his letter to Georgia officials.

"You should understand that your entire department leadership will resign," Donoghue warned Trump. Donoghue, dressed in a T-shirt and muddy jeans, had rushed to make the White House meeting that night and hadn't had time to change. "This is your leadership team. You sent every one of them to the Senate; you got them confirmed. What is that going to say about you, when we all walk out at the same time?"

Donoghue said Clark lacked the qualifications and no one in the department would view him as competent to lead it.

"He's never been a criminal attorney. He's never conducted a criminal investigation in his life," Donoghue said. "He's never been in front of a grand jury, much less a trial jury."

Clark took issue with that summary. "Well, I've done a lot of very complicated appeals and civil litigation, environmental litigation, and things like that," Clark said.

Donoghue turned dismissive: "How about you go back to your office and we'll call you when there's an oil spill."

Trump wasn't convinced. Cipollone warned the president that having the department send Clark's letter to Georgia amounted to "a murder-suicide pact."

"It's going to damage everyone who touches it. And we should have nothing to do with that letter," Cipollone said. "I don't ever want to see that letter again."

Cipollone and his deputy, Philbin, said they would resign as well. Donoghue stressed that many other top Justice officials and U.S. attorneys would likely join them.

Trump finally relented. At the end of the meeting, he turned to Clark:

"I appreciate your willingness to do it," Trump said. "I appreciate you being willing to suffer the abuse. But the reality is, you're not going to get anything done. These guys are going to quit. Everyone else is going to resign. It's going to be a disaster."

At 9:00 p.m., Rosen's deputy, Hovakimian, emailed senior Justice Department leadership, who had been waiting to learn if they would soon be announcing their exits.

"I have limited visibility into this but it sounds like Rosen and the cause of justice won," Hovakimian wrote. He promised a conference call when Rosen and his team returned to the building.

John Demers, the assistant attorney general over national security, shared a grateful, one-word reaction:

"Amazing."

. . .

Early that Sunday morning, the FBI's Washington Field Office, which had overall responsibility within the Bureau for tracking potential violence at the D.C. event, cobbled together a summary of all the incoming warnings about January 6 for the new head of the office, Steven D'Antuono.

D'Antuono, a straight-talking native of working-class Rhode Island, had until recently been the special agent in charge of the Detroit Field Office, where he had overseen the investigation of a militia group's attempt to kidnap Michigan Governor Gretchen Whitmer. Wray had promoted D'Antuono to run the D.C. office, and he had arrived just a month before the presidential election.

Leading up to January 6, D'Antuono had told colleagues that he viewed the expected arrival of the president's supporters and counterprotesters as something akin to an unpredictable East Coast snowstorm. He had grown up in the path of many nor'easters and knew the wintry cyclones were notoriously hard to pin down before they happened. One spot might end up buried in snow, while nearby residents might escape unscathed. D'Antuono told his deputies he had an "icky" feeling about the sixth, unsure if the city would get three feet or a light dusting, but he sure hoped it would be a bust.

Agents in D.C. and across the country had been running ragged since a powerful homemade bomb had exploded in an RV parked in downtown Nashville on Christmas Day, prompting a massive federal investigation that put the FBI on high alert for a similar attack throughout New Year's.

On Saturday, January 2, an increasingly concerned FBI Deputy Director Dave Bowdich had just reached out to D'Antuono to check in and register some concern.

A sudden unease had taken hold at FBI headquarters, in tandem with the escalating level of vitriol in social media posts, as well as new data showing local hotels were almost completely sold out. Bookings for plane and train travel to the nation's capital were similarly spiking for the days remaining before the protest.

FBI and police had for weeks predicted the protests around the sixth would amount to a repeat of testy November and December Stop the Steal rallies that had drawn a few thousand Trump supporters. But the latest data suggested that more than fifty thousand might descend on the city. D'Antuono emailed his deputies that Saturday to update them on the mood at FBI headquarters.

"No one knows what is going to happen and that scares them," D'Antuono wrote. "They want to know what the intel is and plan accordingly."

The FBI was partially in the dark at that point, because for days it had largely operated on its own island from an intelligence standpoint. D.C. Homeland Security officials had grown concerned enough from their own assessment that they had ordered hospitals in D.C. to stock up their blood banks and to staff for possible mass casualty events. They'd begun holding nationwide interagency planning calls, trading information about convoys and known criminal suspects headed for D.C. But the FBI never announced its presence on a single one of those calls.

"If they were there, they were just listening," Donell Harvin, the city's chief of Homeland Security and Intelligence, said, shrugging, to a colleague after one call. The FBI's liaison to his office also hadn't been seen in the office for days.

At the same time, the FBI was suffering from a terribly timed technical snafu. The Washington Field Office had begun using a new social media monitoring service about a week before January 6. But many agents hadn't yet navigated the system to set alerts for warnings the way they previously had.

But FBI agents were beginning to answer D'Antuono's call for information.

Late Saturday night and early Sunday morning, intelligence analysts and staff in the office worked to help D'Antuono answer headquarters' questions. Before 8:00 a.m., they had compiled an informal intelligence summary of threats and concerns the D.C. office was tracking.

Among them was a warning from a Georgia tipster who told the FBI that the Proud Boys and its leader, Enrique Tarrio, were heading to D.C. for the rally.

"These men are coming for violence," the tipster said. "They will cause mass unrest, destruction and potentially kill many people in the streets of D.C. on January 6th."

Also in the January 3 summary was a warning from a person in North Carolina who called the FBI's tipline to report a TikTok video with someone holding a gun and exhorting others: "Storm the Capitol on January 6th."

So far there were sixteen Guardian tips about potential violence on January 6 that the Washington office was assessing. But of those, the FBI had already closed or was about to close fourteen as not credible or not warranting additional investigation.

The intelligence summary that day also noted the Bureau had information that four people then under FBI investigation and linked to domestic terror cases were traveling to Washington for the sixth. Nation-wide, the Bureau had sent agents to knock on the doors of several members of extremist groups that the FBI knew through other investigations and strongly urge them not to attend.

The summary had been produced by a team under the D.C. office's intelligence chief, Jennifer Moore.

Despite these stark calls for violence, it dismissed most of the internet posts as bluster or commentary that was "unsubstantiated."

"FBI WFO does not have any information to suggest these events will involve anything other than [First Amendment] protected activity," an FBI staffer wrote in a January 3 email, summarizing the office's intel.

When D'Antuono got this litany of threats, however, the field office chief decided to forward the entire list "as is" to Bowdich.

"I just sent the whole thing," D'Antuono wrote in an email alerting his counterterrorism deputy, Matt Alcoke, that day. "I don't want him getting a sanitized version of events."

Later that afternoon, three days out from the sixth, McCord sent her contacts at the FBI's Counterterrorism Division an emailed report about militias' increasingly transparent calls to travel to D.C. and to use force.

Again, McCord assumed this new round of information would be added to that of others and reviewed as one big picture. But it would eventually come out that not everything that experts and social media companies were taking the time to share with the Bureau was getting catalogued and weighed in its threat assessments. The Counterterrorism Division had not been following its own protocols to incorporate all incoming warnings and referrals. None of the dozens of warnings that came in from Parler, for example, were used in building any intelligence reports.

Just after 5:00 p.m. the night before the sixth, there was yet another eyebrow-raising report logged through the FBI's main public hotline for tips. It was a warning that rally-goers were taking military-grade weapons, and that they were offering a reward for attacking members of Congress who would not vote to help Trump.

"[T]here is a $350,000 dollar reward for the head on [sic] any of the senators that do not want to certify the election," the tipster had said.

By the day before the sixth, U.S. Capitol Police had found additional worrisome material about the tunnel research. Extremist groups were mentioning their intention to find and block the entrances to those used by members of Congress to get to and from their offices and the House and Senate floors. Other posts suggested protesters hoped to form a perimeter around the Capitol.

Throughout downtown D.C., groups of red-clad Trump supporters were already beginning to spill into the streets. A couple thousand huddled by Freedom Plaza along Pennsylvania Avenue for what felt like part political soapbox and part pregame tailgate party. A group of women carrying red Solo cups and wearing Make America Great Again hats at one point began wandering down the middle of an emptied Pennsylvania Avenue, calling out the names of federal agencies as they passed by. "What's this one?" one asked aloud as they reached the Justice Department. "DOJ," yelled back another. Just then, a group of U.S. Marshals stepped onto a balcony of the building. The women looked up. "What are you, FBI?" a woman asked. "Investigate the fraud!" she yelled. Soon the whole group was heckling the officers over the department's handling of election fraud claims, chanting in unison: "Do your fucking job!"

Less than a mile away, inside the FBI's Washington Field Office, the atmosphere was growing more tense. Moore, the head of intelligence, asked fellow staff to join a conference call about the next day.

"Please sign onto the call," she wrote. "This has a huge potential to be a hot mess."

Later that evening, two field offices far from Washington issued separate alerts. Around 7:00 p.m., the New Orleans office issued an intelligence information report—what the FBI sometimes uses to convey raw, unverified intelligence that could be time-sensitive. It repeated nearly verbatim what McCord had relayed to her FBI contacts two days earlier about extremists' plans for a quick reaction force in northern Virginia.

A little more than a half hour later, another warning came in from the Norfolk Field Office.

"Be ready to fight. Congress needs to hear glass breaking. . . . Stop calling this a march, or rally, or a protest. Go there ready for war," read the post spotted by the Norfolk agents. "We get our President or we die. NOTHING else will achieve this goal."

Just after 8:30 p.m., Moore asked a staffer to send an email to a command post the field office was now standing up. It directed supervisors' attention to TheDonald.win message board. The reports by McCord, SITE, and other extremism researchers had been calling out the site for weeks as a hotbed of planning activity, but the message referred to the forum as "a previously unknown website."

A few blocks away at the J. Edgar Hoover Building, headquarters staffed up its National Crisis Coordination Center. Bowdich visited the field office command post and asked about latest numbers of Guardian reports and expected number of rally-goers and made notes of both. Still, that night the Counterterrorism Division at headquarters, which had been receiving McCord's warnings, saw a hopeful sign. Many Trump supporters were already arriving in town, but the night so far lacked any of the protester-counterprotester violence of the last two pro-Trump gatherings. That was in large part because Black Lives Matter leaders and other Democratic groups urged their members to stay home, seeing the potential for violence as too high.

After 10:00 p.m., a Counterterrorism Division employee emailed agents the FBI's final assessment for the next day: "Only notable event tomorrow that could trigger a flashpoint is a planned POTUS rally/speech on the ellipse at 1100EST. It's estimated that 30,000 participants will then march toward the Capital [sic] which will coincide with the 1300EST scheduled Congressional meetings to certify the electoral college vote."

But it was the final line of the FBI's internal update that revealed how little the Bureau still understood about what was about to transpire. In the official record of the FBI office in D.C., the only real threat the next day was if liberal protesters turned up: "Obvious concerns remain if counterprotests ensue and opposing ideologies clash."

[13]

January 6

At daybreak, roadblocks and a smattering of police officers across downtown Washington revealed that authorities had prepared the nation's capital for large but docile protests. Stages had been erected for speakers. City buses and dump trucks had been parked sideways across streets leading to Pennsylvania Avenue, creating a pedestrian-friendly thoroughfare from the White House to the U.S. Capitol, the way authorities protected festivals or parades. Farther out, minivans full of unarmed National Guard troops had been sent to serve as traffic cops. Out of public view, the patchwork of law enforcement agencies with jurisdiction in D.C. was similarly passive. Federal forces each had their own officers on duty but had stood up no unified, interagency command. Capitol Police and others had allowed many to stay on scheduled leave, with scores out with COVID or for isolation protocols. Members of some of the area's civil disturbance and SWAT teams were still sleeping, scheduled to report for duty at varying times throughout the afternoon for shifts geared toward possible counterprotests late at night.

One of the only hints that officials feared Trump supporters were plotting something violent was the makeshift signs that had been taped to light posts near the White House, warning visitors that carrying a firearm in the nation's capital required a permit, and that guns were banned around any protest. Washington, D.C., Mayor Muriel E. Bowser's staff had hung the photocopies over the previous two days, having grown far more concerned than the FBI about online posts from Trump supporters advising each other to bring guns. But the Secret Service had not erected any of the physical barriers they sometimes used to stop people from sneaking firearms into gatherings, such as the elaborate ring of checkpoints they set up to screen visitors each Inauguration Day.

Trump supporters on the morning of January 6 would be free to roam mostly unmonitored through the deserted downtown core of the nation's capital until they reached a green expanse south of the White House known as the Ellipse. Only there, where Trump would speak, did they encounter a security checkpoint, albeit a voluntary one. Secret Service and Park Police officers manned rows of magnetometers. Trump supporters, if they wanted to get close to the stage erected for the president's address, were expected to file into the fenced-in area, much as they would have for his campaign rallies, or to go through airport security. Outside that, in the two-mile stretch between the White House and the Capitol, D.C. police officers were stationed in ones and twos at intersections. At the Capitol, fewer than two dozen Capitol Police officers could be seen at any one time. Most wore only their regular uniforms, not riot gear, a lot of which remained locked away in storage. The officers perched on steps and had in many places pulled lightweight bike racks across walkways to mark where the public was allowed, and not allowed, to go.

Hours before the planned rally on the Ellipse, there were last-minute warnings that went unheeded. A group wearing MAGA gear stopped into an Au Bon Pain coffee shop across the street from FBI headquarters. An FBI official walked in at nearly the same time and noticed one of the protesters wearing a tactical vest. The Bureau official briefly wondered why the rally-goer needed such protection, before returning to work with his coffee.

Four blocks away, in the Command and Tactical Operations Center of the FBI's Washington Field Office, D'Antuono watched screens displaying images from cable news channels. They showed crowds thickening near the Ellipse.

D'Antuono had viewed his agents' role in the January 6 protests as limited, generally taking a back seat to the patchwork of other agencies with direct responsibility for crowd control. The FBI had already done its job of reviewing incoming tips, D'Antuono told associates, and had found no specific actionable threats. Managing the crowds now gathering on the Ellipse was going to be the responsibility of the Park Police and Secret Service when they stomped the grounds near the White House; the responsibility of D.C. police when they entered city streets; and of Capitol Police when they neared the Capitol's turf. The FBI would watch, and if needed, help.

At the Pentagon, however, the country's military leaders worried about the absence of a bigger Department of Justice presence at what felt like a perilous moment. The Joint Chiefs, who paid for some of the same social media monitoring as the FBI, had seen much of the growing online chatter of violent plans that agents had missed. Acting Defense Secretary Christopher Miller believed that only DOJ could ride herd to tighten the city's defenses, but he fretted that Justice wasn't "owning" the event. Miller and his Pentagon team were unaware that Acting AG Rosen had just survived Trump's version of a Saturday night massacre. Miller pressed Rosen, who then pushed the FBI to stand up the Bureau's national command center, known as the Strategic Information and Operations Center, or SIOC for short. It was purely prophylactic: The center would not command anything, but only monitor events.

D'Antuono and Bowdich did, however, ask the Bureau's tactical units to suit up to deploy if skirmishes got out of hand. D'Antuono had his D.C.-based SWAT team lined up first with "go" bags if they had to be dispatched from the Washington Field Office. Bowdich had ordered another Baltimore-based team to be second in line and assemble that afternoon at a Bureau office about ten miles from downtown, just outside the

Capital Beltway around D.C. They even asked the Bureau's elite Hostage Rescue Team, stationed thirty-five miles away at the FBI's facility in Quantico, Virginia, to be on alert to deploy to D.C.

At one of the first FBI briefings, after 8:00 a.m., one of D'Antuono's deputies asked a Park Police representative if predicted crowd estimates were proving to be accurate. Park Police were always reluctant to say. They had faced lawsuits in the 1990s for estimating that a Million Man March had drawn less than half that many people. A Secret Service rep was more willing to give an estimate, saying the projections for twenty-five thousand to thirty thousand protesters so far appeared close to the mark.

But the Secret Service shared a more concerning update: Their plain-clothes surveillance officers spotted many rally-goers that morning carrying war gear. "Some members of the crowd are wearing ballistic helmets, body armor and carrying radio equipment and military grade backpacks," one undercover officer warned his team on a shared alert system.

The Secret Service soon raised another red flag: People arriving early for Trump's speech were abandoning their backpacks and other personal items, leaving piles of unclaimed bags outside the metal detectors. D'Antuono and his deputies paused. The Secret Service suspected the rally-goers were concealing guns they didn't want confiscated at metal detector checkpoints.

But D'Antuono turned to a more urgent matter: A congressional staffer visiting a hotel downtown had overheard protesters, including one wearing military garb, saying there was a plan to attack the FBI headquarters at 2:00 p.m. D'Antuono dispatched agents to the hotel and gave superiors at the Hoover Building a heads-up.

After 9:00 a.m., there was still another worrisome update, this time from Park Police. Hundreds of protesters were refusing to leave a restricted area around the Washington Monument, and when officers made an arrest, the crowd had turned on them.

"There's a large crowd that's following us. We're going back into the monument with the individual that's under arrest," came the radio dispatch from a Park Police officer. "Units are backed into the monument. Everyone's breaking through the bike racks." Park Police were sending backup to help.

Near the Ellipse, Acting U.S. Attorney Michael Sherwin was getting a firsthand view—and sensing officers' blood pressure rising. Agents were pulling knives and Mace from dozens of people entering the area for the president's speech. But more deadly weapons seemed to be lurking in the crowd. Around them, crackling radio dispatches reported an officer seeing a butt of a gun poking out here, a sling for a rifle there. And everywhere, members of the crowd were uttering ominous threats, echoing one of Trump's latest tweets:

"Alert at 1022 regarding VP being a dead man walking if he doesn't do the right thing," a Secret Service email warned at 10:39 a.m.

Riding around with a deputy D.C. police chief, Sherwin was repeatedly pulled into the crowd by officers to look at components of rifles confiscated from protesters. One was a long, black upper receiver and attached scope for an AR-15-style assault rifle.

"Can we charge him?" an officer asked. Sherwin had worked gang cases and prosecuted gun possession charges in his time as a federal prosecutor in Miami. "No," he shouted over the noise of the crowd after a quick look. Officers were encountering things that looked ominous—protesters with what appeared to be assault rifles. But repeatedly, they turned out to be components that lacked the trigger mechanism that would immediately land their owners in trouble under D.C. gun laws. In this case, the rifle was missing the lower part that requires a federal serial number and allows the gun to fire.

Sherwin told the officer instead to take down the protester's name, seize the gun part, and move on. Many officers' biggest worry was that they didn't know whether the protesters were carrying the parts just to look tough or whether they had split up the components and somewhere nearby another protester had the missing piece to quickly assemble a high-powered assault rifle more commonly associated with the country's grisliest mass shootings than a political protest on the National Mall.

At roughly the same time, at the other end of the Mall, a group of the far-right Proud Boys with body armor bulging from under their clothes appeared near the Capitol and began walking in loose columns.

About twenty minutes before noon, Trump's motorcade was on the move for the short ride from the White House to the Ellipse. As they drove, fresh warnings streamed into earpieces of Secret Service agents.

One told the motorcade team to alert the president's personal protection detail to a possible sniper overhead.

"Make sure PPD knows they have an elevated threat in the trees, south side of Constitution Avenue," the officer said. "Look for the Don't Tread on Me flag, American flag, face mask, cowboy boots, weapon on the right-side hip."

Over a radio frequency shared by local law enforcement in the capital, D.C. police officers reported several more sightings of rally-goers packing weapons, or maybe parts of them.

"A white male, about six feet tall, thin build," one officer radioed in. "Underneath the blue jean jacket, complainants both saw stock of an AR-15."

Two other men with him were wearing green camouflage fatigues and had Glock-style pistols in their waistbands, police warned. Another Metropolitan Police Department officer drew attention to three men flashing more rifles: "I got three men walking down in fatigues carrying AR-15. Copy, at Fourteenth and Independence."

Upon Trump's arrival at a VIP tent near the stage at the Ellipse, the president scanned the setup and quickly waved over his deputy chief of staff, Tony Ornato, to complain: There was still open space and the crowd was thin in places in front of the stage. Aides immediately understood that Trump was worried about the crowd looking sparse on television.

Standing within earshot was Cassidy Hutchinson, an assistant to White House Chief of Staff Mark Meadows. Hutchinson would later say she knew Trump had already been warned about the thin crowd and the reason why: Police believed protesters were hanging back to avoid going through magnetometers, keeping their gear to head down to the National Mall and the Capitol after the speech.

Hutchinson would say she heard Trump demand the Secret Service take away the metal detectors. "They're not here to hurt me," she remembered him saying of the weapons.

Secret Service did not do as Trump demanded, leaving some bare spots close to the stage as thousands remained behind the security fence, spread out in the direction of the Washington Monument. Even so, before Trump took the stage, agents manning the magnetometers had confiscated a small arsenal from those who opted to enter the stage area: 269 knives or blades, 242 canisters of pepper spray, 18 sets of brass knuckles, 29 tasers, 6 pieces of body armor, 3 gas masks, 30 batons or blunt instruments.

A couple of minutes before noon, Trump walked to the podium, positioned so the White House loomed behind him in the frame of waiting cameras. He quickly began recounting baseless conspiracy theories that he'd been repeating since the fall. "They rigged an election, they rigged it like they've never rigged an election before," Trump began. "All of us here today do not want to see our election victory stolen by emboldened radical-left Democrats. . . . We will never give up. We will never concede. It doesn't happen. You don't concede when there's theft involved."

As Trump spun deeper into his fraud claims, a Secret Service employee a short distance from the stage emailed a colleague about the barely hidden threats all around them.

"With so many weapons found so far, you wonder how many are unknown," the Secret Service employee wrote.

Nonetheless, the two agreed with the president's off-the-cuff security assessment. The crowd likely wasn't carrying weapons to hurt him— or them. Their target was still likely counterprotesters, they surmised.

"Could be sporty after dark," the agent wrote of the possible gun battles to come between Trump supporters and Antifa.

"No doubt," his colleague replied. Then he relayed the news he had heard about protesters' next step: "The people at the Ellipse said they are moving to the Capitol after the POTUS speech."

Acting Attorney General Jeffrey Rosen was sitting alone in his office. He had told most of his staff that they could work from home on January 6 to avoid the expected road closures and crowds. He'd started the day's meeting with Bowdich and then repeatedly called Sherwin as he rode along with D.C. police, using the acting U.S. attorney as his eyes and ears outside. Close to 12:40 p.m., he called Sherwin, and the two talked about the crowd size as Trump spoke. Rosen picked up a remote and turned on the television. He muted the president and studied the shots of the crowd. It was big, but perhaps not far off the estimates. In his head, Rosen had broken down the day into four quarters, like a football game. The speech marked the end of the first quarter. Soon, there would be the vote by Congress, the reaction of the crowd, and the possible clashes overnight. No one would know the outcome or be sure the threat to public safety had really subsided until sunrise the next morning.

Unbeknownst to Rosen and Sherwin, the contours of the day were shifting quickly. Capitol Police, along with agents from the FBI and the Bureau of Alcohol, Tobacco, Firearms and Explosives, were being dispatched to investigate reports of a pipe bomb with a timer found outside the Republican National Committee headquarters a couple of blocks from the Capitol.

About fifteen minutes later, more Capitol Police officers sped away from the Capitol toward the nearby Democratic National Committee headquarters. Another pipe bomb had been discovered just outside. The second discovery drew an even bigger police response than the first and sent the U.S. Secret Service into stealthy evacuation mode. Agents didn't want the crowd to know, but Vice President–elect Kamala Harris was inside, and had to be taken out through passing protesters.

In Rosen's office, the phones buzzed with news of the explosive devices. The television was still on mute as Trump wound up his speech. Rosen wouldn't hear as Trump implored the crowd to turn toward the Capitol: "We're going to walk down," Trump said, promising to go with them to push Republican members to "fight" to save his presidency. "We're going to try and give them the kind of pride and boldness that they need to take back our country," the president said to wild applause.

As he spoke, several cable news channels had already broken into split-screen mode. Pence had entered the House Chamber at the Capitol and protesters were already outside. Members of the Proud Boys and others were growing bold, heckling Capitol Police officers. "We are taking our House," yelled a man with a bullhorn. Those around him screamed obscenities in support and launched into a call-and-response: "Whose house?" "Our House."

At 12:53 p.m., away from the television cameras and before Trump had even left the stage, protesters along the West Front of the Capitol became rioters. Two men picked up one of the metal bike-rack barriers and pushed it into Capitol Police officers. They and dozens behind them rushed forward, stomping over the gate and streaming onto the restricted Capitol grounds toward steps where construction crews had erected scaffolding for Biden's inauguration platform. To the west, a river of thousands more protesters poured out of the Ellipse and along Pennsylvania Avenue in their direction.

Capitol Police ordered all available officers to the West Front of the Capitol, and to lock doors to the building. One of the force's civil disturbance units with helmets, arm guards, and batons arrived and was soon in hand-to-hand combat with rioters, but with police vastly outnumbered. Rioters climbing the West steps fired bear spray, aerosol grease, spray paint, and other chemicals. They surged in waves closer and closer, around to the East, and then up a staircase under the inaugural scaffolding, pummeling officers with fists, clubs, hammers, and even flagpoles fashioned into spears. Officers fought back, swinging their batons at rioters' knuckles each time the mob latched on to another barrier to tear down, leading closer to nearby doors.

Television cameramen, themselves becoming targets of the rioters, raced to reposition and capture some of the fighting. Rosen's office was suddenly frenzied. Marc Raimondi, the senior public affairs chief at Justice, turned on his office TV at the urging of a friend on the Hill, who called to report the drama. He saw rioters climbing scaffolding outside the Capitol and thought: "Holy shit." He rushed to Rosen's office to find his cell phone, office phone, and many others in his suite all ringing, with no secretaries or staffers to answer them. Raimondi and the head of the Justice Department's Civil Division together fielded calls, taking down notes and lining up phones on Rosen's desk for him and the deputy attorney general could answer the top-priority ones from the White House and the Pentagon.

Sherwin, the acting U.S. attorney, walked incognito up Pennsylvania Avenue alongside protesters, having broken off from his police escort. Looking ahead, he also spotted rioters climbing the scaffolding and abandoned plans to keep going to the Capitol. He quickly peeled off north to get to his office.

At the FBI's Washington Field Office, D'Antuono watched the unfolding scenes on TV in disbelief. He ordered his SWAT team to prepare to leave for the Capitol but, following FBI protocol, asked his staff's lawyers to verbally agree that the deployment would be justified. After a brief discussion, they agreed it would be.

Before the team left, rioters breached the Capitol. They climbed through smashed-out windows and pushed past Capitol Police on their way to taking control of the Capitol Rotunda. Officers in the House barricaded doors to the ornate chamber where hundreds of members of Congress were meeting. One rioter soon shattered a windowpane and began to shout through the broken glass, prompting a House sergeant at arms and Capitol Police officers beside the lawmakers to pull their pistols and point them at rioters they glimpsed packed into the hallway outside. One yelled to the police to stand back and let them come in: "If this doesn't happen, there's going to be a bigger Civil War, and a lot of bloodshed." Texas Republican Rep. Troy Nehls, a former sheriff, stuck his face close to the window and discouraged the rioters, saying repeatedly that he was "ashamed" of their behavior. Another rioter yelled back that that lawmaker was the one who should be ashamed for going forward to certify Biden as the next president. "I drove fourteen hours to get here and stood in the cold for three and a half hours to find out that Mike Pence is a fucking traitor, man," he yelled. "He could have done the right thing and certified those legislators' electors and we wouldn't be standing here right now with a 9mm pointed at me." As the standoff continued, officers were rushing members of Congress down a back staircase to tunnels and to an undisclosed holding room.

As the FBI SWAT team was about to depart, Bowdich suddenly stomped into the Washington Field Office, having walked the four blocks from the Hoover Building with his entourage of staffers and security detail racing to keep up. "Steve," Bowdich said loudly in D'Antuono's direction as he entered the room, "we need to get the tactical team to . . ." Bowdich paused, turning to yell back into the phone, "Where?" Then he looked back up at D'Antuono as he spoke into the phone: "Room 316, right."

Much of the U.S. Senate was going to hole up in a single hearing room, Capitol Police were fighting off rioters, and the FBI's SWAT team needed to protect the lawmakers, Bowdich told D'Antuono. Bowdich's own SWAT team instincts were bubbling to the surface. He asked D'Antuono where the team was staging so he could rally them as they left. Donoghue, the deputy attorney general, soon arrived, and he and Bowdich began to huddle in a conference room off the side of the command center. But Bowdich quickly emerged, yelling orders a second time. The other SWAT team, the one coming from Baltimore, needed to go to the Capitol, specifically to Senate Majority Leader Mitch McConnell's suite.

There, three senior Republican aides had barely escaped the halls and started to pile furniture in front of the door when passing rioters beat and kicked on the door, chanting for Speaker Pelosi: "Nancy? Where are you, Nancy?" A McConnell staffer opened his contacts on his phone and tried Will Levi, the former chief of staff to the recently departed Bill

Barr. Whispering their location, the aide warned that if reinforcements did not arrive soon, people could die. Levi had called Bowdich and now Bowdich was yelling the information to D'Antuono.

Rosen dialed into a call with White House lawyers, Pentagon commanders, and Trump's national security adviser. The situation was dire and required all hands on deck. From DOJ, one FBI SWAT team was already at the Capitol, the other was racing in from Baltimore, and the Hostage Rescue Team was preparing to leave Quantico. All available D.C. police, as well as troopers and sheriffs from Maryland and Virginia, were converging on the Capitol. Still, more were needed. The Secret Service offered to send all its D.C.-based agents and officers with service weapons. The request for still more help was relayed to Bowdich and D'Antuono, who told his deputies to ask for volunteers. Hundreds of FBI agents, including several in suits and dress shoes, stood up. Many would head into the riot with no more than their FBI-emblazoned windbreakers and sidearms.

To the surprise of many in the field office, Bowdich and Donoghue would soon announce that they wanted to go too. D'Antuono looked at them, stunned. Did the deputy director of the FBI and the deputy attorney general really need to be in the middle of the melee? What if they got surrounded and needed to be extracted? The FBI has technology on most agents' phones that can pinpoint their location to within a few feet. As Bowdich left to get ready, D'Antuono turned to the head of Bowdich's security detail and pointed to the app. "Do you have this on your phone?" The two did not. Unbeknownst to the deputy director, D'Antuono had a staffer install the tracking software on the deputy director's team and put his location beacon up on the board at the command center. D'Antuono was not going to lose the FBI's number 2.

Just how much the Bureau was improvising came into focus a few minutes later at the Capitol Police command center. The FBI's Hostage Rescue Team, experienced in jetting into hostile foreign nations for clandestine missions, was inbound in a helicopter and requesting permission to land its team at the U.S. Capitol.

A longtime Capitol Police commander who fielded the call shuddered at the thought. He knew the FBI team's protocol was often to enter a building with assault rifles at the ready. He closed his eyes and pictured the commandos fast-roping onto the rotunda like Rambo—a bloodbath ensuing on live television. "Negative," he said, "permission denied."

By that point, a Capitol Police officer had shot and killed rioter Ashli Babbitt as she attempted to jump through a broken window into a corridor where officers were evacuating members of Congress. But otherwise officers and agents on the ground had avoided drawing their firearms. Many feared members of the mob were armed too. One shot in the sea of people outside the Capitol, many officers worried, could quickly escalate into an all-out firefight. The Hostage Rescue Team circled around and landed about two miles away. Vans from the Washington Field Office were dispatched to pick them up and drive them to a congressional parking lot where officers were staging to enter the Capitol.

A few blocks away at Main Justice, aides were dashing in and out of Rosen's office with worrisome updates and requests for him to hop on one urgent call after another once the Capitol had been breached, so much so that it became a blur. Most of the calls were aimed at rushing agents and resources to the scene. Then at one point, an aide hurried in with disquieting news.

"You won't believe this," the staffer told Rosen, and then he lifted his phone to show Trump's latest tweet:

"Mike Pence didn't have the courage to do what should have been done to protect our Country and our Constitution," Trump tweeted at 2:24 p.m., seeming to put a target squarely on his own vice president, who, along with his wife and daughter, was still inside the Capitol building. Rosen was surprised and saddened and thought to himself: That's not helpful.

He didn't know the frantic chain reaction Trump's words would set off at the scene. A protester on the Capitol steps read Trump's message aloud through a megaphone to his fellow fighters, some of whom were chanting for Pence's hanging. A few hundred feet away, the vice president, meanwhile, was hiding in an office off the Senate floor with his family, advisers, and security detail. The Secret Service agents had already begun calling their families to say heartfelt goodbyes, convinced the situation could end in the worst possible way. The leader of Pence's detail knew they had to get to a safer location. He and fellow agents rushed Pence from their temporary hiding place, down a staircase, and into a parking garage. At one point during the evacuation, Pence and his family came within just seventy-five feet of a surge of rioters.

Over the coming hours, as Pence and members of Congress hunkered down in hiding places, over five hundred FBI, ATF, U.S. Marshals, and other DOJ officers responded to the Capitol. They joined hundreds of police from D.C., Maryland, and Virginia, and then the first-arriving National Guard troops. Law enforcement finally had the numbers to turn the tide and began to regain control of the building and its surroundings.

As the sun set, battle-weary police and FBI agents inside the Capitol searched offices for hiding rioters, while outside, arriving Guard troops formed a defensive line behind the police. Amid bursts of tear gas and pepper spray, officers in front kept pushing back thousands of still-screaming invaders, one step at a time, down the marble stairs, then across the Capitol lawn, and finally onto the public street.

The officers, many bruised or blood-spattered, made no effort to arrest their attackers. In the wake of the uprising to overturn the election, police focused on making the halls of Congress safe for lawmakers to return that night and formally declare Joe Biden the next president of the United States.

Though Rosen had spoken extensively throughout the afternoon with every senior White House official and Pence himself, there was no sign the president had done anything to quell the mayhem on one of the country's worst days.

At 6:01 p.m., with police restoring order, Trump tweeted his takeaway.

"These are the things and events that happen when a sacred land-slide election victory is so unceremoniously & viciously stripped away from great patriots who have been badly & unfairly treated for so long. Go home with love & in peace. Remember this day forever!"

At 7:00 p.m., Rosen convened a call to update the vice president, McConnell, Chuck Schumer, Nancy Pelosi, and Kevin McCarthy, as well as Pentagon and Homeland Security chiefs. From a remote hookup at the Capitol, Donoghue was beamed in to explain that the ATF had cleared the building from the Senate side into the center, and the FBI had cleared from the House side back toward the Capitol dome. Canine units were still sniffing for explosives, checking every nook and cranny to be sure no trouble remained.

"When can we be back in the building?" Schumer asked.

"At eight p.m.," Donoghue said.

Across the nation's capital, where federal prosecutors charge violent crimes because D.C. lacks statehood and the authority to do so itself, lawyers in the U.S. Attorney's Office were glued to their TVs, exchanging text messages and emails. There would be hundreds—maybe thousands— of arrestees to process by the end of the night, they figured. Many had been working remotely for almost a year during the pandemic but were preparing to go into their office or to the D.C. jail for the first time in months. They started building a schedule to work in shifts through the night. But as Congress came back into session and Biden's victory was confirmed, their phones never rang. Only a handful of charges were ready to process, mostly for a man who parked a truck with eleven Molotov cocktails and several loaded firearms outside the Capitol.

As janitors scrubbed down the Capitol crime scene, Raimondi and Rosen exchanged drafts of a public statement. What should Rosen, the nation's top law enforcement officer, say? What should be the Justice Department's first message to Americans following an attack with no precedent in over two centuries of peaceful transfers of executive power?

Earlier in the afternoon, Barr had called his former spokesperson at the department, Kerri Kupec, asking why neither Rosen nor the Justice Department had yet issued a public statement about the riot. Kupec said she wasn't sure what Rosen planned to do. Barr snorted at the lack of urgency. It was around 4:00 p.m. and the Capitol had been breached two hours earlier. He read aloud his own statement so she could write it down. She would issue it using her personal Twitter feed: "From former Attorney General Bill Barr: 'The violence at the Capitol Building is outrageous and despicable. Federal agencies should move immediately to disperse it.'"

That evening Rosen read and reread various options for his message and approved one slightly milder than Barr's.

"The violence at our Nation's Capitol Building is an intolerable attack on a fundamental institution of our democracy," it began. Justice Department officers, federal agents, and local police had worked to restore order, it read, and would continue "in addressing this unacceptable situation, and we intend to enforce the laws of our land."

The Justice Department could only respond to the events of January 6 with the same hesitation and diffidence with which it had prepared for them.

Part Two

[14]

An Early Distraction
for Investigators

On the morning of January 7, as National Guard soldiers blocked roads to the U.S. Capitol, FBI agents, federal prosecutors, and even Trump's top defenders at the Justice Department agreed that the president's supporters had perpetrated a massive crime against the United States—egged on, it appeared, by Trump himself.

At the U.S. Attorney's Office, staffers watched as the number of people dialing into the Justice Department's first press call topped five hundred, then six hundred. The world was watching, and Michael Sherwin, the fast-talking confidant Barr had installed ten months earlier as the top federal prosecutor in D.C., was about to make news. Since his days as an assistant U.S. attorney in Miami, Sherwin had prided himself on relying on few if any prepared talking points. With only a couple of staffers in the room because of COVID protocols, Sherwin spoke empty-handed, pointing and jabbing his finger at the speakerphone as he fielded questions. How far would the investigation reach? Would DOJ look at the actions of politicians?

"We are looking at all actors here, not only the people that went into the building," Sherwin said. "Were there others that maybe assisted, or facilitated, or played some ancillary role in this? We will look at every actor and all criminal charges."

The DOJ's hesitancy seemed to have evaporated. Sherwin, an exuberant Republican prosecutor, along with his cynical counterpart at the FBI's Washington Field Office, were the unlikely pair in the driver's seat. One of the last decisions Rosen had made the night of the attack was to endorse Sherwin's recommendation that all Capitol riot cases be tried in D.C., not in whatever state rioters were later found and apprehended. On the FBI side, there was never a question whether headquarters would bigfoot the Washington Field Office; Wray insisted field offices quarterback, especially anything that touched politics, as running cases from headquarters had in the past led to accusations of bias.

Before the call was over, Sherwin would make headlines worldwide in responding to a question about Trump's potential culpability in the Capitol attack.

"Are you going to be looking at the role that President Trump played at the rally and, you know, whipping up the crowd before they went to the Capitol?" a reporter asked.

"I'm going to stand by my earlier statement: We're looking at all actors here, and anyone that had a role," Sherwin said. "If the evidence fits the elements of a crime, they're going to be charged."

At Sherwin's answer, one federal prosecutor at his home in the D.C. area fist-pumped the air. It had taken something as unbelievable as the attack on the Capitol, but the years of the Justice Department cowering before Trump appeared to be over. The websites of *The Washington Post* and *The New York Times* soon read that Trump could be investigated for inciting the riot, and that the Justice Department would not rule out charges against the president. Sherwin's comments, wrote *Times* reporter Katie Benner, marked "an extraordinary invocation of the rule of law against a president who has counted on the Justice Department to advance his personal agenda."

As the day progressed, prominent and lower-ranking members of Trump's administration resigned, and some Republicans on Capitol Hill even joined Democrats in calling for the president to be removed from office immediately, either by his cabinet invoking the Twenty-Fifth Amendment or through impeachment by Congress.

At his campaign headquarters in Wilmington, Delaware, President-elect Joe Biden seized on the moment to make clear that in thirteen days, his administration was ready to pick up the pieces and restore order, beginning at the Justice Department. As it happened, news of Biden's selection for attorney general had leaked out the very hour before Trump supporters breached the Capitol. Biden had chosen Merrick Garland, a respected federal appeals court judge. Following the attack, Biden cast Garland as an antidote to Trump's four years of "contempt for our democracy." In fact, behind closed doors, January 6 had amplified all the reasons Biden had come to feel that Garland was the right man for the job.

Back in mid-November, Biden and his incoming White House team had been anxious to vet and name the President-elect's future cabinet quickly, so they could press the Senate for speedy confirmations and hit the ground running.

But the balance of power that Biden would face in the Senate had remained in limbo heading into the New Year, hinging on the outcome of two January 5 runoff elections in Georgia. As a result, Biden's advisers focused on nominees with bipartisan appeal in case Republicans maintained control of the chamber.

For months, three candidates had been in the running for attorney general, with Biden's close advisers and longtime allies at loggerheads over the final choice. Some, including lifetime friends Ted Kaufman and Mark Gitenstein, pressed Biden to name Doug Jones, who had just lost his reelection bid for the U.S. Senate in Alabama. A former federal prosecutor, Jones had risked his reelection chances by voting to impeach Trump for his pressure campaign against Ukraine, and he had known and worked with Biden on issues for more than forty years. Several prominent

Justice hands, meanwhile, lobbied for Sally Yates, the former number 2 at the department under Obama. While serving briefly as acting attorney general in the first weeks of Trump's presidency in 2017, she had become a hero on the left for balking at Trump's travel ban targeting Muslims. Biden's future Chief of Staff Ron Klain urged the president-elect to pick Garland, his longtime friend who had been Obama's choice for the Supreme Court but who had been blocked from consideration by then Senate Majority Leader Mitch McConnell. Klain had been eyeing his friend for a while, and days after the election, Jamie Gorelick, a mentor to Garland and longtime adviser to Democratic presidents on judicial nominees, called Klain to tell him she had spoken to Garland about the idea. For the AG job, he was willing to give up his lifetime seat on the bench.

Garland was a smart man who friends could see early in life had ambitions to the highest rungs of the U.S. justice system and who had allowed himself to imagine achieving that with a seat on the most powerful court in the land. For decades, Garland had seemed to shape his life story and key decisions to survive the minefield of a modern Supreme Court nomination. From the bench, he had studiously avoided contention and sought to tease out compromise in his rulings.

Although Garland retained his powerful post as chief of the D.C. Circuit—often the highest court to hear a case outside the Supreme Court—he had watched with increasing alarm as Trump and Barr had ignored DOJ guidelines to be evenhanded and independent in exercising its vast powers of prosecution. Garland, after all, had helped write the department's rule book. After once sleeping outside the Supreme Court to get a seat to hear arguments related to Watergate, one of Garland's earliest jobs at DOJ had been to help codify post-Watergate reforms. Garland helped write the first draft of a section of the *Principles of Federal Prosecution* having to do with the Justice Department's policy on limiting communications with the White House and keeping at arm's length executive branch political decisions. Four decades later, he had begun confiding to others that it seemed as though Justice was losing its way in maintaining its nonpartisan independence. A column in *The New York*

Times in early 2020, titled "Justice, Weaponized," struck a particular chord. Garland began to discuss whether the best use of his twenty-four years as a judge was to stay on the bench. The Justice Department, he told one confidant, "gets in your blood."

By the end of December, the field for the top job had narrowed to Jones and Garland, even as Biden's team had coalesced around Lisa Monaco for deputy attorney general to run the department day-to-day. Monaco was well known and trusted by Biden, and she was already serving as a key legal hand on the transition, vetting top cabinet picks. Monaco's working relationship with Biden had begun decades earlier, when she had served as a Senate committee adviser for him. Later, she was at Obama's side at the White House for four years as his homeland security and counterterrorism adviser. More importantly, in the intervening decades, she had built one of the best résumés in Washington for the number 2 job, with rare bona fides on both the prosecution and the investigation sides of the department.

A Harvard and Chicago Law grad, Monaco had early in her career served as an adviser to Attorney General Janet Reno. She later worked as a federal prosecutor in the D.C. office before investigating key leaders of the collapsed energy giant Enron and ascending to become the first female assistant attorney general for national security. Monaco was known for her dogged, around-the-clock work ethic and exacting standards. No one came to a meeting better prepared. She also could look the part of a tough national security official, projecting a piercing stare she seemed to have honed during the most formative years of her career in the front office of the FBI as protégée and chief of staff for Mueller. Monaco stood about six inches shorter than the director, and in some corners of the Justice Department had for a time attracted the nickname "mini Mueller." Obama's White House had floated her name for FBI director. In the deputy attorney general spot, she'd remain on a path trod before to the director's chair. Her star was still rising.

A couple of days after New Year's, some of Biden's most trusted confidants along with his transition head, Jeff Zients, gathered in Biden's study in Wilmington to make their dueling cases. Vice President–elect Kamala Harris joined remotely on-screen. Gitenstein, a longtime Biden aide who had been at his side for the most pivotal moments of his career, took the lead to explain why Jones was the best choice. Klain then laid out all the pros for choosing Judge Garland, someone he had been close with since the Clinton administration but whom Biden barely knew. Garland, Klain explained, had a reputation as a moderate Democrat and had been celebrated by both sides of the aisle as a pro-prosecution centrist on the country's most prestigious appellate bench. He was no political activist, which could help him reestablish the department's apolitical credibility after Trump had repeatedly deployed the department for his own political goals. On top of that, Klain said, Garland vacating his judgeship would create an opening and an opportunity for standout jurist Ketanji Brown Jackson. Elevating Brown to fill the vacancy created by Garland's nomination could help Biden fulfill another campaign promise: to nominate the first Black woman to the Supreme Court. Choosing Garland was a great "two-fer," Klain insisted. The president would land a person who had experience at the highest levels of the Justice Department and get a chance to prepare another ideal judge for the Supreme Court.

The discussion was "lively," with Gitenstein arguing that Garland was an outstanding person but he didn't really know Biden and he hadn't been in Justice Department leadership since Clinton was president. Klain argued that choosing Jones, someone he also liked very much, risked giving up a chance to dramatically distinguish Biden from Trump. If Biden picked Jones, he could be accused of choosing a "pol" who was personally loyal to him, as Trump had done with Sessions. Klain urged that Biden could forge a winning team with Garland and Monaco.

On January 5, days after their debate in the library, Biden called Klain with his decision. It was the same day Georgia voters were heading to the polls and would give Democrats control of the Senate, thereby removing the pressure to name an AG who would appeal to Republican senators. But Klain's argument had won out.

"I've made up my mind," Biden said. "I'm going to go with Garland."

On January 6, as Trump supporters began swarming the U.S. Capitol, Garland had been in his attic study in Bethesda, Maryland, just outside the D.C. line, drafting his acceptance speech for the next day. His wife entered the room and told her husband to turn on the television. Garland watched in disbelief and soon began recasting his speech. The full depth of the country's political division was for a moment covered over by the shock of what had happened. The United States needed to recover and move on together, and the Justice Department would have to play a central role.

About twenty-six hours later, Biden took the podium in Wilmington and described January 6 as "one of the darkest days in the history of our nation, an unprecedented assault on our democracy."

Above all, Biden promised that on his watch, Justice would do the thing so dear to Garland's heart, restore independence and integrity. "I want to be clear," he said, gesturing toward Garland, "you won't work for me. You are not the president's or the vice president's lawyer. Your loyalty is not to me—it's to the law, the Constitution, the people of this nation."

The president-elect introduced Garland and Monaco, as well as Vanita Gupta and Kristen Clarke, to oversee DOJ's Civil Division and Civil Rights office, respectively.

Garland had not been on the national stage since his thwarted Supreme Court bid, but he stepped up to the podium and, in a measured if raspy voice, picked up where Biden had left off. Like his illustrious career on the bench, Garland's delivery was even, if mildly emotional as he talked about his grandparents fleeing the Holocaust and emigrating to the United States.

"As everyone who watched yesterday's events in Washington now understands, if they did not understand before, the rule of law is not just some lawyer's turn of phrase, it is the very foundation of our democracy," Garland said.

Far from the quips of Trump's two confirmed attorneys general, Garland was also more professorial. He tried to break down the archaic phrase "rule of law," which he vowed to make the Justice Department's guiding principle once again.

"The essence of the rule of law is that like cases are treated alike: that there not be one rule for Democrats and another for Republicans, one rule for friends, another for foes, one rule for the powerful, and another for the powerless, one rule for the rich and another for the poor."

Garland's brand of studious moderation seemed appropriate. Even Republicans longed for a return to bland, middle-of-the-road leaders.

Garland quoted the acceptance speech of Edward Levi, the attorney general largely credited with rebuilding Justice after President Nixon's abuse of the agency. Garland said it remained true, as Levi had said, that nothing could imperil the nation's shared principles faster than "failure to make clear by words and deed that our law is not the instrument of partisan purpose."

That same day, one of Trump's most aggressive advisers continued a desperate attempt to keep him in power. A little-known conservative law professor, John Eastman had counseled Trump on how to disrupt the January 6 certification to stay in power. He had urged Trump to claim fraud in key swing-state elections, despite no evidence of such fraud, as a means for Trump allies in Congress to justify blocking Biden's victory. On January 7, just a day after the attack, he called Eric Herschmann in the White House counsel's office, saying he wanted to talk through some strategies to preserve Trump's options for appealing the results in the Georgia election.

Herschmann, like nearly every lawyer in the White House, had hotly opposed Eastman's advice. He was now aghast that Eastman was still at it.

"Are you out of your effing mind?" Herschmann asked. "I only want to hear two words coming out of your mouth from now on: 'Orderly transition.' I don't want to hear any other words coming out of your mouth no matter what, other than 'orderly transition.' Repeat those words to me."

As Herschmann grew more insistent, Eastman eventually complied. "Orderly transition," Eastman said quietly.

"Good, John," Herschmann said. "Now I'm going to give you the best free legal advice you're ever getting in your life. Get a great effing criminal defense lawyer. You're going to need it."

And then Herschmann hung up.

Eastman seemed to absorb the message. A few days later, he would privately request that Trump give him a preemptive presidential pardon.

In the days immediately after the attack, Sherwin, the top D.C. prosecutor, and D'Antuono, the head of the FBI's Washington Field Office, spent hours together and realized they were naturally aligned on many of the steps their investigators should take.

In many ways, they first had to compensate for the tactical decision police made not to attempt arrests on the night of January 6. The rioters were fast scattering back across the United States, and Sherwin and D'Antuono wanted to track down and arrest as many as possible before the inauguration. Speaking excitedly about the plan to a confidant, Sherwin said several quick, high-profile arrests would not only help remove the threat of more violence around Biden's swearing in but also give the public "confidence" that the justice system would catch up with the Capitol lawbreakers.

One of the first challenges was sorting through the avalanche of incoming tips to law enforcement agencies and even to members of Congress. Sherwin wanted his office and the FBI to start working from a master spreadsheet, which he dubbed "the matrix." As soon as investigators had a name for a face in a video or still image, the ID for that rioter was added to the matrix and assigned to an agent. When agents found video showing that rioter engaged in a crime, such as assaulting a police officer, one of Sherwin's federal prosecutors was immediately added to the case as well.

Still, investigators knew the matrix needed to evolve into a complete list of all rioters, not just those they had ID'd from tipsters. The day after the attack, agents began serving subpoenas to cell phone providers to get records of people they could identify at the scene. Within a week, the FBI would tap its emergency powers under national security law and serve Google with what were known as geofence warrants. The Bureau demanded that Google identify every phone user who had been on the four-acre area inside or around the Capitol between 2:00 p.m. and 6:30 p.m. on January 6. Using cell phone tower data, Google identified at least 5,723 people who were potentially inside the Capitol or surrounding it in those hours. Then the FBI got Google to subtract users who had been at the Capitol earlier or much later in the day, presumably staffers, police, and members of Congress who were on the scene legally. They then subtracted another category, those who had been at the Capitol on previous days. Eventually, they were left with about 1,500 devices—essentially a master list of phones used by potential suspects that the FBI could work to ID.

The FBI national tip hotline, meanwhile, had to add staff to handle an overwhelming gusher of additional leads, including two hundred thousand about January 6 suspects in the first two weeks. Neighbors, coworkers, and even people on dating apps reported people bragging about having participated in the riot.

With leads stacking up, D'Antuono had the FBI's mobile command post, nicknamed "Big Blue," parked in front of the D.C. Field Office on January 8. Agents were told to begin staffing the trailer as well as desks inside the building around the clock, to search video in shifts, twenty-four hours a day.

Some of the disturbing images they focused on—men crushing a Capitol Police officer in a doorway; a shirtless man wearing horns at the Senate dais; one carrying a Confederate flag; another grinning, his feet propped up on a congressional desk—were also replaying constantly on cable news. Talking to his deputies, Sherwin dubbed those suspects the riot's "internet stars." Every time their actions replayed, the indelible images of the attack were "giving Capitol Police the middle finger," Sherwin said. Charging them needed to be a top priority. Within forty-eight hours of order being restored at the Capitol, thirteen rioters who had left behind some of the most incriminating and viral evidence were named in criminal complaints filed in federal court in D.C.

Among them was Richard "Bigo" Barnett, the man pictured reclining with his feet on a desk in House Speaker Nancy Pelosi's suite, exposing a stun gun on his waist. Barnett had recounted his actions to reporters in a recorded conversation, noting that he'd left a message on the desk: "Hey Nancy," it read, "Bigo was here biotch." Facing a warrant for his arrest, Barnett surrendered to FBI agents the next morning at the Benton County Sheriff's Office in Arkansas. By the end of the night, the arrest process was in motion again, with Sherwin's staff filing a criminal complaint against Jacob Anthony Chansley, aka the horn-wearing Shaman.

To process agents' and prosecutors' growing list of subpoenas and warrants, Sherwin visited Chief Judge Beryl Howell of the U.S. District Court in D.C. with an unusual request. His attorneys' requests were piling up and would only increase and overwhelm the court's single on-duty magistrate judge, he warned. Sherwin asked Howell to create a twenty-four-hour rotation to handle the high volume of requests at all hours of the night. Howell's judges organized a seven-days-a-week coverage plan with backup judges. It was something the court had done in 1968 to handle the high volume of arrests from anti–Vietnam War protests, but no one remembered having done so since.

Yet in one key area, the Justice Department's massive mobilization in response to the Capitol attack would come at a cost.

On the afternoon of January 8, federal investigator Waleska McLellan got some disappointing news: Federal prosecutors in D.C. were so busy investigating the riot that DOJ was taking a pass on pursuing potentially criminal actions leading up to January 6.

McLellan, thirty-seven, worked as the special agent in charge of investigations for a tiny government watchdog, the Inspector General's Office for the National Archives. She had won awards for her detail-oriented approach and over the past four or five weeks had grown increasingly disturbed by pieces that were starting to fit together. Republican Party officials in five states had each submitted phony documents falsely claiming that they were the officially appointed electors for their state party and that Donald Trump had won the election in their respective states.

Like many people, McLellan and her small team were reeling from the bloody riot and finding the televised scenes of the attack particularly horrifying and hard to process. She wondered if these fraudulent elector documents had served some role in training Trump's supporters on the Capitol.

In his speech on the Ellipse, Trump had repeatedly remarked on the obscure issue of disputed electors. "We have come to demand that Congress do the right thing and only count the electors who have been lawfully slated," Trump said.

In the hours that followed, some of Trump's supporters who surrounded and entered the Capitol had parroted the president, boasting on social media that they would keep Congress from performing the little-known process of certifying the election by counting the electors' votes of each state. McLellan asked her team if there might have been a larger objective behind the Trump supporters posing as lawfully slated presidential electors.

McLellan had been tipped off to the first phony elector document in mid-December. That's when she and her boss, Jason Metrick, the assistant inspector general, got an email from a seasoned staff attorney at the National Archives saying the office had received some clearly bogus elector submissions from state GOP officials in several swing states. The first one came from Arizona, but within the next few days the office had received similar fakes from Georgia, Michigan, Nevada, and Pennsylvania. In each, Republican state party members alleged they had been chosen as their state's electors.

Like many investigators working across the federal government, McLellan had to be a jack-of-all-trades. The team of agents she supervised generally focused their limited resources on misconduct allegations or the theft of records and treasures that the National Archives was charged with safekeeping. A string of phony Electoral College submissions was entirely new to her. So Metrick and McLellan arranged a conference call to learn more from Miriam Vincent, the longtime government attorney who had first flagged concerns about the documents and was the department's resident expert on the certification process.

On December 21, Vincent explained on a conference call that she had spotted the strange submissions as frauds straightaway. Inside her office, workers had initially viewed the first submission as a political stunt and were annoyed that nearly two months after the election, some pro-Trump troublemakers were still engaging in shenanigans. Vincent told a colleague: "Damn, this election is never going to die." On the call, the agents asked for the bottom line.

Vincent explained that a pattern of fraudulent submissions was very unusual. The National Archives was responsible for maintaining the official records of the presidential election, and someone trying to slip them multiple forgeries significantly amped up her concern.

"Are you sure they were fakes?" Metrick asked. Vincent said she had no doubt. First, the documents lacked the distinctive and unique state seals. Instead, most of the phony ones had an amateurish typed header in boldface that read "Certificate of the Votes of the Electors" for Arizona, Georgia, and so on.

Next, the documents had been mailed or submitted by private individuals, not by a secretary of state, the normal and official route. Finally, each claimed to record that the state had voted for Donald Trump, rather than the reported and verified winner, Joe Biden.

"Has this ever been prosecuted before?" McLellan asked. Vincent explained she'd never seen a multistate fraud like this; but in 2012, a Virginia man who was part of a fringe political party and suffered from delusions had doctored a certificate, inserting his name as the vice-presidential winner in the state. The faked Virginia submission was never pursued by the Archives, Vincent told the agents. It appeared to be a guy who was a nuisance, not the mastermind of a criminal plot. After the call, Vincent sent the team a scanned package of all the falsified certificates, laying bare the nearly identical language and headings.

Vincent stressed to the agents that legitimate Republican Party members had signed these documents. Indeed, before the fraudulent submissions even arrived, GOP officials in some states had put out press releases or given interviews to report they were casting their own elector votes for Trump.

"They weren't exactly subtle," Vincent explained to the investigators. "They were announcing this to the world."

McLellan told her team she was most troubled by the fact that the submissions appeared to be coordinated—and organized in several cases by GOP state leaders. It looked and smelled like a crime, but she needed to ask the Justice Department for advice. Even before the National Archives officials had met to assess the certificates, McLellan had thought of J. P. Cooney, who oversaw public corruption prosecutions at the U.S. Attorney's Office in Washington, D.C. In a task-force presentation to federal agents the previous fall, Cooney had urged them to come to his office if they came across evidence of election crimes. So, on the evening of December 15, McLellan had emailed the general "duty" email inbox that Cooney told her and other agents to use to report a possible case. She asked in her email for someone in his office to contact her.

By December 21, McLellan had sent two emails but heard nothing back. Armed with more information, she emailed Cooney directly a little before noon on December 30 to report she had a potential election crime and no one in his office was responding. Cooney wrote back almost immediately to apologize, and said one of his line prosecutors would be in touch with her ASAP. Not long after, Amanda Vaughn, a federal prosecutor from Cooney's team, called. McLellan shared with Vaughn the key information about the fake elector documents. Vaughn asked several questions and seemed curious but noncommittal. She said she'd confer with others, and they'd talk again. A week later, when the Capitol was attacked, McLellan was still awaiting an answer.

On January 8, Vaughn and McLellan connected by phone, and

Vaughn said something like: "We just don't think there's a case here." McLellan countered that others did see a potential case. The Arizona State Attorney General's Office had been asking her office questions about the fake elector documents in their state. Vaughn suggested McLellan and her team would be better off pursuing the issue with state investigators. That was it. The feds would not be pursuing the case.

McLellan was disappointed but told her team she empathized with Vaughn and the prosecutors in D.C. There was no doubt the riot investigation was sprawling and demanding all their attention.

State charges were possible. Arizona's Attorney General's Office had said they were considering a probe. Aides to Michigan's Attorney General Dana Nessel said she wanted her state to pursue an investigation. Nevada and Wisconsin were possibilities too. But breaking the case into individual state investigations separated the trees from the forest. Each state focused only on the individual forgery related to their election, and not the questions of whether there had been a coordinated fraud and, if so, who had organized it.

The same day that DOJ turned McLellan down, Trump gave federal authorities another, more pressing matter to worry about: inauguration security.

Trump tweeted that his nearly 75 million supporters "will not be disrespected or treated unfairly in any way, shape or form!!!" An hour later, Trump confirmed in another tweet that he would not attend Biden's inauguration, making him the first president not to attend their successor's ceremony in more than 150 years.

While many commentators focused on Trump's announcement as a brutish insult, the Biden team heard the announcement and worried it might be more sinister. Did Trump know something they did not about potential violence on Inauguration Day? The tweet, as it turned out, would also be Trump's last as president. Within hours, Twitter announced it was permanently suspending Trump's account, saying that the two tweets had to be viewed in "the context of horrific events this week" and Trump's power to glorify and incite violence.

The concern within the Biden camp about additional violence quickly became palpable. Klain reminded the incoming White House team that most of them had found it completely implausible before January 6 that mobs would be willing to attack the Capitol. It seemed wise for them to assume an incensed segment of America might attempt to use armed force to block the inauguration from proceeding peacefully.

On January 13, some of Trump's supporters were outraged yet again. The House of Representatives voted 232–197 to impeach Trump for "incitement of insurrection." Ten Republicans, including the House GOP Leader Kevin McCarthy, joined Democrats in concluding that Trump had committed "high crimes and misdemeanors" in blaming his election loss on fraud, and then riling up his supporters on January 6 to "fight like hell." The single article of impeachment said Trump's statements "encouraged—and foreseeably resulted in—lawless action at the Capitol."

The next day, FBI Director Chris Wray used his first public appearance since the Capitol attack to warn that the Bureau was tracking an extensive amount of "concerning online chatter" about violence surrounding the inauguration. In a briefing for Biden's team, FBI officials said they had detected threats of armed protests around the inauguration in nearly every state. Biden's team decided to cancel plans for the president-elect to travel from Wilmington to D.C. by Amtrak, as he had for decades as a senator. The Pentagon decided it was prudent to take another step: increase the number of soldiers called to D.C. to about twenty-five thousand, the largest-ever military presence for a transfer of power ceremony.

[15]

A Prosecutor's Plan
Is Batted Down

By Inauguration Day, downtown Washington had been transformed into a militarized zone, with bridges closed, a maze of concrete barriers, and checkpoints manned by armed members of the National Guard.

Hours before Biden's motorcade would set off for the Capitol, agents arrived at the Virginia home of John Demers, Trump's assistant attorney general. They would drive the DOJ veteran on an hour-long, circuitous path and then chaperone him through barbed wire to the secure zone of the Justice Department, where he would serve as a bridge until Biden's team could be sworn in.

In the main foyer of the stately Robert F. Kennedy Department of Justice Building, he and one of his top deputies, George Toscas, encountered an almost apocalyptic Hollywood scene of a soldiers' encampment. Piled between the department's Greek columns and frescoes were cases of water bottles and piles of ready-made meals. Clusters of camouflage-clad National Guard troops, some with rifles slung over their shoulders, huddled in groups awaiting orders. Military radios squawked and echoed through the corridors.

On the floors above, only a skeleton staff was on duty to keep the department operating for Trump's final hours in power. In fact, because of the extra security precautions, most of Biden's Day One team could not even access the Justice Department as usual. They reported instead to a satellite campus two miles to the north to be sworn in. The group was Biden's landing team, prepared with drafts of executive orders to roll back Trump's most controversial decisions on criminal prosecutions and treatment of immigrants.

Ahead of the inauguration, Biden's volunteers had begun the normal process of interviewing department staff and had begun to hear some of what they had feared. Many teams had been traumatized by their repeated run-ins with Barr and the president's political henchmen. But they also heard a hopeful refrain: Justice wasn't broken, just bruised. What its career staff craved was a clear signal from the incoming team that they would be supported in returning to the careful legal analysis and decision-making they had been trained to do. The transition leaders got the message.

They had crafted a Day One plan to show that the Biden administration was returning Justice to "normal order."

Within hours of taking the oath of office on January 20, Biden signed executive orders to do just that, and to revoke some Trump policies.

At DOJ the next morning, Biden's fledgling team met for its first big briefing in the attorney general's conference room, primarily focused on the January 6 investigation and domestic terror threats. Sherwin, the acting U.S. attorney, gave a detailed update. The FBI had identified almost four hundred suspects by name, and a crush of charges would soon be coming to court. Video and other evidence pointed to a total pool of eight hundred to one thousand criminal suspects who had entered the Capitol. Scores of agents and prosecutors were chasing other critical threads, including identifying whoever had planted the pipe bombs on the day of the Capitol attack. The Biden team ordered the work to continue.

Separately, the Day One team began prepping a series of statements and orders. One reversed a policy that had led to the separation of immigrant children and the parents who had tried to bring them to the United States. Another rolled back a November 9 policy change Barr had made to allow the FBI and DOJ to publicly investigate allegations of election fraud before a state certified a vote tally. With that, Richard Pilger, the respected director who had resigned rather than accept the Barr policy, agreed to return to lead the Election Crimes Branch.

Biden's landing team soon began to grapple with the immense resources that would be needed to handle the January 6 cases going forward. There wasn't much of an issue on the investigative side. The FBI had spread out the work of January 6 cases to the Bureau's network of agents in field offices across all fifty states.

The prosecution side, however, faced a potential bottleneck. Sherwin had won approval to bring all cases in D.C., and although his deputies had organized the investigation into several buckets of work, there were hundreds more rioters still to be charged and complex trials to begin to prepare for. Biden's team quickly recognized the office needed a rapid influx of help.

A little over a week after the inauguration, Main Justice put out an urgent call to all ninety-three U.S. Attorney's Offices nationwide: Any prosecutor who was interested in a six- or nine-month assignment could volunteer and be placed on loan to help the D.C. office pursue rioter cases. Several Trump-appointed U.S. attorneys who were still in their posts backed the move. Five dozen prosecutors quickly raised their hands.

To give some order to the January 6 investigation, Sherwin created several "branches" of investigation. The Branch 3 team was the largest and cast a vast trawling net looking to snare all rioters, including any "breacher" who had entered the Capitol. When it came to filing cases, however,

Sherwin argued to his deputies that the investigation had to focus first on breachers who had a "plus factor." He didn't want his prosecutors to get bogged down with people who entered the Capitol and took a selfie. But if a breacher stole something, broke something, or hit or pushed an officer, that was a "plus factor" that would mark them for indictment.

Meanwhile, another team—Branch 2—was probing deaths that were caused by the riot. The highest-profile of those was the investigation into the death of Capitol Police Officer Brian Sicknick, who had been in a police line on the Capitol's lowest West terrace when a protester shot pepper spray into his face. A little after 10:00 p.m. that evening, with order restored at the Capitol, Sicknick began slurring his words and collapsed, later suffering two strokes and dying the next day. The team was also responsible for probing the deadly officer-involved shooting of Ashli Babbitt, a pro-Trump rioter who was shot and killed as she defied police warnings trying to break into a restricted area of the Capitol where House members were evacuating.

Branch 1 focused on complex conspiracies, the hard and hugely consequential assignment of unraveling whether militia members or white nationalists who entered the Capitol in military garb with radios in hand had coordinated the attack. The team put points on the board quickly, charging three U.S. military veterans associated with the Oath Keepers group.

But not everyone in the U.S. Attorney's Office in D.C. was convinced that Sherwin had built an investigative machine adequate to address the biggest questions about January 6. There was no doubt that the collective swarm of rioters who had attacked with fists, bear spray, batons, and even flagpoles were a worthy set of investigative targets. Yet their crimes were also obvious: committed in broad daylight and largely caught on tape. Cooney and other prosecutors, who had been trained to investigate political abuse of power, thought that DOJ should be simultaneously figuring out who had summoned the mob and set them in motion—and exactly how high up the political food chain criminal culpability reached.

Cooney had begun to collect bits and pieces of publicly available evidence that at times pointed to boldface names and operators linked to the former president.

A week after the inauguration, for example, reporters at *Vice* who had been poring over video footage from January 6 had spotted a startling link to Trump: Roger Stone. Trump's self-described dirty trickster had been recorded traveling with various Oath Keepers on the day before, as well as on the day of, the attack. They were dressed in paramilitary vests and gear, appearing to protect Stone like a security detail.

New and compelling evidence seemed to be bubbling up almost every day from journalists; from groups monitoring extremists online; and from a new wave of internet sleuths who called themselves sedition hunters and were collectively putting their computer skills to work to identify January 6 participants. In the first week of February, about a month after the Capitol attack, a national security organization called Just Security, based at New York University's law school, obtained more video showing Stone accompanied by Oath Keepers outside the posh Willard Hotel, where both Stone and members of the group appeared to be staying before the attack. A week later, on February 14, *The New York Times* published a photographic report identifying six Oath Keepers with Stone.

For Cooney, this showed a close confidant of the president in direct and repeated contact with members of one of the extremist groups that his office was already investigating for leading the attack. Cooney began to see other clues online indicating connections between rioters and Alex Jones as well as Ali Alexander, one of the lead organizers of the rally. Prosecutors working the cases of the Oath Keepers and Proud Boys began to look for evidence of whether Jones, Alexander, or others had inspired their actions. Cooney was leading a group of prosecutors wanting to go even further and probe why Stone and several people in the president's orbit appeared to be linked to extremists planning the riot.

For Cooney and others, this was an imperative investigation for the nation's mightiest law enforcement agency. In fact, in explaining their votes to acquit Trump of impeachment charges, key Senate Republicans seemed to have just teed up DOJ to look more squarely at the actions of the president and those around him. Senate Majority Leader Mitch McConnell said on February 13 that there was "no question" Trump was "practically and morally responsible for provoking" the attack on the Capitol. But since Trump was no longer in office, McConnell sidestepped the issue, saying he felt the job now rested with the justice system: "Presidents are not immune from being held accountable," he said.

Cooney began brainstorming with a cluster of trusted colleagues, mapping out a broader set of investigative questions that could guide the work. How had the network of extremists come to D.C. on January 6? Who gave them their instructions? Had they communicated or coordinated with advisers and intermediaries for the president? The investigative plan soon filled over twenty PowerPoint slides, some citing publicly available reporting and social media posts.

Cooney chose not to seek the blessing of Sherwin, with whom he had disagreed on prior cases and who would likely soon be replaced by a Biden appointee. Instead, Cooney pitched his idea directly to FBI agents he had worked closely with on public corruption cases in the past. Several agents viewed Cooney as a brother-in-arms, a hard-charging prosecutor often in lockstep with them.

Cooney and a small group of prosecutors presented their slide deck, laying out a multipronged plan to investigate what role Stone and other Trump allies had had in the day's events. Cooney wanted to get Stone's phone records from his service provider and begin subpoenaing membership rolls for key groups that hosted the protest rallies, including Ali Alexander's Stop the Steal organization. He raised the tried-and-true investigator adage of "follow the money," proposing they check financial records to see who financed the groups coming to Washington and who paid for buses and hotels. More broadly, he explained to the agents, he wanted to work with the FBI to identify and bring to justice the attack's masterminds.

But some FBI field office supervisors were worried that Cooney was aiming at top political figures around the former president. Past investigations like Crossfire Hurricane, a probe of Russian interference and contact with Trump's 2016 campaign, had left agents the targets of Trump's attacks.

They saw Cooney's approach as putting agents in the uncomfortable position of investigating people based on political speech and support for Trump, rather than any clear crime. For Stone, for example, they would rely on pictures of the ex-president's longtime adviser associating with militia members who joined in the riot in order to justify seeking subpoenas for more information about his conduct. Over the decades, the FBI had certainly begun investigations based on thinner evidence than what Cooney had collected. But the supervisors alerted D'Antuono to their worries. The head of the FBI's Washington Field Office didn't like it one bit.

D'Antuono made two calls, hoping to nip this Cooney idea in the bud. He rang Sherwin, Cooney's boss, and learned that Sherwin was both in the dark and irked to find out about Cooney's proposal from the FBI. D'Antuono separately alerted the deputy director of the FBI, Paul Abbate, asking for his backup in turning Cooney down.

The issue rose to Matt Axelrod, who had served twelve years in DOJ, mostly as a career prosecutor and then as an appointee under President Obama. Axelrod had returned as part of Biden's Day One team and quickly became the administration's point person on the Capitol riot investigation. He arranged and led a conference call with Sherwin and FBI leaders to sort this out. The plan's main detractors made their case. One proposal, to seek membership rolls for Oath Keepers and groups that had obtained permits ahead of the president's rally, was a problematic way to identify which attendees had been involved in the riot, they said. The Justice Department investigates crimes, not people or organizations, they reminded everyone. Those opposed didn't spend much time on the fact that several people tied to the Oath Keepers had already been charged with rioting and conspiring to plan the assault on the Capitol.

Axelrod was instantly put off. He had been at Justice long enough to have witnessed some of the fallout from times when the department had followed such instincts and deviated from its process-driven playbook. What if the Justice Department had taken the same approach a year earlier in investigating looting that had occurred in connection with protests following the death of George Floyd? he asked. How would it have been received if the FBI had sought lists of all those identifying with Black Lives Matter? Cooney's mention of membership rolls had colored the entire proposal for Axelrod. "If he would propose that," Axelrod worried, the entire plan was on shaky footing.

There was another motivation at play in the moment too: Axelrod was an experienced leader, lauded by some of his staffers for making decisions and owning them. But this was not his department, and he was intent on not making any politically loaded moves while serving as caretaker. He was simply holding down the fort until Garland and Monaco could have their hearings on Capitol Hill and get started. Biden himself had said he was wary of the DOJ investigating his political foe, so Axelrod was not going to tie the incoming bosses to that course. Supervisors on the call agreed before the call even began, and now it was official: There would be no task force to expand the January 6 investigation to Stone and others in Trump's orbit. Senior DOJ officials were consciously choosing not to fast-track an investigation into those around the ex-president for any ties to the Capitol attack. It was as if everything Trump and those around him had done publicly in the lead-up to and on January 6 did not rate as sufficient enough to trigger a criminal probe. Agents and prosecutors would continue focusing on those they could identify as having committed violent crimes at the Capitol. They would follow those investigations wherever the evidence would lead. But unless investigators turned up clues from rioters' phones or financial records that pointed them back toward the president's campaign, the decision effectively walled off Trump and his allies from becoming subjects of an FBI probe.

[16]

Family Feud

O n February 22, 2021, Merrick Garland stood in the Senate Judiciary Committee room, raised his right hand, and testified in the kind of confirmation hearing he'd been denied nearly five years earlier as a nominee to the Supreme Court.

Back at Main Justice, televisions were tuned to the hearing and three messages came through from the future boss: Garland would operate the department free of political influence. His top priority would be bringing perpetrators to justice for January 6. And no one should expect that Garland would come in and suddenly aim the investigative firepower of the Justice Department at Trump or those around him. That came through in his response to a question from Democratic Sen. Sheldon Whitehouse, a former U.S. attorney from Rhode Island.

"I would like to make sure that you are willing to look upstream from the actual occupants who assaulted the building, in the same way that in a drug case you would look upstream from the street dealers to try to find the kingpins," Whitehouse said. Ex-prosecutor to ex-prosecutor, he asked: "You will not rule out investigation of funders, organizers, ringleaders, or aiders and abettors who are not present in the Capitol on January 6?"

"Your law enforcement experience is the same as mine," Garland began, referencing his time as a junior line prosecutor and DOJ supervisor a quarter century earlier. "We begin with the people on the ground, and we work our way up to those who are involved, and further involved, and we will pursue these leads wherever they take us. That is the job of a prosecution." Under Garland, there would be no leapfrogging to look at bigger suspects who might have fomented the riot. Four hours later, Whitehouse asked the final set of questions. He took off his reading glasses, put down his pen, and slumped his head against his hand. Whitehouse seemed to be asking his final question not so much as a member of Congress but as a DOJ alum:

"We all need something to believe in, I think," Whitehouse said. "People who worked in the department very much believe in the Department of Justice. They believe in the merits, and the norms, and the values, and the traditions of their service. . . . And there was a lot that happened in the last administration to cause doubt about whether the Department of Justice met that standard."

Whitehouse gestured toward Garland and asked if he was committed to restoring faith in the department: "salvaging, if necessary; restoring, as needed; and upholding those ideals."

Garland and a team of his incoming aides and assistants had spent days preparing for the hearing, including go-to answers that the nominee might turn to for his closing message. But they now watched as Whitehouse's question elicited an unrehearsed response.

"It's not just that the Department has to do justice," Garland answered. "It's that it has to *appear* to do justice.

"The people of the United States have to believe that it does justice. Otherwise, people lose their faith in the rule of law. They take the law into their own hands. They become cynical about law enforcement; about public servants.

"I would, for the time that I am in the Justice Department, like to turn down the volume on the way in which people view the department—that the Justice Department not be the center of partisan disagreement—and that we return to the days that the department does its law enforcement and criminal justice policy and this is viewed in a bipartisan way."

Garland said that he was not naive. He knew some would always disagree with his decisions. But his hope, Garland said in closing, was that the public would come to "understand that I'm doing what I do because I believe it's the right thing and not out of some improper motive."

Whitehouse nodded to Garland. "Godspeed," he said.

Left unsaid, but driving Garland's seemingly impromptu remarks, was a genuine sense of hope. In the weeks since he had been nominated, Garland had told a few friends that he felt the awfulness of January 6 had in fact "burst a bubble" of hyperpartisanship in the country, and that the United States was ready to pick up the pieces and move on, as it had after Watergate.

In the very days leading up to Garland's confirmation, however, there were already signs that Trump was winning a Republican civil war. He was not isolated at Mar-a-Lago, but holding court, drawing top party donors, wannabe congressional candidates, and plotting to drive from office any Republican he saw as having crossed him or abandoned his futile effort to stay in power.

After leading the January 6 investigation for almost sixty days, Mike Sherwin told colleagues he would soon bow out. He'd stick around for just a few more weeks to help with the handover to Biden's pick for the top prosecutor's job. But then Sherwin got a surprise offer to stay. Despite having been installed by Barr, whose decisions had often horrified Biden's incoming team, Sherwin had reacted assertively to the Capitol attack, forcefully prosecuting Trump's supporters-turned-rioters. Biden's DOJ team saw a benefit to having not only the same prosecutor from Day One, but a Republican one at that, stay on to lead the charge.

The specifics of the offer, however, weren't as enticing. Sherwin wouldn't stay on as U.S. attorney in D.C. but was asked to move back to Main Justice to coordinate the probe with Biden's new U.S. attorney prosecuting the cases. Sherwin declined, instead returning to the federal prosecutor's office in Miami. Before he left, however, Sherwin had some final tasks, including briefing the incoming attorney general.

On March 10, the Senate voted 70–30 to confirm Garland, a larger margin of support than for any of the last three attorney general nominees put up by Presidents Obama and Trump. Senate Majority Leader Chuck Schumer, a Democrat from New York, was jubilant: "America can breathe a sigh of relief that we're going to have someone like Merrick Garland leading the Justice Department."

Garland arrived for work the next morning. He first met with FBI Director Chris Wray for a briefing on the most pressing national security matters. He then assembled his senior staff for his first briefing on the topic of January 6. Due to COVID-19 protocols in federal offices, Garland and more than a dozen aides and deputies wore masks. Sherwin soon took his cue and began running through an eleven-slide presentation. The styles of the briefer and the briefed couldn't have been more different. Sherwin spoke in a propulsive staccato. Garland listened with practiced gentility.

Aides nodded encouragingly as Sherwin ran through the numbers, which showed how much his prosecutors and their FBI partners had accomplished in the span of ten weeks.

As of that morning, Sherwin told them, the Justice Department had charged 278 rioters, including 166 with felonies.

Investigators had also identified a total of 885 suspects and had cases open on 420 of those, he explained. In all, prosecutors had secured over 1,300 subpoenas and agents had executed 709 search warrants since January 6.

"Remarkable," several recalled hearing Garland say, his voice muffled from behind his mask.

Sherwin's shoulders broadened at the remark, and he went on to lay out the teams of prosecutors, which he'd now color-coded. Green was the dragnet for rioters; red, the special investigations into Sicknick, the pipe bombs, and the police shooting of Babbitt; blue, the complex conspiracy team with fifteen prosecutors looking at militias and extremists; and yellow, the discovery team coordinating a library of over fourteen thousand hours of Capitol Police surveillance video and other electronic evidence being soaked up by the FBI.

Within the blue conspiracy team, investigators were focused on clusters of defendants in extremist organizations and had already arrested a combined two dozen members of the Oath Keepers, Proud Boys, and other groups. The team would also be responsible for extremist financing; possible foreign influence; and public officials and influencers implicated in the attack.

For many of the breachers already charged, Sherwin and his deputies had made a novel decision on how to use a fairly standard obstruction charge, known as 1512. They had charged many of the rioters with obstruction of a government proceeding. Prosecutors had in the past most often slapped defendants with a 1512 charge when they obstructed a criminal investigation, including by threatening a witness or giving false information. But part of the statute allowed the charge to apply if a person obstructed an official proceeding. It would be tested in court, but Sherwin was confident that the 1512 charge for disrupting the congressional vote to confirm the next president would hold up as appropriate.

Sherwin also wanted Garland to support another novel charge that was far more historic and would accuse some of conspiring against their government. He thought the charge of seditious conspiracy was tailor-made for the riot's ringleaders: those who had not only breached the Capitol but had planned the attack in advance and then helped lead it.

Sherwin had another motivation. If the government was to move up the chain and figure out the masterminds of the attack, a weighty charge like sedition, which came with a threat of decades in prison, might spur some extremists with knowledge of the highest levels of organization to roll over on the riot leaders and cooperate with the government's investigation.

Before Garland's first day, Sherwin's deputies had drafted a memo laying out the strengths of the charge as well as the evidence that backed it up, and sent it to senior leaders at the National Security Division at Main Justice for review.

The department didn't have a long—or particularly successful—track record with seditious conspiracy, however. The Justice Department had last brought the charge in 2010—under Attorney General Eric Holder and President Obama—against members of an apocalyptic Christian militia group accused of plotting to kill police in Michigan. A judge later tossed the charges, finding the evidence of a concrete plot lacking.

During his briefing with Garland, Sherwin broached the sedition idea as part of a shifting approach he began to advocate for when he reached the last page of his presentation, titled "30–60 Day Outlook." Broadly, Sherwin saw the January 6 investigation as having reached an inflection point. The investigation needed to shift away from the reactionary charges that had dominated prosecutors' and agents' work over the last two months to what he dubbed a "proactive" approach. That would mean focusing on more complex and aggressive investigations to pinpoint the leaders and roots of the riot. Sherwin warned that the department risked getting bogged down in a huge number of relatively minor cases of defendants who seemed to follow others who first breached the Capitol. The outgoing U.S. attorney recommended plea deals for more than 250 of the least violent offenders.

The attorney general didn't comment on or commit to any of Sherwin's proposals. But he thanked him profusely for his service.

The Justice Department's and Garland's glowing view of Sherwin, however, would take a 180-degree turn just eleven days later, when CBS's *60 Minutes* aired an exclusive interview with the newly departed U.S. attorney to discuss the ongoing January 6 investigation.

"Until this past Friday, federal prosecutor Michael Sherwin was leading the largest criminal investigation in U.S. history," began the narration from CBS News correspondent Scott Pelley.

Over the next thirteen minutes on the Sunday, March 22, program, Sherwin shared on national television his first-person account of witnessing the start of the January 6 riot. Then Sherwin pivoted to seditious conspiracy, which he had privately pitched to Garland days earlier. Federal investigators, Sherwin said, had obtained evidence strong enough to likely charge members of extremist groups with conspiring against their government.

Marc Raimondi, the department's deputy director of public affairs, watched the program with a clenched jaw. He had worked in the Trump administration, and had quickly learned how strongly Garland felt about never discussing open cases with the press.

The backstory to the interview was complicated. Back in January, shortly after the attack, CBS producers had sought a sit-down interview with Sherwin. Rosen, then the acting attorney general, didn't think it was a good idea and nixed it. One thing Trump paid close attention to was television. Sherwin believed Rosen didn't want to risk angering Trump with so few days left before he would be gone. As he was preparing to move back to Florida, Sherwin got a call from a CBS producer asking again about doing a *60 Minutes* interview. The producer was a longtime associate of Raimondi's, so Sherwin assumed he had the press office's blessing but didn't check to be sure.

On the Sunday afternoon before the program, Judge Amit Mehta, the federal judge overseeing the prosecution of several members of the Oath Keepers involved in the January 6 attack, happened to be watching a game on television. He noticed the CBS teasers promoting Sherwin's coming interview that evening and tuned in to watch. Mehta had found Sherwin's account of January 6 quite compelling. But he was taken aback to hear Sherwin predict on national television that major new conspiracy charges could be filed; the judge was accustomed to learning about new charges only when prosecutors filed a superseding indictment.

Later that night, *The New York Times*, citing anonymous sources, reported that Main Justice officials had for weeks been in receipt of a memo from Sherwin's prosecutors recommending seditious conspiracy charges. A decision, however, the *Times* reported, had languished at headquarters, and the newly arrived attorney general would likely have the final say.

Less than two weeks into Garland's tenure, the interview and leak of a charging memo detonated like a bomb. Garland was furious. This was not the careful way he had run his courtroom; nor was it how he intended to right the ship at Justice. Acting Deputy Attorney General John Carlin, who had learned about the interview only shortly beforehand, contacted the top ethics official in his office, who then reported Sherwin to the internal ethics unit for a possible misconduct investigation even before the interview aired. After the *Times* story, his aides called over to the office of newly arrived Acting U.S. Attorney Channing Phillips with a burning set of questions. Did anyone there know how the details of the memo got out? And did they know that Sherwin had been planning to go on *60 Minutes*? The answer to both was no.

Senior Justice officials weren't the only ones in high dudgeon. On Tuesday morning, Mehta called a surprise video hearing with prosecutors and defense lawyers for that afternoon to ask what was going on. Militia members and extremists charged in the case were already griping about the interview and Sherwin's claims that they'd likely engaged in sedition. Lawyers for Ethan Nordean, a Proud Boys leader charged with obstructing Congress's certification, sought to use Sherwin's public interview to get Nordean out of jail pending trial. In a court filing, Nordean's lawyer said Sherwin gave prosecutors "marching orders . . . to build seditious and conspiracy charges." Other defense lawyers were quoted in the *Times* article complaining their clients were not guilty of sedition and that they found Sherwin's comments alarming.

On Tuesday afternoon, Mehta opened the remote hearing with disappointment.

"I was surprised—and I'm being restrained in my use of terminology—

to see Mr. Sherwin sitting for an interview about a pending case in an ongoing investigation," Mehta said. "The government, quite frankly in my view, should know better."

Sherwin told confidants he was equally stunned at the sudden outrage. Hadn't anyone been listening to a single previous press conference he'd given about January 6? Sherwin had said shades of his *60 Minutes* interview plenty of times, he felt. Six days after the attack, Sherwin said he had urged a team of prosecutors to look at a range of serious conspiracy charges, including sedition.

"Their only marching orders from me are to build seditious and conspiracy charges related to the most heinous acts that occurred in the Capitol," Sherwin had said in a January 12 news conference.

Two weeks after that, he'd gone further: "We are closely looking at evidence related to the sedition charges," Sherwin said January 26. "We are working on those cases. I think the results will bear fruit very soon."

The department began scurrying to contain the fallout, as well as to recommend punishing Sherwin. Justice officials privately told an astonished Sherwin he had broken internal department rules by failing to get permission for the interview.

In the Mehta hearing, Sherwin's former deputy, John Crabb, on instruction from his bosses at Main Justice, announced publicly that Sherwin had been referred for the internal ethics probe. Behind the scenes, the Deputy Attorney General's Office would later take an even more aggressive step after the department's ethics office concluded that Sherwin had violated professional conduct rules by participating in the interview without permission. The department filed complaints that could lead to Sherwin being disbarred in the two states where he held a license to practice law.

The referral was a nuclear option normally reserved for attorneys found lying to the court, stealing, or leaking to the press. The department had no record of referring another prosecutor to its ethics office for failing to coordinate a media interview. Prosecutors said a normal punishment for this would be getting an angry call from the boss and promising never to do it again. Ohio concluded the allegations didn't warrant further review, and New York conducted a preliminary investigation, but both closed the cases without taking any action.

The Sherwin episode resulted in officials at Main Justice spending valuable time looking inward. Though Garland agreed the case should continue to be run out of the U.S. Attorney's Office, his soon-to-be deputy, Monaco, would micromanage it to the hilt through her aides.

Biden's team felt they had installed a trusted leader in Sherwin's old post. Phillips, a D.C. native, was viewed as a reliable old shoe in the boss's chair. Named after his late father, a well-known civil rights leader and D.C. minister, Phillips had served for more than twenty years in the office, starting as a prosecutor before becoming office spokesperson, senior supervisor, and top prosecutor, In fact, his spring 2021 appointment marked his third tour as acting U.S. attorney in D.C.

However, leading the office not only in the wake of January 6 but after Sherwin's explosive exit, made the job more challenging than it ever had been, Phillips later told trusted colleagues.

Axelrod, based in the Deputy Attorney General's Office, set up a daily Zoom meeting on the January 6 probe between Main Justice and the U.S. Attorney's Office. The day-in, day-out questioning soon felt like an unprecedented amount of oversight from the mother ship. Longtime prosecutors groused this was the first case they'd seen involving a daily check-in with headquarters.

That attention only intensified when Lisa Monaco was confirmed and joined the department as Garland's right hand on April 21. In her hearing before the Senate Judiciary Committee, Monaco had called the Justice Department's response to January 6 "nothing less than the defense of our democracy," and those running the investigation soon understood that no update to her office would be considered too small.

For her first day in the office, Monaco had requested a status meeting on the January 6 investigation. She asked so many questions in that session with Phillips and his deputies that it ran overtime without having covered everything on Monaco's list.

The daily meetings that followed were not perfunctory check-ins either. Normally held at the end of every workday, they included a heavy-hitter team from Main Justice. Joining Axelrod were David Newman, the acting associate deputy attorney general; Rush Atkinson, another protégé of Monaco's, who had been a member of Mueller's special counsel staff; and Matt Blue, the counterterrorism chief in the National Security Division. George Toscas, a longtime career deputy in that division, sometimes joined too. Beaming in by laptops to represent the D.C. office were Phillips, as well as Ken Kohl and Crabb, who had stayed in their respective seats as the office's first assistant and Criminal Division chief.

The meetings could sometimes be dispatched within fifteen minutes or so and at other times ran for an hour and a half. But the intensity of the review never wavered.

The bosses from Main Justice got down into the weeds, asking questions about upcoming arrests and charges that they wanted Phillips and his deputies to ask lower-level prosecutors about and get back to them with answers on. They wanted to know about case decisions on the horizon; the backstory on comments a judge had made in a court earlier in the day; any problems looming in cases still in progress; and even this or that revelation about a January 6 defendant in a news story.

A running concern for the Main Justice team was making sure that rioters were prosecuted consistently—and in line with how defendants had been treated previously. One worry centered on the fact that some D.C. prosecutors had begun levying charges on January 6 rioters that were harsher than the ones federal prosecutors had brought against several Portland protesters who had also vandalized or trespassed on federal property during the previous summer's racial justice protests.

Axelrod, who hadn't been at Justice during the Portland protests, wanted to understand why their treatment had been less punitive. Toscas, who had been around for nearly every domestic terrorism case since

9/11, explained that entering a federal building was bad, but entering it and assaulting officers with the intent to block Congress's certification of an election demanded enhanced punishment. On top of that, some Portland defendants were allowed to plead to lesser charges because the evidence against them had been weak. The opposite was true for January 6 defendants: Almost every crime had been captured on camera. Axelrod was satisfied with the answer. He often was channeling questions from Garland and Monaco, who were keen to understand the rationale, as Trump allies were already accusing the department of being unfairly heavy-handed with the former president's supporters. Another curiosity coming from Main Justice was whether prosecutors were on firm footing charging rioters with trespassing. Could prosecutors charge rioters who entered the Capitol with trespassing if they hadn't been officially warned they were trespassing? Some prosecutors would scratch their heads at this query. But Garland, a voracious and thorough reader, worried after spotting older cases in which trespassing charges on other federal property had been dismissed for lack of a clear notice to the defendants that they were out of bounds. A growing number in the D.C. office chafed at what felt like an extreme level of babysitting in making a trespassing case.

Phillips had also found himself in the middle of a still-simmering feud between some of his prosecutors and Biden's leadership team at Main Justice. The decision to kill the proposal from Cooney and his colleagues had happened days before Phillips arrived, and prosecutors were still a little raw over the rejection. Phillips intuitively understood Main Justice's hesitancy, but told his deputies he knew where Cooney was coming from and saw some of Cooney's proposed investigative steps as logical. A few others, he warned, felt a little aggressive given their proximity to a former president.

Phillips brought up the issue with D'Antuono, his counterpart leading the FBI's Washington Field Office. D'Antuono tried to explain that his deputies were extremely uneasy with saddling up to probe the advisers of the former president without clear-cut evidence of traditional crimes— especially when they had January 6 crimes to solve that were squarely in the FBI's lane. D'Antuono's office, for example, had detailed over fifty agents alone to try to apprehend whoever had planted two pipe bombs discovered January 6 near national offices for the Republican and Democratic parties. The dragnet had ballooned into a massive, nationwide data-collection effort going so far as to identify the brand and model of the suspect's sneakers and trace where each part of the explosive could have been sold. The shoes were Nike Air Max Speed Turfs, and agents pulled sales records for all twenty-three thousand pairs distributed to major retailers across the country. They also traced credit card receipts for every sale of the device parts on the East Coast, and vacuumed up cell phone data in the time frames around each store when the parts were purchased with cash. Agents for a while thought a rare battery connector would prove to be the key to solving the case, but they had conducted over six hundred interviews, inadvertently discovered a different novice bomb-maker in Georgia, and were still on the hunt.

By comparison, D'Antuono and his deputies seemed to have an allergic reaction to even looking into pictures of Oath Keepers and known Trump allies like Stone for having congregated the day before January 6. D'Antuono acknowledged to Phillips that the situation had turned the typical dynamic between agents and prosecutors upside down. Usually, agents were the ones who wanted to run in and investigate while prosecutors got queasy about the legal justification for investigative steps.

"I know it's pretty unusual for prosecutors to be more aggressive than the agents," D'Antuono told Phillips.

Phillips supported D'Antuono's goal of proceeding carefully, he told aides, but he saw an office that was also a little gun-shy of tangoing with Trump again. Some at Main Justice worried about that too.

In March and April, senior department officials asked Jeff Rosen to discreetly share his firsthand account of Trump's brazen moves in his final weeks in office. Rosen told of how Trump had threatened to remove him, and how Trump only folded when a room full of Justice leaders threatened to resign. His description left senior Justice officials flabbergasted and willing to take the highly unusual step of approving a request from Congress to have Rosen testify about the conversations with the president. Typically, DOJ leaders fiercely protected the confidentiality of legal advice given to the president. But they felt the events were so extraordinary it merited breaking with the normal policy.

Still, Garland told his tiny leadership circle he wanted any potential criminal investigation to work its way up organically and did not assign anyone in its vast law enforcement network to open a criminal investigation into the episode. The department's inspector general had announced such a probe following the first news reports of Trump's threat to replace Rosen, but had limited it to scrutinizing the actions of DOJ lawyers and not Trump. But that office later agreed to pause their review due to the department's ongoing riot investigation. The result was that no one was actively investigating Trump's apparent attempt to block the transfer of power.

Feelings between Main Justice and the D.C. prosecutors' office remained prickly that spring. At headquarters, officials were still smarting from the public airing of the department's private debates over seditious conspiracy. The disclosure was so alarming that Matt Axelrod raised the idea of putting the U.S. Attorney's Office under a microscope by launching a full internal leak investigation.

Phillips advised against it. Sherwin had been talking about seditious conspiracy for months. Shortly after the attack someone had even labeled a shared folder in the U.S. attorney's computer system "riots and seditious conspiracy." Since then, so many people in the office had come to know about the memo or at least its general outlines that a leak probe would likely prove inconclusive. Phillips had been through such internal investigations before. He warned this one risked further eroding trust between the dozens of frontline prosecutors and the bosses at Main Justice who needed to be working hand in glove to press forward on so many Capitol breach cases.

On the U.S. attorney's side, there were hard feelings too. Cooney and several colleagues were still baffled by the rejection of the investigative plan to look at the links between Trump's allies and militia members. They also felt insufficient resources had been assigned to look at the ways rally promoters had brought thousands of people to the nation's capital.

Several weeks into Phillips's tenure, officials in Monaco's office hosted a powwow at Main Justice to reset relations between the two offices. Because many aspects of the January 6 investigation remained extremely sensitive, senior representatives of the U.S. Attorney's Office, the FBI, and the deputy attorney general gathered for the meeting in the National Security Division's secure conference room.

The conversation soon resurfaced some of the investigative proposals from Cooney's plan. All eyes this time turned to the most senior FBI official in the room, Deputy Director Paul Abbate.

Abbate was a highly respected FBI leader known for keeping his cool. He'd started as an agent in the New York Field Office working violent crime cases more than a quarter century earlier. He had been a case agent collecting evidence in the wake of 9/11, later led the Detroit Field Office, and rose to become executive assistant director shepherding the Bureau's core criminal investigations. Wray often called his choice of Abbate as the department's second-in-command one of the smartest decisions he'd made.

The question for Abbate hung in the air momentarily. Would the Bureau budge on broadening its investigation? Abbate didn't waste time. He said FBI rules and processes frowned on jumping to higher-level targets. Many Bureau officials saw the Capitol attack investigation as a political minefield if they leapt to pursue a former president or his aides at this stage.

Prosecutors from the U.S. Attorney's Office, however, soon turned the tables, arguing the FBI was not pursuing some obvious evidence of January 6 crimes with equal fervor. While prosecutors in D.C. were largely working in lockstep to be fair but aggressive in charging everyone who had breached the Capitol, some agents were stalling on requests to take standard investigative steps or balking at carrying them out altogether.

Prosecutors also reported they were detecting a disturbing pattern: FBI agents in more rural and conservative areas of the country were the ones most likely to slow-walk or to fail to deliver on prosecutors' requests that they question witnesses, or, in some cases, even to execute arrest warrants.

"It broke down as largely an issue in red states," a prosecutor later described. Some FBI officials also acknowledged the dynamic. In fact, it had become a systemic problem, coming up repeatedly by then at weekly meetings in Phillips's office.

In one instance, an FBI agent in the Southeast and a prosecutor in D.C. had almost stopped communicating about a shared case. The FBI agent had reported to the prosecutor that he'd hit a dead end: The rioter's coworkers didn't want to talk about their buddy's political leanings, the agent reported, so it looked like figuring out the rioter's motive wasn't going to happen. The prosecutor was incensed. Since when did FBI agents investigating a violent crime so easily take no for an answer? Why wasn't the agent seeking subpoenas to compel the coworkers to talk?

In the case of another rioter living in Indiana, prosecutors felt they had everything they needed to make an arrest and to execute a search warrant of his premises. But agents balked at a raid and instead chose to notify the rioter that there was a warrant for his arrest and he should surrender. Again, prosecutors in D.C. were stupefied. The advance notice took away a key element of surprise in finding corroborating evidence. Allowing rioters to turn themselves in gave them time and motivation to delete or destroy incriminating photos, encrypted messages, and other data that might help seal a conviction—or help to piece together a conspiracy. On multiple occasions, prosecutors had groused that agents had even resisted investigative steps involving members of the Proud Boys, who had helped lead the charge, breaking windows and forcing their way into the Capitol.

To prosecutors in D.C., such passive approaches to investigations and arrests felt like a dereliction of duty. Some had begun to pick up on subtle differences in the way agents talked about January 6 suspects.

"If an agent began referring to a [January 6] suspect as a 'knucklehead,' that became my clue that they weren't really thinking of them like a criminal worth investigating," one prosecutor said. "FBI and police don't refer to people they think of as real criminals—bank robbers or drug dealers—as 'knuckleheads.'"

Prosecutors feared the growing criticism of the riot probe on the right had begun to influence the motivation of agents, especially in conservative areas of the country. On May 13, 2021, Republican Reps. Thomas Massie of Kentucky and Chip Roy of Texas wrote a public letter to Garland decrying "hyperpoliticization" of the January 6 investigation. "There are disturbing reports of heavily armed teams of federal agents bursting into family homes to arrest individuals with no history or likelihood of violence," they wrote of the arrests of Capitol rioters. The letter was reported and discussed repeatedly on Newsmax and far-right blogs and podcasts.

Indeed, many FBI agents across the country had complained about the endless hours DOJ officials were insisting that agents devote to chasing down every last person who entered the Capitol—including many whom they considered sheep. Among the suspects that the FBI agents viewed as lesser criminals were grandmothers and blue-collar dads who seemed to have followed the mob into the Capitol. The agents questioned why they would be charged with anything more than misdemeanor trespassing. Many agents blamed DOJ brass for the one-size-fits-all approach. They wanted to focus their energies on the most violent actors and extremist plotters. These frustrated agents felt they were losing critical hours that they should instead use to serve search warrants for drug traffickers and to solve violent crimes in their communities.

One angry agent would later write the FBI ombudsman, demanding that Director Wray and his leadership team explain their priorities: "Please ask them why we break out all the tools to enforce a federal misdemeanor of someone walking through the Capitol on January 6th but people can . . . harass Supreme Court justices in broad daylight on the news and NOTHING is done about it."

FBI supervisors and Phillips's deputies worked out a triage system for recalcitrant agents. Every week, a prosecutor running a standing meeting on January 6 cases would call out for updates on the FBI issue. If you're having problems with agents, she would say, speak up; "we don't want this impacting your cases."

When Phillips's office spotted repeated problems with an agent on a January 6 case, they would call over to D'Antuono at the FBI's Washington Field Office. D'Antuono would then call the field office boss over the problem agent and try to get the case back on track. If that didn't fix it, D'Antuono had the option to elevate the issue to Abbate, but never used it.

D'Antuono tried to make light of the awkward conversations with his counterparts, expressing that he was just following orders to quiet the family feud, and neither of them wanted this to go up to Abbate. "Take care of this so I don't have to call Dad, would you?" D'Antuono later quipped about his approach.

With one hundred fifteen thousand people on its payroll, the Justice Department employed Americans of every stripe, from left-leaning big-city prosecutors to right-leaning conservative law enforcement officers. But to many there was growing disappointment that the January 6 attack on democracy had not closed a political fault line, even among Justice Department colleagues. In fact, only a few months afterward, a divide inside Justice seemed to be growing.

[17]

Unmoved by Trump

I n late March, less than three months after the Capitol attack, Trump was rewriting the events of January 6. Rioters hadn't forced their way into the Capitol and bludgeoned officers with flagpoles but had been "zero threat" and were "hugging and kissing the police," Trump said in a Fox News interview with Laura Ingraham. Trump's most ardent supporters soon amplified and echoed the ex-president's baseless claims. January 6 was a "kerfuffle," one conservative commentator claimed. Worse violence had been perpetrated by Black Lives Matter protesters, argued Sen. Ron Johnson of Wisconsin, a Republican. That Trump's audacious gambit was gaining traction was a sign of his broader political resurgence. Fellow Republicans, including many of those who had previously renounced him in the hours after the siege, were returning to his corner, and that was due at least in part to Trump's calculated attacks on those who had crossed him.

Less than a week after Biden's inauguration, the ex-president and his aides had launched a campaign of retribution to defeat the ten Republican members of the House of Representatives who had voted to impeach Trump for inciting the riot. Donald Trump Jr. went further, putting a target on the most outspoken of his father's intraparty critics, Rep. Liz Cheney of Wyoming. He encouraged Republicans not to wait for the next primary, but to oust Cheney from House party leadership and ostracize her immediately. The former president also went on the offensive with the remaining senators who had been weighing whether to support the House and impeach him.

Trump singled out vulnerable Republicans and floated the idea of starting a third political party that would siphon off donors and voters. Soon, polling on Capitol Hill showed a conviction would fail. A little more than three weeks after Trump left office, only seven Republicans joined Democrats in voting to convict. The final Senate tally—57 guilty to 43 not guilty—fell ten votes short of the threshold needed to bar Trump for life from holding public office. Instead, Trump was acquitted—and emboldened.

Online, his supporters further muddied the water, convincing droves that the attack had been the work of Antifa. Near the end of April, with Biden in office not even one hundred days, Trump began talking publicly about running for president again. Asked by Fox Business host Maria Bartiromo about his plans for 2024, Trump said that he was "100 percent" thinking about seeking a return to the White House. "The polls show that everybody wants me to do it. One hundred percent, I'm thinking about running, and we will, I think, be very successful." Polls showed 53 percent of Republicans identified Trump as their "true president" and believed manipulated vote tallies had in fact kept him from rightfully staying in the White House. Trump's threat to return didn't register at DOJ, but it galvanized Democratic congressional leaders, as well as state officials and government watchdogs, to press on to hold him accountable.

Two days after his acquittal by the Senate, House Speaker Nancy Pelosi urged Congress to at least establish an independent commission, much as it had after September 11, to investigate January 6 and all related efforts to interfere with the peaceful transfer of power. In Georgia, prosecutors in March opened a criminal investigation into Trump's efforts to subvert election results there. The announcement followed a string of stunning news articles revealing the extent to which Trump had personally been involved in pressuring Georgia officials to "find" him enough votes to overturn the state's results. The criminal investigation began after a major story published by *The Washington Post*'s Amy Gardner— complete with audio recordings of Trump to back it up. In one recorded call, Trump could be heard threatening Georgia Secretary of State Brad Raffensperger that he needed to turn up additional votes and could be in political trouble if he didn't. "I just want to find 11,780 votes," Trump said. In another episode the then president had reached deep into the state bureaucracy, personally calling a Georgia elections investigator and urging her to find the "dishonesty" in absentee ballot numbers that he blamed for his unfair loss in the state. "The people of Georgia are so angry at what happened to me," Trump said. "When the right answer comes out, you'll be praised."

A government watchdog group, meanwhile, had gathered copies of the eerily similar fake elector documents that the Justice Department had declined to investigate. The group, American Oversight, published the elector documents that state Republican Party officials and others had signed in swing states and sent to the National Archives, and ultimately Congress.

The group tried to draw public attention to the fact that the documents were suspiciously identical, saying they appeared to show a "coordinated, multi-state effort to cast doubt on the 2020 election and undermine the electoral vote process." American Oversight saw a clear tether between fake documents the Trump campaign had tried to put in play ahead of January 6, and authentic ones that the pro-Trump mob had tried to stop Congress from tallying that day.

By late May, partisan lines on the attack had calcified on Capitol Hill, with some far-right members of the House parroting Trump's revisionist history that January 6 had been little more than a "normal tourist visit." Pelosi's push for an independent, 9/11-style commission died at the end of that month with minority Republicans invoking their first filibuster of the Biden era to keep it from passing.

Inside the attorney general's suite, Garland was paying close attention to the headlines, as always, but was intent on keeping political developments from influencing decisions at the department.

In fact, Garland was finalizing a plan to more formally wall off DOJ decision-making from political influence—starting with his boss in the White House.

After moving into the attorney general's modest corner office, Garland had placed a dog-eared original printing of the *Principles of Federal Prosecution*—complete with the pages he'd first helped draft after Watergate—on a side table visible to anyone who entered the room. In practice, Garland quickly began to live out those pages, pushing back forcefully on any suggestion that the department would ally itself with the White House or Democrats in Congress. Garland's gatekeepers sent word to nearly all divisions: They weren't to communicate with the West Wing or party leaders any longer. That separation had long been the reasonable norm for criminal cases. But some quickly felt the restriction was counterproductive for leaders of civil divisions and policy shops who sought to deliver on the president's agenda. The attorney general even seemed to close off personal relationships that could allow for the perception of conflict.

Garland and his lifelong friend White House Chief of Staff Ron Klain nearly stopped talking altogether in the months after Garland became attorney general, save for pleasantries when Garland visited the White House on official business. Though appointed by Biden and charged with carrying out his policy agenda, Garland rarely spoke to the president, except at formal group meetings and when national security situations necessitated it.

Published as a five-page memo, the attorney general's policy spelled out expectations that Justice Department employees would not give the White House a heads-up about criminal—or civil—matters. Further, as in the decades after Watergate, only the attorney general or deputy attorney general would have authorization to talk to the White House, and even then, only through its lawyers, the White House counsel's office. In a statement accompanying the policy release, Garland said the Justice Department must earn Americans' trust every day, beginning with routinely displaying "independence from inappropriate influences." Garland told senior staff that he was proud of the document and that reaffirming the department's independence from the White House was one of the strongest statements he could make to turn the page from the free-flowing Trump-Barr era, when the president would declare on social media who he thought should be prosecuted and line attorneys far below would soon be left to question if fact-based decisions would hold up.

Inside DOJ, another key difference between Garland and his predecessors was simultaneously coming into focus. Where Barr made snap decisions, Garland did not.

He instead ran the powerful sixth floor of the Justice Department much like an orderly—and slow-moving—judge's chambers.

As judges kept their private thoughts and debates locked inside their chambers, so too did Garland keep his decision-making tightly restricted, often to a handful of his most senior staff and appointed deputies. Long-time Justice Department officials viewed Garland's office as surrounded by a moat of young counselors and assistants who performed a service like the law clerks of his former chambers. In fact, several were his former clerks. These young assistants were dispatched to gather information for the attorney general from the department's many divisions and report back their summaries, creating a buffer, many observed, between the top law enforcement official of the land and the many offices he commanded. Some division heads commiserated with each other, saying that they had frequently briefed the boss in prior administrations but almost never were asked to do so with Garland.

Garland exhibited the highest sensitivity to cases and decisions that might open the department to accusations of pursuing a political goal. Garland had always prided himself on his reputation as a moderate on the bench, and as a judge had gone so far as to encourage his Republican friends to point out to Republican Congress members his measured opinions.

Garland, as well as Monaco, hoped their careful and even approach to the January 6 investigation, would someday cause Republicans and Democrats alike to look back on it as the model for how to handle politically sensitive probes. Garland made clear to his deputies he wanted any charges to be reviewed rigorously before being filed in court. But it was not a speedy process, especially when Garland himself weighed in. In briefings with his closest aides, often on Thursday afternoons, Garland would dive into the January 6 prosecutions, sometimes pulling out statute books to compare the prongs of a charge to the specifics of a defendant's case file. He and his team would kick around a handful of cases, with Garland pressing to know how the government planned to sustain the charges and fend off the possible defenses. Garland sometimes asked to read draft charges. That was a new one for Democratic appointees who had last worked for Attorney General Eric Holder; he'd wanted to know the top line and hadn't felt a need to review his employees' work.

In the reviews, Garland frequently focused on things that could go wrong. He zeroed in at times on ensuring the department would never be accused of suppressing potential evidence and violating their obligations to share anything exculpatory with the defendant prior to trial. Teams of techs working with prosecutors had put in hundreds of hours creating a massive database of all January 6 video and other evidence. At Garland's prodding, they ultimately shared the enormous trove with all defendants, a broad interpretation of the duty of prosecutors that gave the department near certainty it would avoid any claims of withholding evidence. Garland and Monaco stressed to their top aides that the eyes of the world were on this case. They wanted to stop problems and catch flaws before they mushroomed.

As a guiding principle under Garland, the department settled on bringing federal charges against any rioter who entered the Capitol, and seeking jail time for anyone who assaulted an officer. But they rejected

Sherwin's earlier advice to plead out a large batch of nonviolent offenders so they could make time to focus on the higher-level plotters.

Instead, nearly all plea agreements were put on hold when Monaco was confirmed, as she and her team decided they needed to review every proposal to ensure consistency. Usually, federal prosecutors rely on sentencing guidelines to recommend punishments for defendants, as well as good judgment and past practice to let a cooperative defendant plead guilty in exchange for a reduced punishment. But on the daily Zoom meetings with the U.S. Attorney's Office, Monaco's team sometimes asked about the smallest details of a defendant's cooperation. Some prosecutors there complained they had never seen the department's seniormost political appointees wade into such routine matters.

While Garland would occasionally show flashes of impatience at delays on cases involving January 6, he hearkened back to his decades on the bench when it came to making the final decision about whether to move forward with complex ones. In meetings, it was clear to senior staffers that he frequently saw the world through the lens of being reversed on appeal by a higher court. Several senior department heads valued his careful legal analysis, and yet even they worried about the review pace. Garland seemed to operate on a court of appeals clock, where judges often took several months to fashion a ruling.

Garland's caution and strict boundaries began attracting a cadre of internal critics who worried an obsession with safeguarding the perception of an apolitical DOJ was interfering with its core mission in a moment with little historical precedent. To them, the department couldn't uphold the rule of law without bringing the most senior people responsible for January 6 to justice. They viewed the department's decision not to prosecute Trump's attempts to get Georgia election workers to overturn results and instead cede that investigation to state and local officials as a kind of political choice in itself.

In fact, unbeknownst to the public, the department's Public Integrity Section had initially chosen to not pursue that case, but never raised this with Garland. He was the nation's chief law enforcement officer but often relied on the division's career staff to make substantive decisions and did not change this one. Staffers did, however, brief Garland on a tip that Trump had met with members of the Proud Boys in Las Vegas prior to the election. Garland told aides that, if true, this was the kind of shocking development that could turn the investigation toward the ex-president. He had earlier told them he thought one of the only ways a case could quickly build toward Trump would be based on new evidence that Trump or his campaign had provided financial support or direction to rioters. FBI agents ran down the supposed Las Vegas meeting but determined it had never happened. Agents returned their focus to the rioter cases.

In the summer of 2021, the D.C. Circuit hosted its annual reception for law clerks of the court and current and former judges. It was a well-established who's who of Washington's legal elite, including clerks who'd gone on to great successes and esteemed judges who'd joined the Supreme Court. Garland greeted all. In one private conversation, later retold to other reception guests, Garland lamented to a former colleague the difficulty of being a Democratic appointee who would likely disappoint the party.

Garland could sense party leaders growing concerned, but he was simply not going to direct the DOJ to look directly at Trump or those around him without clear-cut evidence of a likely crime.

Under Garland, the department would not make decisions based on "consequences to an election," recalled one person involved in regular discussions about cases with the attorney general. Like "'We have to make sure to get this wrapped up so someone isn't a candidate?' . . . It didn't even need to be said; that would be improper. . . . If you start thinking about politics, that starts to cloud your decisions. . . . You can only keep true north by just doing what you think is right and sticking to the facts and the evidence." Garland reiterated his trust in the bottom-up approach in late June as he announced the Justice Department had by this point arrested more than five hundred suspected rioters. "I assure the American people that the Department of Justice will continue to follow the facts in this case and charge what the evidence supports to hold all January 6 perpetrators accountable," he said.

That would prove particularly complicated, however, when it came to the possibility of charging riot organizers with seditious conspiracy. Garland and Monaco were initially wary of this politically loaded charge, and keenly aware it could spark accusations from the right that the new president was bringing down an unusually heavy hammer on opponents. Filing these charges carried historic weight.

The statute dealing with sedition had been enacted after the Civil War to try to stop Confederate secessionists from continuing to fight the U.S. government. It required proving two elements: a corrupt agreement between two or more people, and a plot to use force against the U.S. government. The suspects could be charged if their plan had any of the following intents: to "overthrow, put down or to destroy by force" the U.S. government; to bring war against it; to oppose its authority; or to block the execution of its laws. D.C. line prosecutors argued that some of the texts and phone messages sent and received by members of the Oath Keepers met the two key elements. They also felt the threshold had been reached for members of the Proud Boys. Several had since been arrested and charged with lesser crimes, but the strongest evidence indicated they had channeled their force to block the government from certifying the results of the presidential election.

Over the summer, a set of proposed plea agreements in more serious cases were indefinitely postponed, as Main Justice had not yet decided on whether to pursue seditious conspiracy charges. Phillips walked a tightrope throughout. He stuck up for his prosecutors' judgments, but he also defended Main Justice's use of a fine-tooth comb to his team. Garland and Monaco and their aides were seeking to safeguard the investigation from accusations of political bias or inequity, Phillips told his attorneys, and they needed to be comfortable with the prosecutors' overall path on a case this historic. While prosecutors rarely discussed their concerns in such blunt terms, some were growing frustrated with the bottom-up approach, and what they viewed as ponderous steps along the way. Some prosecutors assigned to Oath Keepers and Proud Boys cases felt particularly annoyed that Main Justice had still not green-lit the charges. They found it nauseating that, for months after the attack, Stewart Rhodes—the group's eye-patch-wearing founder, who they knew had first summoned his members to come to D.C. on January 6 and communicated with Oath Keepers in the minutes before they advanced on the Capitol in military formations—remained a free man. But agents and prosecutors were still far from an arrest.

Garland and Monaco, meanwhile, discussed another concern. With or without sedition cases, the dozens of extra prosecutors detailed to the U.S. Attorney's Office seemed insufficient to handle the expanding workload. Prosecutors were bogged down in the hundreds of existing cases, with as many or more yet to file. No one seemed to have the bandwidth to pore over the reams of financial data, phone records, and other evidence that the Justice Department had gathered to look for financial ties or other possible connections between militia groups and anyone higher up the political food chain who might have masterminded the attack.

[18]

Hill Investigators Find
"the Scheme"

More than seven months after January 6, the Justice Department still had not broached the question of whether President Trump or those around him were culpable for inciting the attack. But a second group of investigators, one unbound by Main Justice's approach, was about to become the last, best hope for Congress to get answers about the attack. After a 9/11-style, bipartisan commission had been blocked by conservative Senate Republicans, House Speaker Nancy Pelosi formed a temporary committee to investigate. She invited Republican leaders to partner in the effort, but then rejected their proposals to seat two lawmakers who had themselves pushed to overturn the election results, Rep. Jim Jordan of Ohio and Rep. Jim Banks of Indiana. In their place, she appointed two Republican critics of Trump, Rep. Liz Cheney of Wyoming and Rep. Adam Kinzinger of Illinois, drawing howls of protest from Trump supporters that the investigation would be bipartisan in name only. Equally important, however, Pelosi's office began to assemble an unusual committee staff to conduct the probe. Pelosi wanted a rigorous investigation into what she viewed as a treasonous attack, not a half-hearted probe followed by lawmakers making bombastic speeches—something less like Benghazi and more like the investigation of the Kennedy assassination. The Speaker assigned two of her senior advisers, Terry McCullough and Jamie Fleet, to search for and hire a top-notch lead investigator.

The two quickly broke with usual practice on the Hill and, instead of selecting a political staffer, began to focus on former Justice Department officials trained in turning up evidence and putting bad guys in prison. One of their top prospects was Tim Heaphy, a hard-nosed former federal prosecutor and U.S. attorney raised in the Department of Justice. Heaphy was a Democrat but no political errand boy. He had a strong record as a fact finder, including a report he conducted on the white supremacist rally in Charlottesville in 2017 that left one woman dead and thirty injured. Although he had sought out the job, he too had some of the same worries being voiced by political commentators: Would this be a real investigation or a political sham?

In the second week of August 2021, Heaphy joined a prearranged call with Rep. Bennie Thompson for a chance to talk with his prospective new boss. Pelosi has chosen Thompson, the longtime chairman of the House Committee on Homeland Security, to chair the new January 6 panel.

Heaphy, fifty-six, had angular features, a trim build from his running routine and marathon training, and wiry hair now more silver than brown. He was an extrovert who struck up conversations easily. Thompson, seventy-three, bald with a gray beard and a round midsection, wore spectacles and disarmed with his slow Southern drawl. He had lived through the Jim Crow era in Mississippi and been an alderman and mayor in his hometown before winning election to Congress, where he had now served for more than twenty-five years. After respectful pleasantries, Heaphy told the congressman his primary reservation about the job. Would the committee, controlled by the Democratic majority, meddle with the investigation to serve a political agenda, or block him from pursuing uncomfortable facts?

"If it seems this is going to be an investigation with a preordained outcome, I'll have a problem with that," Heaphy said.

Thompson told Heaphy he shared his goal of a fact-based investigation, and said that it was premature to predict anything:

"We don't know exactly what happened."

"I don't want to have a role in something that doesn't have integrity," Heaphy said.

"No, no," Thompson assured him. "We are going to let the facts determine our path."

Heaphy had begun to think about conducting such an investigation even as he watched the attack unfold on television on January 6, while alone in his office in Madison Hall on the University of Virginia's gracious Charlottesville campus, where he worked as the university's general counsel. He told his wife that night he thought there would have to be both a massive criminal dragnet and a large-scale after-action investigation, not unlike his Charlottesville protest report.

Heaphy's life and friendships were dominated by his two decades in the Justice Department. In phone calls on January 6, he shared his shock at the events unfolding on the screen with two fellow Justice pals, Sally Yates and Chris Kavanaugh. Yates, Obama's deputy attorney general, was a close friend who had then recently learned she was no longer in the running to serve as Biden's attorney general. Kavanaugh, whom Heaphy had taught in law school and mentored in his career, was a rising federal prosecutor who would soon join the Justice Department's central office overseeing the criminal investigation into the attack.

As Pelosi's plan for a select committee emerged as the only viable path remaining for Congress to investigate, Heaphy called his law school friend who was now head of the Democratic Congressional Campaign Committee, Sean Patrick Maloney, and asked him to relay his interest to Pelosi's staff. After interviews, McCullough and Fleet hired Heaphy to start on August 17.

Besides being allowed to pursue the facts without political interference, Heaphy had one other condition for taking the job: He insisted on having input in hiring his team. Heaphy envisioned using the committee's congressional subpoena power to run something akin to a federal grand jury investigation. To do that successfully, he knew he needed skilled investigators—and especially prosecutors—to unearth what the president and those around him had done. Those prosecutors would also have to be effective litigators, confronting former White House officials under oath. Heaphy didn't want his contemporaries who were comfortably ensconced as partners at big law firms. Equally, he didn't want green, young law students. Heaphy wanted seasoned attorneys in the middle, those still ascending in their careers—still hungry to find the truth, and with the skills to do it.

In the intervening months since the Capitol attack, Kavanaugh, Heaphy's former student, had been nominated to take Heaphy's old job as U.S. attorney in Charlottesville. When asked for advice about attorneys for the congressional investigation, he steered his old mentor to two standout prosecutors he had worked with: Dan George, an assistant U.S. attorney in Tampa who happened to be looking to move back to the Northeast, and Sean Tonolli, a former federal prosecutor Kavanaugh called "a great homicide guy." A Charlottesville friend and former federal prosecutor in Brooklyn also urged Heaphy to consider his former colleague Soumya Dayananda, who stood out for shepherding complex federal cases there for a decade.

Heaphy also unexpectedly learned of a shrewd McGuireWoods lawyer seeking to return to public service, Casey Lucier. Her name came up when he called the firm's senior partner Richard Cullen, a longtime counselor to Republican politicians, to inquire about interviewing his client, former Vice President Mike Pence. Cullen told Heaphy that he couldn't promise an interview with the vice president but softened the blow, quipping: "You can't have that, but you can have Casey."

In quick succession, Heaphy reached out to George, Tonolli, Dayananda, Lucier, and others, and was soon ecstatic at the response. Each was willing to drop what they were doing and join the team despite no promise of what would come afterward.

George quickly began working to sell his home and move from Tampa to a rental place on Capitol Hill. Tonolli and Lucier gave up the comforts and security of their law firm jobs for what promised to be long hours and more meager pay as congressional staff. Marc Harris, a former DOJ public corruption prosecutor in California whom Rep. Adam Schiff had strongly recommended, also jumped on a plane. At fifty-eight, he was the oldest of the group and rented an apartment in D.C. to join the team.

Within six weeks and unbeknownst to the Justice Department, Heaphy had quietly assembled a kind of shadow U.S. Attorney's Office working from a nondescript congressional office building and divided his staff into color-coded teams. But in stark contrast to the actual D.C. prosecutors' office about a mile away, Heaphy authorized lines of pursuit that remained mostly off-limits to their former colleagues at the Justice Department. Tonolli was asked to lead the Red Team, focusing on January 6 planners and Stop the Steal promoters—an effort that at Justice had already been sidelined as lacking a predicate for FBI agents to vigorously pursue. Dayananda began forming the Blue Team, investigating law enforcement and military planning and response to the attack. Meanwhile, George and Cheney adviser John Wood took charge of the Gold Team and a mission still unexplored at Justice: probing the actions of Donald Trump and the White House to block the transfer of power.

Heaphy's loose timeline for his team was to investigate until spring and put out a report by July 4, before hopefully wrapping up to head home by Labor Day, a year later. Unlike a few blocks away at Main Justice, where Garland forbade any consideration of the political calendar ahead, this group knew they had to finish before the midterms the following November. If Republicans won control of the House, they would surely shut down the investigation and bury its unfinished work in a single day.

When Heaphy had called George to offer him the job, he urged an investigation to scrutinize Trump's role. It started taking shape even before George pulled into D.C.

George had packed the last of the contents of his family's Tampa home into the back of a Penske truck and began driving north with their hound dog at the end of September. He passed a good bit of the fourteen-hour drive listening to the audio version of Bob Woodward and Robert Costa's just-published book, *Peril*. George noted with interest the role of Trump attorney Rudy Giuliani in running a "war room" at the Willard to overturn the election results. He was also intrigued by a memo that Trump legal adviser John Eastman had written suggesting how Congress could throw out election results from states where "alternate" electors insisted Trump had won. In the truck, George began making mental lists of White House aides and other witnesses to interview.

Reaching D.C., George reported to the team's makeshift offices at the O'Neill House Office Building, a former hotel converted into offices for two thousand congressional staffers. In reading everything he could find about the critical last months of Trump's presidency, George noticed a series of developments on December 14, 2020. The Electoral College met then to confirm Biden's victory, and Trump had tweeted that same day that Barr would be stepping down as attorney general. Also that day, Trump senior adviser Stephen Miller gave an interview to Fox News saying the president still had a plan to fight the "fraudulent" election by focusing on alternate electors who were voting in swing states "as we speak." Why was a Trump White House adviser talking about state electors? Nine months earlier, investigator Waleska McLellan had posed a similar question, and unsuccessfully pressed DOJ to look at why so many pro-Trump GOP leaders had been talking about alternate electors in the run-up to January 6. George knew nothing of McLellan's efforts. But he told his teammates Harris and Lucier that it was something he wanted to understand better.

While DOJ was trained on rioters, this team wasted no time going straight to the top for answers.

In George's second week on the job, Lucier arrived for her first day and had to quickly acclimate to the whirlwind she had just joined. After Heaphy introduced the pair, George suggested they get lunch to talk over a few things, including prep for their interview with the former Acting Attorney General Jeff Rosen the next day.

"Oh, sure," Lucier teased. Surely this was a joke, she thought. At a big law firm such a high-profile deposition would take days and possibly weeks to prepare for.

"No, really," George said earnestly. "It's tomorrow."

Before the committee had begun its work, conventional wisdom about Trump's postelection efforts to stay in power centered on assumptions that Trump had desperately pushed on any door he could to find fault with the election's outcome. When one door closed, he simply tried another. But George had spotted a different pattern in a series of publicly available clues: Nearly all of Trump's efforts connected like spokes to this strange idea that alternate state electors could throw the final election results into doubt.

George found another connection while reading a report just released by the Senate Judiciary Committee about Trump's attempt to install Jeffrey Clark as attorney general days before January 6. The October report contained a draft letter that Trump and Clark wanted to send to Georgia election officials at the time, falsely claiming that widespread fraud left Biden's win in doubt. The letter, which Rosen and his deputy Rich Donoghue had secretly refused to approve, emphasized that alternate electors were insisting Trump had won in several states.

George also found it bizarre that so many Trump supporters had traveled to the nation's capital for January 6, thinking Pence could simply choose whether to count some states' electors and thereby set in motion events to overturn the election. This little-known exercise of certifying state electors in a presidential election had always been a pro forma, ceremonial event, yet it had become a key part of the backdrop in luring Trump supporters to Washington.

The January 6 investigators' office in O'Neill was arranged in an open bullpen, with the team leaders sitting at the head of a column of cubicles each facing Heaphy's office. For speed and efficiency, team members routinely shared their work like reporters in a newsroom, popping up from their desks to lean over cubicle walls and announce a new discovery or ask a question.

Less than two weeks on the job, Lucier and George stood up from their desks to discuss George's operating theory. Trump wasn't making desperate lunges to stay in power, George said; he was following a multi-pronged strategy to throw the election results into chaos.

"I really think it is all part of a plan," he said.

George had shown Lucier the five-page investigative blueprint he had drafted so far, with its emphasis on the fake elector scheme and the scanned images of the "alternate" elector certificates. Lucier agreed with George that it was glaringly obvious: These strange and similar certificates were obviously coordinated and were critical to investigate more deeply.

Gold Team members soon became among the last to leave the office and dubbed their frequent late-night brainstorming sessions "the Golden Hour." It was when George, Wood, Harris, and other members of the team could be found scribbling the latest key moments on a huge wall-size whiteboard in the office, connecting all the ways the electors cropped up in those final weeks before January 6, and vetting them with other staff and members of the committee.

George urged the group to consider the possibility that all Trump's pressure tactics—on states, the Justice Department, and eventually the vice president—were part of the same legal strategy. The ginned-up electors dispute might be the centerpiece of his plan to cling to power.

Some of the investigators pushed back constructively: Had Team Trump ever really been that organized? But as the initial round of interviews continued, George told colleagues he was growing more convinced. His and Wood's finalized investigative plan now listed central questions for the Gold Team to answer. Among them: Were the alternate electors created with the express goal of getting Congress to reject the results of the Electoral College vote on January 6?

The Gold Team began pumping out subpoenas. One for Clark had already been issued; next up was Eastman. But it was more obscure names added to the list that showed just how much the prosecutors-turned-congressional staffers were still approaching the job as if they worked for the Justice Department.

Heaphy was curious about some he'd never heard of, like Angela Mc-Callum. George explained that she had been a low-level Trump campaign staffer. His team had noticed a December 2020 Michigan news article that mentioned a voicemail McCallum left for Republican state legislators. McCallum's recorded message stated: "We want to know when there's a resolution in the House to appoint electors for Trump, if the president can count on you to join and support." She had also been mentioned in the story as having attended a meeting with Rudy Giuliani. McCallum, it seemed, knew something about the alternate elector strategy and had probably been given instructions from higher-ups in the campaign.

George wasn't sure how yet, but he told Heaphy he thought perhaps testimony and documents from someone on the lower rungs like McCallum could help break open the case.

At Main Justice, the House committee's rapidly expanding investigation into the area of an ongoing criminal investigation would eventually produce a raft of headaches for prosecutors, but the first one came as a surprise.

On October 15, 2021, President Biden had traveled to the campus of the University of Connecticut to help dedicate a center for human rights in the name of his longtime friend and former Senate colleague Chris Dodd. Returning to the White House, Biden stopped to answer questions from reporters. CNN correspondent Kaitlan Collins shouted out the key question on the topic that had been consuming Capitol Hill. The previous day, Trump adviser Steve Bannon had defied a subpoena from the House Select Committee, refusing to appear for an interview. The committee's lawmakers were now scheduled to meet to discuss whether to recommend that the Justice Department criminally prosecute Bannon for contempt.

Biden didn't hold back.

"I hope that the committee goes after them and holds them accountable," Biden said.

Collins pressed further, asking Biden if he thought the Department of Justice should prosecute people like Bannon who ignored their subpoenas.

"I do, yes," Biden answered.

It was close to 6:00 p.m. on October 15, a Friday. Anthony Coley, the chief spokesperson for the Department of Justice, had gotten back to his Capitol Hill home and poured himself a glass of wine. But just then his phone rang. It was Evan Perez, who covered the department for CNN. He told Coley to get ready because the president had just made some news.

"Aw, don't fuck up my night, man," Coley teased the beat reporter, then turned serious. "What did he say?"

Perez explained Biden had said he believed the Justice Department should prosecute people like Steve Bannon and others who defied congressional subpoenas in the January 6 investigation.

Coley shook his head. "No. He didn't."

Yes, Perez said. He did.

Compared to the way that former President Trump had berated then FBI Director James Comey to consider jailing members of the media and later pressed his attorney general to indict Comey himself, Biden's comments were anodyne. But Garland had less than a year earlier come into office vowing a return to absolute independence for the Justice Department.

Coley told Perez he'd get back to him and hung up. Before long, Garland, Monaco, and their senior staff members were on a conference call.

"Read me exactly what was said," Garland said over the conference line to Coley. Coley suggested the Justice Department immediately respond with language to make clear DOJ would make this decision independent of anything the president said. He said they shouldn't wait until Monday. Silence might stoke a weekend of news stories questioning the department's independence, he said. Garland and others on the call agreed. Coley read aloud his proposed statement a few times.

After a couple tweaks from his bosses, Coley released the national law enforcement agency's crisp response just fifty-one minutes after Biden's comments were first aired:

"The Department of Justice will make its own independent decisions in all prosecutions based solely on the facts and the law. Period. Full stop."

The statement put an end to the news cycle but left one audience fuming. Top White House officials, including in the press secretary's shop, were ticked off. They knew Biden had put his foot over the line, but they were upset that Garland had immediately blown the whistle and chosen to make such a defiant statement rather than let the White House have a chance to clarify and walk back Biden's off-the-cuff response.

But career staff at the department were delighted, and emailed and texted Coley their encouragement. Many said they were proud of the department for sticking up for itself and taking on a White House that had strayed, if ever so mildly, across the proper boundaries.

Coley had never gotten so much positive feedback from the staff before, including from many lawyers who were strangers to him. As one wrote: "Saw your statement. That is exactly right."

A week later, on October 21, the House voted to refer Bannon to the Justice Department for criminal contempt in his defiance of a congressional subpoena. Chairman Thompson said the committee needed Bannon to answer their questions, including those about his communications with then President Trump before the assault on the Capitol. Bannon had famously foreshadowed the attack, commenting the day before that "all hell is going to break loose."

The same day, Garland happened to be on Capitol Hill, testifying for the first time since becoming attorney general seven months earlier. Garland said he was proud of prosecutors' work on the January 6 investigation, but repeatedly deflected questions about what the department would do about Bannon. His agency was still not actively investigating Trump for his role in January 6, but Garland refused to confirm or deny that. "The Department of Justice has a long-standing policy of not commenting on investigations," Garland said. "I'm going to have to rest on that."

[19]

The Lone Prosecutor

By November 2021, the Justice Department had been investigating the horrendous assault on the Capitol for nearly ten months, and, finally, two of President Biden's critical nominees to spearhead the investigation and make big decisions were about to arrive. Matthew M. Graves, Biden's choice for U.S. attorney for the District of Columbia, and Matthew G. Olsen, the president's pick to be assistant attorney general for national security, had been long delayed.

Biden had not nominated Olsen until May, and Graves until July. Then both approvals took months to wend their way through Capitol Hill. Sen. Ron Johnson for a time blocked Graves's nomination, demanding information on how rioters were being treated in jail.

The absence of permanent leaders had contributed to significant delays and what some considered paralysis in making key decisions to advance the probe. Garland's focus on returning Justice to "regular order" meant in large measure that prosecutors in the field drove the decisions of when to open new investigations or to pull the trigger on seeking indictments.

Olsen, fifty-nine, was the son of a congressional staffer and a school nurse, and a rare homegrown Washingtonian. He'd clerked for a judge in the D.C. federal courthouse out of law school, and then spent two years as a civil rights lawyer in Main Justice before moving to prosecuting crimes in the D.C. U.S. Attorney's Office. Olsen had made an early mark in his decade there by putting away murderous drug dealers and gang leaders. Then the September 11 terror attacks led him to rejoin Main Justice to help stand up the newly formed National Security Division to interrupt further terror plots.

When Olsen arrived in November, it was immediately clear to his staff that he'd spent his time in confirmation purgatory making to-do lists. For starters, he began asking why the National Security Division had almost no involvement in the January 6 probe, especially since FBI Director Wray had publicly declared this an investigation of domestic terror. Olsen's acting predecessor told Olsen that Monaco and her team had largely been running the show, monitoring the D.C. prosecutors. The National Security Division, Olsen soon told his staff, had final say on sedition charges under Justice Department protocol, and its attorneys should be rolling up their sleeves to push those decisions along.

Graves, forty-six, also was returning to an office where he had excelled. As an assistant U.S. attorney almost fifteen years earlier, Graves had worked his way up, handling local violent crime, drug trafficking, and illegal firearms cases before beginning to prosecute fraud and public corruption cases in 2010. He earned the respect of FBI agents in investigating how former Congressman Jesse L. Jackson Jr. had embezzled $750,000 in campaign funds for jewelry, furs, and other luxuries. Graves had risen to acting chief of the Fraud and Public Corruption Section, then left for private practice before the 2016 election.

Upon his return, Graves told friends he felt he was joining a weary team of former colleagues only partway through a grueling marathon. Scores of the office's top prosecutors from its national security and fraud and public corruption units had sprinted to indict rioters in the immediate aftermath of the attack. Some prosecutors working other violent crimes, financial, and even foreign cases had been pulling double duty, often helping get the most violent rioters locked up.

Graves quickly realized that the office was not organized to handle the new reality of their workload, and set out to revamp teams of prosecutors and assignments, especially regarding January 6 cases. Graves also received a staff addition that his boss, Monaco, and her team had arranged to help with a uniquely sensitive part of the probe. Sitting among stacks of papers on Graves's desk on his first day was a memo to approve transferring Thomas Windom, a little-known prosecutor based in Maryland, to his D.C. office.

At forty-three, Windom had salt-and-pepper hair but still boyish good looks. He'd also come from a politically prominent lineage. His stepmother was a presiding judge of an Alabama state criminal appeals court, and his father had been the state's lieutenant governor. Monaco and her team liked his track record: Windom had racked up impressive wins in eighteen years as a federal prosecutor in the U.S. Attorney's Office based in Greenbelt, Maryland, including a recent investigation of a white supremacist organization that called itself "the Base" and plotted to launch a race war, kill minorities, and topple the government. Windom had secured lengthy prison sentences for some of the members by using gun and domestic terror charges. Two of Monaco's top lieutenants overseeing the January 6 investigation vouched for Windom. Chris Kavanaugh had been friends with him since law school at the University of Virginia, and Rush Atkinson's wife worked with Windom in the Maryland office and recommended him. Windom had made clear he was looking for a change.

Throughout the summer, Kavanaugh had been on temporary assignment to Monaco's office while awaiting his own Senate confirmation and won high marks for helping to cool the tensions between Main Justice and the U.S. Attorney's Office. He ratcheted down the daily check-in calls on January 6 cases. Garland and Monaco, mindful of new leads and reporting that fall that pointed to the pre–January 6 planning of Trump's top allies, began to see a need to expand the bandwidth of the D.C. U.S. Attorney's Office. They wanted someone dedicated exclusively to reviewing evidence of possible connections between people in Trump's orbit and the attack.

Woodward and Costa's book, *Peril*, followed by reporting by *The Washington Post*, provided fresh leads on a command center that Trump's allies had been running from the Willard Hotel to try to overturn the election. Not only had Roger Stone been operating from the hotel near the White House before and on January 6 with Oath Keepers escorts but Rudy Giuliani, Bannon, former New York City Police Commissioner Bernard Kerik, and John Eastman, author of the memos laying out the strategy for upending the election, had also been hunkered down at the hotel. There, they'd made calls and coordinated efforts, including reaching out to state legislative officials in hopes the election could be pushed back to states by Congress. Eastman had actually referred to the Willard operation as a "war room" back in May during an appearance on a talk show. And Kerik had billed Trump's campaign $55,295 for Willard rooms for legal team members for two weeks before January 6, the *Post* reported.

The Maryland prosecutor's first weeks in the office were awkward at best, with no announcement as to why he was there or what he was doing. Some attorneys working around his cubicle texted friends in the Maryland U.S. Attorney's Office to figure out his story. John Crabb, the chief of the office's Criminal Division and technically Windom's boss, told others that Windom's assignment wasn't yet entirely clear. But within a few weeks, Graves created a new "Investigations Unit," with Windom as its first member. Graves, his deputies, and counselors to Monaco sketched out Windom's initial task. Rather than searching for evidence on any particular rioter, he would sift through the mountains of evidence collected so far to spot connections or signs of a broader conspiracy. These were big, broad questions that the office's prosecutors had not yet explored.

On Monday, November 15, 2021, Olsen and Graves arrived at the

FBI's Washington Field Office to receive their first soup-to-nuts briefing on the January 6 investigation. Atkinson, now the sole point person overseeing the investigation for Monaco after Kavanaugh left for his U.S. attorney post, accompanied them. Windom, with only a handful of senior Justice officials aware of his remit, sat along a back wall as the presentation began.

Steve D'Antuono, the director of the field office, opened the meeting with an overview of the investigation. During the next three hours, senior FBI supervisors took turns breaking down the number of people charged with breaching the Capitol, vandalizing the halls of Congress, and assaulting police. Other agents delved into the intense and increasingly frustrated search for the culprit who placed pipe bombs outside Democratic and Republican Party headquarters. And the presentation went deep into the evidence of advance planning by some Oath Keepers, Proud Boys, and other extremists to deploy violence on January 6.

In his first days, Olsen had already been clued in about charges being considered for members of those groups. When the briefers got to discussing the Oath Keepers evidence, one mentioned that the U.S. Attorney's Office in D.C. had drafted a memo that urged charging some of these plotters with seditious conspiracy. Olsen took note of the mention of the criminal statute—2384—a charge his division had to approve if it was ever used. By this point, memos and debates about charging some riot plotters with seditious conspiracy had been floating around Main Justice and the U.S. Attorney's Office for over eight months.

Depending on where one sat around the table that day at the FBI field office, the reasons for the delay on seditious conspiracy looked vastly different. Some prosecutors assigned to the Oath Keepers and Proud Boys cases in the U.S. Attorney's Offices had heard their February recommendation for seditious conspiracy had been stalled for months in an opaque appellate "risk" review at Main Justice, at the request of the attorney general. But the Deputy Attorney General's Office believed prosecutors were still preparing a draft indictment—the main way Main Justice could assess its strength—but had yet to finish. The D.C. office, though, was meanwhile adding defendants and newly gathered facts to its draft. Atkinson, at Monaco's urging, had succeeded in October in obtaining an internal working draft from the U.S. Attorney's Office—what became known as a "bootlegged" copy—in hopes that appellate lawyers could soon get a jump and begin stress-testing it.

Leaving the FBI briefing together, Olsen and Atkinson hopped into a waiting Justice Department van. On the way back to their office, Olsen asked Atkinson about the status of the seditious conspiracy charges.

"That's something you're going to need to get into," Atkinson told him.

Graves and Olsen had the Senate-confirmed authority to sign off on the rare charge. Olsen called Graves after the November 15 briefing and they agreed they needed to figure this out together: Was the evidence against some of the Oath Keepers strong enough for sedition? If so, they should present that case to the attorney general as soon as possible to clear this logjam slowing down the largest investigation in the department's history.

[20]

"I'm Not Subpoenaing
the Friggin' Willard"

Just a few days before Thanksgiving, Thomas Windom took a big step to try to make quick leaps forward on his assignment. He and an old friend stepped out of their respective offices on opposite sides of the National Mall and, at roughly the same time, began approaching a park bench near the Hirshhorn Sculpture Garden, nestled between the Capitol and the Washington Monument.

It was a cold, brisk day in the high forties, not ideal for an outdoor meeting in suit jackets. The subject to be discussed, however, was one of the hottest topics in town, and for that, the ground rules had to be clear: This chat between friends now working for different branches of government was explicitly unofficial.

The more senior of the two was Windom's old friend Tim Heaphy, the chief investigative counsel of the House Select Committee on January 6. Heaphy's congressional team was nearly three months deep into identifying targets, interviewing witnesses, and reviewing subpoenaed records, with dozens more interviews and demands for records on the runway. Windom, on the other hand, was still a one-man show. At this moment, the prosecutor turned to his old teacher and mentor for advice. Heaphy had taught Windom in his law school class at the University of Virginia more than fifteen years earlier. He had advised Windom in his career and tried to help him along, recommending Windom at one point to U.S. Attorney Rod Rosenstein for the prosecutor job in the Maryland office.

Heaphy greeted Windom with a hearty hello and congratulated him on landing his new job at the U.S. Attorney's Office in D.C. Windom avoided sharing a lot of details about his work but said he was going to be looking beyond who had hit cops and broken through the Capitol's doors and windows. He said he wanted to study the motivations for the riot and possible links between the rally promoters and the attack.

Heaphy considered this an encouraging sign, and an opportunity for two trusted friends to build a good-faith bridge between the committee and the department that had been his home for decades—as both tried to unspool the truth. Heaphy expected Windom's assignment would inevitably lead DOJ to former President Donald Trump. Over the last eleven months, he saw a Justice Department consumed by the "blue-collar" crimes of January 6, the rioters who harmed police and broke into the Capitol. To his dismay, the department had so far avoided examining the evidence of the "white-collar" crimes, or Trump and his allies fomenting the attack and seeking to block the certification of the election.

Heaphy knew the telltale signs of a DOJ investigation, and so far his team had encountered zero evidence of Justice poking around in Donald Trump's orbit. Not one of the administration or campaign witnesses that Heaphy's committee had interviewed had been contacted by federal prosecutors. Members of Heaphy's team remarked on it frequently, with some shock. "We're the first footprints in the snow," Heaphy told them. Congress was almost never first to interview witnesses in a serious criminal investigation, and Heaphy and his team believed this case might end up being the single greatest crime against America's government since the Civil War. Yet the Justice Department was nowhere to be found.

He told Windom this was a great move—for him and for the department.

"You're totally ready for this," he said.

Windom responded with accolades for the House committee's quick start.

"You guys are doing a great job," Windom said. "I know you've been immersed in this. I need to get up to speed."

Windom said he was eager to hear any insights that Heaphy could share about what the congressional committee was doing.

Names of nearly everyone interviewed by the committee ended up being leaked to the press shortly after the witnesses left their Hill interview rooms, so tidbits of each new development had been available on the front pages of national newspapers. By this point, the committee had interviewed former Acting Attorney General Jeff Rosen and Acting Deputy Attorney General Richard Donoghue, and had gathered surprising details from inside the rooms where Trump had pressured Vice President Pence not to certify the election.

"I know you guys are ahead of us," Windom said.

Windom said he planned to take advantage of work that had already been done to date by the riot investigators at the FBI and U.S. Attorney's Office.

Heaphy was guarded too but told Windom his big takeaway so far: The events leading up to January 6 had some markers of a classic conspiracy case.

"There's a lot there that could lead to criminal charges," he said.

Heaphy then pitched his idea to Windom: an informal, two-way communication channel he had been keen to establish with Justice. Heaphy said he didn't expect to get any special or sensitive material from Windom—he sure wasn't asking for the FBI 302s, the forms agents used to record notes from witness interviews. But he would like to stay in touch so they could give each other a heads-up on significant developments, when appropriate. Heaphy said he hoped to get some useful information and genuinely believed they had the same goal.

"We have a shared interest in developing facts and getting to accountability," Heaphy said.

Windom said creating this channel sounded good to him in principle but he was still finding his way in the D.C. office. Windom would later learn such an unofficial channel was frowned upon, and the two would not talk again.

Over the first three weeks of December, Windom began outlining an investigative plan to present to his bosses. He needed to drill down and to understand better the activity in the days before January 6 at the Willard—both by Oath Keepers and by so many in Trump's orbit who were present. Also, the office still needed to get to the bottom of the president's attempt to install Clark as acting attorney general in the days before January 6. Windom finished the plan over a weekend and circulated it on a Sunday, about a week before Christmas. Graves and the Deputy Attorney General's Office were on board. One of the first steps was to get critical buy-in from the investigative branch of the department.

In D.C., a handful of long blocks separate the U.S. Attorney's Office and the FBI's Washington Field Office. On a nice day, the distance can easily be covered by foot in less than ten minutes. But this time, Windom and federal prosecutors were stepping into hostile territory. Accompanied by his boss, Crabb, as well as Atkinson, who had joined them from Monaco's office, the new D.C. prosecutor entered an oversize conference room and met D'Antuono, flanked by his field office deputies. The two sides greeted one another with professional nods and slightly awkward hellos.

D'Antuono had heard from a prosecutor pal at the U.S. Attorney's Office that nobody there really knew this new guy Windom or what exactly he was assigned to do, only that the Deputy Attorney General's Office had arranged to have Windom move to the D.C. office. That had been enough for the old FBI agent to identify Windom as Monaco's guy.

Across the table, Monaco's guy got to the point. His argument, put most simply, was that there was reason to suspect a link between Trump's orbit, people like Roger Stone and others at the Willard, and Oath Keepers at the riot, and it should be examined. Windom asked D'Antuono to open an investigation and assist in bringing material to a grand jury, beginning with subpoenaing the Willard for guests' reservations and billing information during those critical days before January 6. Windom conveyed a certain eagerness, leaning over the conference table to make his points. D'Antuono, on the other hand, who had clocked two decades in the Bureau, sat back, looking curious and mildly skeptical.

D'Antuono had been consumed ever since January 6 with tracking down evidence implicating the rioters engaged in violence. The work of his agents had since proven through phone records and recordings that some of the lead rioters had planned their assault for weeks in advance. Opening a criminal investigation into what politicians intended or didn't intend to happen on January 6, however, felt like a danger zone. In fact, it sounded a lot like what Cooney had proposed to D'Antuono's field office in February 2021, and which D'Antuono had helped kill. For D'Antuono, little had changed. He'd learned as a young agent on one of the 1990s corruption probes of the infamous Providence mayor Vincent "Buddy" Cianci that the Bureau could have a seeming mountain of evidence and still barely win a case. The FBI should always use extreme caution in investigating politicians, was his takeaway.

As D'Antuono had told aides repeatedly since January 6, Trump could argue many of his supporters were engaged in their constitutionally protected right to free speech in challenging the election results and that they never intended for the riot to turn violent. And he had frequently warned that the FBI must meet a higher bar to probe politicians because any investigation created an impression of guilt, even if no charges were brought.

After a pause, D'Antuono turned to his two top deputies in the room for feedback, starting with Michael Glasheen, the special agent in charge of counterterrorism cases in his office. Did the FBI have any evidence of Stone or any other Trump advisers being connected in incriminating telephone communications with the Oath Keepers identified in the riot?

"No, sir," Glasheen said. "There's no evidence of that."

Were there any indications Trump's campaign aides had helped finance the militia groups coming to Washington? D'Antuono asked. Glasheen again said: "No, sir."

D'Antuono asked Timothy Thibault, one of the Bureau's most seasoned public corruption investigators and his assistant special agent in charge of the teams running white-collar cases, for his reaction. FBI headquarters had decided the field office should run the January 6 investigation out of its Counterterrorism Division, which Glasheen now oversaw, not the criminal one that Thibault helped supervise. D'Antuono asked if, based on everything publicly known about the Willard, his criminal chief could identify any reasonable suspicion of a crime on the part of Trump campaign members.

Thibault said there were unknowns, including news reports about Trump campaign advisers organizing alternate electors from the hotel. But the FBI had not opened an investigation into that topic, and generally, no, there was nothing obviously criminal about the known actions of Trump associates at the Willard.

The prosecutors kept pressing. The new public clues suggested Trump and his lieutenants were pushing the country toward the January 6 conflict from the hotel, they said. The Department of Justice had a good factual basis to probe what Trump allies had been up to at the Willard, they argued.

D'Antuono and his team were growing frustrated. They heard nothing that sounded like sufficient predicate to open a case on the president's advisers. Thibault, who had worked on nearly every sensitive case involving a president since Whitewater, demanded clearer signs of a crime. If you want the Bureau to engage, he said, raising his voice, "give me a scheme to defraud."

194

After listening to Windom and his own deputies, D'Antuono re-peated for Windom many of the criticisms he'd leveled against Cooney's plan. He could defend his agents pressing to learn if the rioters who had been present and committed crimes were linked to people around Trump. Fine, no problem. But to start in the other direction felt like a leap, looking for guilt by association.

"It looks like you don't have an articulable basis to open a case," D'Antuono told Windom.

Windom and Crabb tried one more approach. Couldn't some of the hotel's guest records they were seeking flow logically from the Bureau's open investigation of Oath Keepers?

The agents disliked this idea, seeing it as an effort to shoehorn the president's advisers into the rioter investigation. The specific hotel re-cords Windom wanted also gave D'Antuono hives for a separate reason: a potential invasion of privacy. What if some married person was using the hotel for a tryst, totally unrelated to January 6? A subpoena for these records could be an improper invasion into the private lives of poten-tially anyone else staying at the hotel. Both would be hard for the FBI to justify, he felt.

"I'm not subpoenaing the friggin' Willard," D'Antuono said. "Sorry. You don't have it."

Windom, looking surprised at the reaction of his DOJ counterparts, tried a few more times. D'Antuono continued to resist but offered Win-dom an opportunity to build a better argument. The FBI chief said he would give Windom a key to the treasure trove of data the FBI had gath-ered about the rioters, allowing Windom to peruse all the transcripts of interviews, phone records, and financial transactions to see if he could find any connections between the Trump allies, the Willard, and the breach. The FBI chief said he'd toss in a parking pass to the garage so Windom could come and go as he liked. Windom thanked him and left.

A day or two later, Abbate called D'Antuono for a regular check-in. He grew incredulous hearing that D.C. prosecutors were raising this a third time without new evidence.

After so many jabs at the FBI by Trump when he was president, D'Antuono wasn't going to give the department's critics on the right a weapon to stab them with again. He told Abbate how he'd turned Windom down. "DOJ won't get blasted for this," D'Antuono said. "We will."

Abbate asked a few more questions and D'Antuono could tell he had his boss's support. D'Antuono ultimately answered to Abbate, FBI Director Chris Wray, and, finally, Deputy Attorney General Lisa Monaco. If any of them told him to open an investigation, he knew he would have to do it.

But none ever did. Garland and Monaco almost never gave a top-down order to the FBI, and certainly would not in a case with these political trip wires. For a third time since January 6, the Justice Department's leaders couldn't agree on whether there was an adequate basis to turn its powerful investigative spotlight on evidence linking January 6 to Team Trump.

Around the holidays, Windom caught up with Jonathan Lenzner, his old boss from the Maryland U.S. Attorney's Office, who knew well Windom's impressive past work on domestic terrorism cases. Lenzner asked him how the new job in D.C. was going. Windom offered sparing details, but mentioned the FBI's Washington Field Office wouldn't help him on a case, so he was now looking for investigators from other agencies. It was a fortuitous encounter. Lenzner was about to be named Chris Wray's new chief of staff at the FBI.

At Main Justice, word of D'Antuono's rebuff had spread too, but Atkinson had reported that Graves and the team at the U.S. Attorney's Office thought the FBI would eventually come around. Garland and Wray both favored a firm and broad consensus and would let it build organically, said one person involved in the discussions: "If we're going to go forward with this, there's going to have to be a lot of hands on the knife."

[21]

One Year Later

As the one-year anniversary of the Capitol attack approached, the chasm widened between the Justice Department's and the House Select Committee's investigations of January 6. The committee was about to vote to refer former Trump Chief of Staff Mark Meadows for contempt of Congress charges for refusing to testify. Liz Cheney, the House committee's vice chair, underscored the gravity of the situation: Trump may have committed a crime, she suggested for the first time, and Meadows's account was critical to understanding what had happened. She then read aloud several eye-popping text messages the committee had obtained that were to and from Meadows around the time of the attack. One by one, on the afternoon of January 6, as rioters assaulted police and tramped through the halls of Congress, a series of Fox News hosts urged Meadows to get Trump to stop the violence.

"Hey Mark, the president needs to tell people in the Capitol to go home . . . this is hurting all of us . . . he is destroying his legacy," Laura Ingraham pressed.

"Please get him on tv. Destroying everything you have accomplished," host Brian Kilmeade wrote.

"Can he make a statement?" Sean Hannity wrote. "Ask people to leave the Capitol."

Shortly after 2:30 p.m., the president had issued a tweet asking protesters to support the U.S. Capitol Police and "be peaceful." But his son Donald Trump Jr. insisted it wasn't enough, urging something stronger.

"He's got to condemn this shit Asap. The Capitol Police tweet is not enough," Don Jr.'s text read.

"I'm pushing it hard," Meadows replied. "I agree."

After her dramatic reading of the text threads, Cheney said the evidence suggested Trump had been derelict in his duty as commander in chief during a raging domestic terror attack, a moral failure. But she made clear the committee was also looking at whether Trump broke the law and helped plot the larger scheme. "Did Donald Trump, through action or inaction, corruptly seek to obstruct or impede Congress's official proceeding to count electoral votes?" Cheney asked.

The line closely—and intentionally—tracked the statutory language for a 1512 felony under the U.S. Criminal Code. A few blocks down Pennsylvania Avenue, the Justice Department had used that charge for rioters but had still not gotten close to seeing former President Trump's actions as possible crimes.

In early December, U.S. Attorney Graves and Assistant Attorney General Olsen had spoken every few days about whether to charge Oath Keepers with seditious conspiracy for their plot to block the election results. Ever since their November 15 briefing, both had grown increasingly certain the department should pursue the novel charge, which, nine months earlier, Sherwin had said on national television would likely fit the bill. Graves told staffers he was proud of his complex conspiracy team's methodical work to prove the militia members' planning. Olsen agreed the charges were a no-brainer.

"If this isn't seditious conspiracy, I don't know what is," Olsen said when reviewing the statute with his staff. "The conduct fits the crime exactly."

Graves and Olsen disagreed strenuously, however, on how many of the Oath Keepers and their allies should be charged with sedition. Olsen wanted to trim the list to suspects who explicitly agreed to use force to help stop the January 6 certification. Graves pushed back against narrowing the case, saying his team felt confident they would win convictions for militia members who, for example, readied themselves with guns in Virginia but didn't come to D.C. Theirs was an intense back-and-forth, cerebral, but not personal. The stakes for both Graves and Olsen were extremely high. Charging—and then losing—a seditious conspiracy case involving the politically contentious attack on the Capitol could damage the department; Graves, who would sign the charging documents and whose office would win or lose at trial, would be most exposed.

At Graves's urging, John Crabb and Jocelyn Ballantine, two skilled prosecutors in his office, made a presentation to Olsen on how they would make their case in court for sedition for those who had not entered the Capitol. Olsen, experienced in the risks of prosecuting complex conspiracy cases in the same office, remained unpersuaded. A D.C. jury might well convict, he told them, but they could lose on appeal. Taking that risk on a drug conspiracy case might be OK, but it wasn't good enough for one of this significance.

The attorney general also wanted to ensure this charge could survive potential challenges all the way to the Supreme Court. Word spread that the Solicitor General's Office had tapped some former Supreme Court clerks who now worked at Justice and who were predicting the arguments that a Justice Alito or Justice Kavanaugh would make to overturn a January 6 seditious conspiracy conviction.

The last time Justice had won a seditious conspiracy case was in 1995, when Garland was working as a political appointee in the Justice Department under Attorney General Janet Reno. Federal prosecutors in New York convicted the "Blind Sheikh," Omar Abdel Rahman, and nine codefendants of seditious conspiracy for their roles in plotting to attack or bomb a series of New York landmarks, including the World Trade Center, in 1993.

Garland was not a gambling man, and from his two decades on the

D.C. Circuit, he, too, knew well the leanings of most of the Supreme Court justices who might ultimately hear such a case. To bulletproof the charges, Garland endorsed a kind of trial before a trial, using a red team of legal eagles and seasoned appellate lawyers at Main Justice who had no connection to the cases to stress-test whether the facts they had uncovered matched the statute's requirements.

"They took all this stuff to them and played it out: What would the text messages show? What would the emails show? What would the cooperators say? And taking all this evidence together, would it hit the threshold for seditious conspiracy?" said someone involved in the discussions.

One crucial adviser for vetting seditious conspiracy was Patty Stemler, an appellate guru who had worked in the department for three decades and upon whom nine previous attorneys general had relied to build unassailable cases. Stemler and Atkinson, Monaco's deputy overseeing the riot probe, had asked why the department wouldn't just charge the Oath Keepers group with a 1512. That charge involved proving the same facts as sedition and sentencing rioters to the same amount of prison time if they were convicted.

But Graves and Olsen were firm. Graves insisted this conduct was far worse and sedition charges signaled that. In a meeting in the Deputy Attorney General's Office a few weeks into his tenure, Graves won over Atkinson and others by arguing the Justice Department had a responsibility not to shy away from charging the crime that best captured the motive and violence of an act. Congress was at the time revisiting whether to make lynching a federal hate crime, nearly seventy years after the killing of Emmett Till. The Justice Department, Graves argued, needed to think about the imperative to charge seditious conspiracy the way it felt compelled to charge a killing as not just murder but as a civil rights violation when that is what clearly happened.

"Charges give name to the thing that has been done," Graves said. His legal argument galvanized support in the room to move forward.

Through early December, Graves and Olsen pored over indictment drafts, redlining their changes, talking by secure phone, and inviting feedback from Stemler. Olsen and his national security team ultimately whittled the defendants down to a core group of thirteen, including their leader, Stewart Rhodes.

On Thursday, December 16, 2021, Olsen headed to the standing weekly briefing with the attorney general to present the decision he had reached. He had been regularly updating Garland on his and Graves's review. This time Olsen told Garland of their plans to finally indict using this almost-never-invoked charge. The normal group was in attendance, including Garland's chief of staff, Matt Klapper, Monaco, and Atkinson.

Olsen summarized his reasons for charging sedition. Garland pulled out his statute book and read aloud key passages, asking Olsen to spell out how he would prove each element. Olsen explained that he'd worked closely with Stemler to spot and address any vulnerabilities in the case. Monaco gave her endorsement.

"Matt and his team have really pressure-tested this," she said, narrowing it to the tightest, strongest case. Garland nodded approvingly.

"OK," Garland said.

That was it. The attorney general had given his approval.

After the meeting broke up, Olsen reported the good news to Graves. They could proceed with the indictments. Graves and his office began finalizing the charging documents through the Christmas holidays, adopting the changes Olsen had recommended. Unfortunately, Graves had caught COVID during those holidays, making the precise editing of the charging documents even more grueling. In an extended and final videoconference with his counterparts at Main Justice, a quarantined Graves had to beam in from his home office, but he still wore his standard uniform—suit and tie. Because of his fever, Graves was visibly sweating through his shirt and the folds of his suit as the conference call wore on. A DOJ lawyer on his own screen humorously praised Graves for his dedication.

"This is your Flu Game, man," he said, referencing Michael Jordan's famous NBA finals win while suffering dehydration, dizziness, and other flu symptoms.

That week, Garland personally drafted and then rehearsed a speech to mark the one-year anniversary of the Capitol attack while knowing indictments on seditious conspiracy were likely only days away. The work the department had just done on that case—the careful internal debate and case preparation that the public would mostly never see—represented the best traditions of the Justice Department in extraordinary times, Garland sought to convey.

Still, with criticism of the pace of the Justice Department's investigation having only intensified as the House committee had put Trump in the crosshairs, a handful of top department officials urged that the speech needed to say more about how far beyond the rioters the department was willing to go. The group included Garland's chief of staff and Vanita Gupta, the department's associate attorney general. The group workshopped one of the speech's most quoted lines until hours before Garland delivered it. Even then, Garland barely went as far as Sherwin had a year earlier, on the morning after the attack:

"The Justice Department remains committed to holding all January sixth perpetrators, at any level, accountable under law—whether they were present that day or were otherwise criminally responsible for the assault on our democracy. We will follow the facts wherever they lead."

[22]

"Weapon Left at the Crime Scene"

The week of January 10, a string of news stories pegged to the one-year anniversary of the attack snowballed into a maelstrom of criticism of the Justice Department. One key question dominated the airwaves: Why were prosecutors MIA in investigating evidence that Donald Trump and his allies had illegally tried to overturn an election?

It started when *The Detroit News* reported that Michigan Attorney General Dana Nessel hadn't taken any action in the fake elector case she opened more than a year earlier. *Politico*, meanwhile, revealed the copious evidence the House Select Committee was gathering on the Trump campaign's push to gin up fake electors. Rachel Maddow complained to her millions of MSNBC viewers there were no signs of DOJ probing either that scheme or other well-documented aspects of Trump's attempted election interference, "while Attorney General Merrick Garland has made sort of vague patriotic statements about no one being above the law."

On January 13, 2022, the Justice Department revealed what had been dominating its attention. The evening before, the department had filed its long-awaited indictment on seditious conspiracy, charging Oath Keepers founder Stewart Rhodes and ten other members of the group with the Civil War–era felony, writing that the defendants had "planned to stop the lawful transfer of presidential power" by force.

One year and one week after the attack, Rhodes was arrested and instantly became the most high-profile person charged in connection with January 6. The indictment laid out, often in Rhodes's own words, captured in recordings and writings, how for months before the attack he had guided members toward a violent clash to keep Trump in power. Two days before the election, Rhodes wrote to fellow Oath Keepers on an encrypted group chat: "We aren't getting through this without a civil war. Too late for that. Prepare your mind, body, spirit."

An article in the nonpartisan *Lawfare* blog said the seditious conspiracy indictment showed a Justice Department still focused on Trump followers: "While this constrained model of a conspiracy may well maximize the chances of holding Rhodes and other similarly situated defendants accountable, it most likely excludes those political leaders who drove the events of January 6—including the man who many believe bears the greatest responsibility, former President Donald Trump."

The night of Rhodes's arrest, Maddow spent several minutes of her 9:00 p.m. show asking why it had taken so long when prosecutors had talked about sedition within days of the attack.

"But now, it's of course more than a year after the attack. This is the first time they've actually used it in the indictment unsealed today."

On the night of Thursday, January 13, Attorney General Nessel, who was facing questions at home about her lack of action on her state electors case, joined Maddow's program as a guest with news to share.

Michigan's top law enforcement official said she now believed there was sufficient evidence to charge as many as sixteen Republican electors with state crimes of forgery for their part in Trump's scheme to stay in office. Nessel's office did not explain why she was acting on the case now or why she was urgently announcing it on Maddow's late-night show. But since Michigan was just one of several states where party officials had tried to pull a fast one on the country, she said she had that day referred the Michigan case to Justice Department prosecutors based in the Western District of Michigan. Rather than pursuing a state case, she was recommending they consider a criminal probe.

"And we hope that Main Justice, the Department of Justice, will become involved and use the information they already have to better understand exactly what happened that day so that federal charges can be evaluated," Nessel said, adding later: "I think that you're talking about a conspiracy, really, to overthrow the United States government."

Back in Washington, however, a group of little-known federal investigators privately seethed at Nessel's nationally televised news. The investigators knew an entirely different—and unflattering—backstory that called into question Nessel's motives.

This small, close-knit team of investigators hailed from the Inspector General's Office for the National Archives. Assistant Inspector General Jason Metrick had set his phone to alert him to news reports mentioning the office and received a ping that evening about Maddow's program. He immediately messaged the team in their shared chat thread, sending a link to the Nessel news with a note along the lines of: "What the hell?"

As the attorneys and investigators in the chat began circulating and watching a clip of the show, everyone on the thread shared their disbelief.

A full year earlier, this team had first tried to sound the alarm about fake Republican electors with Justice Department prosecutors in Washington, D.C. But the prosecutors in the U.S. Attorney's Office, who specialized in election crimes and who coordinated with Main Justice on such investigations, had turned them down. The prosecutors, who worked for Cooney, had recommended the investigators instead try to partner with states to see if there were charges that should be brought.

For twelve months, the Archives investigators had repeatedly encouraged state attorneys general to pursue those fake elector cases—and had gotten exactly nowhere. Working with Nessel's Michigan office had in fact been one of the team's worst experiences. The agents had initially received indications that Nessel's office was interested. But their offers of help had then been brushed off. Just a month before, in fact, the Archives investigators had just received notification from Nessel's office on December 7, 2021, that her team had decided it would *not* pursue the electors fraud case. What the hell, indeed, had changed? the investigators asked now.

In Michigan, the probe had in fact bogged down from the very beginning. Nessel had decided the previous year that she had to refer the case to a county prosecutor, Carol Siemon, explaining that as a top Democrat running for reelection she had the appearance of a conflict.

Nessel had confided to fellow prosecutors that on its face, the case seemed like "a slam dunk," but Siemon and another prosecutor in her office concluded that under state statutes, it wasn't a strong or advisable case. They found the fraud the GOP officials had attempted despicable, but felt that proving wrongdoing under state law would be a challenge. One statute required proof their action had cheated someone out of a financial stake, which wasn't the case. The other required proof the officials had an intent to deceive, and that wasn't publicly documented, though the state hadn't interviewed anyone to learn more. Siemon's assistant prosecutor recommended against going through the hassle. Siemon, a Democrat, agreed it could appear petty and political to spend state resources bringing misdemeanor charges against the opposing party's leaders, including a Michigan GOP national committeewoman. Siemon, of course, wasn't looking at the nearly identical frauds carried out in six other states or the way Trump allies used the certificates to pressure Vice President Pence not to certify the election on January 6. Focused only on Michigan, Siemon reported to Nessel's office that it wasn't worth using state time to prosecute this strange "political prank" that would likely never happen again.

A month later, the night of Nessel's prime-time announcement, Metrick texted his staff that he wanted answers about Michigan's about-face. Waleska McLellan, the head of investigations for the office, told her agent who had been in contact with Michigan officials to get to the bottom of it. She told him he had either been misled or something funky was happening.

The Archives team worried about how this would play with their new boss, the inspector general. He—and the public—might wrongly assume their office had dropped the ball.

The next morning, Nessel's aides tried to smooth things over with Metrick and McLellan in a conference call. Metrick didn't hide his anger.

"Wait, we tried to get you to follow this case for a year," he said. "You had no interest. Now you care so much?"

Nessel's aides kept apologizing but also didn't explain what had changed. They stressed that the attorney general and her staff had the discretion to change their minds.

Metrick delivered his blunt take on the dramatic turnaround by Nessel, a Democrat, who was running for reelection that fall.

"This feels political to me," he said.

Nessel's U-turn tossed a softball to her Democratic allies atop the Justice Department, giving them clear cover to launch a federal probe and catch up to what the House January 6 committee was quickly concluding: The elector scheme was obviously coordinated and linked to Trump's larger plan to stay in office.

Members of the Archives team soon reached out to the acting U.S. attorney in the Western District of Michigan, Andrew Birge, to find out whether his office planned to pursue the case. Birge's office explained they were taking their lead from Deputy Attorney General Lisa Monaco, and waiting to hear from her office on how they should proceed.

That same day, McLellan reached out to the Justice Department's Public Integrity Section at Inspector General Baker's suggestion. Metrick told her not to get too invested. They would check the box by contacting the feds one more time and then move on, he told her. He didn't want the team to help the state or the feds with any political show or ass-covering. Late that afternoon, however, another email zipped in the opposite direction, arriving in McLellan's inbox from a prosecutor she hadn't spoken to in a few years: Thomas Windom.

Windom's note was a bit cryptic, asking if McLellan had time for a call. McLellan knew Windom from a case the two had been paired up on years earlier in suburban Maryland, where a repository for the Archives sits just a few miles from Windom's old U.S. Attorney's Office. She hadn't known Windom had joined the D.C. office. McLellan took a wry tone in her reply, saying that it was quite a coincidence that Windom wanted to talk. She, too, had something she wanted to discuss.

They arranged a Google Meet video call at about 8:00 p.m. Windom was in the office; McLellan was working from home that day. When they connected, he explained that his office was, in fact, considering a possible probe of the fake electors issue. He asked if she and any of her team of agents from the Archives' Inspector General's Office would like to help the U.S. Attorney's Office as investigators. It was an unusual request; both he and McLellan recognized that reality with a pause.

Why would federal prosecutors in D.C. not tap into the hundreds of FBI agents working a few blocks away at the field office in downtown D.C.? Windom confided that the FBI wasn't working with him, at least not yet. He said it was something he was trying to change; he and the FBI were "in discussions."

"You are the first on board," Windom told her.

Agent and prosecutor both talked a bit about the facts of the case. They later told colleagues they got a good vibe from each other. They both spoke precisely, avoiding any drama. They had a feeling of sharing the same goal: figure out this fraud and how high it went, and, if the facts warranted it, charge the people responsible. It had been over a year since McLellan first suggested a federal probe; they needed to stop wasting time.

At Windom's request, two members of the inspector general's team would soon be the first agents to join his investigation. At the Archives, the investigators were asked on January 21 to reopen their case files, due to "renewed" interest by federal prosecutors.

Within a day or two, DOJ's press office called Evan Perez of CNN to grant a revived request he had been making for months to get an on-camera interview with Lisa Monaco. Perez and Monaco taped the interview the afternoon of January 25, and press officers quietly tipped beat reporters to watch CNN air the conversation that night: The boss might break some news. Perez, a respected Justice correspondent, took the opportunity to ask Monaco about the fake electors of the 2020 election.

"What can you say to assure people?" Perez asked. "Because there's very little that we've seen publicly said by this department on this issue."

"Well, first, on the issue you raised, in terms of fraudulent elector certifications, as has been reported, we've received those referrals," Monaco said. "Our prosecutors are looking at those, and I can't say, uh, anything more on ongoing investigations."

The line might have washed over many viewers as a bureaucrat's clipped nonanswer, but Perez and other editors and reporters immediately recognized this as a big development. The Justice Department usually abided by an informal rule never to confirm or deny the existence of a nonpublic investigation. Garland's DOJ had been even more tight-lipped. The department's number 2 official had just acknowledged "ongoing investigations." Monaco had indeed broken news.

Her remarks also broke the news to FBI agents, who would be a logical choice to investigate the matter. Early the next morning at the Washington Field Office, Steve D'Antuono read Monaco's announcement with a grimace. Recognizing her unusual admission, he predicted it wouldn't be long before he'd be asked to consider investigating election interference by Trump allies after declining Windom's request about the Willard.

"Watch," D'Antuono told his deputies. "We're going to get a call."

Behind the scenes, and coordinating with Monaco's office, U.S. Attorney Matt Graves and Windom had in the weeks since last visiting D'Antuono identified five significant potential crimes at play for those who trafficked in the fake elector documents. They included wire and mail fraud, the same charges McLellan had tentatively proposed that this office investigate a year earlier, along with falsification of federal records, conspiracy, and obstruction of a government proceeding.

As D'Antuono predicted, Graves and Windom called him to ask for a meeting at his office. When they gathered several days later, the two prosecutors said they had identified eighty-four people who had signed the alternate elector documents and whom they knew they wanted to interview.

Compared to the last time Windom was in the office, D'Antuono quickly warmed to this narrower framing for an investigation. People had signed documents. There might be mail receipts. These were the kinds of nuts and bolts needed to build a case. D'Antuono said he was willing to consider an investigation. Yet despite the straightforward nature of this suspected crime, approving and launching the probe would take months. That glacial pace had become a pattern at DOJ and FBI for every matter that involved Donald Trump. A genuine federal investigation was underway, but the agents conducting it had lost a year.

As one of the Archives team members would later lament, the failure to more quickly investigate was hard to justify. There had been documents and signatures, evidence in black and white, even before January 6. As is often the case, when they began looking, agents found far more than had first been apparent. "That's true with every investigation. You have to look in order to know how serious something is," said one of the investigators. "It was so much more serious than we first thought."

Like Dan George had done starting in September at the House investigation, Justice investigators needed to focus on the fake elector documents that had been sitting in front of them all along.

"At a point, you realize," said a person who met frequently with Garland at the time and was regularly briefed on the start of Windom's investigation into the fake elector documents, "it was the weapon left at the crime scene."

[23]

A New Matter

In the final weeks of January 2022, a private battle between a little-known federal agency and Donald Trump was about to explode into public view. Over the previous eight months, that fight had pitted a cerebral and fastidious career government lawyer, Gary Stern, against the famously chaotic and disorderly operation that surrounded the former president.

Stern, who had been the general counsel of the National Archives for more than two decades, was a proud advocate for his agency's mission of preserving the history of the United States—some twelve billion pages of documents, including records that chronicled forty-five presidencies and moments both monumental and mundane. In his sixties, Stern was as lean and wiry as he had been as a young Yale Law School graduate arriving in Washington eager for a career in public service. With a thin white beard and wire-rim spectacles, he remained a fierce stickler for the rules.

Throughout his career, Stern had dogged agencies and outgoing administrations to save the presidential history that belonged to the public. But since May 2021, Stern had quietly waged one of his most unusual campaigns ever. He'd been nagging and pressing Trump's lawyers and aides to return well-known presidential records that had gone missing. Presumably, they had been packed up and taken from the White House by Trump's aides in January 2021. In his first email to Trump attorneys and aides, Stern had explained that the Archives had learned that some twenty-four boxes of official records in the Trump residence had not been properly transferred to them, seemingly in violation of the Presidential Records Act.

"For example, the original correspondence between President Trump and North Korean Leader Kim Jong-un were not transferred to us," Stern wrote. Another missing piece was a letter President Obama had been publicly known to have left for President Trump on his first day in office.

"We know things were very chaotic, as they always are in the course of a one-term transition," Stern wrote, but "it is absolutely necessary that we obtain and account for all original Presidential records." Stern gave his cell phone number, adding: "Please let us know as soon as you can how we can get these issues resolved."

In follow-up calls and emails through that summer, though, Stern got no satisfaction. One Trump adviser quickly said he'd look into it, then said they had located the Kim Jong-un letters in Trump's Florida club, Mar-a-Lago. But nothing came.

"I am out of patience," Archivist David Ferriero emailed Stern after reading another round of vague promises from Trump attorneys.

In early September, the general counsel and the archivist had pulled out a big threat. If they didn't fork over the missing papers soon, they told Trump's lawyers, they were going to have to notify Congress and the Department of Justice.

"At this point, I am assuming they have been destroyed," an exasperated Ferriero told Mark Meadows by email. "In which case, I am obligated to report it to the Hill, DOJ and the White House."

That got Trump World's attention. In a flurry of calls and emails, Meadows and Trump's former Deputy White House Counsel Pat Philbin vowed to help figure this out. Eric Herschmann, the former White House counselor to Trump, met with the former president in November to offer some advice as a family friend.

"Give them back the documents," he warned. "Don't give them a noble excuse to indict you. They're going to take it."

Days before Christmas, Trump attorney Alex Cannon alerted Stern that Trump's staff had found twelve boxes of potential presidential records at Mar-a-Lago. That was only half the number that a White House recordkeeper had told Stern were loaded up and driven away from 1600 Pennsylvania Avenue. Nevertheless, the Archives staff began eagerly arranging for a trucking company to go to Palm Beach to pick them up and return them after the holidays.

Weeks later, on January 18, a total of fifteen boxes from Mar-a-Lago arrived safely at the Archives loading docks, and for a few hours, Stern began to feel triumphant.

Almost immediately, however, the situation unexpectedly turned more serious.

An Archives staffer named John Laster, who specialized in White House records, had begun a preliminary inventory of the boxes and within minutes made a shocking discovery. Inside a haphazardly packed banker's box, tucked in between newspaper clippings and notes, Laster encountered a document with classified markings. Soon he came upon another, then another. Some bore markings that Laster recognized as the telltale acronyms for the government's most closely held secrets, and yet many were also missing the color-coded folders typically used to shield their contents.

Laster immediately took the boxes to a secure room designed to review sensitive documents to continue his inventory.

"I wasn't joking about the classified docs just showing up in the midst of a stack of newspapers," Laster wrote to Stern and other Archives leaders in an urgent email summarizing his review just before midnight that night. The lack of any organization was consistent throughout the boxes. "There are a lot of classified records," he wrote. Some of the documents were part of the President's Daily Brief (PDF) books. Others involved highly classified operations, known as SAPs, or Special Access Programs. Knowledge of their existence was typically limited to a handful of government officials, who normally had to be authorized to be read into the program by a cabinet member or the president himself.

"I saw several docs that I think are PDBs," Laster wrote. "I also found an incredibly sensitive SAP document."

And a little more than a dozen of those carried the classification markings that were red sirens signaling they should never be out in the open. Some were marked TS/HCS/SCI, indicating that they involved human intelligence operations that were among the national security agencies' most carefully guarded secrets.

This wasn't what Stern had expected, and it had never happened before, presenting a huge question. What now? The documents had been White House documents, so Stern began by contacting a deputy White House counsel. That attorney, however, told Stern he should contact the office of Garland's number 2, Lisa Monaco, to get the Justice Department's advice. A top Monaco deputy, David Newman, instructed Stern to refer this unprecedented discovery to the inspectors general for both the Archives and the Office of the Director of National Intelligence. Newman also gave Stern a way to contact the heads of two Justice Department units that were almost always called in to investigate when there were instances of mishandling of classified records: the Public Integrity Section and the Counterintelligence and Export Control Section. There was, Stern quickly learned, an elaborate federal protocol for moments when classified documents were found "in the wind," and it got very serious, very fast.

The following week, Stern notified his own Inspector General's Office of the classified records discovery. It stunned the special agent in charge, Waleska McLellan, who had just been brought into the fraudulent electors probe.

The irony was thick. For more than a year, McLellan had wanted the Justice Department or other state investigators to take seriously the fake elector documents. For the first time, the department was finally doing just that. And yet McLellan had no choice but to temporarily turn her attention to this new matter involving classified records. Federal court dockets were littered with instances of government officials found wrongly possessing classified documents; by one count there had been over a hundred cases in the past five years. Their motives often hadn't really mattered to judges and juries. The stacks of highly sensitive government records shipped back from Mar-a-Lago were, by themselves, likely evidence of a federal crime that needed to be sorted out quickly. It was unclear who had seen the documents and if the country's intelligence-gathering methods had been compromised, up to and including possibly the lives of covert operatives abroad.

As the Archives' top investigator, McLellan now had to summarize the recovered records and evidence suggesting Trump or his staff might have committed crimes of mishandling classified records and violating the Espionage Act. Obviously, the Archives had had previous cases of sensitive missing or stolen government records. But the volume of classified records and the identity of the person who had possessed them made this unparalleled. When she was done, McLellan drafted a formal referral that explained the nature of the classified documents the Archives had discovered and asked the FBI to consider opening a criminal investigation into their mishandling.

In Washington, such a development was not going to stay secret for very long. At 6:00 a.m. on Monday, February 7, *The Washington Post* published a scoop that revealed the existence of the fifteen boxes. Within hours, the Archives released a statement confirming the find and saying Trump's aides had agreed to keep looking for any additional records that may have been taken to the president's Florida club. Without knowing that a criminal referral was already in the works, Democrats in Congress pounced. Trump had won the White House in large part by casting Hillary Clinton as a criminal for having retained and deleted government emails from a private server in her New York home. Suddenly, Trump, who had been impeached twice and was still in Congress's crosshairs for inciting January 6, looked like a hypocrite. By the end of the day, House

Oversight Committee Chairwoman Carolyn B. Maloney, a New York Democrat, vowed Congress would investigate.

The next morning, McLellan emailed her carefully documented referral for a possible criminal investigation to the Justice Department's leaders. That afternoon, a small cluster of officials at the Archives' Inspector General's Office dialed into a conference call with top leadership of Justice's National Security Division. The three senior-most officials responsible for prosecuting the mishandling of classified information, longtime colleagues reunited in the same office, stood around a desk phone set on speaker mode at Justice Department headquarters.

There was Olsen, plus two career deputies with whom he had overlapped over decades. Jay Bratt, the chief of the division's Counterintelligence and Export Control Office Section, which prosecuted classified document cases, had been a line prosecutor alongside Olsen in the D.C. U.S. Attorney's Office many years before. George Toscas, the deputy assistant attorney general for counterterrorism and counterespionage, was a Justice Department lifer and veteran of its most sensitive spy probes. Toscas felt lucky to have spent his career doing such meaningful work. As a college student, he had landed an internship in the U.S. Attorney's Office in his hometown of Chicago. Straight out of law school, he was hired as a trial lawyer as part of the Attorney General's Honors Program, the path for promising rookie lawyers to get training in exchange for their service. Toscas kept moving up the ladder, taking on bigger counterterrorism and counterintelligence jobs, including as counselor to the National Security Division, which Olsen helped stand up in 2006.

After a round of brief introductions, Archives officials explained the referral and summarized the fight the National Archives had waged to get Trump to return missing presidential records; the return of the boxes after the threat to draw in Congress; and the staff's discovery shortly thereafter of more than one hundred classified records scattered inside.

At the start of the call, Bratt, Toscas, and Olsen had been standing around with arms crossed, looking down at the speakerphone, listening to the chronology of events. The three remained expressionless, but

Bratt, Toscas, and Olsen would later tell colleagues they were floored by the details of what Trump had apparently taken from the White House. They were familiar with a few classified records here and there being improperly stored, or even some accidentally left on a desk, but this was a huge number of government secrets to discover unsecured for more than a year. Also, a significant number were marked as containing the government's most closely guarded secrets, programs that were "need-to-know" only and could involve covert operations and undercover spies. That a departing president had put these in cardboard boxes and kept them in his Florida club was stunning.

Toscas was the first to speak when they clicked off the line with the Archives. He had a flair for storytelling, but also several years of painful experience in politically contentious cases to back up what he was about to say. He had helped oversee key elements of a highly sensitive investigation called Midyear Exam, the probe into Hillary Clinton's use of a private email server in the summer of 2015, as well as the highly sensitive Crossfire Hurricane probe. Both investigations had created enormous headaches, controversies, and painful self-examination for the Justice Department, challenging Justice officials to take steps involving two potential presidents in the middle of an active campaign and even afterward.

"You should know this is a big deal," Toscas said. "Take a minute. Remember where you were when we got this call."

He underscored the unprecedented nature of the moment: They had just effectively been asked to open a criminal investigation into the forty-fifth president of the United States. Toscas's two colleagues smirked at his dramatic tone.

"For good or bad, this is history," Toscas insisted. "You were part of history."

Olsen gave Toscas a bemused eye roll.

"Aww, George," Olsen said teasingly. "Really?"

Toscas wasn't laughing.

"You watch," he said.

Toscas and Bratt then called Alan Kohler at FBI headquarters to give him the news. Kohler was the FBI's seasoned, no-nonsense assistant director for counterintelligence, and had been working in that field for more than two decades. With broad shoulders and a six-foot-one frame, as well as a shaved head, Kohler was imposing. He prided himself on reacting logically in the face of crisis; his job demanded it. In the hours after the 9/11 terror attacks, he'd been part of the FBI team sorting through evidence and clues at the burning crash site of the Pentagon. He later rose to run counterintelligence investigations of Russian threats and stood up the task force to track Russian efforts to interfere in U.S. presidential elections in 2017.

At the time, the counterintelligence boss had no fewer than six hundred terror and intelligence threats either literally or figuratively stacked on his desk, all requiring some kind of monitoring, assessment, or action. The last thing he and the FBI's counterintelligence unit needed was the job of chasing down classified documents that the former president may have spirited away to his part-time home and club. And few things knocked him for a loop, but after the call with his DOJ partners, he walked out of his office and into the larger suite outside looking dazed. Staffers noticed and waited for him to speak.

"You're never gonna believe the call I just got," he told his deputies.

Several of the faces of the teammates loosely clustered around the assistant director fell. Kohler took a beat to remind himself and his team they couldn't get worked up and start worrying about the fact that this referral centered on the former president.

"We just have to work the problem," Kohler told them.

When the story became public the next day, the reaction from both sides of the political spectrum was demonstrative. Months of growing frustration among Democrats over the Justice Department's lack of action suddenly swirled together with the new, concrete revelations that Trump had left the White House with sensitive government secrets. It sent left-leaning lawyers, politicians, Hollywood celebrities, and other influencers into paroxysms of anger at the department's seeming reluctance to hold Trump accountable. More than ever, that frustration was directed at the attorney general.

"Gosh it seems everyone and every institution in the USA is calling on the DOJ to DO ITS FUCKING JOB," actor John Cusack wrote to his 1.8 million followers on Twitter, reacting to a post about the Archives' referral to DOJ. "Every day garland cowers from his responsibilities another asshole is emboldened to do whatever the fuck they want. . . . Why should anyone respect the law? AG garland?"

[24]

Operation "Arctic Frost"

Unbeknownst to Garland's vocal critics, 391 days after the attack on the U.S. Capitol, the Justice Department took one of the first critical steps to gather evidence about a possible fake electors scheme to keep Donald Trump in power. On Monday, January 31, 2022, federal prosecutor Thomas Windom secretly convened a grand jury that could be used to authorize subpoenas for cell-phone records, documents, and interviews.

The next day, Windom and his boss, U.S. Attorney Matt Graves, led a meeting via secure video link with his counterpart U.S. attorneys from the seven states where fake elector documents originated. Each could have independently investigated the matter. But Graves made the argument that any charges involving the fabricated documents should be filed in D.C., where the January 6 case was based and where Trump allies had submitted the doctored certificates to Congress and the National Archives. Windom walked the seven U.S. attorneys through the available evidence and possible charges: 18 USC 1512—obstruction of a government proceeding; 1519—alteration of government documents;

371—conspiracy. And there were potentially others, including mail fraud and wire fraud. Windom said he and his D.C. team had identified eighty-four people nationwide who might have been involved in forging, signing, and couriering the documents, and he had an even longer list of additional people to interview. There was little debate on the call. Graves had the support of Main Justice, and his counterparts agreed not to launch any separate probes.

Though the U.S. government was finally probing a possible criminal conspiracy to obstruct the congressional certification of the 2020 presidential election result, Windom remained the only full-time prosecutor on the case out of one hundred thirteen thousand on the DOJ payroll. None of the thirty-eight thousand FBI employees were yet cleared to join. Instead, with the help of McLellan, Windom had cobbled together a makeshift team of two inspector general agents from the National Archives and agents at the U.S. Postal Inspection Service.

Deputies to Graves and D'Antuono went back and forth over the first weeks of February on the factual justification to allow the FBI to open an investigation, trading drafts of a Bureau document known as an EC, for the authority it grants agents to get suspects' phone and other electronic communications. Until the bosses signed off, FBI agents were not cleared to subpoena evidence or interview potential subjects. On February 14, Timothy Thibault, the head of the Criminal Division under D'Antuono in the Washington Field Office, circulated a nearly final version—and that would open a "full" investigation, Bureau code for allowing agents to use all the FBI's vast tools for the case. "This full investigation is predicated on information subjects conspired to provide knowingly false statements to the United States Government for the purpose of corrupting the 2020 US Presidential election."

The draft for Operation "Arctic Frost" cited as justification a series of facts that had been publicly available for nearly a year.

It included copies of the fraudulent certificates that appeared to be coordinated; American Oversight had published them in March 2021, eleven months earlier. This was the same evidence that McLellan of the National Archives had spotted weeks before January 6 and unsuccessfully urged the U.S. Attorney's Office to investigate.

Additionally, the FBI draft cited other facts known publicly before the attack, including December 2020 statements by GOP officials in swing states that they would use "alternate electors" to challenge Biden's win. It also quoted top Trump legal advisers Eastman and Boris Epshteyn in an appearance on Steve Bannon's *War Room* podcast on January 2, 2021—four days before the attack. Epshteyn and Eastman had gone further, discussing that if electors disagreed about who won, Pence had the power to reject some state results and refuse to certify the election. When an EC involves a politician or people close to one, Bureau lawyers deem a case a SIM, or "sensitive investigative matter." Approving a SIM is a tense undertaking, because the subject's identity could become public during the probe. The proposed subject of this SIM made it the ultimate sensitive matter.

On February 24, Thibault emailed Crabb in the U.S. Attorney's Office with news of the FBI investigators' decision on subjects. After review, "we believe there to be predication to include former President of the United States Donald J. Trump as a predicated subject." Trump wasn't the only one. He was atop a long list of electors who signed the fraudulent elector documents, as well as his campaign and people who had acted on its behalf.

Because this was a SIM that could involve the former president, it also triggered what agents referred to simply as "the Barr memo," which the former attorney general had issued in the wake of the Mueller investigation. In this case, it required that both the attorney general and the FBI director sign off on opening the investigation. Prosecutors in the D.C. office waited for weeks, and kept checking. Why hadn't the FBI produced the EC yet? But inside the FBI, the notion of again investigating Trump and his campaign had revived painful comparisons to the FBI's controversial Crossfire Hurricane investigation, the origins of the Mueller probe. Wray had not been in the director's chair when the probe of

Russian contacts with Trump's campaign began, although he had fought GOP attempts to undermine the FBI over its role and Trump's threats to fire him for it. This time, Wray wanted to make sure that the Bureau's decision-making stood up to future scrutiny. If the Bureau opened a case file on anyone close to the former president, there could be no mistake.

Garland was content to wait. Returning the department to regular order meant letting decisions—especially those that could be viewed as touching on politics—bubble up to him.

As the FBI's hand-wringing continued, criticism of Garland approached a fever pitch in the weeks after the Mar-a-Lago documents scandal burst into public view. The attorney general and several of his top aides found the growing chorus of critics confounding. The naysayers were overwhelmingly on the left. Didn't they see he was differentiating himself from Barr and rebuilding the institution's integrity by being careful and deliberate?

Eager to address the growing criticism, Garland's staff encouraged him to accept a media interview with longtime Justice Department reporter Carrie Johnson at NPR to mark the one-year anniversary of his Senate confirmation and time as attorney general. Garland told Johnson the investigation of the riot and the attempt to interfere with the country's tradition of the peaceful transfer of power was the "most urgent investigation in the history of the Justice Department." Garland had been attentive and engaged on the many threads of the January 6 riot investigation. But the longtime appellate judge's definition of urgency was up for debate, especially around the question of Trump's responsibility for the attack.

In March 2022, while the FBI was still secretly debating whether it had reasonable basis to open an investigation into Trump's role in the fake electors scam, George and the other federal prosecutors leading the congressional investigation were half a year ahead of DOJ. The Gold Team were a weary bunch, having interviewed more than one hundred Trump advisers, White House aides, and other witnesses. They faced another packed week of interviews ahead. They typically had to prepare for and conduct four interviews a week, each running up to nine hours long. The small team would wrap one interview, grab another cup of coffee at the end of a long day, then spend the rest of the night preparing for the next day's session. The grueling pace had paid off: The team had learned fascinating new details about, and in some areas, whole new chapters of, the brazen plans Trump entertained and sometimes acted on to try to hold on to power. Just that month, staff secretary Derek Lyons described to them an unhinged Oval Office meeting in late December 2020 at which Trump discussed with aides a secret plan to access voting machine data and software in Georgia.

Also in March, members of the Gold Team were about to hit pay dirt in court.

After Trump's election night defeat, Eastman penned a barefaced theory he shared with Trump advisers for how the president could remain in power. The memo, which had been revealed in Woodward and Costa's *Peril*, had jumped out to George because it imagined a scenario in which seven swing states sent "dual" slates of electors to Congress, with the second set challenging Biden's win. Eastman claimed Vice President Pence, presiding over Congress's certification of the electoral vote on January 6, could cite the competing slates as justification to either cast Biden's win into question or unilaterally declare Trump the next president.

The team learned that Pence's lawyer, Greg Jacobs, had dubbed Eastman "the serpent in Trump's ear."

Like others, the white-haired, blue-eyed Eastman had refused to answer the committee's questions, citing attorney-client privilege. But the Gold Team spotted a potential opening. If the president had let a random law professor sit in on discussions with campaign lawyers, maybe a judge would find his emails weren't protected by privilege.

The team also noticed a Southern California institution they could approach for records. Eastman used a chapman.edu email in some of his consultations with Trump and other administration officials about disputing the election. It was his email address as a former dean and professor at Chapman law school, and not his personal or any White House account.

The fight for Eastman's emails set off a chain reaction that would propel the House investigation forward, and in ways even the Gold Team did not foresee. Eastman had sued to block the Gold Team's subpoena in federal court in California, drawing in as a referee of sorts a no-nonsense federal judge named David O. Carter. When Carter was randomly assigned to the case, Lucier, the young standout corporate lawyer who had been recommended for the congressional investigation by none other than Pence's attorney, called her Gold Team colleague Marc Harris for intel. Harris had worked many cases in Carter's courthouse and knew the judge by reputation. The Clinton appointee was a former lieutenant in the Marine Corps who had fought in Vietnam and the battle of Khe Sanh and had won the Bronze Star and Purple Heart.

"What do you know about this judge?" she asked.

"Carter will work really hard, and he'll make others work really hard too," Harris told Lucier. He typically got into the weeds of his cases quickly and expected the lawyers to keep up with his pace, Harris added. That proved true straight out of the gate. Eastman sued on a Thursday; Carter scheduled a hearing for the following Monday.

About two-thirds of the way through that first hearing, Carter surprised the House investigators with a critical question: Did they think it likely that former President Donald Trump, whom Eastman was advising on his effort to stay in power, had engaged in a crime in seeking to reject and block the 2020 election results?

The judge turned to Doug Letter, the general counsel for the House of Representatives, and the investigator's lawyer, about the argument he hadn't heard the committee make.

"Mr. Letter," the judge began, "if the House Select Committee's purpose involves investigating sedition, which is a federal crime, why is the committee not raising the crime-fraud exception?"

The idea went to the heart of the committee's investigation: Had Trump engaged in a crime and relied on Eastman's legal advice to do so?

Lucier and her colleagues felt a jolt as they listened remotely from their office back in O'Neill. Carter had just handed the Gold Team an opportunity—an invitation even—to think more boldly about whether they had sufficient evidence to argue Donald Trump's efforts to stay in power were criminal.

Letter tap-danced to give the committee time to weigh the move. "Your Honor, that is something that, if there were further proceedings in this case, we would certainly look very closely at."

Members and senior staff deliberated over the following days and then gave investigators their marching orders: It was time to seize the opening by Judge Carter and lay out the case that Trump had engaged in a crime, with Eastman as his loyal henchman.

"We have to assert the crime-fraud exception," Liz Cheney said in a weekend conference call.

George, used to carefully assembling criminal prosecutions in the U.S. Attorney's Office in Florida, told some that he shared the team's excitement about what a possible crime-fraud ruling in the House's favor would mean for the investigation, but warned that Trump supporters could spin a ruling against the committee as exoneration.

Over the next two weeks, the Gold Team and their House lawyers frantically worked on pieces of what became known as the Frankenstein Brief. Small subteams were responsible for drafting separate sections that argued different reasons they felt Eastman's documents weren't protected and should be turned over. A big blank space was left in the draft with the words "Insert crime-fraud here?" As that section was drafted, George and others became a sort of red team, looking for vulnerabilities in each claim that Eastman had likely participated in a crime.

Cheney made clear the committee *would* pull that trigger and argue to Carter that Trump had more likely than not acted criminally in their next pleading, due March 2. A newly hired lawyer, Brittany Record, a former clerk to Justices Ruth Bader Ginsburg and Stephen Breyer, teamed up with Lucier on the draft. Together the factual evidence the pair laid out became devastatingly sharp.

Even George now resoundingly agreed. Their brief made two claims. The first was that Trump, with Eastman's counsel, had tried to obstruct an official proceeding, the certification of the vote by Congress. Next, they alleged Trump engaged in a conspiracy to defraud the United States, by also conspiring to block the certification. On March 28, just four weeks after receiving their filing, Judge Carter handed down his decision. The pages crafted by Record and Lucier won the day.

"Dr. [John] Eastman and President Trump launched a campaign to overturn a democratic election, an action unprecedented in American history," Carter wrote in his opinion. "Their campaign was not confined to the ivory tower—it was a coup in search of a legal theory. The plan spurred violent attacks on the seat of our nation's government, led to the deaths of several law enforcement officers, and deepened public distrust in our political process."

He continued: "Based on the evidence, the Court finds it more likely than not that President Trump corruptly attempted to obstruct the Joint Session of Congress on January 6, 2021."

These were also some of the same crimes that Windom's fledgling team at Justice had just begun to eye in their fake electors case. They were also the crimes that, on the day of Carter's ruling, the FBI's lawyers and supervisors were still debating whether they should formally begin investigating.

In his written opinion, Judge Carter took the opportunity to speak harshly and directly to the Department of Justice. He asked whether and when the country's premier law enforcement agency ever planned to act on such extensive evidence of crimes. He said the facts demanded that those responsible for this Machiavellian caper be held accountable, something neither he nor the House committee could do in their civil case centered on whether a professor-turned-Trump adviser had to fork over emails.

"More than a year after the attack on our Capitol, the public is still searching for accountability. This case cannot provide it," Carter wrote. "If Dr. Eastman and President Trump's plan had worked, it would have permanently ended the peaceful transition of power, undermining American democracy and the Constitution. If the country does not commit to investigating and pursuing accountability for those responsible, the Court fears January 6 will repeat itself."

Carter's decision spurred a defensive flinch for some back in Washington, especially on the seventh floor of the FBI's Hoover Building. It was the end of March and the Bureau had by that time spent two months in debate without approving the contours of its investigation of the fake electors scheme. It turned out that the recommendation by FBI case agents to name Trump as a subject of the probe had touched off an intense internal review, and was contributing to the delay.

No judge's opinion changed the fact that to investigate any American, the FBI had to pass its own rigorous tests. Wray insisted that senior leadership take an active role.

Wray, a standout lawyer in his own right, asked his counsel Jason Jones to conduct a deep analysis of whether the evidence linking Trump was solid enough to justify naming him. Jones had started out as a federal prosecutor in Brooklyn and risen to senior Justice Department ranks before working at the same firm as Wray.

Jones pored over the agents' draft, and then sought more information from Graves and Crabb at the U.S. Attorney's Office. Amid the daily deluge of incoming national security and other pressing decisions—including how to deal with the just-discovered classified documents found at the ex-president's home in Florida—the review had stretched out over a month, and then into another. Jones eventually told Graves and Crabb that he saw plenty of reason to name several Trump advisers as well as the president's campaign, but without having agents begin the actual work of investigating, he saw no information that Trump himself should be named as an investigative target.

Atop the FBI building, Jones, Wray, his chief of staff, Jonathan Lenzner, and Deputy Director Paul Abbate discussed this high-stakes matter repeatedly. It was a near certainty that the Bureau would eventually be called before Congress and possibly internal watchdogs to explain and defend taking the consequential step—again—of investigating a U.S. president.

Reviewing the evidence one more time, Jones recommended the FBI name the campaign but not Trump. If agents found more direct evidence linking Trump, he said, "You can always add someone later."

Briefed on the decision, Monaco's deputies huddled with Graves to discuss the impact. Would this impede the investigation? Graves said he didn't think so. With or without naming Trump, he mostly wanted the Bureau to decide and open the case so that Windom would have the agents needed to conduct dozens of interviews and other work.

Finally, on the morning of April 14, a couple of Wray's deputies appeared at Garland's routine morning threats briefing to present a document for the attorney general's review. The subject was highly sensitive and shared only on an absolutely-need-to-know basis, so only a few of Garland's deputies were allowed to stay behind when it was time for Wray's staff to explain the contours of the electors investigation the FBI was prepared to open. The attorney general, who had been briefed on previous drafts, quickly read this final document once and signed it on the spot and handed it back to a member of Wray's staff.

When Wray's team had departed the AG's conference room and some of Garland's aides returned, they found Garland's surprisingly quick go-ahead on this consequential new investigation had created a mildly embarrassing problem. Justice Department leadership had no copy of the document opening one of the single most sensitive domestic investigations that Garland might ever authorize as attorney general.

"This is a pretty important document," said one person involved. Top DOJ staff were sent scrambling, and later in the day the FBI located the original and sent back a signed copy.

With the all-clear, Jamie Garman and Michelle Ball, the two seasoned FBI public corruption agents who had been tentatively assigned to the case, could now fully join the probe and begin interviewing witnesses. The FBI could also officially start using its electronic case management system to track and log evidence, and flex its extensive muscle to demand that witnesses hand over their laptops and cell phones. Garman, a former federal prosecutor in Miami, had already won over the team with her smart questions. Once Archives agents finished bringing Garman up to speed on the pieces of the fake electors plot, they privately remarked that they saw a switch flip inside her as she grasped the scheme.

The coalescing team recognized the good chemistry the FBI agents added to the government's fledgling investigation. But a new point of tension with the much more advanced congressional investigation was about to flare.

Six days after Wray and Garland approved the FBI opening an investigation into Trump's close advisers and his 2020 presidential campaign, the Justice Department formally asked the House Select Committee to turn over its trove of evidence to the federal agency beginning a criminal probe. The April 20 letter, signed by Graves and Assistant Attorney General Kenneth A. Polite Jr., who headed the Criminal Division at Main Justice, was sent to the committee without public fanfare. It asked the committee for access to transcripts of the testimony of all witnesses who had given the committee their accounts of events, and for witnesses it might interview in the future. By this stage, the committee asserted it had interviewed and obtained documents from more than one thousand people. This was a highly unusual break in the natural order of how DOJ operated. The feds almost never came behind a congressional investigation, and this awkward reversal of the normal pecking order proved why Justice nearly always took first position. Coming second significantly weakened the department's hand.

As Justice ramped up its probe, Graves and Monaco and their deputies knew that transcripts of the committee's witness interviews could deliver both gold and protection for the federal investigation. First, the interview transcripts could provide leads to help speed up the DOJ's work. More importantly, federal investigators had to know exactly what witnesses had already said under oath to Congress to avoid problems with challenges to their accounts later. Even the most well-intentioned, cooperative witnesses could inadvertently describe the same event differently on two separate occasions and risk having their testimony tossed out as worthless at trial.

In a private briefing, Heaphy told the committee's lawmakers he had no objections to providing some select information, though DOJ said they wanted all transcripts. "Let's try to find a compromise," Heaphy replied. But Heaphy's clients, the members of the House committee, did not want to share their work product. The committee had blazed a trail long before DOJ indicated an interest in the subject of Trump's attempt to overthrow a democratic American election. Their work had pieced together Trump's multipronged plot to block Biden's victory, and Heaphy's investigators were now sketching out a plan for a string of televised hearings on their findings. They hoped to launch the big reveal in a prime-time television broadcast in May.

Chairman Bennie Thompson and Vice Chair Liz Cheney were adamant; they weren't going to hand over their hard-earned discoveries to the Justice Department and possibly jeopardize their fact-finding. The members of congress sent word. The answer was no. Justice would have to start its investigation from scratch. "Congress is not DOJ's staff," Cheney told her inner circle.

[25]

"I Don't Want Anybody Looking Through My Boxes"

The Justice Department's priority in cases involving missing classified material had long been to move quickly to recover the nation's mishandled secrets. That had been the guiding principle even in the rare instances when doing so risked embarrassing a military general or other prominent government official.

But in the late spring of 2022, Justice Department leaders discovered that same sense of urgency didn't seem to apply when it came to classified records that had turned up haphazardly in boxes that former President Trump returned to the National Archives. Instead, FBI agents were reluctant to press and didn't see a need to search his properties for additional records. Trump, after all, was no usual case. He had sat in the Oval Office with the power to decide if government secrets were classified or not, and despite leaving office under the cloud of January 6, he had managed to remain a mighty power in national politics. This new conflict was quickly dredging up a stress-inducing dynamic the Bureau rank and file were all too familiar with.

For the first half of 2022, Trump chose to publicly dispute that the

Archives had found anything improper, characterizing his transfer of documents back to D.C. in December 2021 as voluntary and routine for a former president. He sought to control the narrative and put National Archives and Justice Department investigators on the defensive.

"Much of this material will someday be displayed in the Donald J. Trump Presidential Library for the public to view my Administration's incredible accomplishments for the American People," he said in one February statement.

Trump also feigned outrage, blaming the media for unfairly casting aspersions on what he called a minor misunderstanding about presidential records. Working with the Archives to secure his legacy was a "great honor," he said, and the appropriate documents had been sent to the government records agency following "collaborative and respectful discussions."

Behind closed doors at his luxury beach club, however, Trump privately fumed, in May and June of 2022, that these records were his personal property that he had a right to keep, both for posterity and possible future leverage. As federal investigators kept pressing for a full accounting, Trump acted deviously when his lawyers were out of sight. Aides had initially moved nearly seventy boxes to Mar-a-Lago when he left the White House in January 2021. After he had relinquished a fraction of those, Trump instructed a trusted valet he had brought from the White House to help move—and seemingly conceal—portions of the remaining trove. Back in Washington, FBI Director Chris Wray set out dueling goals for how the Bureau would approach the sensitive investigation. In discussions with his leadership team that were soon conveyed down the chain as orders, Wray wanted agents to treat the case like any other. The FBI had a duty to retrieve and secure highly sensitive documents that should never have left government custody, he told them. It didn't matter to Wray that the unsecured location of these government documents was a part-time home of a former president, one who had several times threatened to fire him. He repeated his well-worn mantra that by now his deputies had memorized.

"We follow the facts where they lead, wherever they lead, to whomever they lead," the director so often said.

Yet a competing Wray directive kept agents and supervisors from moving as quickly as they had in many previous missing records cases. Wray—and Garland—wanted the Bureau to proceed with caution, so that every *i* was dotted and every *t* crossed. In early February, Abbate gave Alan Kohler, the FBI's assistant director of counterintelligence, approval for an early-stage investigation, after asking several questions to be sure it was appropriate. The agents soon wanted to eyeball the classified documents that Trump had returned in order to gauge the seriousness of the situation. In late February, the agents learned just how much top-secret material had exited the White House. The Archives staff reported they had found 767 pages of classified records, scattered in twelve of the fifteen returned boxes. Some were ho-hum documents that didn't set off alarms—classified as secret as a matter of course. Those included memos chronicling some of Trump's diplomatic calls with foreign leaders. But 140 pages were marked top secret or referred to top-secret subjects.

By Bureau standards, the sheer volume and nature of the returned documents necessitated serious and quick action. On March 30, two months after the Archives first alerted the Justice Department to their discovery of classified documents, Garland and Wray formally approved a full criminal investigation into who was responsible for the sensitive documents being spirited to Mar-a-Lago and for the possible resulting damage to national security. Compared to many previous classified documents cases, this was slow and already enough time to search a property, arrest a suspect, and begin preparing for prosecution. But due to complexities of the documents involving a former president, agents in the Mar-a-Lago case had not even been able to see the documents and begin assessing the potential damage to the country from having such documents in the wind.

First, the Department of Justice had to ask President Biden formally to let the FBI look at these sensitive presidential records. Biden granted that request on April 11, and through his White House counsel asked the Archives to give agents access. The next day, the Archives tackled their next legal hurdle: notifying former President Trump so he or his lawyers could have the opportunity to review the documents, before or at the same time the agents did. According to a competing law, former President Trump had a right to look over his own presidential records from the fifteen boxes.

"The Presidential Records Act was not written with the idea of a president withholding classified records," one senior Justice official later said with a shrug.

In a private meeting in mid-April, Attorney General Merrick Garland shared a concern with Olsen about whether more sensitive records might be stashed at Mar-a-Lago. Should they consider a search warrant? Olsen told his national security team and they wrestled with the question for about thirty minutes before reaching agreement: They just didn't have probable cause yet to suspect Trump or his staff were engaged in the crime of withholding other records.

Over the month of April, Trump's new lawyer running point on the documents case, Evan Corcoran, used his client's special status to plead for time. Corcoran, like several other Trump lawyers, lacked the security clearance to review the documents now in the Archives' storage vault and struggled to find someone who did. He didn't mention that obstacle in his letters to the Archives, but repeatedly asked them to delay letting the FBI look at the records. In a follow-up letter at the end of April, Corcoran made the bold claim that Trump likely had a right to assert executive privilege over some of the records and thereby withhold them from investigators.

While the FBI was awaiting clearance to review the documents in April and early May, Jay Bratt, the National Security Division prosecutor overseeing the documents probe at Main Justice, focused on opening a grand jury to investigate the likely criminal mishandling of these sensitive documents.

A new archivist, Debra Seidel Wall, had just taken over running the Archives for her retiring predecessor that week. She consulted with a bevy of government lawyers about the matter and concluded that Corcoran's privilege claim didn't hold up. On May 10, an exasperated-sounding Wall notified Corcoran by email that these delays in such an urgent matter couldn't continue. She told him the former president was not the final arbiter of which documents should be shielded due to executive privilege; President Biden was.

"I have concluded that there is no reason to grant your request for a further delay before the FBI and others in the Intelligence Community begin their reviews," Wall wrote. "Accordingly, NARA will provide the FBI access to the records in question, as requested by the incumbent President, beginning as early as Thursday, May 12, 2022."

At the same time, the attorney general told Olsen he remained highly concerned about state secrets that might still remain at Mar-a-Lago and could be obtained by foreign adversaries. This time, when Olsen met with his national security prosecutors, including Bratt, they agreed on a middle path. They would begin drafting a subpoena demanding that Trump return any outstanding documents.

The next day, May 11, was a big one. The FBI was cleared to begin its review, but faced a logistical challenge. Due to the highly sensitive nature of the documents, FBI agents had to locate special copiers used only for imaging top-secret papers—and then truck them over to the Archives' headquarters. Agents spent hours copying the key records so they could take them to their own SCIF and spend time carefully reading and analyzing them. The same day, Bratt issued a subpoena he had drafted. Addressed to the office of the former president and transmitted to Corcoran, the document seemed historic. It demanded that Trump and his advisers return "any and all documents or writings" in Trump's custody that bore specific classification markings. Without knowing what specific sensitive records might be at Mar-a-Lago, Bratt simply repeated the long list of classification categories found in the fifteen boxes Trump had already returned. The response deadline was in two weeks, May 24, but Bratt told Corcoran he could extend the date.

With brown hair and pale skin and a short, stocky build, Bratt had worked many years in the D.C. U.S. Attorney's Office before heading to the Main Justice office that rode herd on cases of mishandled classified records. He was known for his careful, even persnickety approach. Amiable but not chatty, Bratt generally sought to keep a low profile and keep his personal opinions and emotions on lock. But this case tested his normally cool demeanor.

He worked closely with Julie Edelstein, who was DOJ's resident expert on securing national secrets and had participated in almost every significant investigation of government officials taking or mishandling classified records. Amid all the delays that prosecutors and agents encountered that spring, the duo had worried most about possible additional documents remaining at Mar-a-Lago. The two had come to the consensus that the FBI should conduct a search at Mar-a-Lago as soon as possible to ensure there were no other national security secrets in the wind. They had even begun planning how to get a warrant.

A search—whether voluntary or a court-ordered surprise—was a natural next step in a classified documents case, especially because such top-secret documents had already been discovered. Plus, the Archives still hadn't accounted for all the high-profile records it suspected were missing. Trump also had been known to retire to the White House residence at night with papers from the Oval Office. Archive staffers had found some of those papers mixed in with his personal mementos. It seemed entirely possible there could be more of both. Many agents recalled the search of FBI analyst Kendra Kingsbury's home, where they found evidence she was routinely taking classified records from work. At the time of the indictment, a year prior, the FBI leadership praised the Bureau's devotion to holding even their own to account.

"The defendant, who's well trained in handling classified information, put her country's sensitive secrets at risk," Kohler said in a news release the day Kingsbury was arrested and charged with felonies—crimes for which she later pleaded guilty and was sent to prison. "The FBI will go to great lengths to investigate individuals who put their own interests above U.S. national security, including when the individual is an FBI employee."

But Bratt warned Toscas and Olsen that the normally gung-ho squad at the FBI's Washington Field Office was still unusually skittish.

"We may have a problem," Bratt said. "These guys do not want to do a search."

The idea of rifling through the home of a former president made the Washington Field Office agents and even FBI supervisors in headquarters like Kohler recoil, Bratt explained to his DOJ bosses. Since 2016, FBI agents had taken a beating. They faced accusations they were political tools when they had investigated Hillary Clinton and again when investigating Trump's campaign for its contacts with Russian operatives.

The May 11 subpoena to turn over any remaining classified documents was the compromise that Bratt, Toscas, and Olsen reached to protect any remaining sensitive records while the criminal investigation proceeded.

On May 18, Bratt and two FBI agents from the Washington Field Office traveled to Palm Beach, Florida, to interview Trump aides. Just before 10:00 a.m., they met in a lawyer's rented office space in Lake Worth with a Trump aide who provided a turning point in the probe. Molly Michael had previously worked in the Trump White House as an assistant just outside the Oval Office and had followed him to Florida to again serve as an assistant in his postpresidential office. She was cooperative but seemed nervous as the interview started; investigators noticed Michael was shivering at times and hoped it wasn't from fear but the office's frigid air-conditioning and her sleeveless dress. Michael felt loyal to Trump and didn't want to hurt him, but she had a duty to tell the truth. Her lawyer Dan Benson knew that she had important evidence to share.

After a break in the interview, agents asked about records that might still be at Mar-a-Lago, and Michael pulled out a printed copy of a picture that was worth a thousand words: It showed rows and rows of boxes, some the same brown boxes Trump used to store documents from his time at the White House and some white ones staff used to pack up for his departure. There were as many as eighty or ninety, stacked up against an outer wall of the club storage room. It made clear that Trump possessed far more than the fifteen boxes he returned to the Archives in January. Michael, in fact, said she saw many such boxes remaining *after* Trump advisers made their January shipment to the Archives. In theory, there was little reason for Trump to have so many. Nearly all Trump's documents from the White House were public records that the law required the Archives to maintain. Plus, why did Trump still have so many more when he claimed he had returned everything of import in January?

Michael provided a general timeline of Trump's move from the White House and described how so many documents ended up at Mar-a-Lago. Though she couldn't recall some specific dates, she had transformed the fledgling investigation.

Bratt and the agents returned to the FBI's West Palm Beach office immediately after the interview to brief Toscas and FBI superiors by phone.

"There are more boxes," Bratt said.

Olsen, the assistant attorney general, winced when Toscas shared the update from Florida. This increased the risk that classified records were at the club and could be compromised by foreign foes.

"We should have done a search," Olsen told his team.

The assistant attorney general knew investigators would normally press for an urgent search based on this witness's information. But because of the Justice Department's compromise subpoena, served just a week earlier, Olsen argued the best course now was to wait for Trump and his lawyers to respond by the May 24 deadline.

Garland, upon being briefed by Olsen about this development, wasn't convinced of that. Shouldn't they search Mar-a-Lago? he asked. Olsen advised they now needed to wait for Trump's response to the subpoena.

"But . . . wouldn't we have searched anyone else's property with these circumstances?" Garland asked.

In subsequent meetings on the case, the attorney general kept pressing prosecutors to explain why a search wasn't warranted. Toscas told Garland they had certainly executed searches at this stage in other records cases, but they needed to wait the few days for Trump's response. Some took small comfort knowing they had ordered Trump staff to install a lock on the storage room to secure the records.

"Sir, this is the way we're going to do it. Step by step," Toscas said. "The threat here is different."

At the FBI Washington Field Office, some supervisors wanted to pump the brakes harder. The word of one aide wasn't sufficient evidence to take the bold step of searching a former president's home. Derek Pieper, a D'Antuono deputy, said a witness seeing boxes of records wasn't the same as seeing classified documents. Kohler backed the agents' insistence that they get more evidence before taking that leap. A search of Trump's club would require an airtight case that Trump or someone in his orbit had withheld documents, he argued.

"What if the person who said there are classified documents still at Mar-a-Lago is a donor to Hillary Clinton?" Kohler reasoned with his DOJ counterparts. "We're gonna look stupid."

The FBI agents began researching the witness's background to be safe.

At a meeting in Main Justice in late May, Garland, Wray, and their deputies discussed how to proceed based on this new lead. Some DOJ officials in the room were leaning toward seeking a judge's approval for a search warrant. A senior adviser to the deputy attorney general repeated one of Garland's mantras.

"We're going to treat this case like we treat all cases," the aide said. "We're going to treat this like a regular case."

Kohler and Wray exchanged a look, enough so that others in the room noticed. Kohler wasn't too shy to say what he was thinking.

"The fact that we're in a room together talking about this makes clear: This is not a regular case," Kohler said. The attorney general, the FBI director and assistant director "don't handle search warrants."

Meanwhile, at Mar-a-Lago, Trump was unaware of the investigators' new lead and scheduled to meet with his two criminal defense attorneys on that very issue of responding to the subpoena. On May 23, lawyers Evan Corcoran and Jennifer Little flew to Palm Beach to explain the gravity of the situation to their client and to urge him to comply with the now twelve-day-old federal subpoena. Corcoran felt assured Bratt would extend the deadline a week or so. Once inside the grand lobby of Trump's club, the pair was escorted to Trump's private office, and there they planned to walk him through the steps for doing as the government demanded.

Six-foot-two and silver-haired, Corcoran had many years earlier worked as a federal prosecutor in the U.S. Attorney's Office in D.C. Having come to Trump's attention when he had represented Steve Bannon on a contempt charge, Corcoran had just weeks earlier decided to take on this famous and famously difficult client whom some of the nation's best criminal defense lawyers had politely declined. Corcoran, who hadn't practiced law for more than six years, told close friends he saw this new job representing one of the most recognized political figures in the world as a possible banner comeback.

Trump had earlier hired Little, a criminal defense lawyer out of Atlanta, and her firm to represent him in a Georgia investigation. More than a year earlier, a county prosecutor there had taken up what Justice hadn't and begun looking at Trump's pressure on state election officials to declare fraud in the Georgia election. Young and pretty, with blond highlights in her long hair, Little resembled many of the women Trump had hired as White House assistants. She also had a strong track record as a Georgia prosecutor and, before Corcoran's arrival, was one of the few Trump lawyers with criminal defense experience.

But immediately Corcoran and Little faced both bluster and

headwinds from Trump. The former president started by lambasting the Justice Department for unfairly targeting him.

Without a break, Trump then proceeded for several more minutes to lay out how well he was doing in extremely early polling for the 2024 election and his plan to announce his candidacy for president. Corcoran, normally parsimonious with his words and not given to grandstanding, tried to interrupt Trump and return the conversation to the subpoena they were there to discuss. Corcoran warned Trump they had to conduct a review to make sure they returned any classified records still on the property.

"I don't want anybody looking through my boxes, I really don't," Trump told the two lawyers. "I don't want you looking through my boxes."

Trump paused for a moment, looking at the two, seeming to still wish the issue away:

"Wouldn't it be better if we just told them we don't have anything here?"

Corcoran warned Trump gently of the risk of the FBI showing up at his property to forcibly collect the records. "There's a prospect that they could go to a judge and get a search warrant, and that they could arrive here," he said.

During a break in the meeting, Little privately shared with Corcoran the warning she'd received from another Trump lawyer: that Trump would "go ballistic" over complying with the subpoena and "that he was going to deny that there were any more boxes at all."

Little warned Trump of the new legal jeopardy he faced. Unlike with the Archives' unenforceable requests, Little said, Trump and his lawyers would now have to sign a document swearing to a court that they had done a diligent search for any classified records and returned all that they found. "Once this is signed—if anything else is located—it's going to be a crime," she warned.

Trump looked surprised, then said: "OK, I get it."

Trump proposed that Corcoran return June 2 to search for any remaining classified records in the boxes at the property. Trump and his aides had indicated all White House–era records were in a storage room under the club's main dining room. Corcoran figured he could turn over any sensitive records to the government by June 3. He flew back to Baltimore, arriving at midnight, then rose at dawn the next day to drive to his daughter's graduation at Princeton. In his car, he spoke aloud notes into his iPhone, using the long drive to make a record of his conversation with his client. But two things were happening that Corcoran had no idea about.

First, Bratt had been trying to connect with Corcoran to convey the government's urgent need for Trump to return all outstanding documents by the date on the subpoena, May 24. Bratt finally reached Corcoran on his cell phone in Princeton that evening.

"You gotta give us the documents tomorrow," Bratt said.

Corcoran was angry, not only at being interrupted at his daughter's celebration, but at Bratt now refusing to be flexible: "This is fucking bullshit—you are reneging on the deal."

Trump's lawyer said Bratt would have to issue a new subpoena, and they might have to sort this out with a judge. The second thing Corcoran didn't know was that Trump had plans to review the records himself before Corcoran returned. Late on May 23, Trump told his valet, Walt Nauta, he needed his help. The next evening, on May 24, Nauta removed three boxes from the storage room. On the morning of May 30, Trump and Nauta spoke by phone briefly. An hour later, Nauta removed a much larger number—about fifty boxes—and placed them in Trump's residence. Two days later, just after noon on June 1, Nauta moved another eleven boxes to Trump's residence, making a total of sixty-four boxes removed from the storage room.

Melania Trump had noticed the boxes piling up in the family's private rooms. On the Monday before the couple's scheduled Friday departure for Bedminster for the season, she politely texted Nauta just after lunch to register a concern.

"Good afternoon, Walt. Happy Memorial Day!" she wrote. "I saw you put boxes to Potus room. Just FYI and I will tell him as well: Not sure how many he wants to take on Friday on the plane. We will NOT have room for them. Plane will be full with luggage. Thank you."

Nauta told the former First Lady not to worry. Her husband didn't plan to take the boxes; he just wanted them nearby so he could look over and pick through them.

The morning of June 2, hours before Corcoran was to arrive, Trump called Nauta with new instructions. Working at Trump's direction, Nauta and another Trump worker, Carlos De Oliveira, returned roughly thirty of the boxes that had been moved to Trump's private rooms for his review.

Corcoran arrived later that afternoon, unaware of the movement of records. He began going through the contents of the boxes in the storage room below the club's dining room, starting about 3:50 p.m. By the time he finished his review two and a half hours later, he had identified thirty-eight documents that had classification markings and carefully pulled them out of the boxes and placed them in a Redweld accordion-style folder.

Nauta, who didn't mention his work moving boxes since Corcoran's last visit, escorted the lawyer to the Mar-a-Lago dining room to give Trump his report.

"Did you find anything?" Trump asked when Corcoran confirmed he had finished his task. "Is it bad? Good?"

Corcoran explained what he'd found. Trump made a funny plucking motion that Corcoran interpreted as taking documents out of the folder and getting rid of them. Trump seemed to be suggesting the lawyer take out and remove any "bad" documents. Corcoran ignored this.

Evening was arriving at Mar-a-Lago. It was time for Trump to go to dinner and breeze out among his guests. After Corcoran and Trump parted ways, Corcoran emailed Bratt at about 7:40 p.m. to request an FBI agent meet him at Mar-a-Lago the next day so he could hand over an envelope of documents. Corcoran also called for Christina Bobb, an in-house lawyer for Trump, to come the next day and sign the certification as the custodian of records, attesting that a diligent search had been completed and any remaining sensitive records had been turned over.

Bobb wanted to help "the Boss" but she was also hesitant; she had had no role in reviewing the documents and knew nothing about Corcoran's search. She agreed to sign the statement after Corcoran added a large caveat. She would pledge that a diligent search had been conducted "based upon the information that has been provided to me."

Bratt flew down the next morning and arrived at Mar-a-Lago with three FBI agents before noon to find a motorcade lined up to take the Trump family to the airport soon. A Secret Service supervisor led the investigators into the club's dimly lit dining room, now closed for the summer season, where Bobb and Corcoran were silhouettes surrounded by uncovered banquet tables. Corcoran introduced Bobb. He then handed Bratt the Redweld envelope where he had secured thirty-eight classified documents, seventeen of them marked top secret, with double-wrapped tape. He also handed over Bobb's sworn certification that no other classified records remained at Mar-a-Lago. Bratt read the certification and then asked Corcoran who did the search and how he knew he had all the records. The lawyer, with whom Bratt had briefly overlapped as a fellow prosecutor in the U.S. Attorney's Office, gave some vague answers.

Then there was a flurry of activity in the adjoining living room and Trump emerged through the dining-room entryway. Trump welcomed his visitors heartily, and Corcoran offered introductions, starting with the FBI agents.

"Oh, FBI," Trump said. "You do great work."

Then Corcoran introduced Bratt.

"Oh, DOJ," Trump said. "Great reputation."

Trump explained he wanted to make sure his visitors knew they had his full cooperation.

"I'm an open book," Trump said. "Anything you want I'll give it to you."

Corcoran explained that he and Bratt had worked together as prosecutors. The former president then asked Bratt to give him his review of Corcoran.

"How was he?" Trump asked.

"He had a very good reputation in the office, sir," Bratt said.

In the comfortable chatter of a host, Trump asked the federal investigators if they'd had a comfortable flight. Bratt told Trump they had been delayed leaving D.C., not by weather, but a missing crew member.

"That's the problem today," Trump said with a sigh. "Nobody wants to work. Nobody wants to work."

After Trump said his goodbyes, Bratt asked if they could see the storage room where Corcoran had conducted his search.

"If it were up to me alone, I would not let you," Corcoran said. But he added: "I asked the president and he said I should let you see the room."

Corcoran led Bratt and the agents down a spiral staircase to a dank and hot underground tunnel that led to a storage room with a door spray-painted gold. This crowded but air-conditioned room was where Trump's lawyers said all the boxes of records from the White House had been kept. Once inside, the feds immediately saw that things had been moved and reorganized since Michael had taken her picture. There were far fewer boxes. A long coatrack held a line of Trump's signature blue Brioni suits in dry-cleaning bags. A stack of picture frames leaned against a wall.

Corcoran said they could not open any of the document boxes. The irony wasn't lost on the team; not quite an open book.

Bratt and the agents were hopelessly unaware of Trump's brazenness. They had no idea yet that the former president had misled his own attorney and meddled with the room just before his attorney had been instructed to search. But that wasn't all. Just a few hours before Trump greeted the federal investigators, Nauta, at Trump's instruction, worked with two other aides to load about ten to fifteen boxes onto a supporter's private plane at the nearby West Palm Beach airport. That afternoon, as Bratt and agents were finishing their futile tour of Mar-a-Lago, the plane flew Trump, his wife, Melania, their son, Barron, and Melania's parents to his Bedminster golf club, where the family normally decamped for the summer. More than four months after investigators at the National Archives had alerted the FBI, the possibility of a full accounting of what the former president and his staff had taken from the White House was slipping through investigators' fingers.

[26]

House Investigation
Blindsides DOJ

In June 2022, almost a year and a half after the attack on the Capitol, it was time for House Select Committee investigators to reveal what they had uncovered in congressional hearings that would serve as a made-for-TV trial.

The committee had gathered a mountain of never-before-seen witness accounts showing Trump's increasingly desperate attempts to hold on to power after losing the 2020 election. In firsthand testimony, White House advisers had described Trump's repeated bullying of his senior staff and state election officials to find ways to overturn his election loss. The committee's interviews had also opened a window onto Trump's state of mind. The committee's witnesses would reveal that Trump's aides had repeatedly told him there was no factual basis to dispute his loss even as he pushed his followers to come to D.C. to protest. One powerful new voice the committee had was the verbatim account of Attorney General Barr, who recounted in a taped interview how he told an infuriated

Trump that the claims of widespread election fraud were "bullshit." The committee teed up additional witnesses to show that Barr wasn't the only one who had tried to halt Trump from undermining the election results. Jeffrey Rosen, Barr's successor, added shock value with his account of the threatened mass resignation to stop Trump from using the Justice Department to cast doubt on Biden's victory. The committee also had in hand nearly one hundred forty thousand documents that offered new insider accounts. Among them were the texts and emails to and from Trump's former Chief of Staff Mark Meadows.

Over the weeks leading up to early June, with the help of former ABC News President James Goldston, congressional investigators edited their best interviews and video clips for public consumption. The level of pre-production planning felt like another first for a congressional committee. Again, Cheney was leading the process. Having already been stripped of her party leadership position for criticizing Trump, Cheney was now aghast at the way the former president was attempting to rebrand the attack as mostly peaceful and no real threat to democracy. Cheney was adamant that the hearings bring the public face-to-face with the reality of the attack and appropriately jolt the American consciousness.

Goldston, who for a time led ABC's respected news program *Nightline* and earned a reputation for producing compelling documentaries, had met with Cheney and found her argument convincing that the country needed a true accounting of January 6. However, Goldston and the small team he assembled quickly found that the thousands of hours of taped interviews would make for lousy viewing. The recordings had been an afterthought by the committee's attorneys. Many looked like the worst kind of legal deposition videos: blurry, out of focus, and failing at times to show the person speaking, including the former president's daughter, Ivanka Trump. But their first-person descriptions of events, including private and tense conversations at the White House, were gripping, and Goldston began to piece their words together like an oral history.

The result was a multipart miniseries. Goldston broke the hearings down into episodes, each showing how Trump had been the driver who set the attack in motion. First, they would highlight how the president ignored evidence that he lost and instead promoted conspiracy theories of widespread voter fraud. Another episode would show how he fueled the false notion that Vice President Mike Pence had authority to upend Biden's electoral win and had pressured Pence to carry out that radical last-ditch plan. A tranche of episodes would examine the hours before the attack itself, showing how Trump whipped supporters into a mob and then abandoned his oath of office by doing nothing for hours to stop his supporters ransacking the Capitol and instead watching television coverage of the violence.

The committee's first hearing would air in prime time on the night of June 9. Even though so many Americans had watched coverage of the attack when it happened, and had since seen countless snippets of video, the new footage brought a silence over the House hearing room.

An eleven-minute compilation moved from one gory scene to the next, as Trump's supporters left his rally and swarmed the Capitol. They were next shown turning violent, breaking through police barricades and then attacking officers with bear spray, rough-fashioned spears, and even a fire extinguisher. The video footage cut to protesters responding to Trump's tweet at 2:24 p.m. that day complaining that his vice president "didn't have the courage" to challenge the election results. A supporter with a megaphone read Trump's tweet aloud, and members of the crowd surrounding the Capitol grew visibly angry and began chanting, "Hang Mike Pence."

Cheney said the committee had learned Trump's response: "Maybe our supporters have the right idea. Mike Pence deserves it," she quoted Trump saying.

U.S. Capitol Police Officer Caroline Edwards described being in the melee as protesters unexpectedly wielded a metal bike rack to push her backward onto her head, knocking her unconscious. When she came to, Edwards found herself engaged for hours in a medieval kind of hand-to-hand combat.

"What I saw was just a war scene," she said. "I was slipping in people's blood. . . . It was carnage. It was chaos."

Goldston's team ended the video with Trump's voice, from an interview he'd given to Fox News six months after the attack. "They were peaceful people. These were great people," Trump said. "The love in the air—I've never seen anything like it."

The committee's opening day of "trial" drew over nineteen million viewers, more than most Monday Night Football games or the series finale of the record-breaking series *Game of Thrones*.

But half the country heard a completely different story, or nothing at all about the hearings. Unlike every other cable news network, Fox News and Trump's increasingly frequent go-to, Newsmax, did not air most of the hearings. On Fox, Tucker Carlson began his show saying the network wouldn't air Democrats' propaganda. "They are lying," Carlson said, "and we are not going to help them do it." Newsmax aired the eleven-minute video revealing the assault officers faced at the Capitol, but then equated the scenes to the vandalism and conflicts between some crowds and police officers following Black Lives Matter protests and the killing of George Floyd. "We saw a lot worse in the summer of 2020, spurred on by comments from the other side of the aisle, that burned major cities in this country down," said Newsmax host Rob Schmitt. "Where's the hearing on that?" On his social media platform, Truth Social, Trump launched a tirade of more than a dozen messages. The committee was a bunch of "HACKS," letting a "documentary maker from Fake News ABC to spin only negative footage." Also, Barr was a "weak and frightened" attorney general, Trump wrote; "(he sucked!)." Above all, the former president did not waver but further leaned into his rewriting of January 6: "It represented the greatest movement in the history of our Country to Make America Great Again," Trump wrote. "It was about an Election that was Rigged and Stolen, and a Country that was about to go to HELL."

The committee's second hearing, broadcast four days later, during the daytime on June 13, showcased the accounts of one Republican Trump aide and adviser after another describing Trump publicly clinging to fabulist conspiracy theories about widespread election fraud—even after his own investigators had checked them out and found them, in the words of Barr, "bogus and silly." Trump demanded that his Justice Department run down each new and nuttier claim of fraud to the point that senior DOJ officials began viewing it as a game of "whac-a-mole."

"I made it clear I did not agree with the idea of saying the election was stolen and putting out this stuff, which I told the president was bullshit," Barr said in his videotaped interview. "I thought, boy, if he really believes this stuff, he has, you know . . . become detached from reality."

The same day, Garland appeared at an unrelated event and declined to answer questions about January 6 investigations or to discuss the committee's findings but acknowledged his keen interest in the presentations.

"I am watching, I will be watching all of the hearings," Garland said. "I may not be able to watch all of it live, but I'm sure I will be watching all of it, and I can assure you the January 6 prosecutors are watching all of the hearings as well."

From Garland's first day as attorney general, he typically began the day with a summary of big developments and reports overnight, and he often peppered senior aides with questions about the news stories that might impact the department. He expected aides to keep him in the loop on major news and similarly vacuumed up every detail. But when the House committee began airing lengthy, nationally televised hearings divulging testimony from those around Trump on the day of the Capitol attack, Garland wanted to know as soon as possible what impact the latest revelations might have on the investigation he'd promised would be the Justice Department's top and most urgent priority.

Schedulers in Garland's office began clearing a block of time at the end of each hearing day for what aides began referring to as the "hot wash" of the day's discoveries in committee. Garland would begin by asking his senior staff if the department had learned anything it hadn't already known. When the new items were presented before him on the table, Garland's questions shifted to whether the fact pattern identified by the congressional committee changed the department's understanding of any of its existing cases in court against rioters or militia members—or, embarrassingly, revealed facts that Windom's team might not yet even be pursuing about Trump and his allies. Often, the hearings said little to nothing about riot cases the Justice Department had charged. Rather, the Justice Department was, as much as the public, learning for the first time about Trump's schemes and hearing the firsthand accounts of so many people in his orbit.

On June 15, two days after the January 6 congressional committee's second live hearing, Graves and two other senior Justice Department officials wrote a stern letter to Heaphy, the committee's chief counsel, insisting the committee now finally turn over the full transcripts of their interviews. The three officials were all close past work colleagues of Heaphy's: Assistant Attorneys General Matt Olsen and Kenneth Polite, who oversaw the National Security and Criminal divisions, respectively, and were friends, and Graves, who long before taking over the D.C. office had worked there as an attorney when Heaphy had.

"It is now readily apparent that the interviews the Select Committee conducted are not just potentially relevant to our overall criminal investigations, but are likely relevant to specific prosecutions that have already commenced," their letter read, referencing obliquely the Proud Boys case that was scheduled to go to trial that summer. It is "critical that the Department be able to evaluate the credibility of witnesses who have provided statements to the multiple governmental entities in assessing the strength of any potential criminal prosecutions," they wrote.

But Representatives Bennie Thomson, Liz Cheney, and Jamie Raskin, Heaphy's clients, had repeatedly questioned why the Justice Department had been seemingly MIA for over a year. Heaphy himself had tried to open a back channel with Justice more than six months earlier, and a federal judge had said a month before that Trump had likely committed a crime related to January 6. The lawmakers scoffed at the fresh outrage.

Their position hadn't changed since Justice first asked in April; they weren't willing to hand over the fruits of their long labor yet—at least not before their TV trial was done.

Graves was furious. Without the transcripts, he'd told colleagues the office would be forced to agree to postpone the trial of the first Proud Boys indicted for helping organize the Capitol attack. What's more, his office's ignorance of key witness accounts risked dozens of additional future prosecutions. But as the January 6 committee's investigation threatened to ice its Proud Boys case, the pace of Justice's fake electors probe quickened.

On Tuesday, June 21, the committee's fourth hearing featured the live testimony of Arizona and Georgia election officials who described the intense pressure they faced directly from President Trump to reject their state vote counts due to alleged election fraud, which the state officials were confident had not occurred.

Rusty Bowers, the Republican Speaker of the Arizona House of Representatives, recounted Trump and his attorney Rudy Giuliani pressuring him in a phone call, asking him to hold a special legislative hearing to investigate voter fraud. Trump and Giuliani explained their goal was to remove Biden's electors and replace them if fraud was corroborated.

"Look, you are asking me to do something that is counter to my oath when I swore to the Constitution to uphold it," he said. "This is totally foreign to me. . . . I will not break my oath."

The hearing revealed the firsthand accounts of top Republican Party officials who described Trump and a handful of advisers as the architects of the alternate electors scheme. The plot, as the committee concluded, was to create enough smoke and doubt about election fraud to prevent Congress from certifying all fifty states' results on January 6.

That evening, Graves's office asked the judge in the Proud Boys case to delay a trial, citing the continued congressional hearings and the department's lack of knowledge about what else witnesses might have told the committee. "The parties' inability to prepare their respective cases to account for such additional information is potentially prejudicial—to all parties."

The next morning, on Wednesday, June 22, the measure of how far behind DOJ was became clear. FBI agents with Windom's electors probe fanned out to swing states that appeared central to Trump's plot. They arrived at the homes of several Republican officials who had participated in crafting these fake elector slates for Trump in Georgia, Arizona, New Mexico, and Michigan. The FBI visited the home of Brad Carver, a Georgia lawyer who was reported to have signed on as a Trump elector for his state, and the home of Thomas Lane, a Virginia lawyer who worked on the Trump campaign's efforts in Arizona and New Mexico. The feds also dropped a series of subpoenas for records and email correspondence on people who had signed as alternate electors for Trump in Michigan and elsewhere, including David Shafer, the head of Arizona's Republican Party.

Early that same morning, Windom's team surprised Jeffrey Clark, coming through the door of his Virginia home. Agents from the Inspector General's Office of the Department of Justice whom Windom had asked to help his small task force, instructed Clark to come outside. He stood in his driveway while several agents and police officers searched his home for hours, taking his phones and all other electronic devices as evidence. Clark appeared on Tucker Carlson's Fox News program the following night and called the Justice Department search "highly politicized." He compared the surprise search to the secret police of Cold War–era East Germany.

Meanwhile, the committee was about to debut one of its biggest surprises. In early June, Liz Cheney had been quietly contacted by a low-profile witness who had already been questioned three times by committee investigators earlier that year. Cassidy Hutchinson, the former aide to White House Chief of Staff Mark Meadows, was a pretty brunette who sometimes gave clipped answers and had so far provided little in the way of revelatory information.

When investigator Dan George asked her in a February session what she had heard Trump say at an informal Oval Office gathering the night before the January 6 rally, Hutchinson said: "I believe just being excited for the rally the next day."

Behind the scenes, though, the witness confided something quite different to a good friend and former White House aide, Alyssa Farah Griffin, who had resigned in December, disturbed by Trump's baseless claims of a rigged election. Hutchinson told Griffin the committee didn't ask her about the most important events she knew about in the days and hours surrounding the riot.

"There is more I want to share that was not asked," Hutchinson told Griffin. "How do we do this?'"

Hutchinson told Griffin her interviews had been stifled somewhat by advice she was getting from the attorney the Trump political campaign had arranged to represent her. That attorney would later fiercely dispute this, saying he had advocated for her ethically and professionally based on the interests she communicated to him.

Griffin, whom Cheney had encouraged to testify, felt sorry for her friend and called Cheney to see what she would suggest Hutchinson do. Cheney said the committee would need to contact Hutchinson through her lawyer. Now the lawmaker knew the former aide had more to say.

The end result was that on Monday, June 20, at 1:00 p.m., Hutchinson sat with the committee for her fourth interview. This time it was a secretly arranged meeting held in HT-64, a small, inconspicuous basement office in the House wing of the Capitol. Only Cheney and George sat on the questioners' side of the table, and Hutchinson, with new counsel at her side, now recounted how Trump had been warned that his rally-goers were carrying weapons and angrily demanded they be waved into the rally. Trump, she said, insisted they weren't going to hurt him.

She told of learning after his speech at the Ellipse that Trump had grown incensed and lunged for the steering wheel inside his SUV when his security detail leader refused to take him to the U.S. Capitol. Agents in the car with Trump would later dispute that.

Toward the end of the week, Cheney conferred with senior staff. She said she wanted Hutchinson to testify early the following week in a live televised hearing about the stunning moments Hutchinson had just revealed in her closed testimony. Tim Heaphy, the panel's chief investigator, warned senior staff that it was dangerous to do without more homework.

"I think it's a mistake," he told the group.

First, Hutchinson's new account was very different from what she had said under oath previously, he cautioned. Her account also didn't jibe with that of Secret Service agents Bobby Engel, the head of Trump's detail, and Tony Ornato, an agent then temporarily acting as White House deputy chief of staff. The agents may have omitted this information, Heaphy said, but they needed to be asked.

On Saturday morning, June 25, Cheney, Speaker Nancy Pelosi's senior adviser Jamie Fleet, Pelosi's chief of staff, Terri McCullough, and senior committee staff dialed into a conference call to go over the pros and cons of a surprise Tuesday hearing.

Heaphy told the group he worried about damaging their very successful investigation if they didn't first vet these claims with other witnesses or records. "It would be irresponsible" to put Hutchinson in a public hearing this quickly, the chief investigative counsel said.

Cheney, McCullough, and Fleet disagreed. They said other witnesses had given dubious accounts. Now the public deserved to hear from an insider, their surprise star witness.

Cheney said there was another reason to go forward: Hutchinson had received not-so-subtle threats from Trump allies.

"It's going to leak anyway if we don't get it out there," Cheney said. "She's going to be in danger."

Cheney, as she often did, had the final word. They were doing the hearing Tuesday but under extreme secrecy. A Cheney deputy instructed several committee staff to take the day off on Monday, ultimately keeping the plan a secret even from them.

Late on Monday, June 27, the House committee announced a televised hearing for the following day to "present recently obtained evidence and receive witness testimony" from an unnamed witness. Hutchinson got a warning that some Trump White House alums had heard rumors she might be the surprise witness. That evening, Liz Horning, a longtime aide to Trump White House counsel Pat Cipollone, texted her friend, concerned she might be testifying under duress.

"Cassidy, plz tell me you are not testifying tomorrow."

She never responded.

That Tuesday morning, on June 28, Hutchinson swore to tell Congress the truth about what she saw at the White House. For the next two hours, this once trusted Trump aide described how the president railed to stay in power and largely did nothing when violence erupted at the Capitol. Wearing a plain white blazer over a black scoop-neck top and trousers, she recounted jaw-dropping moments. She described an unhinged and chaotic Trump. She said she had to wipe ketchup off an Oval Office wall, where Trump threw a plate in fury after Barr told the AP that there was no substantial election fraud to erase Joe Biden's victory. Hutchinson said she knew Trump had demanded that supporters suspected of carrying weapons be waved through magnetometers at his rally. She described trying to get Meadows, her cell-phone-scrolling boss, to "snap out of it" on January 6 and get Trump to do something about people beating police and trying to break into the Capitol. Meadows had asked Trump's daughter Ivanka to join him in convincing Trump to later tweet a message urging his supporters to stand down.

As the hearing continued, one group was missing from the audience. Several of the former federal prosecutors serving as the committee's investigators couldn't bring themselves to watch and had departed for drinks at Bullfeathers, a Capitol Hill bar. They shared an uneasy feeling that all the months of work they'd put into the investigation and the ironclad case of Trump's dereliction of duty could be called into question by one unvetted witness.

Heaphy's team of former federal prosecutors had put their reputations on the line to impartially and rigorously investigate every aspect of January 6 when they didn't see DOJ or the full Congress stepping up to do it. Several were more than disappointed with the risky move the committee had just made. Heaphy tried to reach a few by phone to discuss next steps, and got an earful from one about how premature and dangerous it had been. Heaphy told the investigator he'd pushed back as much as he could but he had given his advice and the client—the lawmakers—had made the decision.

"I can't believe you rolled over," the investigator said.

"I didn't roll over. But I lost," Heaphy said.

Fully vetted or not, this witness and her explosive testimony showed another gaping hole in the Justice Department's investigation.

No one in the attorney general's suite had ever heard of Cassidy Hutchinson as a potential key witness. The attorney general turned to Rush Atkinson, who was still helping Garland and Monaco monitor the U.S. attorney's five-month-old investigation of the Trump campaign and its effort to overturn the election.

"Did we know about this witness and her account?" Garland asked.

No, Atkinson said. Not that he knew of.

Atkinson was dispatched to ask Graves and Windom a barrage of questions about which rocks his team had yet to turn over, and what investigative steps it had and had not taken. What had Windom and his fledgling investigation determined about key White House aides' account of events before and during the riot? Did they understand Meadows's role in these critical events?

The same day, Windom for the first time contacted Meadows's lawyer, asking him about obtaining the Meadows texts and emails from the end of Trump's time in the White House. These were the same communications that the committee had obtained six months earlier and had scrutinized for clues and links.

Two days later, Graves sent an office-wide email announcing a significant expansion of the Investigations Unit in the U.S. Attorney's Office that was cast as having been in the works for a while but some saw as further reaction. Graves had already sent a couple of prosecutors to work with Windom, but new plans called for building up the team by ten to twelve more. Graves had asked Cooney, who stirred controversy early in Biden's tenure by proposing to focus a line of inquiry on January 6 directly on ties to those in Trump's orbit, to supervise Windom's new beefed-up team.

On July 6, Windom received Meadows's texts and emails. As DOJ sped up to cover the ground exposed by the hearings, the left would increasingly question why it was taking so long to prosecute what the committee had portrayed as obvious. The right would paint the Justice Department as doing Democrats' bidding. Garland's goal of rebuilding the Justice Department's image as that of a fair, apolitical broker was quickly evaporating.

[27]

Family Feud—Part II

In the wake of the congressional hearings, Windom's team issued another burst of subpoenas and his agents searched several more Trump advisers' homes. Federal prosecutors and FBI agents were now fully aligned and actively probing who in the former president's circle might bear criminal responsibility for January 6.

In those very same weeks, however, the two sides were once again scrapping and stalled on the second federal probe involving Trump's possession of classified documents. Bratt, the lead prosecutor, had returned to D.C. after his June 3 visit to Mar-a-Lago convinced that Trump was still holding back records. Steve D'Antuono and his top supervisors in the FBI's Washington Field Office felt that in voluntarily turning over the additional documents, the president had complied with the subpoena and the Bureau might even be able to soon close the criminal case. A former president of the United States and his lawyer had said he had returned everything. What else was Justice really going to do?

Bratt told D'Antuono's team that he saw the next step as obvious: The FBI had to search Mar-a-Lago. Trump aide Molly Michael had shown them a picture of many more boxes at the president's club, and the government couldn't risk having top-secret information among them. Indeed, the day after her May 18 interview, Bratt's deputy, Julie Edelstein, had drafted a search warrant to prepare for that inevitability. Derek Pieper, one of D'Antuono's lieutenants, pushed back, saying that after the Trump team's claim they had turned over everything, the Bureau no longer had probable cause for a search. Inside the D.C. Field Office, supervisors grumbled privately that they suspected Bratt had an anti-Trump bias and that it was fueling his overly aggressive push for a search. Bratt believed the evidence compelled them to take these steps.

Because Bratt and the field office kept butting heads over a search, the FBI's assistant director for counterintelligence, Kohler, was tasked with working with Toscas and Olsen to reach common ground. Kohler agreed with D'Antuono to an extent: The government was not in the business of assuming an attorney was lying.

To bridge the divide between the Bureau's reluctant Washington Field Office supervisors and the department's frustrated prosecutors, Kohler offered an idea that had bubbled up from the squad working the case. Some of the agents who had accompanied Bratt on the June 3 visit to Mar-a-Lago had seen surveillance cameras positioned around the club and even in hallways leading to the storage room. Bratt could subpoena the recordings of those surveillance cameras to see what they might learn, Kohler suggested. It might turn up more evidence about what was going on at Mar-a-Lago. Bratt agreed, but still D'Antuono's deputies resisted, questioning why this step was needed. They suggested the National Archives instead ask Trump about the remaining boxes, with the presumption they might just contain presidential rather than classified records. Eventually, Bratt sent the subpoena to the Trump Organization's attorneys in New York on June 24.

In the first week of July, the Trump Organization's general counsel, Alan Garten, provided the FBI with a hard drive with the surveillance tape for the previous several months, but the FBI initially struggled to figure out how to view the material. In about ten days, the agents watched the tape, and the FBI resistance to a search melted away.

The tapes showed Trump's valet and the other staffers moving boxes into and out of the storage room where agents had been told all the records shipped from Washington had been kept. The nature and timing of these movements were also highly suspicious. They could see how the staff had removed dozens of boxes after Trump received his subpoena, and then that his staff had returned roughly half as many boxes just before Trump's lawyer was scheduled to conduct a government-ordered search. "It's clear now," said one FBI supervisor after viewing the tapes. Somebody was trying to hide something—and not just from the government, it seemed, but even from Trump's own lawyer.

Wray, Kohler, and other senior leaders had initially been wary of a search, but now saw a solid basis to believe that someone, and possibly Trump himself, had tried to criminally obstruct the investigation. It was also vindication, Kohler told Bureau leaders, of the best traditions of the FBI's methodical approach to investigation. Call it cautious or thorough, but by slowing down and taking the extra step of getting the surveillance video, the department not only had ample justification to obtain a warrant but could one day show skeptical Trump supporters or Republican Congress members this unprecedented step had been necessary.

The FBI was on board with requesting a warrant to search the former president's home, but still, from Wray on down, the few Bureau personnel briefed on the case knew this was a huge decision. The unannounced search would have to be carefully planned and executed. Over the first weeks of July, agents on the case squad began making extensive preparations to finesse how they would enter the property. To avoid a dramatic standoff, they needed to be sure to pick a day when Trump was not there, made easier by the fact that he rarely stayed at the club in the summer months. To lower the profile of the search, they would use unmarked vehicles and agents would wear khakis and polo shirts rather than the jackets emblazoned with "FBI" in big, block lettering that many donned for raids. Normally, agents would also go to local city planning offices days ahead of time to get the blueprints of the structures they were going to search to avoid any surprises. But to avoid a potential leak, they decided against it. They also planned to ask the Secret Service to send Trump's normal security detail elsewhere and staff Mar-a-Lago with a replacement crew during the search to avoid any potential conflict for agents who had become personally close to the former president. But one significant voice inside the FBI still wanted to fight the surprise search. D'Antuono was ready to put up whatever clout he had to block it, telling colleagues he was convinced the search was a bad idea.

Word of D'Antuono's and his deputies' opposition began to spread through Main Justice in late July, just as his case agents were busy preparing for the search and as Bratt was working on the affidavit the team would present to a judge. Bratt relayed the news of the pushback to his boss.

Olsen, the assistant attorney general, was known to generally prefer honey over vinegar to settle internal strife. He called a meeting of the key decision-makers at DOJ and FBI for Monday, August 1, at 10:30 a.m. He proposed they meet on the FBI's turf, the Hoover Building, and specifically in the conference room of Wray's general counsel, Jason Jones, on the seventh floor.

Jones and Kohler knew D'Antuono couldn't be the Bureau's final word on this decision. The two Wray deputies were in lockstep; they didn't agree with Garland and his aides that this was just like any other case, but they knew the Bureau had to do a search. The two FBI leaders also supported Olsen's goal of winning over D'Antuono.

In the room, they were joined by Olsen and Bratt from Main Justice and D'Antuono and his deputy Tony Riedlinger from the Washington Field Office. Toscas joined by phone. Bratt carried with him the draft affidavit for the search warrant. Olsen helped open the meeting by going over the evidence to date.

"We think we've got enough for probable cause," Olsen said. "We want to apply for a search warrant."

D'Antuono asked why they couldn't contact Trump through his lawyer Evan Corcoran and get a voluntary search with Trump's permission.

Bratt explained the video showed the lawyer was obviously being misled by his client. They risked allowing Trump or his aides to destroy documents if Trump knew ahead of time of an FBI search. Bratt emphasized the video evidence gave them sufficient probable cause to believe their investigation was being messed with, a serious crime by itself, if true.

"Maybe we have enough, but I still don't want to do it," D'Antuono said. "It's not a good look for us."

Kohler took a turn trying to use reason.

"Think about how it looks if we don't do it and there are records there," he said to D'Antuono. "How will that look?"

Toscas had an unusually good and trusting relationship with the Washington Field Office and especially the counterintelligence agents after all the work they'd done together on the Hillary Clinton email probe and in the early days of the Russian interference investigation. Toscas told D'Antuono that he too had been reluctant early on to agree to a surprise search, but the evidence had swayed him to conclude it was now the only safe option.

"George, that's great, but you haven't swayed me," D'Antuono replied.

D'Antuono said the whole thing made him uncomfortable. What he didn't say out loud was that he had felt that way since Bratt insisted on a search following the Molly Michael interview in mid-May. D'Antuono confided to his deputies that it felt like Bratt and DOJ attorneys in general were assuming Trump was guilty because they were mostly Democrats who detested and distrusted the former president. D'Antuono believed investigators should be showing a tad more respect for the office.

What he said out loud to the group in his conference room was that a surprise search was a big deal and would make it appear that Trump was a criminal. There was a possibility, he noted, that agents might only find the missing folders that should house some of the documents Trump had already returned. It would be a technical violation, yes, but an embarrassment if the Bureau conducted a search and turned up nothing more.

"We are not the presidential records police," D'Antuono said. When

Bratt objected and stressed that they were talking about securing classified records that could fall into the wrong hands, D'Antuono then asked if DOJ had officially designated Trump as a subject of the criminal investigation.

"What does that matter?" Bratt replied, irritated. The purpose of a search warrant was to investigate a suspected crime, and whose house they were searching was legally irrelevant.

The emotional temperature in the room kept rising. Bratt was visibly frustrated. D'Antuono didn't yell but he was stone-faced and frowning. Toscas, known for a temper when he felt strongly, tried now to reason with D'Antuono, saying this wasn't how the FBI handled this kind of evidence of obstruction. A search was justified.

"This would not be my recommendation, not this way," D'Antuono said. "Someone's gonna have to order me to do it."

Jones and Kohler, who both had reputations for poker faces, frowned in resignation. Kohler let out a deep sigh. So that's how it was going to be, their expressions said. Taking turns, they told D'Antuono that the next time they met with the FBI's deputy director, they would recommend to him that the field office proceed with the search.

With that, the meeting ended, and D'Antuono's guests said polite goodbyes. Later, a bewildered Olsen and Toscas talked with Kohler privately and asked him to decipher what they had just heard from his FBI colleague. It felt to the attorneys like they had simply been asking the FBI to do what agents normally ask to do all the time. In ninety-nine out of a hundred cases, they said, agents were the ones pressing cautious attorneys to green-light a raid or a subpoena to gather more evidence.

"What the hell, Alan?" Toscas asked.

Kohler said they had to appreciate the pressure the Washington Field Office had been under for years with respect to investigations of presidential candidates. Working the Hillary Clinton email investigation hadn't boosted anyone's career and had left some of those agents feeling tarnished. Similarly, agents who had last handled a case this politically charged—the investigation of Russian interference in the 2016 election and contacts with Trump's campaign—continued to pay a price. Years later, those agents remained stuck on desk duty, answering questions from internal affairs and inspectors general about their conduct and decision-making in that probe.

"You gotta understand," Kohler told them. "The guys over there are still stepping over the bodies of Crossfire Hurricane."

Kohler didn't want Olsen and Toscas to misunderstand. He explained he didn't mean that agents were afraid to do their jobs, or even afraid of Trump. But they were rightly cautious about handling this kind of political TNT.

At an FBI briefing the next morning, Olsen told Abbate, the FBI deputy director, his summary of the meeting and expressed worry about D'Antuono's insistence on doing a voluntary search despite the obvious risks.

Abbate told Olsen he'd look into it. He conferred with Kohler and Jones, who also argued it was past time for a search.

Later that morning, Abbate called D'Antuono. The two men were longtime colleagues who had worked together or overlapped in the same field offices for years. D'Antuono had taken Abbate's old job overseeing the Detroit office when Abbate got promoted to headquarters; D'Antuono had followed in Abbate's footsteps again in taking over the Washington Field Office after Abbate moved to headquarters. There were no cross words.

D'Antuono aired his concerns to Abbate but his arguments received little sympathy; the Washington Field Office chief understood the decision was made. He suggested that DOJ at least give Corcoran a decent heads-up—more than a few minutes. Abbate alerted Olsen about the FBI's wish to do so. Tempers soon flared again, though, when Toscas insisted they do the search at the end of the week, and D'Antuono said it would have to wait until the following week and explained he would give the attorney a courtesy call.

"You are way out of line," Toscas emailed him. "You and your leadership seem to have gone from cautious to fearful." D'Antuono told Toscas he was trying do things the right way, and he wasn't going to get in a personal email battle with him.

With the plan finally in motion to search August 8, Wray was briefed, and he sought further restrictions. He thought agents should only search areas where Trump had routine access. Parts of the club that were rented to other guests and were unavailable to Trump didn't need to be scoured. On the morning of August 8, the FBI's chief spokesperson, Cathy Milhoan, had a public statement ready and waiting for the right time. She and her team had worked out the language with the Justice Department's public affairs office. The FBI wanted to explain through the press that a court had approved this search if and when it became public. Kohler called Milhoan in the late afternoon to let her know agents had completed their search. They had entered the compound at 10:00 a.m., after calling Trump's attorney to alert him, and left by 4:00 p.m.

"It's done," he said.

A local Florida politics website broke the story around 6:40 p.m. Soon, Fox News ran a grainy nighttime video of an agent carrying a long gun amid the palm trees on the club property. Kohler was furious. There had been no FBI agents on the property carrying such a gun or wearing such gear. The cable news station was rerunning stock footage, and it was obviously a U.S. Secret Service officer pictured in the video, he concluded.

Trump, who was in New York and had been alerted to the unfolding search, then made things worse. He seethed as he watched clips of agents moving through the property from the same security cameras whose earlier recordings had given investigators the basis for the search. Just before 7:00 p.m., he issued a lengthy statement through his political action committee. It accused Democrats of weaponizing the Justice Department to try to prevent him from returning to the White House. He complained that agents "even broke into my safe."

"These are dark times for our Nation, as my beautiful home, Mar-A-Lago in Palm Beach, Florida, is currently under siege, raided, and occupied by a large group of FBI agents," Trump wrote on his social media site, Truth Social. In truth, the search team had left hours ago.

"It is prosecutorial misconduct, the weaponization of the Justice System, and an attack by Radical Left Democrats who desperately don't want me to run for President in 2024."

Milhoan knew this was the time to release the statement. But just then, a Justice Department spokesperson called to say the FBI couldn't release it. Senior DOJ officials had put the brakes on the statement, fearing it could cause chaos.

When Kohler heard this, he was flummoxed. Wouldn't the department want to at least explain that a court had approved this unprecedented step of searching a former president's home? The old video of an agent with a long gun quickly stirred up online criticism of the government. Soon, Trump was further amping up that vitriol with his own rhetoric.

Kohler called Olsen, wanting to know why DOJ was blocking his team from issuing the agreed-upon statement that they normally released after conducting a search.

"What the hell, dude?" Kohler asked Olsen.

"I don't know," said Olsen, who hadn't sought the block and was focused on the documents recovered.

Late that night, preliminary results from the search were, in Bratt's description, "extraordinary." Beforehand, some at the Justice Department had rightly feared the consequences if they descended on Trump's residence and agents ultimately found no classified documents.

Instead, they had found hundreds of pages of secret records. What's more, the sensitivity of the material they found was terrifyingly high, with top-secret documents nearly spilling out of boxes in Trump's personal office, his residence, and even a bathroom shower.

Olsen convened a late evening conference call with his far-flung national security prosecutors, including two who had been on-site for the search, to go over the findings. Olsen, a veteran terror prosecutor who had little hands-on experience investigating mishandled classified documents, asked his experts:

"What else do we need to do?"

Edelstein, the Justice Department's living library on classified document cases, replied dryly. Knowingly taking classified documents outside of a secure government facility was a crime, plain and simple. Edelstein said she knew how the department had responded to such clear evidence of a crime in dozens of cases before. But with Trump, all bets were off.

"If it was anybody else," Edelstein said, "we would arrest him tomorrow."

That night, the FBI began the first careful steps of assessing the classified documents they had found, and as they took in each document one by one over the next many hours, they discovered part of that work would be extremely delicate. Some of the most senior counterintelligence officials in the Justice Department, the people trained to do this work, weren't even authorized to look at or handle a few of the documents, they found.

The very next day that they were both in D.C., Kohler gave Garland and Monaco their first briefing on the results of the search. He ticked through the basics, how the search had gone smoothly, how many top-secret documents were recovered, the assorted places they were found in Trump's private residence, in his personal office, and other spots. Kohler then summarized the agents' inventory so far. Monaco, who had lived so many hours of her life reviewing classified secrets in SCIFs and in the White House Situation Room, immediately leapt to the urgent tasks at hand. They had to contain the potential damage to national security. She asked Kohler which agencies needed to be warned about their secrets having been in uncontrolled boxes in Mar-a-Lago for more than a year.

"Who do we need to call right now?" Monaco asked Kohler.

Kohler, who prided himself on being able to read a room, saw the mild disappointment in Garland's and Monaco's eyes. They had just authorized a search of a former president's home—one of the biggest and most sensitive decisions they might make in their careers. Both were natural micromanagers and detail-oriented. Their questions revealed they were looking for Kohler to give them a far more granular degree of knowledge about the documents that had been recovered. Monaco, especially, had a keen sense of the caliber of government secrets that flowed through the Oval Office, and her reaction indicated the department would treat each government secret as not just hoarded by the former president but now compromised. Kohler promised more details soon.

The next day, Kohler arranged to visit the Washington Field Office to put his own eyes on the recovered documents.

Olsen realized he too should review the materials.

When he arrived at the field office, a case agent assigned as Olsen's handler steered him to a secure room where all the classified documents retrieved from Trump's possession had been laid out in three piles. One stack contained all the documents returned to the National Archives by Trump's staff in January. A second small pile involved the documents returned by Corcoran in the Redweld folder in June. The final pile—considerably taller than the one from the voluntarily returned folder—held the documents seized in the search.

Olsen was handed a pair of rubber gloves to wear as he looked through the stacks, now with two people standing by as minders. The gloves underscored one point: These pages were evidence in a criminal case.

Olsen didn't try to read every word, but he needed to be familiar with how serious the national security threat was to have had these documents out of the government's safekeeping.

Then Olsen learned from his minders there was a fourth stack of documents, stored in a separate safe, and only one agent in the field office was approved to handle them. Each of the documents in the safe bore a ticket with coding that described its unique handling instructions—above and beyond the strict approvals for highly sensitive top secret/sensitive compartmented information.

Olsen got on the phone with his counsel to confirm for each ticketed item whether he had the clearance to review it. He read the codes aloud, one by one. Some of the documents were so restricted that top Justice Department security officials reacted with surprise: They had never even heard of the code names before. Some involved special access programs that usually only the president or a cabinet member could authorize access to.

In this way, Olsen, the assistant attorney general responsible for the Justice Department's efforts to protect national security, learned that a handful of documents that had been sitting in boxes in a Florida resort were so sensitive that even he didn't have authorization to look at them.

Outside of DOJ, Trump's claims that the search proved the FBI had been weaponized against him activated his most militant supporters in ways that had lain dormant since January 6.

In western Pennsylvania, a Trump supporter began posting threatening messages on the far-right social media website Gab, saying that after the raid, "Every single piece of shit who works for the FBI in any capacity . . . deserves to die. You've declared war on us and now it's open season on YOU."

A day later and three hundred miles away in Cincinnati, another set of threats turned real. A Navy veteran who had been posting about the search tried to break through bulletproof glass in the visitors' entrance of the FBI's Cincinnati Field Office wielding an AR-15-style assault rifle and a nail gun. The gunman fled after failing to break through the glass and was killed by police six hours later following a standoff. Beginning after the Mar-a-Lago search, postings in the suspect's name on Trump's Truth Social site warned everyone to "get whatever you need to be ready for combat. We must not tolerate this once."

The same day as the attack, the FBI agents who had signed the search warrant paperwork for Mar-a-Lago were evacuated temporarily from their homes for their own safety after documents with their names began to circulate online. The agents' identities had been redacted from filings on the court's website, but a copy of the paperwork had been left at Mar-a-Lago. FBI officials quickly surmised and others speculated publicly that Trump's team had leaked the paperwork, putting a bull's-eye on the agents—as well as on magistrate judge who signed the warrant.

By the end of the day, the FBI and the Department of Homeland Security had put out a nationwide alert to law enforcement, warning of increased threats of violence against officers, including a threat to place a "dirty bomb" in front of FBI headquarters. Wray also sent an email to the FBI's entire global staff saying employee safety was the Bureau's number one concern.

On a prescheduled trip to Omaha, Wray took questions, saying he couldn't speak about the documents investigation but denouncing the threats against Bureau personnel that had followed.

"As I'm sure you can appreciate, that's not something I can talk about," Wray said of the search, calling such threats to law enforcement "deplorable and dangerous." He added: "Violence against law enforcement is not the answer, no matter what anybody is upset about or who they are upset with."

Even inside the FBI, supervisors in the field were calling Kohler and emailing Abbate demanding to know why in the world the Bureau would conduct a surprise search of a former president's home. An email from one top supervisor to the FBI ombudsman on April 11 reflected the shock in the field:

"Did this really just happen?" he wrote. "Am I dreaming? The FBI served a search warrant on a former president. . . . Over documents? I've lost just about all faith in our leadership. They obviously forgot Crossfire Hurricane."

On August 22, two weeks after the search, Trump once again came for the investigators. He sued the Justice Department and the FBI, with his lawyers arguing the department had used its extraordinary power to hurt Donald Trump politically. They asked Aileen Cannon, the South Florida judge newly named to the court by Trump and now overseeing the documents case, to take the extraordinary step of appointing a special master to review the government records seized in the search—a move that would temporarily halt the Justice Department from continuing its investigation of Trump.

"Law enforcement is a shield that protects Americans," Trump's legal team wrote in their complaint. "It cannot be used as a weapon for political purposes. Therefore, we seek judicial assistance in the aftermath of an unprecedented and unnecessary raid on President Trump's home at Mar-a-Lago in Palm Beach, Florida."

Trump's lawyers insisted Trump had "voluntarily" accepted a subpoena and offered to help the government in every way to return sensitive and presidential records. They accused the Justice Department and FBI of a pattern of trying to unfairly harass Trump, the expected future candidate for president in 2024, and to besmirch his reputation. His lawyers laid out a highly misleading picture of the FBI's previous investigation of Russian contacts with Trump's 2020 campaign.

"The FBI and DOJ have demonstrated a willingness to treat President Trump differently than any other citizen," they wrote.

Justice Department lawyers in the National Security Division internally dubbed the Trump legal filing "the crazy motion," one that they believed Judge Cannon would have to immediately reject. Based on years of established case law, the government had sole authority and responsibility to declare certain government secrets as classified, and thus was the primary owner of classified documents. No one had ever suggested they should be assessed by some outside third party. But Cannon would surprise the DOJ in what was either her ignorance—or her rejection—of established law. Cannon asked the government to reply within the next ten days to Trump's complaints and his request for a halt in their probe.

Under that pressure from the court, the Justice Department on August 26 released parts of the FBI affidavit it had filed in secret to justify the surprise search. The Justice Department, however, heavily redacted the document. Most importantly, it didn't share why investigators had come to believe Trump had concealed classified records on the property. Prosecutors generally held their specific evidence close during an investigation and only released the full affidavit after charges were filed and the trial had arrived.

At the FBI, however, Wray and Kohler were eager to get out more of an explanation to the public—and just as importantly, to their own agents across the country. They had confessed to feeling somewhat naive for believing that the public would trust them that such a search must be warranted.

Kohler argued to DOJ lawyers that Trump's legal screed had given the FBI a huge opening to show their receipts. Trump's lawyers had inaccurately portrayed the former president as a cooperative martyr targeted by a rabid FBI led by his foe Joe Biden. This was the Bureau's and DOJ's chance to lay out for the public all the chances the government had given Trump to turn over records—and the worrisome evidence they had gathered indicating Trump had intentionally hidden documents that could harm national security.

The FBI had pictures of dozens of classified documents found in the search. The photos showed documents stored haphazardly without any security, in boxes that were sometimes stacked on a public ballroom stage and even on a bathroom floor next to a shower. They had witnesses who told them about the documents still kept by Trump at the club after he claimed to have returned everything. As well as videotape of Trump aides moving boxes into and out of a storage closet after he received a subpoena to return these records.

Kohler argued they should now release as much of the affidavit on the court's public website as they could. "Let's make sure everyone knows why we did what we did."

The national security prosecutors at Main Justice—Edelstein, Bratt, and Toscas—strenuously disagreed with the idea of sharing more of the affidavit and evidence that led them to conclude Trump was hiding records. Their position was firm and based on the department's tradition: DOJ usually didn't release this kind of information before trial. Doing so could create a bad precedent. Olsen, however, sided with the FBI.

"No, Trump's legal team has made an error here," Olsen said. "We can show how hard we tried—and still protect witnesses. We can defend ourselves now. With the facts."

Soon after, Kohler raised the idea at Garland's 9:45 a.m. meeting, saying the Bureau felt strongly. Kohler got the green light to huddle with Olsen and Toscas and decide what portions of the affidavit and evidence DOJ could release. But the debate in the smaller group quickly got tense.

"We don't do this," Toscas said. "We've never done this. We shouldn't do this."

Kohler wasn't backing down either: "We have guys attacking our field offices," he said. "We have to tell the story of what happened here."

The argument was between two people who had endless trust in each other's integrity and commitment to their job, which made their dispute all the more challenging and even a little painful. Kohler and Toscas had known each other since working together in the 2000s on Operation Ghost Stories, a landmark investigation of Russian spies living under deep cover as Americans.

The two men were struggling to find common ground. They agreed to assign Edelstein and one of Kohler's deputies to work together on a draft reply to release some of the affidavit language. But Edelstein agreed with Toscas: It was dangerous territory to say anything before criminal charges were filed. Kohler learned that Edelstein had redlined out two-thirds of the evidence that the FBI had proposed making public.

As the deadline for the government's reply drew closer, Wray added his own heft to the swirling dispute and weighed in at the next morning meeting he attended with Garland.

"It's very important to me," he told the assembled group, saying the department needed to be forward-leaning and transparent in the court filing. "The facts need to get out to the American people."

With that, Garland asked Toscas and Kohler to try to work out a compromise again, and this time, the DOJ lawyer's absolutist tone softened a bit. Toscas finally agreed to Kohler's repeated request to include some photos from the search.

Just a day or two before the government's reply was due, Toscas briefed the attorney general and his advisers on the reply and information the government planned to release. Kohler again objected and again Toscas fought back. But this time they were fighting rather vehemently in front of the attorney general, because that's how strongly they both felt. Toscas told Kohler flatly this was the amount of information the DOJ could safely file.

"Sir, we don't agree," Kohler told Garland. "We feel there are more things that can go in there."

Each was under some of the most tremendous pressure of his career. Garland, who could be a mensch when the moment called for it, came around to Kohler's side of the large conference table to assure the FBI chief he was committed to figuring out a way forward.

"I'm sorry; I thought we had this worked out," Garland said.

He put a hand on Kohler's shoulder.

"Alan, we're going to find a way," Garland said. "I understand what the FBI is going through. We will work it out."

On the night of August 30, Wray's chief of staff, Jonathan Lenzner, and Olsen's top deputy, David Newman, sent final edits back and forth before the Justice Department filed with the court a powerful reply to Trump's narrative. It revealed for the first time some of the reasons the government had had probable cause to suspect they would find evidence of a crime at Mar-a-Lago in their search twenty-two days earlier. The government described all the ways Trump and his aides had obstructed the government's attempt to retrieve both unclassified and classified records, and how his aides had secretly moved boxes of documents prior to Trump's lawyer's search. The prosecutors explained their focus on a Mar-a-Lago storage closet and growing evidence that made them confident "government records were likely concealed and removed . . . and that efforts were likely taken to obstruct the government's investigation." Within another ten days, the government would formally approve the court's releasing more of its partially unredacted affidavit—as Kohler had wanted.

Perhaps the most dramatic material the Justice Department released in response to Trump's accusations was a simple photograph appended to its August 30 court filing. The image made some former prosecutors gasp—in both surprise and a bit of admiration for the government's rejoinder to Trump.

It showed a slew of classified documents, including five bright yellow folders marked top secret, all spread randomly on a rug at Trump's club after FBI agents searched his property and found them in his office. Trump's lawyers had insisted that the Justice Department, by launching an "unprecedented, unnecessary, and legally unsupported raid" on Mar-a-Lago, was "criminalizing a former President's possession of personal and Presidential records in a secure setting." The photo of the documents told a different story. It proved at least two of Trump's claims were no longer plausible. Pictures didn't lie.

[28]

No Choice

With stacks of classified documents retrieved from Trump's club, Attorney General Merrick Garland could no longer see a way around a collision with the country's next presidential race.

At the start of September 2022, FBI agents and federal prosecutors were engaged in two full-blown investigations into the former president. As with any investigation, they had leads to pursue, evidence to gather, witnesses to subpoena, and, in the documents case, likely charges to debate. Racing ahead at full speed, neither would reach indictment or closure for months. And that was if the Justice Department never let off the gas. But unbeknownst to the public, starting on Labor Day, Garland froze both investigations. For months, investigators would have to wait to issue subpoenas or interview witnesses to gather new information.

Garland had chosen to impose a very conservative interpretation of what DOJ officials called the "60-day rule." The policy, which was not really a rule, urged prosecutors to avoid taking public or "overt" investigative steps within two months of Election Day when it involved candidates in that election.

The National Security Division team running the classified documents case was dumbfounded. They had been preparing to subpoena Meadows, a key witness to Trump's handling of sensitive documents, for interviews before the grand jury. They also wanted to bring in Susie Wiles, the head of Trump's Save America political action committee and his informal chief of staff in 2022. Investigators had received an insider tip that Trump had shown Wiles a classified map when they were traveling together on his plane, and they wanted to ask her about it. The team argued that Trump didn't qualify as a candidate under DOJ policy; he wasn't running for office in the November midterms, members noted. Garland disagreed.

"He's the head of the Republican Party," at least for practical purposes, Garland told his deputies. "I consider him to essentially be a candidate."

The team argued that issuing a subpoena for testimony wasn't a public or overt act. Garland said the department took a risk either way.

"They are likely to make it public," he said.

Similarly, investigators on the January 6 case had spent the summer executing searches and conducting interviews and were still finding more leads to pursue. They would now have to pause that kind of work for sixty days. In September, the team used this quiet period to review something they'd only recently obtained: communications on Rudy Giuliani's phone, which New York–based prosecutors had collected in a foreign lobbying case more than a year earlier and now planned not to pursue.

That wasn't the only challenge for the probes. For almost a year, Trump had been hinting that he would announce a comeback run for the White House. "I know what I'm going to do, but we're not supposed to be talking about it yet, from the standpoint of campaign finance laws," Trump had said back in the fall of 2021. Over the summer, Trump had only grown more bold, campaigning to oust Republicans whom he had come to view as disloyal, especially the dozen that had joined Democrats in voting to impeach him for inciting the January 6 attack. Trump had especially celebrated the defeat of Liz Cheney in Wyoming. He planned to speak at a Labor Day weekend event advertised as "Pennsylvania Trump Ticket." Any day, it seemed, Trump could blurt out that he was running for president.

Garland's boss also showed no signs of turning over the 2024 race to the Democratic Party's next generation, as he suggested he would in his 2021 campaign. Garland wrestled with the path forward. The attorney general was increasingly discussing with a small group of advisers the few short sentences near the top of Title 28, Part 600, of the Code of Federal Regulations: the guidelines for when to appoint a special counsel.

Under the law, it was the attorney general's responsibility to appoint an outside prosecutor to take over an investigation when running that case from inside the Justice Department would present a conflict of interest. Those around Garland saw him as reluctant to declare a conflict, believing it was the job of the Justice Department to rise above politics and always be independent and fair. Still, with no end in sight to the two Trump investigations, Garland told aides that having to name a special counsel was likely inevitable.

Deputy Attorney General Lisa Monaco tapped Atkinson, who had served as a prosecutor in Mueller's office, to begin quietly assembling a short list of candidates. Soon, Garland, Monaco, her principal deputy, Marshall L. Miller, and Atkinson began meeting regularly to talk through the possible names.

The earliest conversations were animated as much by what Garland didn't want as by what he did. They discussed the ongoing work of Special Counsel John Durham, a former U.S. attorney who had been charged by Barr in 2020 to investigate potential misconduct in the FBI's Trump-Russia probe. That investigation was about to enter its third year, with no end in sight. Mission creep and seemingly endless investigations were always a danger with special counsels. The federal guidelines called for a special counsel to work expeditiously, and Garland made clear he too wanted someone who would move quickly, "make a decision," and move on.

The group began looking for prosecutors who had demonstrated that they had been dispassionate about the facts of a case, equally comfortable going forward if justified or making the tough call to abandon a dubious or weak prosecution.

Each discussion seemed to whittle away another name. One, however, kept standing out on the page: Jack Smith, then a top war crimes prosecutor at the International Criminal Court in The Hague. A decade earlier, Smith had worked his way up to running Main Justice's Public Integrity Section. Formed after Watergate and known for its swagger, the unit had handled many of DOJ's biggest public corruption cases over the last half century but had been stung by the dismissal of the case against Republican Sen. Ted Stevens of Alaska in 2009. Top DOJ officials thought Public Integrity needed a reset, including clearing out a backlog of slow-moving investigations. They saw Smith as the kind of rare prosecutor who could review evidence impartially and act decisively. When Smith took over the division the subsequent year, he ordered a review of cases and closed several, including those of four sitting Republican members of Congress and one Democrat.

Smith rebuffed criticism at the time that DOJ was going soft or was gun-shy to take on politicians in the wake of the Stevens case. "I understand why the question is asked," Smith told *The New York Times* in 2010. "But if I were the sort of person who could be cowed—'I know we should bring this case, I know the person did it, but we could lose, and that will look bad'—I would find another line of work."

The quote provided a small window on Smith's prosecutorial approach that intrigued Garland. Marshall Miller, who had worked with Smith when they were young prosecutors in the Eastern District of New York, vouched for him, describing him as a "prosecutor's prosecutor." He made well-calculated decisions without wasting time and had proven he wasn't afraid of pursuing challenging cases or cutting the cord when a seemingly "righteous" case had serious flaws that would imperil a successful conviction.

The attorney general wanted to meet Smith, but his advisers didn't want someone spotting Smith and asking why the former Justice Depart-ment official had made the trip from Europe to headquarters. So Gar-land's aides arranged a cover story: They would ask Smith to fly back for meetings with the DOJ's Human Rights and Special Prosecutions Sec-tion. Once inside Main Justice, he would be whisked through a back hall-way for a seemingly impromptu audience with Garland. The meeting went off largely as planned and cemented for Garland that Smith was his top choice—if he'd take the job.

Justice Department attorneys began to vet Smith for problems. And because of Trump's earlier attacks on McCabe and other DOJ officials, they also began vetting his wife and looking into any political positions she had previously staked out.

The big question left for Garland was when he would have to pull the trigger. Trump had repeatedly teased a run, but Garland decided that un-til the former president officially filed as a candidate, naming a special counsel was premature. But when that happened, Garland told aides he had no other option.

As one person close to the attorney general for those debates said: "If the subject is the presumed front-runner against the AG's boss, it creates a conflict. Period."

In early September, Olsen, the assistant attorney general, gathered with his prosecutors on the classified documents case at their standing 11:00 a.m. meeting in the National Security Division. They typically convened then, or whenever Olsen returned from going over the President's Daily Brief with the attorney general.

Olsen had added a talented new member to the band after the search: David Raskin. Spry and boyish despite nearing sixty, Raskin was a leg-end at Main Justice for his rigorous terror prosecutions and winning ways with a jury. A product of the Southern District of New York, he had worked on the case of the only 9/11 plotter ever convicted in a U.S. court. He had left government for a lucrative law firm job, but soon missed the righteous work of DOJ and took a junior line prosecutor job in Kansas City to get back on the public service side. Just a few months before the search of Mar-a-Lago, Raskin had overseen the prosecution of an FBI analyst in Kansas City who, like Trump, had taken hundreds of classified documents to her home from work. At that moment, the evidence of Trump's obstruction was building, as was the probability of DOJ bringing criminal charges against him. Olsen added Raskin to the team, realizing he had to prepare for the likelihood of a Trump indictment and would need an experienced closer for trial.

Olsen told the team not to get consumed with Cannon's legally dubious decision to appoint a special master and temporarily halt the review of documents. The department's appellate lawyers would handle the effort to overturn her ruling with the Eleventh Circuit Court of Appeals. Instead, Olsen said, the team had to dig into the case they already had built and try their best to ignore that their suspect was the former president.

It was important, Olsen warned them, that they "not be afraid to do the normal thing."

Olsen raised the general point Edelstein had made after agents had found so many classified documents. The normal thing to do would be to act expeditiously. Analyze the facts of the case and see if charges would stick or not.

"You need to start working on a prosecution or declination memo," Olsen said.

The work would fall to Bratt and Edelstein, an encyclopedia on the Espionage Act that governs classified records, had months earlier been planning to leave and join a D.C. law firm. But after the Mar-a-Lago search she officially turned down the offer.

Based on a long list of prior cases, they all knew they likely had more than enough to indict Trump. But Toscas emphasized that the only way to know was for Bratt and the team to lay out the strengths and weaknesses of the case in standard DOJ form.

"Get it written so we can make a recommendation on whether to prosecute or decline," Toscas said.

Several weeks later, in early October, the attorney general alerted his top advisers that he was preparing for the near certainty he would name a special counsel to take over the election interference and classified documents investigations, based on the expectation that Trump would announce his candidacy. In a news report the first week of October, Trump was described as itching to begin his campaign.

In the second week of October, Olsen asked Bratt to come up to his office for a private chat. He told him Garland was eyeing a special counsel for the case. As Bratt would later tell colleagues, Olsen was one of the best bosses he had ever had, a guy who felt honored to help protect the country and catch bad actors, and it was clear he didn't want to lose this case. He urged Bratt to get cranking on his memo.

"We don't have a lot of time," Olsen said.

But Bratt was also working on responses to Trump's legal arguments and the newly appointed special master. He knew there were so many other questions that he had to answer, some he couldn't during the pause for the sixty-day rule, before he could start drafting anything in earnest; for him and his team this was premature.

On November 3, the team stress-tested a possible Trump defense that had been tossed out by one of Trump's loyal foot soldiers. They interviewed Kash Patel, a former Trump White House aide and Pentagon official, before a grand jury that day. When the documents investigation first became public, Patel had claimed in media interviews that the probe was fatally flawed because he knew Trump had declassified broad sets of sensitive records. Was Patel just bluffing for right-wing audiences, or did he actually know something important to their case? Prosecutors had to grant Patel limited immunity to get him in the witness box that day. Patel's lawyer successfully convinced a judge in closed proceedings that Patel reasonably feared being charged with a crime if he answered honestly. After hours of testimony, prosecutors would later tell others in an update, Patel pulled back somewhat from his on-air statements, saying he only knew about Trump's efforts to declassify a specific set of documents, and didn't know about the larger expanse of records found at Mar-a-Lago.

Bratt and Julie Edelstein also still needed to talk to Mark Meadows. Trump had named his former chief of staff as one of his authorized representatives to the National Archives in the handling of his presidential records. Meadows had also been the man handling nearly everything regarding Trump to the bitter end of his presidency. Bratt called Meadows's lawyer, prominent veteran white-collar attorney George Terwilliger, to seek some of Meadows's documents and communications regarding Trump's departure from the White House and return to Mar-a-Lago.

Terwilliger, seventy-one, a former U.S. attorney in Vermont appointed by President Reagan who had served as deputy attorney general in the George H. W. Bush administration, was a lifelong Republican and about the most experienced defense lawyer Meadows could hope for. After leaving the Justice Department, he had spent the next two decades building McGuireWoods's white-collar practice and played a leading role in the legal fight over the 2000 election recount that put George W. Bush, rather than Al Gore, in the White House. Like many old-school Republicans, including his longtime friend Bill Barr, Terwilliger was disturbed by Trump's role in building the fire that led to the January 6 riot at the Capitol. He felt Trump's greatest exposure for potential criminal charges, though, was his mishandling of national defense information. He had represented Meadows during the House investigation, but now realized he had to get up to speed on a whole new set of facts. He had to learn everything Meadows knew and did as Trump left the White House with a truckload of boxes littered with classified documents.

In studying his client's role, however, Terwilliger learned that a White House staffer had warned about likely government records stacked up in Trump's residence in the final days of Trump's tenure. Meadows had directed that all presidential or sensitive records be packed up and put on a truck heading to the National Archives. Any that might be Trump's personal property could be returned later.

"If there's any dispute, take the records to the Archives" was one of the exhortations Meadows repeatedly gave the staff, his lawyer heard.

Terwilliger saw no way that Meadows had played any role in helping

Trump abscond with sensitive documents. But he needed to know if Bratt considered Meadows a potential subject or target of the probe, so he asked to meet with him in person in early November after he handed over the documents Bratt requested.

Their first meeting was consumed by Terwilliger and his partner explaining what Meadows knew and didn't know about Trump's handling of the records. By the second November meeting with Meadows's lawyers, Bratt was firm in declaring that the prosecutors considered Meadows's real value to them was as a witness.

"Look, we have to call him a subject because he was involved, but he's so far away from being one and far on the periphery," Bratt said.

That's what Terwilliger needed to hear. He was now far more comfortable and would soon agree to his client's answering the government's questions in an investigation that Terwilliger considered a true threat to Donald Trump's freedom.

On November 14, many political reporters in D.C. were making arrangements to fly down to Palm Beach for a "very big announcement" Trump promised to make the next day at his private club. At Justice Department headquarters, the attorney general decided to prepare too. He called Smith to know for sure if he had a special counsel at the ready.

"If I offered you the position, would you accept it?" Garland asked.

Smith said he would. But neither Garland nor his aides knew the horrific shape Smith was in.

Smith was an intense athlete who was virtually always in training for his next triathlon. He had raced in more than one hundred of the swim-bike-run contests starting in his thirties, including several Ironman races, and regularly biked to work. But about two weeks earlier, on November 3, Smith had been hit by a moped while commuting to work on his bicycle. He had already undergone one surgery and was scheduled to undergo a second operation to reconstruct his fractured leg the next day, November 15. Garland's office knew about the accident, but didn't know its severity. When Smith had first been brought to the hospital, emergency technicians commented that his leg moved like a noodle, as if there were no bone inside. After the first operation to stabilize the leg, Smith had been screaming so loudly from the pain that doctors had moved him out of one hospital ward to another section so his fellow patients could sleep.

While Smith was still in a recovery room in the Netherlands, Trump took the stage in the ballroom of his Mar-a-Lago club on the evening of November 15. He announced he would run for reelection for president of the United States. It marked the first time in more than eighty years that a president defeated after his first term launched a campaign to regain the Oval Office.

"America's comeback starts right now," Trump told the crowd of aides and supporters in the same space that, three months earlier, had been temporarily controlled by FBI agents conducting a surprise search to recover government secrets. Trump had several goals in announcing his campaign when he did; among them was to beat the U.S. Justice Department to the punch. Many Trump advisers feared the former president could conceivably be indicted at any time in the classified documents case, and hoped this announcement could stymie investigators.

The announcement sent Garland's office scurrying. To recover from his second leg surgery, Smith had been prescribed powerful painkillers, and now the attorney general's aides rushed to learn whether such sedatives would compromise Smith's ability to legally take the oath of office to become special counsel. Smith decided to leave no doubt about his fitness to do so. He discharged himself from the hospital against doctor's orders. At home, he went cold turkey, taking no prescription drugs.

Finally, Garland was ready to break his own news—first to his troops and then to the public. Early on the morning of Friday, November 18, Raskin got a call from a Justice colleague.

"I'm glad you are in the building," the prosecutor told Raskin. "The attorney general is going to appoint a special counsel and ask you all to join his team."

Within minutes, Garland's office instructed top bosses to personally summon the D.C.-based prosecutors working on the January 6 conspiracy probe as well as those in the National Security Division investigating the classified records at Trump's resort. They had a little less than two hours' notice to report to the attorney general's conference room at Main Justice. Some prosecutors working at their desktops in jeans and button-downs that Friday in the D.C. U.S. Attorney's Office joked with team members that they were especially glad that they kept suits hanging in their offices just in case they had an emergency court hearing.

A little after 1:00 p.m., the attorney general told the assembled group that to ensure the appearance of independence in the two probes scrutinizing Biden's possible political rival for office, he would appoint a special counsel that same day. Trump's announcement of a presidential run had left the department no choice, he said.

"If there was ever a time when a special counsel was required, it's this case," Garland said. "We have someone who's named himself as a candidate for president."

Garland told them his pick was Smith. Younger prosecutors in the room had no reaction, having little knowledge of the guy and only a fuzzy idea of his bio. Raskin was among those old enough to remember the no-drama prosecutor from his early days running cases in New York and quietly cheered. Garland told the gathered prosecutors he was very proud of their hard work and public service to date on these two very difficult, sensitive cases and recognized the public heat they had sometimes had to endure because of it. He said he knew their work product would prove "immensely important" to the new special counsel. Then he turned to the future.

"It's up to each of you to decide what you do next," Garland told the group. But he urged them to continue this public service and join Smith's team to finish the job.

Deputy Attorney General Monaco noted the investigation would continue on the same track.

"It's the same team," she said. "We're just decapitating the leadership."

A few eyebrows went up; some in the room chuckled softly.

"OK, maybe 'decapitate' isn't the best word," she said, smiling.

The news was quick to leak to the world outside. While Garland was still talking, prosecutors noticed alerts on their phones, with a few news outlets saying they had breaking news. Sources said the attorney general planned to name a special counsel for the politically sensitive probes encircling former President—and now candidate—Trump.

And indeed, immediately after talking to the prosecutors, Garland headed to the briefing room to make the announcement to reporters who had been summoned for just this news.

The prosecutors on the documents case reconvened at their National Security Division offices. Raskin tried to soothe those who knew little of Smith and worried about losing Olsen and Garland for a mystery boss.

"He's the real deal," Raskin assured them. "A prosecutor's prosecutor."

One career lifer who had also been in the room discussing the new special counsel was Toscas, the trusted heart and soul of the National Security Division. He was worried. Toscas had learned of the likelihood of Garland naming a special counsel weeks before and had summoned the courage to warn the attorney general against naming one person to oversee both probes. For months, Toscas had been uncomfortable with Justice and FBI officials even privately briefing Garland on both the documents and election cases in the same meeting, which he feared would later be mischaracterized as "the attorney general's anti-Trump briefing." He warned Garland that the optics of this single appointment could be worse.

"It's going to look like the anti-Trump investigation," Toscas said.

Part Three

[29]

Existential Threat

J. P. Cooney liked to move fast on a big case. He knew his old boss and mentor, Jack Smith, did too. So it surprised no one that within hours of Garland naming Smith as special counsel, Cooney was in the U.S. Attorney's office asking for approval to fly to Amsterdam the next day. By Saturday, November 20, Cooney was on the other side of the Atlantic, sitting down with Smith to begin reading him in on the election interference case that Cooney had been supervising for over four months. Alongside the classified documents probe, it was one of the two most sensitive criminal investigations underway in the United States, and Smith was suddenly in charge of both.

Smith told Cooney he didn't want to pause the investigations while he evaluated what he was taking over. Rather, he wanted to keep up the momentum on both and quickly get up to speed as they pushed forward. Just four days after his appointment, on Tuesday, November 22, Smith was deeply engaged. He approved fresh subpoenas to county and state election officials in Arizona, Michigan, and Wisconsin, seeking all their communications with Trump and his campaign advisers and attorneys. The House Select Committee had already obtained many of those documents, but Smith's nascent team wanted to be sure they had everything. The special counsel's requests named Trump's advisers whose communications they were eyeing, including Bill Stepien, John Eastman, Rudy Giuliani, Boris Epshteyn, Sidney Powell, and Cleta Mitchell.

He also conferred by phone that Tuesday with Jay Bratt, a lead prosecutor on the classified documents case. The team was ready to issue search warrants to collect the cell phones of Trump's valet, Walt Nauta, whom they had spotted moving boxes on surveillance tapes. Smith suggested they hold off a few days: He said he needed to alert the Deputy Attorney General's Office to such a significant investigative step that could become public.

Smith had accepted an unprecedented high-wire assignment as well as an imperative to beat an urgently ticking clock. Without a doubt, Smith was also the first to begin such a challenge from a hospital bed in a foreign country.

On the night of November 27, the Sunday after Thanksgiving, Bratt and Edelstein flew to Amsterdam to brief Smith on the documents investigation.

The two prosecutors landed around 7:00 a.m. on Monday, November 28, got some breakfast, freshened up at their city center hotel, and at about 10:00 a.m., walked to Smith's nearby home in the charming Museum Quarter. Inside the tidy, older-style house, they found Smith now confined for the most part to his first floor, where a metal hospital bed had been set up for him to sleep in place of his family's kitchen table. As other visitors had noticed, Smith would wince silently when he moved. Nevertheless, he welcomed the pair and ushered them to sit at the dining-room table, where he joined them after methodically propping his reconstructed left leg on a nearby chair.

Smith's reputed intensity quickly became evident. From his grasp of the evidence to date, the two could tell he had read every pleading, document, and case outline that Bratt and Edelstein had emailed to him several days before the visit. Smith also had questions about each of the eight key topics the pair had come to discuss, and he asked about nearly every witness and their level of cooperation. The two also briefed Smith on the then still secret move by the government to get the chief judge in Washington, D.C., to order Trump to turn over any other records he might have at his Florida home or stored elsewhere. With only short breaks for coffee and meals, the briefing lasted eleven and a half hours, and the prosecutors departed for their hotel at 9:30 p.m.

The next morning, the trio was back around the dining-room table at 9:00 a.m. Smith had new questions about the strengths and weaknesses of the evidence. He queried the prosecutors about the Justice Department's effort to overturn Judge Cannon's appointment of a special master and the oral arguments before the Eleventh Circuit the previous week. The Florida district court judge's ruling, roundly criticized by legal practitioners as a bizarre departure from the norm of not interfering in a criminal investigation, had created a huge obstacle for Bratt and Edelstein by enjoining government investigators from taking control of the government's own records.

The group took a two-hour break midday, when a physical therapist arrived for a scheduled session with the injured Smith, then they reconvened to wrap up. Smith told them he planned to name Cooney as his deputy. "J.P. gets shit done," Smith said.

For expediency, he would soon need to organize the team into specific tasks, and told the pair he wanted them to get going on creating a detailed to-do list of sorts, outlining the next steps the team needed to take quickly in the investigation. The prosecutors parted sometime after 6:30 p.m.

Edelstein was all-in and told Smith she looked forward to the work ahead. As they parted, she said something along the lines of: "See you in the States."

The visit had been demanding and invigorating for both, but also clarifying for Bratt. Before Garland had named a special counsel, Bratt had led the documents case alongside his work as chief of the

Counterintelligence and Export Control Section in the National Security Division. To keep going with the documents case, however, Bratt would have to step away from the influential post. After Smith assured him that he would remain a lead prosecutor on his team, Bratt returned to D.C., planning to stay with Smith until he reached a decision about whether to indict the former president. With all the evidence Bratt had seen, he had little doubt which way Smith would ultimately tilt.

Next, Ray Hulser, a former deputy of Smith's at the Public Integrity Section whom he had brought aboard, along with Cooney and Windom, flew to the Netherlands for a similarly extended briefing on the election interference case. They outlined the five lanes of inquiry into Trump that prosecutors were probing: 1) the fake electors scheme; 2) false claims to state officials to get them to upend vote tallies; 3) the effort to install Jeffrey Clark and misuse the Justice Department; 4) the pressure on the vice president to subvert the will of voters; and 5) false claims about election fraud to instigate the Capitol riot—and to then benefit from the chaos to delay certification of Biden as the next president. They were also tracking who had financed efforts to promote the fraudulent claims of a rigged election and the January 6 rally. Smith chose to leave the investigation proceeding on its many tracks.

In those early weeks, Smith gave one address to the staff by video link and seemed to be stiffly reciting much of what Garland had said in announcing his appointment. Upon returning to the States, Cooney and Hulser pressed the team for frequent briefing memos to share their progress and next steps with Smith. Also back in D.C., Edelstein and Bratt set off for an important scheduled interview: Mark Meadows. The prosecutors had long viewed the elusive man at Trump's side for the last eleven months of his presidency as key to both investigations.

The prosecutors met Meadows where they thought he would be most comfortable: the downtown D.C. offices of his lawyer George Terwilliger's firm, McGuireWoods. They had also agreed to hold a proffer session, a less formal type of interview that could help shield Meadows from potential charges by showing his willingness to share information. Bratt and Edelstein had hours of questions: How had Trump handled classified records while president? Did he take classified records back to his residence? Had Meadows ever seen Trump with classified material after he left office?

Sitting beside his attorney, Meadows started cautiously but grew more comfortable, giving the investigators their first peek into the White House through his eyes. Trump's chief of staff said he had been in the president's bedroom in the residence only once—when Trump had COVID—and noticed boxes of records there but didn't know their contents. Meadows said various intelligence and military officials showed Trump classified records on a daily basis, but it was chiefly the National Security Council's job to track them. He knew of the president's push in his final days in office to declassify Crossfire Hurricane records and others related to the Russia investigation. Meadows told prosecutors that, despite Trump claiming after the Mar-a-Lago search that he had a standing policy of declassifying everything he took to his residence, the chief knew of no such policy.

In response to questions, the former chief of staff also recounted an October 2021 visit he made to Mar-a-Lago that prosecutors hadn't heard about before: Meadows, one of Trump's chosen representatives to the Archives, was friendly with Archivist David Ferriero and offered to help Trump locate records that the Archives was by then pressing him to return. Trump turned down Meadows's offer, saying something to the effect of: "We'll see what we have." But after the interview ended, Meadows told Terwilliger he remembered something he hadn't mentioned to prosecutors. Terwilliger called Bratt, who put Edelstein on the line. Soon the lawyer shared the stunning recollection.

Not long after Trump left office, Meadows had recalled, the ghostwriter and publisher of Meadows's memoir were interviewing Trump in person at his Bedminster, New Jersey, golf club. Meadows had been on the phone listening. During the chat, Trump mentioned highly sensitive records he wanted to discuss. "Trump was making a reference to having classified records related to the bombing of Iran," Terwilliger said.

The prosecutors fell silent.

"Just thought you'd want to know," Terwilliger added.

If confirmed, this could be a huge new development. Did Trump have a classified war plan he was discussing with random citizens who certainly lacked security clearances? They thanked Terwilliger. If the tip also panned out about Trump showing Wiles a government map, could there be two times the former president had flashed classified documents?

Finally cleared by his doctors to travel, Smith flew on Christmas Day to D.C., where he had put Cooney and Hulser, his trusted Public Integrity lieutenants from a decade ago, in charge of helping him run the office. He would soon add another from his old PIN team: David Harbach, to help lead the documents case.

The next day, December 26, was a federal holiday, but Bratt, Cooney, and Hulser were among those who greeted Smith at the special counsel's new office space at the building that DOJers called 2CON. The Justice Department's unremarkable glass-and-steel structure in Northeast Washington provided overflow office space for its attorneys, but few would know that walking past. Smith temporarily camped out on the sixth floor until building maintenance could get the third-floor offices equipped and ready to become the team's long-term home. Some on the team found one feature limiting initially: Until he closed up shop and moved out, Special Counsel John Durham's team was typically occupying the third floor's only large SCIF for secure meetings.

Smith spent a few days that holiday week between December 26 and New Year's Day reviewing for the first time the classified documents retrieved from Mar-a-Lago, most of which he could inspect in a secure room at the FBI's Washington Field Office. The remaining set of records—fourteen documents categorized as SSMs for the special security measures they required—revealed details of intelligence and military programs so sensitive that they had been moved to an access-controlled safe at FBI headquarters.

On New Year's Day 2023, in Smith's second week in the office, the special counsel's team was eager to finally receive a long-awaited trove of information they hoped would push the investigation forward: the transcripts of interviews conducted by the House Select Committee. DOJ had been seeking that information with thinning patience for most of the previous year. Smith's team knew after Republicans won control of the House in November, the committee would likely be shut down and retrieving records could become impossible. After the committee released its final, 845-page report on December 22, Smith's team implored committee staffers to finally share their documents. In the final days of the year, a handful of attorneys and staffers who remained in the committee office engaged in a frenetic, last-minute scramble to review and share their evidentiary documents with the special counsel.

On January 1, less than forty-eight hours before Republicans could lock down all the evidence or perhaps delete it entirely, a committee staffer summoned an attorney from Smith's team to Capitol Hill to receive a hard drive containing the committee's work. But after the appointed hour for the handoff had come and gone, the meeting was called off as staffers were still working to compile and review the documents. The next day, Cooney drove to the Capitol and at the last minute succeeded in collecting two hard drives containing about two hundred interview transcripts, less than twenty-four hours before Republicans began shutting down the committee's website. Many transcripts were dense, running hundreds of pages. The drives also contained videos of additional interviews and notes of others—plus voluminous phone call records of Trump advisers and campaign staffers leading up to January 6. Smith nonetheless gave his team a rush deadline: They had one week to read everything and synthesize their findings.

Smith set a grinding tone in his first days in office, which would thereafter pace the work of the special counsel's team.

One afternoon in the first week of January, Smith held an introductory meeting with all his team attorneys in the oversize, windowless break room in the center of the third-floor office that the group dubbed the Secret Kitchen. Hulser had bought cans of soft drinks and plates of cookies from a nearby Harris Teeter and placed them on the table for the occasion. Smith told them he knew he had inherited a "great team" that would work hard. He said the evidence would guide them in deciding whether to charge Trump or anyone else.

"No decision has been made or will get made until all the facts are on the table," he said.

Several felt an awkwardness in the room that Smith seemed unable to smooth over. Many people didn't know each other and, other than Cooney and Hulser, Smith really didn't know them.

In a larger meeting the next week, Smith gathered the election interference, or EI, team and the classified documents, or CDI, team, plus FBI agents and other support staff. He said he could tolerate no leaks about Special Counsel's Office operations. Prosecutors knew instinctively how secretive their work had to be. Soon they would fly all over the country to talk to witnesses about whether the former president had committed crimes, and other than explaining their departures to spouses, could never share with anyone outside the office what they were doing.

Inside, the investigators took precautions too. For daily meetings, the two teams took turns gathering in a back corner conference room they called Dog Park; it happened to overlook an apartment building's dog park, but they kept the blinds closed to avoid having any curious apartment dwellers on higher floors looking in. For large or more sensitive meetings, including weekly updates with FBI agents, they gathered around the long table in the Secret Kitchen, a room with awkward countertops but no appliances, creating the feel of a space that construction crews never quite finished.

In those first weeks, attorneys found Smith led with two key operating principles: He wanted to know and study every fact and event himself, and he pushed progress through to-do lists and deadlines. From the day he started in the office, he had daily meetings with both teams, at which attorneys briefed him on what they'd learned and what they were doing next. Later, as the two cases took firmer shape, the "tell Jack everything" meetings were cut back to three a week. In one of Smith's early meetings with the election interference team, he made clear that he expected attorneys to put in long hours when needed.

"We don't have as much time as you think," Smith said.

Some in the room considered it an odd comment. These accomplished attorneys had given up other jobs, some with significantly higher pay, to join the office and believed they'd shown their commitment to this complex, historic case. The urgency was also obvious: They could all hear the loud, ticking clock driving the work. Smith, chosen for the job because of his reputation for decisiveness, told his deputies they couldn't leave the public wondering or Trump battling unsettled allegations of wrongdoing; in the interest of justice, he had to give both sides definitive answers by either charging or not before the election.

In his first briefings with Bratt and Edelstein, Smith proposed they finish the probe and decide whether to indict Trump in three months—by March. Bratt and Edelstein knew Smith had little experience with classified records cases and explained it would take many weeks just to negotiate with U.S. intelligence agencies which documents the prosecutors could use as evidence and how they could describe them. The pair suggested six months. Smith nodded and tried to hold firm to that timetable.

"Here's the date, and we're triaging to get to that," Smith said.

His pacesetting was accompanied by a push to coordinate and prioritize next investigative steps, something many of the prosecutors on the team valued. In team meetings, flat screens or whiteboards at the front of a conference room charted streams of work, what subpoenas had to go out, who was doing what, what was left to tackle. Smith and Cooney told prosecutors to stop chasing some answers; they weren't essential. Cooney often served as Smith's enforcer, sharing Smith's orders or concerns, but in his own loud, go-get-'em, team captain persona. He kept on top of the tasks accomplished and those not yet completed.

Smith had intense rules for witness interviews. He required that every one be recorded rather than the standard of having FBI agents take notes and summarize the conversation in a 302 form. Smith didn't want someone to later whip up a conspiracy and dispute the FBI agents' notes. He also required that prosecutors produce a list or memo of their proposed questions for every witness for him to review, two days before the interview, along with exhibits and evidence they might use. If they did not, he could ask to postpone the interview. Many respected this level of intensity, but smirked when Smith tried to tell them how to do something they'd done for years. He sometimes urged his attorneys to plunge headlong into the most critical questions as soon as they got the witness seated, when seasoned prosecutors knew from experience that they often got more cooperation using a gradual, softer approach.

The good part about the process, some attorneys saw, was that it brought Smith directly into the team's latest thinking on the cases and made him intimately familiar with each piece of evidence and witness and their potential contribution to a future indictment. They found the prep sessions tedious, however. Smith sometimes asked an attorney to predict how a witness would answer each question, hoping that would help the team spot an irregularity or something that could advance the case.

On the last day of January, Windom and Gregory Bernstein, a dogged assistant U.S. attorney who had worked with Windom for years in Maryland and returned from California to join him on the special counsel staff, had their own scheduled interview with Meadows. Smith's office now questioned the chief of staff using information from emails they had obtained in a secret court proceeding in late December. They involved topics that Meadows claimed were protected by executive privilege, including advice and discussions with the president. Some of the emails also contained descriptions and clues about Trump's many schemes to claim a rigged election to stay in power. Meadows, who had never been eager for this moment with prosecutors, nonetheless had answers at the ready. He explained to the prosecutors his overview of those last fifteen weeks of Trump's presidency: Starting on November 5, he believed fraud had very likely tainted the election. But over the next three weeks, Giuliani and other campaign lawyers kept losing cases in court after court. After a lengthy briefing with FBI Director Chris Wray, Barr also declared Justice attorneys and agents had found no substantial fraud. Meadows told prosecutors of a December 2021 West Wing meeting when Sen. Lindsey Graham confronted Giuliani, demanding that if he had any hard evidence of election fraud, it was time to "show me the beef." Giuliani's answers were so flimsy, Meadows said, that he concluded there was nothing there.

During a coffee break on the first day of questioning, Meadows's lawyer shared a story with Windom and Jamie Garman, a lead FBI agent on the case, about a client he'd had in a different special counsel investigation decades earlier. Patrick Fitzgerald, a legendarily tough and upstanding prosecutor, was then investigating who in the George W. Bush White House had illegally leaked the classified identity of an undercover CIA operative named Valerie Plame. Fitzgerald suspected Plame's cover was blown as retaliation after her husband publicly disputed the Bush White House's justification for going to war with Iraq.

Terwilliger recounted how Fitzgerald had asked for a break in the middle of interviewing his nervous client, an administration official, and asked to speak with Terwilliger outside the interview room for a moment.

"You need to have a talk with your guy, because some of the things he's saying are not lining up," Fitzgerald told him.

His client in the Plame case had not been trying to hide anything, but was either misremembering the facts or making nervous mistakes. Terwilliger told this new special counsel team that he had been grateful for Fitzgerald's honorable treatment back then. Fitzgerald was focused on getting the truth, he explained, not catching a side player in a false statement.

The very next day, ironically, it was Meadows who arrived in the interview room agitated and nervous, as if he feared misspeaking—and getting indicted for it. Prosecutors began the morning as they had the previous one, asking about emails in which Meadows appeared to be an ardent supporter of a strategy to use "alternate" electors from swing states to challenge Biden's victory. Meadows's answers came off as stilted. Terwilliger asked Meadows if he'd like to take a break and took the chance to speak to Windom outside.

"You see that he is a different person today," Terwilliger said. "He's very worried that his openness is walking him right into a perjury trap. . . . If there's anything you can do, it would be appreciated."

Windom listened without responding. But when the interview resumed, Windom said something on the record to Meadows before asking his next round of questions.

The sentiment of Windom's message was clear: "This isn't a trap. We're just trying to get to the truth." He said prosecutors appreciated that Meadows was there and trying to help.

It was as close as Meadows was going to get to an assurance he was not a target of the investigation himself. All they really cared about was figuring out whether then President Trump had committed a crime. Meadows answered the rest of their questions with more ease.

Smith worked tirelessly, and often spent from morning till night holding meetings around the small conference table in his office. Increasingly, he conferred privately with his trusted inner circle, mostly Cooney and Husler, and sometimes Windom on election interference. Later, he would include Bratt and Harbach in these closed sessions regarding classified documents. But he largely left other attorneys on both teams in the dark. Smith was a one-way street, demanding information but sharing it with his teams sparingly or not at all.

Smith's insular and siloed management style ruffled some feathers; his methods left some talented prosecutors, who took pride in learning their cases inside and out and feeling relied upon for their expertise in complex frauds or national security, seething.

A federal prosecutor who had worked with members of Smith's inner circle sympathized with a colleague about the emerging office dynamic. "It's not just that they think they are great lawyers—which they are. It's that they don't countenance that other people could be great lawyers too."

Some dubbed the bubble forming around Smith as FOJs—Friends of Jack. Another called it "the Cult of Jack": People invited in revered him, but the so many others left on the outside, not so much.

The result was an office that wasn't exactly whistling while it worked. The toughest blows for prosecutors came when Smith made decisions without ever asking their opinion on material they knew best, or gave the pretense of asking them when he had already decided.

To those often seated inside Smith's corner office and to those who had known him for decades, Smith had nothing to apologize for. The attorney general had asked him to be special counsel, and it was Smith who would ultimately have to answer for his work. He wasn't going to run the office by committee.

In February, Smith asked Hulser to start a running draft for a prosecution memo in the documents case. Smith hadn't made a final decision to indict Trump, but wanted to prepare for that likelihood. Hulser had no direct hands-on knowledge of the case, but he had Smith's trust. Team members were asked to send critical information to Hulser, who followed up with more questions and assembled a series of drafts that evolved as prosecutors brought in new evidence and details.

Smith also tasked James I. Pearce, a talented appellate lawyer who had worked at Public Integrity, to analyze where the team should bring its charges: in D.C., the place where Trump had taken the records from, or in Florida, where he had conspired to conceal them.

Some of the new details that came into the documents case that spring were holy-shit shocking—and prosecutors were salivating at the wow factor they would have at trial one day. Harbach and Edelstein had also obtained the tape recording that Meadows's ghostwriter had made of his Bedminster meeting with Trump on July 21, 2021.

Some listened with mouths agape as they played the recording in Smith's office. Trump repeatedly complained that Mark Milley, his former chairman of the Joint Chiefs of Staff, was a dangerous hawk and had proposed ways to attack Iran.

"He said that I wanted to attack Iran. Isn't it amazing?" Trump said in the recording, referring to Milley's claim. The former president then told his audience he had papers, Pentagon war plans, that showed this was the Defense Department's proposal, not his. "These are the papers! This was done by the military and given to me."

Trump at one point indicated the documents he was flapping around were classified.

"See, as president I could have declassified it," Trump said. "Now I can't, you know, but this is still a secret."

The team added another great arrow to its quiver when Judge Howell ordered in March that Corcoran, Trump's lawyer, turn over the notes of iPhone recordings he had dictated, like a personal journal to himself. They revealed a nearly contemporaneous record of Trump's reluctance to turn over the documents, and the former president at times misleading Corcoran.

"Well, what if we, what happens if we just don't respond at all or don't play ball with them?" Trump asked Corcoran, according to his phone notes. "Wouldn't it be better if we just told them we don't have anything here?"

On another subject, Raskin had been tasked with understanding everything about the classified records Trump had hidden in his club. He had come up with a powerful narrative plan for describing the key records they would use at trial and showing the jurors the harm that would befall Americans' safety if the documents had landed in the wrong hands.

Raskin also unraveled a painful truth about the White House: It had a less than airtight system for tracking and recovering classified records shared with then President Trump. Along with Brett Reynolds, another CDI attorney, Edelstein, and FBI agents, Raskin reverse engineered the trail of these highly sensitive maps and memos that the FBI found at Mar-a-Lago, tracking them back to the veteran intelligence officials and generals who first showed them to Trump in the Oval Office. In interviews, they described how Trump frequently just picked a document up from the table where they were conferring and walked off.

Raskin had asked several of these officials a version of the same question: Did you ask Trump for it back when he took it?

"No," said one, incredulous at the question. "He's the *president*."

After obtaining the email and phone records of Trump aides, Bratt learned that on the morning of June 3, as he and FBI agents had been driving from the airport to Mar-a-Lago to pick up the additional classified records, Trump aides were driving the opposite way with an SUV filled with boxes from Mar-a-Lago. Trump's valet had instructed them to load the boxes onto Trump's plane, the government later found. Records concealed from the government would now accompany the family as they departed for Bedminster for the summer.

Meanwhile, the election interference case was similarly gaining steam that spring—and had amassed powerful evidence. In March, Windom asked Bernstein, Timothy "Tad" Duree, and Mary Dohrmann, all experienced line attorneys in the office, to begin outlining a draft prosecution memo. Within weeks, the draft had swelled to a daunting length. The fake electors plot took dozens of pages to explain, as did Trump's pressure campaign on officials in each swing state. They then described Trump's threat to replace the acting attorney general with Jeffrey Clark, who promised to use the department to claim election fraud.

Meanwhile, Smith's team was gathering new information about Trump's pressure on Pence not to certify the election. The team knew a little of their exchanges from the House committee probe and Pence's autobiography, *So Help Me God*, published in late 2022. But Smith's team learned that Pence had kept notes and journals about lengthy meetings that he'd described in his book with just a sentence or two.

Windom commissioned a memo to analyze all the evidence and possible charges, which prompted a discussion about Section 241 of the criminal code, Conspiracy Against Rights. The felony charge had been written into federal law in the aftermath of the Civil War, when the Ku Klux Klan and other white supremacist groups had coordinated to terrorize Black residents and keep them from exercising their newfound voting rights. Prosecutors had used 241 to convict John Ehrlichman, a Nixon aide, of authorizing a burglary in the aftermath of the Pentagon Papers. Smith and his deputies saw evidence that Trump's attempt to upend vote tallies in some states that were unfavorable to him was essentially stripping some Americans of their fundamental right to vote.

Duree, meanwhile, set out to verify that every one of Trump's many claims about election fraud ahead of January 6 was indeed false, an effort Smith came to see as important to the strength of their case. Prosecutors would face ridicule if even one of Trump's claims about deceased voters, double voting, uncounted ballots, or other fraud proved true, Duree stressed to the team.

By listening to Trump's speech on the Ellipse on the morning of January 6, Duree and others identified more than forty individual claims of fraud. By studying his additional claims on Twitter and at rallies, they added over ten more. Over several months, they contacted state election officials, reviewed ballot records and electronic voting systems, and eventually found not one of Trump's claims could be affirmatively proved true.

Aided by House interview transcripts and follow-up interviews, Smith's team also fleshed out the fake electors scheme. Some Republicans who had signed the fabricated documents, and who had previously declined to talk to congressional investigators, told Smith's team that they had felt misled by surrogates for the Trump campaign. Several said they had signed their names having been told to think of their roles as akin to those who had cast disputed electoral votes decades earlier in Hawaii after the 1960 presidential contest.

The prosecutors and agents on Smith's team came to view many of the 2020 electors as rubes. There were a few who had realized the potential illegality of signing the fake documents and refused to do so. One of those, a Republican in Pennsylvania, even told Smith's team that he recognized the plan as an attempt to "overthrow" the government. But most seemed clueless about having done anything improper. Smith's team discovered that top advisers to Trump and possibly the president himself understood the larger scheme: to use them to pressure Pence to put off certifying the election results on January 6.

"Did anyone ever inform you that the documents you were signing on December 14, 2020, might be used as a reason not to count Georgia's electoral votes during the certification of the election on January 6, 2021?" one of Smith's investigators asked an elector who signed a forged document. "No, nobody told me," the Republican replied. "Would you have agreed to that?" an investigator asked. "No," the witness said.

Smith's team also learned from an interview with Republican National Committee Chairwoman Ronna McDaniel that more than a week before the Electoral College met on December 14, Trump himself had encouraged her to help implement the elector plan. Trump and Eastman called McDaniel on December 6 and told her it was important that the RNC organize the electors meeting in several states. Afterward, Trump continued to communicate about electors with Eastman and Rudy Giuliani.

Smith's team discovered that on December 13, the day before the elector votes, Trump followed up, asking a senior campaign adviser "what was going on" with electors. Trump that day also urged his campaign to publicize the effort, putting out a "statement on electors." Several campaign officials, however, refused. "Here's the thing," Trump's deputy campaign manager wrote to others in a group text, "the way this has morphed it's a crazy play so I don't think anyone wants to put their names on it." Another adviser replied to the group, suggesting the fake electors scheme had crossed into the realm of "Certifying illegal votes."

On the evening of December 14, the RNC's McDaniel had received an update for Trump, and she sent an email to his executive assistant at the White House under the subject line "Electors Recap—Final." The email contained an accounting of fake electors who had cast ballots that day for Trump in Arizona, Georgia, Michigan, Nevada, Pennsylvania, and Wisconsin, even though Biden had won all of them. Trump's assistant responded to McDaniel: "It's in front of him!"

Smith's team had hit dead ends in confirming one of the most provocative accounts the House Select Committee presented in its televised hearings. Smith had early on asked his team to figure out whether they could corroborate key episodes that former White House aide Cassidy Hutchinson had described. Smith was especially interested in her claim that a White House deputy chief of staff alerted Trump that some of his supporters had not entered a rally stage area because they were likely armed. She testified that she overheard a furious Trump insist they remove the magnetometer checkpoints, which agents suspected the supporters were avoiding so police would not confiscate their weapons. "They're not here to hurt me," she testified that Trump said. "Take the fucking mags away."

Smith had wondered whether some of Hutchinson's claims might be relied upon at trial. Duree and others conducted multiple follow-up interviews with Hutchinson. But as they probed her account with others, they could not corroborate certain elements. Still, at one point, Smith told the elections team he wasn't ready to give up on Hutchinson's account, so the interviews continued. Ultimately, however, former Trump administration officials uniformly and fiercely disputed her accounts under oath. Prosecutors told Smith they wouldn't want to use Hutchinson as a witness in court. Smith agreed.

As each new tranche of information about fake electors came in, members of Smith's team intermittently raised the idea of opening separate case files on Giuliani, Eastman, and others. Each time, however, Smith dismissed the idea. He said he did not want the office getting bogged down in potentially prosecuting those around Trump. Each former administration and campaign official charged could create their own web of complications and delays, affecting a case against the former president.

Anyone working in the office knew Smith felt the clock. He had not declared a go or no-go date to bring charges, but he told his staff that if they asked a grand jury to indict, they had to do so as far ahead of the 2024 election as possible.

When the team raised the prospect of charging co-conspirators, Smith told prosecutors to stay focused on the main reason the office had been created: to handle the unique sensitivities of investigating Donald Trump. He didn't want the team ending up like Mueller's special counsel operation, he said, splintering into "cottage industries" of smaller side investigations that failed to address their main charge. Smith and his top deputies did individually weigh decisions about whether to go forward with cases against six co-conspirators whose interactions with Trump would be central to the case but decided against seeking indictments at the same time as those against Trump.

"Jack always felt like he was hired—that we had a special counsel—because of the political sensitivity of prosecuting a former president who also happened to be a candidate for a future presidency," said one person who spoke with Smith repeatedly at the time. "If the D.C. U.S. Attorney's Office wanted to prosecute the other guys, they could go ahead later and do so."

The team didn't dwell on the political reality: If Trump won reelection in 2024, the co-conspirators would surely never face charges.

In April, when Hulser circulated what he considered a close-to-final copy of the prosecution memo for the documents case, the team recoiled; his draft contained several factual errors. It wasn't Hulser's fault; he was a great prosecutor. He had Smith's trust, but he had no hands-on role in the probe. Some on the team worried it also lacked a clear narrative that pulled together the story of Trump's plot to put some of the nation's most sensitive secrets at risk and lie to keep them. In reaction, the team piled on with a raft of suggestions and corrections, the beginning of a series of rewrites. Bratt took over writing an executive summary; Harbach and other team members got busy revising the rest.

In mid-April, Smith contacted the U.S. attorney in Miami with a series of secret requests. He wanted to know if he could borrow his grand jury in the Southern District of Florida. The special counsel had decided he needed to make a big change of plans—but hadn't told everyone on the team.

Raskin had always assumed the document case would be charged in the District of Columbia, where they had been presenting all the evidence to a grand jury and where the judges had extensive experience with classified records cases. He was stunned one day in the office hallway when Bratt told him of Smith's decision to indict Trump in Florida.

"What?" Raskin said, sounding surprised.

"Yeah, Jack has decided," Bratt said. The case law generally favored the prosecutors bringing these charges in Florida, Bratt said. Smith had conferred with his inner circle, as well as Bratt and Edelstein, and all had agreed.

"We have a memo," Bratt said, referencing Pearce's analysis. "It makes sense. I'll explain it to you."

"You all are fucking insane," Raskin said.

Raskin's gut instincts weren't anything to scoff at. Olsen had first asked him to join the documents case after the August 2022 search of Mar-a-Lago for a reason. Raskin was one of a tiny handful of the most experienced national security prosecutors in the country and had an impressive batting average in trials. While Smith had very little experience in prosecuting national security cases or classified records crimes, Raskin had a lot of it, on top of his extensive trial experience. But the special counsel was only seeking the advice of his core team.

Raskin soon got a copy of the memo and agreed its analysis leaned toward bringing the charges in Florida. But so what? Raskin asked Bratt. Prosecutors made their own venue decisions all the time. Whether the law favored going to Florida or not, prosecutors could legally choose. He told teammates they first had to ensure their case had the best chance of being properly heard.

To Raskin, Judge Cannon had handed the special counsel's team a huge gift in late 2022. She had appeared biased and willing to ignore the law, as well as the decisions of scores of previous judges before her. It was a big neon sign for the team to stay far, far away from her district. He argued to his teammates that the prosecutors' top priority was getting to first base—getting a fair hearing—and not first obsessing over the possible appeal.

"This is an existential threat to the case," Raskin told them.

Raskin liked and respected Smith. Quite a lot. They hailed from the same generation of DOJ trial lawyers and had the same pure motivations about putting the case first. Each was proud to be called a "prosecutor's prosecutor," the highest compliment a trial attorney could receive from his peers. But Raskin told colleagues he was starting to realize something unsettling: He disagreed with Smith on most of the big decisions he had made so far.

[30]

Great Story, Not a Great Case

By the start of May, Smith's leg was healing and he was training again, working up to what would become twenty-five-mile bike rides before going to the office in the morning, and that would leave his security detail gasping for air. Word spread in the office that to keep pace, his agents began trading places mid-ride, and eventually turned to e-bikes. Smith's operation was also hitting stride. The special counsel had reached his decision on the classified documents case and invited Olsen and Toscas, the heads of the National Security Division at Main Justice, to review the team's draft prosecution memo. To say the document was closely held was putting it mildly. It bore a cover with bold lettering that read:

"Eyes Only. Copy 1 of 2."

Opening the folder revealed a document unprecedented in American history, a plan to charge a former U.S. president and his personal valet with conspiring to mishandle and conceal classified documents.

Toscas and Olsen, two seasoned prosecutors who could quickly spot a mediocre case from a strong one, dug in—and were impressed. Importantly, they noticed, Smith's team had gathered critical new evidence in the past six months since Olsen had relinquished his National Security Division team to the Special Counsel's Office. Under Smith, the team now had found evidence that Trump had misled his own lawyer Evan Corcoran about where to search for the remaining classified records. They could also show that when Trump knew he was required to turn over remaining documents, he nonetheless instructed aides to move boxes away from his lawyer and federal investigators. They even had Trump on tape after leaving office, boasting about still having a classified war-planning document in hand and describing it to visitors at his Bedminster club.

"Good fact," Toscas later remarked to his colleagues.

Olsen and Toscas, as well as David Newman, Olsen's principal deputy, had a few days to review it before Smith and his team were scheduled to make a presentation in person. Smith was accompanied by Bratt, Cooney, and Hulser.

Olsen told Smith and his team he wasn't there to tell them whether to indict Trump and what charges to bring. But he wanted to make sure Smith's prosecution plan was generally within the bounds of the way the National Security Division would tackle this kind of alleged crime of mishandling classified documents.

Smith's memo had laid out the pros and cons of indicting Trump in D.C. versus Florida, and summarized Pearce's analysis. Smith's team saw a risk the government could be overturned if they charged Trump in D.C. with the Espionage Act crimes under Section 793. Those charges formed the heart of the government's case, in which they claimed that Trump willfully retained thirty-two national defense documents whose release could harm national security. The potential vulnerability of those espionage charges was that the government had ample evidence Trump knew he was sitting on a pile of sensitive records at Mar-a-Lago, but had somewhat less convincing proof that he had broken the law when taking records out of Washington, D.C., some on the day of Biden's inauguration. That was because a moving company had trucked a portion of boxes that prosecutors believed contained some classified records to Mar-a-Lago on January 17, when Trump was still president. Trump had taken another set of boxes with him on Air Force One on January 20, just hours before he would no longer be president and would lack authority to take them anywhere. Smith considered it a safer bet to charge him in Florida, where they had extensive evidence of the steps Trump had taken to willfully withhold and conceal the records. They also couldn't charge Trump with making false statements in D.C.

Prosecutors have a lot of discretion in where to bring a charge, as long as some portion of the criminal conduct occurred in that district. But Smith's choice was Florida.

The National Security Division chiefs, who together had overseen the prosecution of scads of national security cases in D.C., saw the logic of the memo, but didn't think Florida was their only option. Olsen had expected to bring charges in D.C. if his team decided to prosecute Trump. Newman, who recognized the legal argument for Florida, nevertheless warned Smith and his lieutenants that the greatest danger of charging in Miami was to have the prosecution over before it even began.

"The biggest risk you have is Cannon gets the case," he said. "Then it's dead."

Smith knew the risks, but he hadn't experienced the battle that the National Security Division had waged against Cannon starting in August 2022, when she was assigned to oversee what initially seemed like a laughable legal bid by Trump to retain some power over the evidence that FBI agents had seized from Mar-a-Lago. He hadn't been there when she made what DOJ alums of both Republican and Democratic stripes called "egregious" and "unprecedented" rulings in Trump's favor, moving to block investigators from reviewing government-owned documents seized in a court-ordered search.

Smith had a bit of bravado. "I'm not worried about Florida," he said. The case was very strong, he told Newman and his colleagues. They could handle whatever happened in court.

In similar fashion, Smith sent copies of the prosecution memo to the Attorney General's Office, and a few days later he and his team presented the plan to Garland in person. The attorney general didn't raise issues with the evidence or strength of the case, but he did want to know more about the decision to seek an indictment in Florida. Smith and his team again explained the risk to the Espionage Act charges in D.C.

At the end of the day, Smith said he thought the worst risk was to have the conviction overturned based on venue. In avoiding one risk, he was willing to expose the case to another.

After the team left, Garland asked his staff to stress-test Smith's position on Florida and, specifically, whether the 793 charges could be doomed, or seriously endangered, in D.C. Senior counselor Rush Atkinson and others from Main Justice consulted with J. P. Cooney and reported back that the 793 concerns seemed sound. Smith's team, they reported, had also analyzed the specific risk Newman had raised and that others at DOJ feared. They initially calculated the odds of Judge Cannon being randomly assigned to the Trump documents case at just one in six, Main Justice officials were told. Said another way, it looked like the U.S. government had a better than 80 percent chance of landing before another federal judge.

Garland and his staff considered two other potential pitfalls in bringing the documents case in D.C. Trump's attorneys would likely file for a change of venue right off the bat, paralyzing the case. Trump would surely accuse the department of jury shopping; Washington voted overwhelmingly for Democrats and its jurors had convicted 100 percent of Capitol rioters.

Smith's team soon realized that, due to judges' caseloads in the Florida district, the chance of drawing Cannon was far worse, about 31 percent, or nearly one in three. But to Smith and Garland, the roulette numbers didn't matter. The legal analysis showed the best case was in Florida. They would simply have to face that possibility.

In the second week of May, Smith's documents team flew down to Miami, checked into a hotel under a phony corporation's name, and began secretly re-presenting all their evidence to a grand jury there. It took five weeks. Reporters didn't figure out the special counsel had relocated to Florida until a couple of days before the team asked a grand jury to vote on whether to indict Trump.

On June 6, CNN reporters surprised many others covering the special counsel's work with the scoop that a federal grand jury had been empaneled in Miami in the classified records case. It set off a flurry of activity, with reporters from other outlets staking out the courthouse and trying to determine if Smith planned to try to indict Trump there.

Meanwhile, Smith's team received a surprise of its own. On June 7, the squad supervisor for the FBI's agents on the documents case called Bratt to share a closely held secret. She said the FBI had to complete some new paperwork that day in a hurry, which required updating their investigative file. They had to say they were now officially investigating Trump.

"We're going to redo this investigation and say he is the subject of the investigation," the female supervisory agent explained.

Bratt was floored. For nearly eighteen months, the DOJ and FBI had been investigating whether the former president hoarded classified records and sought to conceal that from the government. They had conducted an unannounced search of his home. A judge had agreed to force his lawyer to testify about his private and normally privileged conversations with Trump, because the prosecutors and agents showed Trump had likely used his lawyer in his criminal plot.

"You gotta be kidding me," Bratt said, mentioning the FBI's code name for the probe. "Nowhere in Plasmic Echo files did you say that Trump was a subject of this? After all this?"

Bratt shared the news with the team. Some concluded this further showed the FBI's continued angst about tussling with Donald Trump. Yet the FBI had its own arcane ways; counterintelligence probes like Plasmic Echo typically didn't name subjects, so nobody had rushed to add the former president's name.

The next day, Thursday, June 8, sometime after 3:30 p.m., a grand jury operating in secret voted to indict Trump. And as was often the case, it was Trump who broke the news and took the opportunity to frame it in his terms. That evening, a little before 7:30 p.m., he posted on Truth Social that he had been criminally charged and had been ordered to appear in court in Miami the following Tuesday.

"The corrupt Biden Administration has informed my attorneys that I have been Indicted, seemingly over the Boxes Hoax," Trump wrote. He claimed he was being treated unfairly. "I never thought it possible that such a thing could happen to a former President of the United States," he said in a campaign website post that ended, in part: "I AM AN INNO-CENT MAN!"

A jury of twenty-three members, however, had agreed there was probable cause to believe former President Donald Trump had engaged in thirty-three felony counts of mishandling classified records, conspiring to obstruct a criminal probe, and making false statements. The indictment, and all the details that revealed the team's hard work, wouldn't be unsealed for the public until the next morning.

A thunderstorm was rolling in that afternoon over Miami, darkening the sky as if it were night. Sometime between 5:00 and 5:30 p.m., the CDI team learned on the federal court's electronic website which judge had been assigned to the case. Some gasped seeing the initials at the top of the docket: AMC.

Bratt called Olsen to tell them the fate of the judicial wheel: Aileen Mercedes Cannon.

"You're not going to believe it," Bratt said. "We got Cannon."

It was the worst news.

"We're screwed," Olsen said.

Bratt had first notified Smith, who was back in Washington with many of the team members. Smith didn't really react but thanked him for the update.

On Friday, June 9, the next day, Smith's trusted inner circle was insisting everything would be fine. Cooney called Newman, who had worried about just this event, saying the Special Counsel's Office would just play it straight and show Cannon the facts.

He delivered a similar message to Atkinson.

Garland, however, was nervous, staffers sensed. Cannon had acted so erratically, no one could say how she might be able to jam up and delay the government's case.

Bratt and Harbach flew back from Miami on a midmorning flight, arriving at Reagan National Airport at about 1:00 p.m., and headed straight for the office. Harbach, who had teamed with Bratt to handle all the arguments in court, said he remained eager to get in front of Cannon. With such powerful evidence, he said, they had a good chance to win her over.

Bratt poked his head into Smith's office.

"This is really not good," he said.

"We'll see. We'll see," Smith replied. "We don't know yet. Give her a chance."

Smith recognized the seismic shift in the case, however, and the need to do some hand-holding, which was far from his natural mode. That Friday, the special counsel went from office to office, giving one-on-one pep talks to the worried members of the CDI team—some of them despondent. He told them not to forget all the hard work they had put in to gather the evidence, and that now they needed to present their best case.

"We've got to keep our focus and hope for the best," Smith told them.

Early on the afternoon of June 13, 2023, former President Trump stepped out of his Doral golf resort and walked to a waiting motorcade for a twelve-mile drive to the federal courthouse in downtown Miami. Police had closed off some major thoroughfares for the lengthy procession, and Secret Service agents armed with long guns stood guard, much as if Trump were still commander in chief. From inside one of the fast-moving government Suburbans, Trump lobbed accusations that the Justice Department was unfairly persecuting him.

In posts to his 5.4 million followers on Truth Social, Trump had earlier published a video in which he denied the charges and framed the indictment as a naked attempt to interfere with his campaign to return to the White House.

"Our country is going to hell, and they come after Donald Trump, weaponizing the Justice Department, weaponizing the FBI," Trump said, equating the documents case with the Mueller investigation from his first term. "A boxes hoax, like the Russia, Russia, Russia hoax," he said. "This is what they do, what they do so well . . . They're trying to destroy a reputation so they can win an election."

Trump's trip to the courthouse for his arraignment fell on the eve of his seventy-seventh birthday. He reposted a story about Smith, writing over the special counsel's face: "This is the Thug . . . that Biden and his CORRUPT Injustice Department stuck on me." Smith, he wrote, was a "Trump Hater . . . who probably 'planted' information in the 'boxes.'" From the cocoon of the motorcade, Trump fired off a final message in all caps: "ON MY WAY TO THE COURTHOUSE. WITCH HUNT!!! MAGA."

As the entourage pulled into the courthouse complex, a smattering of Trump's supporters, some holding up signs that read SHAM INDICTMENT. WEAPONIZED DOJ, broke into a ragged rendition of "God Bless America." Counterprotesters cheered Trump's arrival to be tried as a federal defendant, with some thrusting placards in the air that read NOBODY IS ABOVE THE LAW. One woman held up a piece of white paper that simply read FINALLY. After whisking him inside, U.S. Marshals booked Trump, requiring him to place his hands on a scanner to take digital copies of his fingerprints, but they stopped short of asking him to pose for a mug shot. Soon, Trump was escorted to the thirteenth floor and into a wood-paneled courtroom with blue carpeting. A clerk called criminal case No. 80101. Three attorneys from Smith's team were at the prosecutor's table. Trump stood about twenty feet away at the defendant's table. Asked by a magistrate judge how the former president would plead, his attorney Todd Blanche, a former federal prosecutor, said:

"We most certainly enter a plea of not guilty."

With Smith looking on from the second row of the gallery, his team offered to release Trump on his own recognizance, without bail. Within an hour, the courthouse spectacle was over, and Trump made a point of immediately making a campaign stop. At a Cuban coffee shop, he posed for pictures while grumbling. "Some birthday," Trump said, pursing his lips, "some birthday."

That same day, back in Washington, a contingent of Trump's most loyal allies in Congress went on the offensive, staging an event to amplify Trump's emerging campaign message that with its two-pronged Special Counsel's Office investigation, the Justice Department was again on a full-blown "witch hunt" against Trump to gin up wrongdoing, not only with the alleged document crimes but also around January 6. At almost the same time that Trump was standing at the defense table in Florida, Rep. Matt Gaetz, Republican from Florida, and other Republicans convened their own hearing in the Capitol Visitor Center. With a bank of cameras lined up for conservative outlets, the hearing had the feel of alternative programming to the day's unflattering events for Trump.

Gaetz, Rep. Paul Gosar, and lawyers for rioters unspooled conspiracy theories, questioning whether the entire attack had been secretly instigated by government agents who had infiltrated the crowd. They also alleged that the DOJ had unfairly corralled rioters in an illegal dragnet, having set up a "trespass trap" by not labeling Capitol hallways as off-limits to the public and then scooping up cell phone data of those who had been in the building during the riot.

Among those at the official hearing's witness table was Jeffrey Clark, the Trump Justice Department official who had nearly succeeded in a plan to send a letter to officials in Georgia ahead of January 6. The Republican congressmen, however, did not ask Clark to explain his planned interference in a statewide election. Instead, they gave him a platform to question whether Americans really saw what they saw on January 6. Prosecutors and the media, Clark said, had pushed a "fake narrative that an insurrection had occurred."

Sitting beside Clark was Ed Martin, an attorney representing three

January 6 defendants, who had taken to calling those who had been incarcerated for January 6 "survivors." Martin took the opportunity with the cameras rolling to blast his courtroom opponents from the D.C. U.S. Attorney's Office. Such allegations had already fallen flat in court, but he charged that the government's attorneys had targeted the rioters, lied, and leaked information to hurt his clients' and other rioters' cases. "The system that we rely on, the due process that's been at the heart of America, has been denied to the individuals here," Martin said.

Unbeknownst to Trump or his supporters, Smith was at that moment, in June 2023, well on his way to indicting Trump a second time in federal court.

Cooney and Windom had called the election interference team together for a meeting at Dog Park to share the outcome of a series of high-level huddles in Smith's office. Smith laid out the four charges and proposed indictment he wanted to bring against the former president: the civil rights count, 241; two charges linked to obstructing the congressional certification, 1512; and a charge of conspiracy to defraud the United States, 371. In its simplest, most distilled form, the Special Counsel's Office would charge that Donald Trump had perpetrated a fraud on the United States. As president, he had spread baseless lies to Americans that he would have won reelection but for vote tallies having been manipulated in key states. Then, despite repeated warnings that the conspiracy theories were wrong, the president engaged in unlawful efforts to push states to discount legitimate votes or set aside tallies to award him electoral votes to stay in power. Smith's deputies went around the room asking if prosecutors agreed with the plan. "Is everyone on board?"

Some had mild reservations about how the civil rights charge would play in court. But it was clear Smith had decided, some felt, and their approval was a perfunctory exercise.

Smith set a deadline of early July to send the case to the attorney general for review.

Again, Smith's team planned to hand-deliver a closely held draft to Main Justice: both a prosecution memo and a 350-page, book-length document called the Evidence Summary, or ES, laying out every shred of proof to support the charges. At 6:55 one evening, just a few days before they planned to share the document, Bernstein and a group of line attorneys were still making final edits to the Evidence Summary when Cooney passed through the office and demanded they hit the print button.

Garland, Monaco, and their most senior advisers read copies ahead of time. But this time, as Smith, flanked by Cooney and Hulser, presented the planned charges, the attorney general's reception was decidedly more cautious.

Ahead of Smith's arrival, Garland and Monaco and their top aides compared notes: The draft seemed rather long, and mostly covered already well-known actions and efforts by Trump and his advisers. Broadly, Smith had framed the case as a conspiracy to commit fraud, but the details of the fake electors scheme, the pressure campaigns, and the Clark drama did not always fit into one simple narrative. In short, Trump and his advisers' multifront effort to overturn the election was, as it always had been, complicated. Compared to the documents case, it was not an open-and-shut, black-and-white tale. Here the prosecutors had no pictures of an ex-president's private shower room filled with classified documents and a trusted aide caught on camera moving away boxes before a search.

At his conference table with Smith, Garland was visibly unenthusiastic. He recommended they continue working to stress-test the charges. In particular, he wanted to be sure that the indictment was not vulnerable to claims that its accusations interfered with Trump's right to free speech, his right as a candidate to say what he believed.

Garland also wanted Solicitor General Elizabeth Prelogar to work with Smith on how the evidence supported the fraud. It was a rare step for prosecutors to work with the premier appellate office before an indictment, and unprecedented to consult with the solicitor general herself. But criminal charges against a former president were unprecedented too. Smith, in fact, had already sought her office's advice on some matters.

"You need to have further consultation," Garland told Smith. The congenial attorney general didn't often criticize in large settings, so the circumspect remarks landed hard. Back at the Special Counsel's Office, Smith huddled for a debrief. The staff dove back into the draft that evening and, within a couple days, met with Prelogar, a former Garland law clerk who had the attorney general's implicit trust. If Prelogar signed off, many aides knew, the attorney general likely would too.

Prelogar and Smith's attorneys together streamlined the argument for the conspiracy charge. Her staff also recommended whittling down references to Trump riling up the crowd on January 6, something Garland had also found worrisome. One main concern seemed to be driving the solicitor general: She didn't want to leave an opening for a judge to question whether the government was on safe footing and get into a position of debating with the bench whether any single charge or part of a charge should be allowed to proceed. Doing so could cause delays, but losing any single prong was also a pet peeve of the attorney general. It was not acceptable, and certainly not on this case, for a judge to find the government had not locked down its case.

Within a couple weeks, Smith's team had a revised draft of the charges but found it challenging to get it in front of decision-makers. It was summertime in D.C. Congress and most of the nation's top judges had gaveled their sessions to a close and left town. Justice Department attorneys were also juggling the rare window for family vacations. In mid-July Smith was able to return to Main Justice to present the slimmed-down memo.

One senior Justice Department attorney reading the case cold wondered how it would play out. A jury might initially convict, but would it survive on appeal? He knew well that for any successful fraud case, prosecutors have to show efforts on the part of the defendant that are based on "deceit, craft or trickery, or at least means that are dishonest."

Trump had never publicly wavered in insisting he had won. Even privately, he'd only left open the possibility he knew otherwise a few times. In a moment with family members, he said: "It doesn't matter if you won or lost the election, you still have to fight like hell." Once, when Biden was on television, Trump had said to a staffer, "Can you believe I lost to this f'ing guy?"

Senior Justice Department lawyers reviewing the case saw copious evidence that Trump had abused his office to stay in power, and behaved reprehensibly by pushing a lie to the public and bullying his fellow public servants to keep him in power. But to some, the evidence for the core claim that Trump plotted to defraud the American public seemed thin.

Smith anticipated a fight at trial over whether Trump had been clear in knowing he'd lost, and he planted an early flag in the opening lines of the indictment, filed on August 1: "The Defendant spread lies that there had been outcome-determinative fraud in the election and that he had actually won. These claims were false, and the Defendant knew that they were false," it read. In its opening pages, the indictment also included an eight-point section to further make the case for Trump's deceit. It was titled "The Defendant's Knowledge of the Falsity of His Election Fraud Claims."

By Smith's reading of the *Principles of Federal Prosecution*, he had an obligation to seek an indictment and charge Trump. It was the only way to protect the integrity of the electoral process and the future of the country's tradition of a peaceful transfer of power.

The senior DOJ attorney concerned about the charges understood the duty to charge the former president, but he feared a rocky road ahead.

"My reaction was it was missing something critical. You think if you are going to have the president doing all this stuff . . . then you would have Trump saying to someone 'I know this is bullshit' or 'I know I lost.' But it wasn't in there.

"It was a great story, a corrupt guy pushing a lie, but not a great criminal case."

[31]

"The President Is Now a King"

O n August 3, 2023, Donald Trump stood in a federal courtroom in D.C. to face charges that his lies had seeded the deadly attack that shattered the United States' tradition of peaceful transfers of presidential power. As Jack Smith sat in the front row and his lead attorneys looked on from the prosecutor's table, Trump told the magistrate judge his plea: "Not guilty."

It was the second time in a little more than seven weeks that the two sides had gone through this formal step. But another number associated with Trump that day illustrated how long the Justice Department had tarried in getting to this moment. In the two years, six months, and twenty-eight days since rioters had waged a violent attack on the Capitol, the Justice Department had identified, investigated, and charged 1,077 people for their involvement.

Trump—the one who had urged his supporters to come to the Capitol and "fight like hell," the person the special counsel now argued had started it all—was defendant number 1,078.

Judge Tanya S. Chutkan, who had been randomly assigned to preside over the case, watched a magistrate judge arraigning Trump from a remote courtroom receiving a live feed. Chutkan, sixty-one, a former public defender and white-collar defense attorney who had been appointed to the bench by President Obama, asked the magistrate to relay a message from her to the lawyers on both sides: They needed to get ready to pick a trial date.

Chutkan had earlier told fellow judges she hoped she didn't get Trump's case. Given Trump's profile as Republican nominee and his divisive role in America, his prosecution would bring intense scrutiny and disrupt the life of whichever judge presided. Chutkan loved her work, but detested the spotlight.

"I've had enough," Chutkan had earlier told fellow judges, referring to the waves of pro-Trump, anti-Chutkan hate mail she received when she sentenced several January 6 rioters to prison.

When Chutkan was new to the bench, a friendly federal appellate judge, Robert Wilkins, asked her about her goals.

"To never see my name in *The Washington Post*," she said, grinning.

"Good luck with that," Wilkins chuckled.

Soon her name would be in news pages everywhere, aided by the social media posts of Donald Trump.

The morning after Trump's Tuesday indictment, staff from the court's security office arrived at Chutkan's chambers to tell her they were immediately assigning her a security detail. Chutkan, a Black woman who had been born in Jamaica, had never flinched at a case and didn't now. Colleagues attributed her self-assuredness to decades of experience in D.C. courtrooms and weathering second-guessing by critics.

"For a lot of people, I seem to check a lot of boxes," Chutkan said in an interview for a courthouse profile published the year before. "Immigrant, woman, Black, Asian. Your qualifications are always going to be subject to criticism and you have to develop a thick skin."

She would need it with Trump, who quickly leapt into attack mode. He reformulated the criminal charges against him into rocket fuel for his campaign. He accused a "biased" judge and "Crooked Joe's Department of InJustice" of unfairly persecuting him in order to remove him as a political threat. On August 4, the day after his arraignment, Trump sounded a battle cry for a new war he would wage: "IF YOU GO AFTER ME, I'M COMING AFTER YOU!"

Trump's supporters quickly took their leader's words to heart. The next day, on August 5, Abigail Jo Shry, a Texas woman, called Judge Chutkan's chambers and threatened to kill her.

"If Trump doesn't get elected in 2024, we are coming to kill you, so tread lightly, bitch," she said in her message. "You will be targeted personally, publicly, your family, all of it." Shry would later plead guilty to federal charges of making threats.

Chutkan didn't worry for her safety. A team of U.S. Marshals now accompanied her everywhere she went. They joined her when she jogged in the early mornings around her hilly Northwest Washington neighborhood near Rock Creek Park. At their request, she stopped biking to the courthouse, and instead the marshals escorted her there. When she returned home, two large security vans stayed parked outside as sentries.

Trump didn't soften his attacks. In an August 14 social media post, he called her a partisan who was out to get him. He noted that Chutkan had chided a January 6 defendant, saying that she and others mobbed the Capitol in "blind loyalty to one person who, by the way, remains free to this day."

"She obviously wants me behind bars," Trump wrote in his post. "VERY BIASED & UNFAIR."

Chutkan had asked Trump's defense lawyers and Smith's team to propose when the trial should begin. Smith pushed for a January 2024 start date, just a little over four months away. Trump's team, by contrast, argued Chutkan had to postpone the case until long after the presidential contest, and proposed April 2026, then two years and seven months off.

In a late August hearing, just weeks after taking over the case, Chutkan announced she had chosen a trial date of March 4, 2024. She said the court had to be guided by the Speedy Trial Act, and that meant doing what was fair not just for the defendant but also for the public.

"The public has an interest in the fair and timely administration of justice," the judge said. That meant the trial would begin a day before Super Tuesday, when the greatest number of states hold presidential primary elections, a sign that the case would inevitably run into election-year politics. But Chutkan said the court would have to divorce that fact from its obligation to evaluate Trump's guilt or innocence.

"Mr. Trump, like any defendant, will have to make the trial date work regardless of his schedule," Chutkan said.

Amid Trump's continued barrage of attacks on the judge, the special counsel, and the DOJ, Smith's team requested that Chutkan order Trump to stop trying to intimidate people and taint the jury pool. Trump claimed that a jury in "filthy and crime-ridden" D.C. would never give him a fair shake and echoed supporters' claims that Chutkan was "a fraud dressed up as a judge in Washington, D.C." and a "radical Obama hack."

Chutkan had been reluctant to restrict Trump's speech, but on October 16, she agreed to a narrow gag order, worried most that Trump's megaphone was hard for D.C. jurors to avoid.

"This is not about whether I like the language Mr. Trump uses," Chutkan said. "This is about language that presents a danger to the administration of justice."

Trump's dual strategy throughout a lifetime of legal travails had been attack and delay. This strategy had worked brilliantly when he was president and repeatedly put off giving an interview to Special Counsel Robert Mueller. Trump's new attorneys, John F. Lauro and Todd Blanche, had fully latched on to his successful playbook, working to either push off the trial or have it thrown out altogether.

But Chutkan was a hard no on any more delays.

"This trial will not yield to the election cycle," she said.

At the same time, though, Lauro and Blanche were pursuing an audacious plan to get the special counsel's case dismissed. The two had argued Trump was president at the time of the alleged offenses and therefore couldn't be charged. Presidents, they insisted in a fifty-two-page pleading filed October 5, weren't only immune from prosecution while in office, as the Justice Department had long held, and which

Mueller had concluded left him unable to even decide whether Trump had obstructed justice. Rather, presidents had "absolute immunity" from criminal prosecution—and forever—for acts they'd taken while in office, Trump's team claimed.

"As the Constitution, the Supreme Court, and hundreds of years of history and tradition all make clear, the President's motivations are not for the prosecution or this Court to decide. Rather, where, as here, the President's actions are within the ambit of his office, he is absolutely immune from prosecution," they wrote.

Trump was now staking out a newly convenient position that happened to be the opposite of what another attorney of his had argued in successfully keeping the Senate from convicting Trump in his impeachment related to the Capitol attack. In that earlier justification, Trump attorney David Schoen said in February 2021 that Congress shouldn't bother with impeachment because it was the Justice Department's job to prosecute a former president if he had engaged in wrongdoing.

"We have a judicial process in this country. We have an investigative process in this country to which no former officeholder is immune. That is the process that should be running its course."

Slate magazine published an article with a headline that called out the galling reversal of his legal position: "The Most 'Heads I Win, Tails You Lose' Trump Argument Ever."

But even lodging this argument carried unique power. Unlike most challenges in a criminal case, which can't be appealed until after the case is over, the claim that Trump was immune had to be addressed before the trial could proceed. Chutkan paused to rule on Trump's motion. The assignment was daunting; she'd be the first district court judge in a half century to rule on whether a president was immune from criminal prosecution. Chutkan had persuaded one of her departing clerks to stay on, giving her four rather than three clerks to help her research and draft the opinion and run her normal caseload.

Lauro and Blanche argued that all of Trump's actions that prosecutors claimed were criminal election interference, like calling out election fraud and talking to state officials about vote counts, could just as equally be viewed as Trump having faithfully executed his duties to ensure a fair federal election process. "The prosecution falsely claims that President Trump's motives were impure—that he purportedly 'knew' that the widespread reports of fraud and election irregularities were untrue," the filing read.

Inside Smith's office, prosecutors had expected the immunity claim, but considered it brazen to recast Trump's actions to undermine the election as benevolent. A prosecutor on Smith's team had come to believe that Trump was, as former FBI Director James Comey once said, a man of "above average intelligence." For him to have repeated one or two lies about fraud could have been written off as mistakes. But his decision to repeatedly amplify over fifty different baseless claims was, he believed, a coordinated disinformation campaign. The special counsel's staff filed a fiery fifty-four-page response arguing that nothing in the Constitution, history, or Supreme Court precedent "supports the absolute immunity he asks the Court to create for him." Trump's "novel approach to immunity would contravene the fundamental principle that '[n]o man in this country is so high that he is above the law,'" prosecutors wrote.

On December 1, Chutkan sided with prosecutors and rejected the absolute immunity claim.

"No court—or any other branch of government—has ever accepted it," she wrote, "and this court will not so hold."

Further, "The United States has only one Chief Executive at a time, and that position does not confer a lifelong "get-out-of-jail-free" pass," she wrote. "Former Presidents enjoy no special conditions on their federal criminal liability."

Trump's legal team wasn't really trying to win over Chutkan. Rather, Lauro and Blanche could now appeal and indefinitely freeze the case in its tracks based on their immunity claim. They predicted the Supreme Court justices might very well feel compelled to address the weighty separation of powers question the Trump case raised and might further delay the planned March trial date.

Smith's team had made the same calculation. The trial team recognized the near inevitability that the Supreme Court would want to review the matter. So Smith's office quickly attempted an end run and petitioned the Supreme Court to take up the case directly in hopes of avoiding a monthslong pit stop at the court of appeals. Smith warned the high court that if it did not make the rare decision to take up the case out of order, Trump's trial could be postponed beyond the 2024 election. "The United States recognizes that this is an extraordinary request. This is an extraordinary case," Smith wrote. Two weeks later, the Supreme Court issued a one-line, unsigned opinion declining to hear the case out of order. Nevertheless, just two weeks after that, on January 5, the justices agreed to an expedited hearing for a different case that threatened Trump's campaign: A Colorado court had barred Trump from the Republican primary ballot under a state law that prohibited those who engaged in insurrection from seeking high office.

Judge Chutkan and the chief of the court, Judge James "Jeb" Boasberg, watched this development with concern. The two judges had then been meeting every few weeks with the U.S. Marshals and court staff to work out the security logistics of holding Trump's trial. To ensure security for everyone, they had decided to move the trial from Chutkan's court to another at the end of a back hallway with limited public access. They planned to install a second set of magnetometers, to screen people not just when they entered the building but again when they entered this courtroom. The court staff were assessing the most secure way for Trump to enter the building each day.

But the Supremes' refusal to hear the immunity challenge quickly gave the two district court judges their first reason to doubt the election case would be heard that year. The high court's choice to let the appeals court go first, all but ensured two rounds of appeals court challenges because the Supremes could likely feel compelled to review a court loss by a former president. That could consume more than a year's time. The tension was rising: Would this historic case have a chance of going to trial before the presidential election? The two judges paused some of their logistics planning.

"It's clearly going to delay things," Chutkan warned her clerks. On January 9 a three-judge panel of the U.S. Court of Appeals convened to hear oral arguments on the immunity fight. James Pearce argued for Smith's team. Absolute immunity, Pearce said, was a dangerous concept. "Never before has there been allegations that a sitting president has, with private individuals, and using the levers of power, sought to fundamentally subvert the democratic republic and electoral system," Pearce said, "and frankly, if that kind of fact pattern arises again, I think it would be awfully scary if there weren't some sort of mechanism by which to reach that criminally."

The three appeals court judges—Karen Henderson, Florence Pan, and Michelle Childs—all sounded critical of Trump's claim when questioning the two sides, but as weeks stretched on afterward without a ruling, the process began to have Team Trump's desired effect. At the end of January, Chutkan put the special counsel's case on ice. She also took off her calendar a weekslong block she had long reserved to preside over the trial in March. As January turned to February, the appeals court judges themselves became a focal point of gossip and rumor at political gatherings in D.C. Could Henderson, a George H. W. Bush appointee, be holding up the process?

But on February 6, the appeals court issued what many saw as an even more forceful ruling than Chutkan had. "We cannot accept former President Trump's claim that a President has unbounded authority to commit crimes that would neutralize the most fundamental check on executive power—the recognition and implementation of election results," the panel wrote. "At bottom, former President Trump's stance would collapse our system of separated powers by placing the President beyond the reach of all three Branches."

Again, Team Trump appealed—without knowing just how angry and eager Chief Justice John Roberts was to overturn the lower appellate court. On February 22, Roberts sent a private message to his fellow justices ripping into the appeals court ruling and urging them to hear the appeal. The lower court's reasoning was weak, he said, and had "failed to grapple with the most difficult questions" about presidential immunity. In his message, later revealed by *The New York Times*, Roberts predicted: "I think it likely that we will view the separation of powers analysis differently."

Less than a week later, on February 28, the Supreme Court agreed to grant limited review of the case, but focused on one question that Roberts had sculpted: *"Whether and if so to what extent does a former President enjoy presidential immunity from criminal prosecution for conduct alleged to involve official acts during his tenure in office."*

The order seemed straightforward, if somewhat technical, but judges in D.C., including in the circuit and district courts, saw something else. This amounted to the death knell for getting the Trump case to trial before the November election. There were two reasons. The justices had set oral arguments for the last day of their calendar before the fall session, adding more delay. And the court's "to what extent" question seemed like the opening salvo to spark a fresh round of appeals. In the most likely scenario, after the court ruled, Chutkan would have to analyze which specific acts by Trump were immune and which were not. Trump would then appeal her findings. All of that could take another year. At Mar-a-Lago that night, Trump's advisers celebrated their rising confidence that the case would never see a courtroom before November. "They were popping champagne," one reporter later said they had heard.

Smith's team had planned on presenting a forceful case against Donald Trump in March and April. Political pundits had spent months pondering what it could do to Trump's campaign to have the darkest day of his presidency retold in Technicolor at the height of the primary calendar. Instead, that spring, with the election interference case on ice, Trump found himself in a New York courtroom as prosecutors rehashed one of the oldest scandals of his political career, his payments to cover up sex with adult film actress Stormy Daniels.

The case had been resurrected by Manhattan District Attorney Alvin

Bragg, who now wanted to hold Trump criminally responsible for hiding the costs of paying off Daniels. The case was widely seen as the weakest of those against Trump—as well as the most politically controversial because of the age of the claims. Because the facts were so well known, it was also the least consequential with voters—at least, that was, until Trump turned the court into the backdrop for his own daily press conference.

On the first day of the tawdry court spectacle, Trump emerged to a gaggle of television cameras and reporters and immediately capitalized on the captive audience. With Blanche at his side, Trump turned the day's news away from jury selection and to how he was being persecuted, right down to the judge possibly preventing him from attending his son Barron's high school graduation.

"He was looking forward for years to have graduation with his mother and father there and it looks like the judge isn't going to allow me to escape this scam trial," Trump said. "The graduation of my son, who has worked very, very hard."

A couple of days later, Trump's live, televised diatribe focused on the court's dirty bathrooms. Then he returned to complaining, inaccurately, that Judge Juan Merchan would not let him attend Barron's graduation. Trump discussed anything, really, other than the facts of the case itself. His campaign even began timing fundraising email blasts to Trump's courthouse stand-ups. "The heartless thugs are forcing me to skip my son's graduation," one read. Trump's backers then took to social media to bash the judge as well, calling him a "Leftist NYC judge" and predicting blowback for "this Marxist tyranny." One Facebook video poster told viewers: "I never thought I would disrespect a Judge but F*** Justice Juan M. Merchan. This man is the Devil!"

The truth never had a chance. Judge Merchan had said he needed time to rule on Trump's request to postpone the trial, but could adjourn the trial for a day or two to accommodate a break for his son's graduation.

. . .

Back in D.C., Smith's team and attorneys from the Solicitor General's Office were busy preparing for the Supreme Court hearing on immunity. With Trump being the first former president charged with crimes, they had little law to work with. Trump's team liked to point to a 1982 decision finding that former President Nixon should be absolutely immune from damages liability "for acts within the 'outer perimeter' of his official responsibility." Attorneys on Smith's team dismissed that civil immunity case and argued a Nixon case from 1974 was far more relevant. In that case the court ruled Nixon had to comply with a subpoena for tapes of White House conversations and rejected the claim that presidents enjoyed an "absolute, unqualified presidential privilege of immunity from the judicial process." Smith's team called this the "closest historical analogue" and said that when Nixon accepted President Ford's pardon, it showed the two men's "recognition that a former President was subject to prosecution."

Smith had asked Michael Dreeben, the department's longtime deputy solicitor general who had argued over one hundred cases before the high court, to make the historic argument on April 25. In a secret moot court a few days before, Dreeben, bald and sporting a thin beard, stepped to the podium to face the jabbing questions of several colleagues serving as stand-in justices. Three hours in, the room was getting hot, water bottles were running empty, but no one paused for a break. Even when the group wrapped the questioning, it went straight into a nearly two-hour postmortem analyzing weak spots they had identified.

Some on Smith's team looked on, shocked by the emerging consensus among the department's top appellate lawyers. Smith's team had won so convincingly at the district and appeals court levels, they said, but it looked like they could easily lose conservatives on the Supreme Court. Members of Smith's team left the room, discussing the likelihood they would have to contend with some compromise decision by the court.

On the morning of the oral arguments, bright sunlight reflected off the nearby Capitol dome as the western front of the Court and the four words chiseled atop its entrance remained in shadows: EQUAL JUSTICE UNDER LAW. Judge Chutkan was jogging around the Capitol, her U.S. Marshals alongside, and spotted the crowds outside the court. The press room was abuzz with more reporters than had been on hand for any hearing that session. Taking their seats at the government's table were Dreeben, James Pearce, Jack Smith, and J. P. Cooney. The special counsel's top supervisors and senior litigators, Ray Hulser, John Pellettieri, Cecil VanDevender, Molly Gaston, and Thomas Windom, sat in a line behind.

"Oyez, oyez, oyez," announced the marshal as the justices entered. "God Save the United States and this Honorable Court."

From the first sentence, Trump attorney John Sauer left no doubt that the case was monumental. "Mr. Chief Justice, and may it please the Court: Without presidential immunity from criminal prosecution, there can be no presidency as we know it," Sauer began. "If a president can be charged, put on trial, and imprisoned for his most controversial decisions as soon as he leaves office, that looming threat will distort the president's decision-making precisely when bold and fearless action is most needed." To allow otherwise, Sauer warned, would lead to occupants of the Oval Office governing in fear of what their political rivals might do to them when their terms expired.

Dreeben, in his opening, was no less emphatic. "This Court has never recognized absolute criminal immunity for any public official," he said. To accept Trump's novel theory that such a blanket protection exists "would immunize former presidents from criminal liability for bribery, treason, sedition, murder, and, here, conspiring to use fraud to overturn the results of an election and perpetuate himself in power."

The back-and-forth that followed led to nearly three hours of the most bizarre hypothetical arguments that longtime court reporters could recall. Justices threw out one untenable situation after another, debating actions that future presidents could in theory claim were official acts for which they were later immune from prosecution.

"If the president decides that his rival is a corrupt person and he orders the military or orders someone to assassinate him, is that within his official acts that—for which he can get immunity?" asked Justice Sonia Sotomayor.

Sauer said it potentially could. "It would depend on the hypothetical," he replied, "but we can see that could well be an official act."

Justice Samuel Alito raised the specter of the president calling in SEAL Team 6, but said officers would be a check, bound by military rules not to follow an unlawful order.

But what if such activity was discovered after a president left office? Justice Elena Kagan asked. "Let's say this president who ordered the military to stage a coup, he's no longer president. . . . You're saying that's an official act? . . . That's immune?"

Again, "it would depend," Sauer said. The only backstop in Trump's model was that a president could be prosecuted after leaving office if they were first impeached by the House and convicted by the Senate.

By the end of the hearing, the justices seemed to have rejected the extremes presented by both sides, but any possible consensus on official acts with immunity was unclear. It also didn't seem likely the court would quickly decide the case at hand. Justice Neil Gorsuch, a Trump appointee, said near the end of the hearing that the court had to write a rule "for the ages." Justice Brett Kavanaugh, another Trump appointee, agreed: "This case has huge implications for the presidency, for the future of the presidency, for the future of the country."

Whatever the justices decided would have profound consequences for a document gathering dust back at Smith's office. The court's decision would determine how much of the special counsel's roughly hundred-page trial plan would ever see the light of day.

Shortly after 10:30 a.m. on Monday, July 1, a staffer delivered a freshly printed copy of the Supreme Court decision to Attorney General Merrick Garland. He began reading, and before the end of the first page, he was in disbelief. In a 6–3 vote, the court's conservatives had redefined two centuries of presidential power, giving the nation's chief executive complete immunity from future prosecution for acts considered part of his core responsibilities, and a "presumption" of immunity for any other act taken in his capacity as president:

"The nature of Presidential power entitles a former President to absolute immunity from criminal prosecution for actions within his conclusive and preclusive constitutional authority," it read. *"And he is entitled to at least presumptive immunity from prosecution for all his official acts."*

The decision, authored by Chief Justice Roberts, was jarring in theory, but enraging as Garland and others got into the specifics.

Any conversation the president had about installing Jeffrey Clark or misusing the Justice Department to sow distrust about the election in Georgia or elsewhere would have to come out of the special counsel's case:

"Because the President cannot be prosecuted for conduct within his exclusive constitutional authority, Trump is absolutely immune from prosecution for the alleged conduct involving his discussions with Justice Department officials."

Similarly, Smith's team would be hard-pressed to argue that Trump's pressure campaign on Vice President Pence was also not shielded from prosecution:

"Whenever the President and Vice President discuss their official responsibilities, they engage in official conduct," Roberts had written. Any claims Trump made on Twitter or in speaking at the Ellipse ahead of the Capitol riot also had a high chance of being protected and immune.

"[M]ost of a President's public communications are likely to fall comfortably within the outer perimeter of his official responsibilities," the decision said.

As for what remained of the special counsel's indictment of Trump—his pressuring state officials, asking state elections officials to "find" him votes, engaging in a fake electors scheme—the court remanded each of those back to Judge Chutkan to undertake a laborious examination.

She'd have to assess whether they counted as official acts, as Trump contended, or unofficial ones, as the special counsel argued.

Roberts was deeply and personally invested in shielding a president from prosecution for steps the president felt warranted at the time, and this was based on his own time in the White House as an associate counsel to President Ronald Reagan. He expected his decision to rise above the politics of the day. Near the end of the majority opinion, Roberts seemed eager to underscore his broader goal. As bad as Trump's actions might have been, a larger threat could loom in successive prosecutions of each president by his political opponents. It was the argument Sauer had made, and it had won over the court's conservatives:

"When may a former President be prosecuted for official acts taken during his Presidency? Our Nation has never before needed an answer. But in addressing that question today, unlike the political branches and the public at large, we cannot afford to fixate exclusively, or even primarily, on present exigencies. In a case like this one, focusing on 'transient results' may have profound consequences for the separation of powers and for the future of our Republic."

Garland was floored. So was everyone in the Solicitor General's Office, Smith's office, and throughout DOJ. The decision seemed to toss aside what little precedent there was and radically alter the balance of federal power in favor of the presidency.

"I mean, they reversed Nixon," one Justice Department official said incredulously. If this Supreme Court had been in charge, it appeared, Nixon would never have been ordered to turn over the White House tapes that proved his role in the criminal Watergate cover-up.

But Garland's shock was informed by something deeper. He knew these justices well, knew most of them personally, knew how they'd decided other cases. He knew they had to be aware of the precedents they were trampling over.

"They know this is wrong," Garland later told a confidant.

Chutkan read the opinion in her chambers with resignation. She was disappointed, she told colleagues, but not shocked. In February, she had predicted this result when the Supremes took the case. Now it was all but official, there would be no trial before the election.

Some Justice Department alums, especially Democrats, issued blistering critiques on social media. Former Attorney General Eric Holder posted on X, calling the ruling "absurd and dangerous" and a "monstrosity." Trump, for his part, quickly hailed the decision as an absolute victory, and made the pivot that the ruling "should end" not only the election interference case but all the prosecutions against him. His campaign fired off a series of fundraising pitches on the news: "BIG WIN FOR DEMOCRACY & OUR CONSTITUTION!" read one.

Justice Sotomayor, writing for the court's three liberals, became the only balm for those seeking some consequences for Trump's crimes. She outlined all the ways the court's conservative majority had blessed a president to engage in horrific acts and remain insulated from criminal prosecution.

"*Orders the Navy's Seal Team 6 to assassinate a political rival? Immune. Organizes a military coup to hold on to power? Immune. Takes a bribe in exchange for a pardon? Immune. Immune, immune, immune,*" she wrote. "*. . . Even if these nightmare scenarios never play out, and I pray they never do, the damage has been done.*"

"*In every use of official power, the President is now a king above the law,*" Sotomayor concluded. "*Never in the history of our Republic has a President had reason to believe that he would be immunie from criminal prosecution if he used the trappings of his office to violate the criminal law. Moving forward, however. . . . If the occupant of that office misuses official power for personal gain, the criminal law that the rest of us must abide will not provide a backstop.*

"*With fear for our democracy, I dissent.*"

The special counsel's case was badly wounded. Inside the Solicitor General's Office, advisers met and wondered if the case could even be salvaged. They gave Trump "everything he wanted and more," said Dreeben.

Garland's aides called Smith and his team the day of the SCOTUS opinion to get their initial reaction. They said they needed time to consider, to regroup. They acknowledged they weren't sure which parts of the case would remain in the wake of the ruling. Smith told Garland he would evaluate and get back to him.

Back at their third-floor offices at 2CON, members of the election interference team the next day began reviewing the trial plan with an eye for everything a jury would now likely never hear.

There was example after example that the special counsel had not yet made public but that the trial team thought would help establish that Trump knew his claims of election fraud were bogus.

Back in February 2020, right before the pandemic. Trump had received a detailed briefing in the Oval Office about tightened election security since 2016 from national security, FBI, and Department of Homeland Security officials. "This is great," Trump said toward the end of the meeting. He asked why Americans weren't talking about how good election security was—and then concluded it was because "I'm not talking about it." Trump said they should hold a press conference to tell the country, according to one person who had been in the room and whom Smith's team interveiwed. Before the pandemic, Trump was completely confident he would win reelection. But as the virus gripped the nation, he ended up never holding a press conference to publicize the security improvements.

Prosecutors also had several meetings they could reconstruct between cabinet members and Trump, with each warning the president that his election fraud claims were not true. Before the January 6 attack, John Ratcliffe had told Trump that the intelligence community had looked into all claims of foreign influence, and they had found nothing that could have altered the outcome of the election.

In their analysis, members of Smith's team also became worried about how the immunity decision would impact the classified documents case in Florida. Trump was surely going to use it as grounds to upend that prosecution as well, and when he did so, a small part of the Supreme Court ruling could have an outsize influence.

In addition to saying the president had immunity for a core set of activities, the Supreme Court said prosecutors couldn't use evidence from that arena to prove a case elsewhere. That came into play in the documents case because investigators had, for instance, interviewed dozens of senior staffers to understand whether Trump had a process for declassifying documents. It helped establish that the documents found in Mar-a-Lago had never been declassified. But because those conversations could all now be shielded, prosecutors might be barred from presenting any of that evidence at trial.

"It wasn't that we were trying to prosecute the president for those. They were simply using those conversations as evidence related to an entirely separate offense," said one of the prosecutors. "That's one of the things that came out of left field for us. If the president was exercising some kind of presidential power, you couldn't prosecute that exercise, but you also couldn't mention it in court to a jury, period, even if you were prosecuting something else."

Smith and his team, however, weren't giving up. In fact, crowded into Dog Park, Smith didn't sugarcoat the decision but sought to rally his attorneys to find a way through the minefield of the Supreme Court ruling. It was worse than he or anyone around the table had imagined. In fact, some in the room fretted that the office would be remembered most not for indicting Trump for election interference but for having inadvertently created some of the worst case law on executive power in U.S. history. Regardless of who became president in 2024 or after, the country's balance of power had undoubtedly tilted toward the White House, as Sotomayor opined, creating "a king above the law." Smith said those in the office still had a job to do. They had to rebuild their case without the central tension of Trump having abused his presidential power to stay in office. It was, Smith said, an opportunity to "show what kind of lawyers we are."

On July 13, however, Donald Trump came within an inch of being assassinated at a campaign rally in Butler, Pennsylvania. A twenty-year-old whose house had Trump signs in the yard had scurried atop the roof of a sheet-metal building overlooking the stage where Trump would speak. Due to a string of Secret Service security failures, Thomas Crooks had a clear shot at the man of the hour. As he began firing, one of Crooks's bullets grazed Trump's ear and others killed a spectator and injured two. Trump thrust his fist in the air as Secret Service agents who had rushed to surround his body evacuated him to a bulletproof SUV. Trump had miraculously survived.

Two days later, Trump emerged victorious again. Judge Cannon shocked the Justice Department by embracing another long-shot bid by Trump and upending what had appeared to be settled law. Cannon ruled that Smith had not been lawfully appointed and confirmed by Congress as a special counsel, something that had not been done in decades of previous special counsel appointments. To justify her decision, Cannon cited a nonbinding, concurrent opinion by conservative Justice Clarence Thomas, which he issued alongside the court's immunity ruling. In it, Thomas had written that he was "not sure that any office for the Special Counsel had been 'established by Law,' as the Constitution requires." No other member of the Supreme Court signed Thomas's opinion. Still, Cannon cited it to dismiss the entire classified documents case.

In the span of fourteen days, Republican-appointed judges had left both special counsel investigations of Trump hanging by a thread.

[3 2]

"The Judiciary Failed"

On July 18, five days after he survived an assassination attempt and three days after Judge Cannon's ruling in his favor, Trump took the stage at the Republican National Convention to accept the party's nomination for president. With a square white bandage covering his right earlobe, Trump soon celebrated the "very big news" of Cannon's dismissal of the special counsel's case in Florida. "The prosecutor and the fake documents case against me were totally unconstitutional," Trump claimed. He then mocked how much attention the charges had drawn, given their demise. "With all of that publicity," he said wryly, "thrown out of court."

Trump not so subtly married the attempt on his life with his years-long campaign to cast himself as a target of politically motivated prosecutions. "The Democratic Party should immediately stop weaponizing the justice system and labeling their political opponent as an enemy of democracy." Trump's adoring convention crowd burst into applause.

Three days after Trump accepted the Republican nomination, the contest experienced another earthquake. Having stumbled through a halting debate performance weeks before and with Trump clearly ascendant, President Biden on July 21 dropped out of the race and endorsed Vice President Kamala Harris to run in his stead.

Harris picked up the baton, criticizing Trump for recklessly keeping classified documents and for having incited his supporters to attack the Capitol on January 6. But with both cases growing cold, the attacks landed flat with voters, who were increasingly pointing to the economy and inflation as their primary voting issues. For his part, Trump claimed a new mystique for having vanquished the mighty Justice Department.

"They weaponized the government against the political opponent. Can you imagine?" he told a rally crowd in Arizona in August. "I'm the only one that ever happened to where my numbers went up."

As the summer wore on, work inside the special counsel's office slowed following the back-to-back court losses. Since the first indictment in June, about ten attorneys had left the counsel's office. Some had left at Smith's strong suggestion; others knew they'd finished their core assignment and had no desire to stick around if Smith continued to give key assignments only to his trusted inner circle. The classified documents team had shelved its trial prep and diverted to researching and drafting a challenge to Cannon's ruling. The immunity ruling would also constrain their case, so now the team had the dual concerns of resurrecting their dismissed case and reshaping it. The elections interference team, meanwhile, was still ripping apart its case, debating which pieces of evidence, and, therefore, which charges prosecutors could continue to bring under the Supreme Court's decision. As the workflow slowed, Jack Smith's demeanor in the office also eased.

Smith told his team the Special Counsel's Office would no longer push the court to act quickly. The chance of the election interference case reaching trial before the election was nil. In fact, they had gamed out how the appellate challenges could ping-pong through the courts and estimated it would take at least another year—until late 2025, or into 2026—to reach a jury.

They would simply retool the case and let Chutkan set the pace for her tedious work of defining the boundaries of presidential immunity. With that, the constant deadlines Smith had set over so many months began to dissipate. Where many prosecutors on the election team had viewed Smith as aggressive—and admirably so—in being willing to put his name to novel charges against a former president, they now saw him as more apprehensive. Smith repeatedly expressed concern to prosecutors drafting the rewrite that it would have to look and feel different to Supreme Court justices when they read the new indictment in the course of some future appeal by Trump. Smith urged the team to be cautious, and to cauterize the case where they had to rely on conversations and actions by Trump that the president could argue were part of his official duties and therefore immune from prosecution under the Supreme Court's ruling.

"The Justices can't read this and think, 'Those guys at the special counsel don't get it; they don't understand what we were trying to do here,'" Smith told them. Smith wanted to make sure the team could defend its logic for claiming that evidence it presented didn't encroach on the president's "official acts," now immunized by the Court.

In August 2024, Smith and his team were finishing up their motion to appeal Cannon's dismissal of the case. What no one outside of a handful of people knew was that Smith also believed his team had ample grounds to ask the appellate court to remove Cannon as the presiding judge. At the same time that Smith presented the appeal to the solicitor general to review, as the special counsel regulations required, he sought her approval to ask the appeals court to toss Cannon off the case.

Smith's team had charted the many choices Cannon had made that strained the law or bypassed precedent, and also favored Trump. One shocker that only a tiny group knew about had happened a full year earlier—in August 2023. In a sealed order, on Monday, August 7, Cannon had of her own volition launched an investigation from the bench into potential prosecutorial misconduct in the case, citing "news reports."

Cannon didn't specify what reports she was hearing. But on August 6, the day before her order, the conservative Fox News television program *Life, Liberty & Levin* had featured a Trump defense attorney making allegations of strong-arm tactics by Smith's team that she sought to dig into.

The final straw for Smith came when Cannon dismissed the documents case, citing as a basis Thomas's concurring opinion, which carried zero legal weight, making the choice a striking departure from judicial standards.

Solicitor General Elizabeth Prelogar ultimately approved the appeal of Cannon's ruling. But the former Garland law clerk rejected Smith's plan to seek to have Cannon recused, saying he didn't have enough evidence to try to remove her.

Smith could have asked Garland to reconsider his trusted counselor's position, but he did not. If Garland turned him down, it would have to be reported to Congress.

In the last week of August, Smith's team was ready to press forward on both cases.

On August 26, the classified documents team filed an appeal with the Eleventh Circuit Court of Appeals, arguing that Cannon had been flatly wrong in asserting that Smith should have been confirmed by Congress. Smith pointed out that Congress had for over a century vested in the attorney general the power to commission special assistants and attorneys to prosecute violations of law. Since 1999, the department had also published guidelines for how and when it used special counsels, and the Senate had held hearings on those plans. What's more, in response to a 1974 challenge by Nixon, arguing he shouldn't have to turn over White House recordings, the Supreme Court had ruled that the attorney general did have the power to appoint special prosecutors.

The next day in D.C., the special counsel also revealed its response to the Supreme Court's decision. Smith's team had put the case back before a grand jury, stripped of the parts where Trump's actions were likely immune. The team still maintained that Trump had committed all four of the original charges, but as a candidate trying to get reelected, rather than as a president.

Where the first indictment had read "The Defendant, Donald J. Trump, was the forty-fifth President of the United States and a candidate for re-election in 2020," the new filing described him simply as "a candidate for President of the United States in 2020."

More substantively, the filing excised one whole line of alleged misuse of his authority. To abide by the Supreme Court ruling, Smith erased all references to how Trump had sought to install Jeffrey Clark and deploy the Justice Department in a last-ditch effort to undermine the election.

When it came to Pence, however, Smith made clear he was ready to keep arguing that there was no valid case to make that a sitting president should have pressured his vice president to ignore states' certified election results and instead manipulate the congressional certification. Some justices had suggested in oral arguments that any conversation between the president and vice president would occur in the course of the president's official duties, so even pressuring Pence not to certify the results might not be admissible. But Smith's team coalesced around an argument that, in pressuring his vice president, Trump had not been acting in his capacity as president but as a candidate.

"The Defendant had no official responsibilities related to the certification proceeding, but he did have a personal interest as a candidate in being named the winner of the election," the new indictment read.

But there was another way that the entire underpinning of the election interference case had been weakened. The through line of the special counsel's legal argument remained that Trump had committed a fraud by claiming there had been voting irregularities on a scale big enough to have altered the outcome of the race. But the section on Trump's "Knowledge of the Falsity"—that he knew his election claims were not true— would have to proceed without key evidence. They deleted from the new indictment almost an entire page listing all of Trump's senior and trusted aides who had told him his election claims didn't pan out. The prosecution's case had always rested in part on the repetitive but circumstantial evidence that so many people Trump relied upon for advice had told him his election claims were untrue. The case lopped off the warnings that senior leaders of the Justice Department, his director of national intelligence, senior officials at his Department of Homeland Security, and senior White House lawyers had consistently given Trump: He had lost the election.

Back in court on September 5, Chutkan said she intended to keep going and work through the Supreme Court's order to decide which of Trump's actions would be immune from prosecution. To accomplish that, the Special Counsel's Office proposed delivering one comprehensive brief, laying out all the special counsel's evidence to support its position that all the criminal acts remaining in the indictment involved Trump acting as a private candidate. Trump's lawyers John Lauro and Todd Blanche objected, arguing that each aspect should be litigated separately. Plus, they said, any filings that potentially divulged new evidence on the eve of the election would be inappropriate.

Chutkan, who had at times used the analogy that she would not change the court's schedule to accommodate a star athlete, was not swayed. "This court is not concerned with the electoral schedule," she said. Chutkan ordered Smith's team to submit its underlying evidence for all charges against Trump by late September. Smith's team did so, filing the evidence under seal, begetting a new round of legal sparring over what facts could be released. Trump's lawyers alleged in a motion that the "true motivation" behind the comprehensive filing was that the special counsel "wants their politically motivated manifesto to be public . . . in the final weeks of the 2024 Presidential election."

On October 2, a little more than a month before Election Day, Chutkan released a redacted version of Smith's 165-page filing. It revealed private conversations and other snippets showing that Trump had been indifferent to whether the claims he'd made about the election results were true or not. At one point, when a White House lawyer warned him that his theories wouldn't survive scrutiny in court, Trump responded: "The details don't matter." And on January 6, when an aide told Trump that Pence might be in danger as rioting began, Trump again showed indifference, replying, "So what?"

The new touchpoints seemed to change few minds, but further emboldened Trump to promise he would gut the Justice Department and target his perceived enemies if voters returned him to power.

On Truth Social, Trump reposted and amplified messages calling Chutkan's release of the additional evidence preposterous and Smith's filing itself prejudicial so close to the election. He settled on the phrase "enemy from within" in an interview on Fox News, and used it through October to alternately refer to Democratic members of Congress, Kamala Harris, Smith, and others. "They are so bad and frankly, they're evil," Trump said. "They're evil, what they've done. They've weaponized, they've weaponized our elections. They've done things that nobody thought was even possible."

And Trump's threats continued up until Election Day. Even as he remained the only candidate ever to run for president while facing felony charges, Trump assumed the role of aggressor. In a series of social media posts, he threatened anyone who "cheated" with massive criminal penalties. "WHEN I WIN, those people that CHEATED will be prosecuted to the fullest extent of the Law, which will include long term prison sentences so that this Depravity of Justice does not happen again," Trump wrote on October 25. He also alluded to prosecuting any lawyers, political operatives, or donors who sought to organize or fund postelection recounts or challenges.

On Election Day, as the polls closed and vote tallies began rolling in, it became clear that the country need not worry about recounts or a protracted battle over the results. Trump was leading in every swing state. Fox News, which had drawn Trump's ire by projecting Biden the winner in key states four years earlier, was among the first to call the race. The remaining members of the Special Counsel's Office watched the election returns in their homes and went to bed knowing what Trump's victory would mean for their work.

While both of the teams' prosecution cases were deeply wounded and hampered, they hadn't yet been dismissed. But they all saw the writing on the wall. Come January 20, Trump would extinguish the Special Counsel's Office.

The next day, close to lunchtime, Smith asked everyone still in the office to gather in the Secret Kitchen.

He began by praising them for the hard work they had done to investigate the now future president of the United States. Then he pivoted.

"We all need to focus on what's good in our lives," Smith said. "I have a wife I don't deserve. And I have a daughter I love to death. I'm so blessed with things I never thought I would have."

He continued: "That's what is important in life and that's what we should take to heart."

At FBI headquarters that day, Wray held his morning threat briefings listening to the latest on cyber intrusions without mentioning the election results. Abbate kept up the all-business demeanor in meetings with supervisors. The message emanating from bosses down to agents through the day seemed clear: Don't get distracted, just keep doing your job. They had already been through a Trump presidency once before.

Across the street at Main Justice, however, senior Justice officials and aides to Garland and Monaco were despondent. They held back-to-back consultations with worried staff who were concerned about their futures in a Trump DOJ, including those who had played central roles in the Trump investigations, but many others with no link to the case also saw a major decision. Should they stay and try to uphold the principles of this institution, or go and avoid witnessing its demise?

"This place is going to be shredded," said one top adviser to Garland.

It didn't take long for Trump's transition team to ready the wood chipper. Two days after the election, Mark Paoletta, an attorney leading Trump's transition team at Justice, warned that Trump could dictate whom and what DOJ investigated, and even who got charged. "He has the duty to supervise DOJ, including, if necessary, on specific cases," Paoletta wrote on November 7.

Trump's Republican allies in the House the next day also broadcast their plan to help the incoming president settle scores. Ohio Rep. Jim Jordan, chairman of the House Judiciary Committee, put Smith at the top of his list. Jordan and Rep. Barry Loudermilk of Georgia sent a letter to the special counsel demanding Smith's office preserve all records "surrounding the Biden-Harris Administration's politicized prosecutions of President Donald Trump."

For his part, Smith that day asked Chutkan to pause all deadlines in the felony election interference case against President-elect Trump. The office needed time to "assess this unprecedented circumstance and determine the appropriate course going forward," read the filing.

After three more days, Paoletta issued a preemptive ultimatum that working at the Justice Department would be different in Trump's second term: DOJ staffers should prepare to implement Trump's agenda or leave, he warned. "Those employees who engage in so-called 'resistance' against the duly-elected President's lawful agenda would be subverting American democracy" and subject to termination, Paoletta wrote.

On November 13, Trump delivered a rebuke to the Justice Department when he announced his pick for his attorney general. He had chosen Rep. Matt Gaetz, a Trump loyalist whom the Justice Department had investigated and whom his peers on the House Ethics Committee had secretly found evidence he had paid multiple women for sex, including a minor, and had possessed several illicit drugs.

The nomination lasted eight days before Gaetz withdrew amid signs the House committee might release its confidential report into Gaetz's indiscretions. Hours later, Trump named his second pick: Pam Bondi, a former Florida attorney general who had previously defended Trump and amplified his false election claims. As state attorney general, Bondi had dropped plans for Florida to join a fraud lawsuit against Trump University days after receiving a campaign check from Trump's family foundation. She appeared regularly on Fox News to laud the wisdom of his first-term policies. And in 2020, she had served as one of his defense attorneys in his impeachment trial for seeking to pressure Ukraine's president to announce an investigation of Joe Biden and his family. After Election Day in 2020, Bondi had raced to Philadelphia to push Trump's false election claims as vote-counting continued two days after the election. Standing in a crowd with an amplifier, she alleged without evidence that election officials were manipulating the vote. "They are not letting every legal vote count," Bondi said. "They are letting anything come in." During Trump's second presidential campaign, Bondi vowed that Republicans would root out the "deep state" from the Justice Department. "When Republicans take back the White House . . . you know what's going to happen? The Department of Justice, the prosecutors will be prosecuted—the bad ones—the investigators will be investigated," Bondi said on Fox News in 2023.

A little over a week later, Trump named a nominee who struck the most fear into Biden's outgoing Justice Department team: Kash Patel for FBI director. Patel had displayed cunning in Trump's first term in national security roles. He'd also made clear his disdain for abiding by traditional democratic guardrails. In podcast appearances and in a book he had written, *Government Gangsters*, Patel had said he would shutter FBI headquarters and bring the Bureau "to heel" and published a list of sixty supposed "deep state" members. Patel said Republicans should investigate them and other Trump political foes as soon as they had the power to do so.

"We're going to come after the people in the media who lied about American citizens, who helped Joe Biden rig presidential elections," Patel said on a Steve Bannon podcast in December 2023. "We're going to come after you. Whether it's criminally or civilly, we'll figure that out."

The last time Trump suggested Patel to help lead the FBI—as deputy director—Attorney General Bill Barr had threatened to resign, warning the White House chief of staff that Patel lacked experience as an agent or a senior manager.

On November 22, *The Washington Post* reported that Trump would fire the entire staff of career Justice Department employees who had worked for Jack Smith. Asked about the scoop, Trump press secretary Karoline Leavitt issued a statement that did not deny the plan: "President Trump campaigned on firing rogue bureaucrats who have engaged in the illegal weaponization of our American justice system, and the American people can expect he will deliver on that promise," Leavitt wrote.

Three days later, on Monday, November 25, Smith's team filed motions to dismiss all charges against Trump in the election inference and classified documents cases. After all the criminal evidence they had uncovered about a former president, the department simply could not prosecute a sitting president. Within a few hours, Judge Chutkan and the Eleventh Circuit Court of Appeals granted the requests, wiping away the charges. Their cases, their witnesses, their hard-fought evidence, none of it had ever made it to a jury.

Judge John D. Bates shared his disappointment with fellow jurists in private discussions. Bates, a federal judge since President George W. Bush appointed him in 2001, was no liberal activist. Chief Justice Roberts had handpicked him to run the foreign surveillance court, and he and Justice Kavanaugh became friends working on the Whitewater investigation. But Bates had earned broad respect for his neutral and careful reading of the law. He told his colleagues the Supreme Court and Cannon, as well as the Department of Justice, had together failed to let a jury weigh the facts in these two cases of momentous importance for the American justice system.

"That these cases didn't get to trial is a failure," he said. "The judiciary failed the American people."

Everyone in the FBI knew that the incoming president would fire Director Chris Wray as soon as he had a chance; on November 30, he promised to nominate Patel and ax Wray. It had long been near the top of Trump's to-do list in his forthcoming revenge tour, a sweet punishment for the FBI searching Mar-a-Lago. Privately, Wray agonized over whether to leave or stay for the inevitable karate chop. He told his wife and chief of staff that he was not worried about getting fired; he had planned for it and expected it repeatedly during Trump's first term. But he had also spent a good part of his tenure trying to help the Bureau recover from the trauma of Trump having abruptly decapitated the agency by firing Comey. Wray brought in more and more people for advice and decided he would announce plans to step down effective the Sunday before Trump's inauguration.

On December 11, in a message beamed to all Bureau employees from the headquarters podium, Wray announced his decision to step down to "avoid dragging the Bureau deeper into the fray." But he also had a parting message for agents: Above all, protect the American people and the Constitution, he said. "What absolutely, positively, cannot, must not change is our commitment to doing the right thing, in the right way, every time," he said. "Our dedication to independence, objectivity, and the rule of law—those fundamental aspects of who we are—must never change."

On Saturday, December 14, the members of the special counsel's team were invited to a holiday party at Cooney's house in Arlington, Virginia. The mood at the gathering wasn't grim or morose, surprisingly. The attorneys and agents seemed to genuinely enjoy seeing each other, sipping beers together, joking about the free time they now had, and reconnecting with teammates who had left months earlier.

Jack Smith was there, but a few attorneys privately remarked to each other that it made sense Cooney was the one hosting the party rather than Smith. Cooney had been a tough enforcer for Smith at times, the one who had to sometimes deliver bad news—such as "Oh, Jack's not happy with your memo," and "Jack thinks it's time for you to leave the office." But Cooney had also played the role of coach and was quick to encourage team members.

After a while, Cooney gathered the group. He had arranged to present a parting gift to each member, a token to remember their time with the office and its righteous, if now ill-fated, mission. Each team member was invited to take a symbolic ornament from the tree. Some received a shiny judge's gavel, a symbol of fairness and lawfulness. Several picked out a tiny gold statuette of Lady Justice. She was blindfolded to represent impartiality and holding a scale to reflect how Justice carefully weighs arguments and evidence. The figurine even held a tiny sword, the symbol of authority and swiftness with which justice can be delivered.

At an otherwise upbeat party, the gift prompted a moment of sad reflection for some of the Smith team members as they absorbed the irony of how their work had ended.

FBI agents, even those who weren't big fans of Wray, had begun to brace for their future under Patel. In his book, he had called for an eradication of "government tyranny" within the FBI by firing "the top ranks" and prosecuting "to the fullest extent of the law" anyone who "in any way abused their authority for political ends."

"The FBI has become so thoroughly compromised that it will remain a threat to the people unless drastic measures are taken," Patel wrote.

Natalie Bara, the president of the FBI Agents Association, wanted to figure out a path forward with Patel. She arranged to meet with him just after New Year's Day on Capitol Hill. They talked in an empty conference room in Sen. Mike Lee's office, where Patel was camped out while visiting members. Bara had two priority requests of Patel. First, she said it was critical for the Bureau that he choose a seasoned and active agent to be the deputy director, as had been the case for as long as anyone could remember. This person would have to make decisions that put the staff's lives in harm's way and had to have operational know-how and agents' respect.

"Totally agree," Patel said. "Who do you think it should be?"

Bara said that Bobby Wells and Mike Nordwall, two top assistant directors already on the seventh floor, were great choices; they had broad experience and knew how to run the place. The troops also recognized Jim Dennehy, the assistant director in charge of the New York office, as a superior leader, she said.

She said she recognized that Trump and Patel believed agents had engaged in misconduct in pursuing the "sensitive" cases—those involving Trump and January 6. Her second request was that Patel not take drastic action to fire anyone until he got confirmed and arrived in the office, so he could see case files and extensive internal investigations of their work for himself.

"We're not trying to absolve bad behavior," she said. "But don't just start ripping through or firing people for being in a case."

Again, Patel agreed.

Bara reported to her members the upshot of her meeting with Patel. Across the country, field office leaders shared cautious optimism. Maybe all of Patel's rhetoric about firing scores of agents and torching the Bureau was simply that: exaggerated talk for MAGA world. Maybe he would respect the agents and the Bureau's work after all.

[33]

Servare Vitas

At forty-five, Brian Driscoll had enjoyed a standout career in the FBI and a rewarding set of assignments, eighteen years' worth. On Monday, January 13, despite all the leadership changes atop the Bureau, he was getting pumped about a new promotion.

Since joining the FBI in 2007, Driscoll had risen from his first job as a violent crimes investigator and SWAT team member in the powerful and tight-knit New York Field Office to become the commander of the FBI's Hostage Rescue Team and section chief of the Critical Incident Response Group. That meant he led the equivalent of the Bureau's Delta Force, a string of elite teams and specialized operators who responded to terror attacks, gathered key evidence in mass casualties, negotiated with hostage takers, parachuted into tense standoffs, and tracked down abducted children. HRT's motto was "Servare Vitas": To Save Lives. And Driscoll could honestly say he'd saved quite a few.

Early in his career, first as a criminal investigator for the Navy and then at the Bureau, he had kept his face clean-shaven, his hair cut short. Now, after so many years in counterterrorism task forces and undercover ops, he had let his curly ringlets grow out and wore a thick mustache and goatee.

For one of his last acts as director of the FBI, Chris Wray planned to announce the next day, on Tuesday, January 14, that he was promoting Driscoll to one of the crowning achievements of an agent's career: special agent in charge. Driscoll would now head up the Bureau's Newark Field Office. The promotion had been in the works for a while, and after Driscoll's many years working in the Greater New York area, this was a chance to be the big boss on his home turf.

But that same day, Driscoll got a call from a person he didn't know, who said he worked on the president-elect's transition team. The person said the incoming Trump administration needed Driscoll to come down to Washington. Instead of running the field office with a couple of hundred employees in New Jersey, they wanted him to serve as acting deputy director over the entire FBI—and start the job next week. Driscoll learned they were also asking another well-respected and longtime New York agent, Rob Kissane, to serve as acting director until the Senate confirmed the president's nominee.

Next week? Driscoll asked. Really? He was stunned, but he also couldn't help but be excited.

"Guess what?" he told a close friend. "I'm going down to Washington to be the acting deputy."

It turned out that Patel, a former counterterrorism prosecutor, had endorsed the choice of Kissane and Driscoll. He knew them both professionally, but not very well. Patel had met Kissane during the agent's counterterror work in Africa. He knew of Driscoll from his leadership role at the FBI's Hostage Rescue Team, but they had never formally met.

Driscoll had never worked at headquarters before. This was a big job, a big opportunity, even if only for a short time. But very quickly, Driscoll ran headlong into some thorny problems.

First, an incoming Trump White House liaison to the Justice Department called Driscoll with some pretty odd questions, and separately called Kissane with the same. The staffer, Paul Ingrassia, wanted to know: Who did Driscoll vote for in the 2024 election? Next, had he ever voted for or donated to a Democrat in the last five years? Finally, would he be willing to go after anyone in the FBI—from its leaders on down to the rank and file—for what they did in investigating January 6? The highly political nature of the inquiry was a shock to them both. They balked at this interrogation, and the personnel aide said this was the standard list they were asking all new agency leaders.

The conversation got testy as Driscoll told Ingrassia he was a career agent, not a potential cabinet member.

"I'm not answering this," he said. "This is not something an FBI agent should be answering."

He soon warned close confidants he might never get to headquarters after all.

"I might be getting fired for not answering these questions," he said.

By design, the FBI had never been in this situation before. Congress had set ten-year terms for directors to maintain continuity and to keep the nation's mightiest law enforcement agency free from the political shifts between presidential administrations. So this political loyalty test was entirely bizarre to the two agents. Eventually, after Driscoll and Kissane complained, Trump's landing team at DOJ intervened and Ingrassia seemed to give up on getting the two agents' answers.

Kissane and Driscoll faced another worry, however. Transition staffers had told them they would take over the Bureau on the day of the inauguration, but they learned no one had told Deputy Director Abbate. Neither one wanted to leave the well-respected deputy in the dark. Driscoll and Kissane arranged to speak with Abbate by phone and told him what the Trump team was planning.

Abbate, who had already assumed some of Wray's responsibilities and was scheduled to officially become acting director on the Sunday before the inauguration, had heard rumblings. James Dennehy, the assistant director in charge of the FBI's New York Field Office, alerted Abbate in early January that he too had been contacted by the Trump transition about taking one of the Bureau's top jobs.

A series of calls that followed with Dennehy, Driscoll, and Kissane reinforced for Abbate that he would have to be nimble. His tenure as acting director might turn out to be the shortest ever.

Abbate intended to stay in his job as close as possible to the moment that Trump was sworn in to keep on top of national security threats. But if Trump's team signaled its plan to replace him, he would announce he was leaving before Trump could claim a first scalp at DOJ.

Abbate had turned fifty-seven, the Bureau's mandatory retirement age for special agents, days earlier and had planned long before the presidential election to depart by April, staying a few extra months at Wray's request to get his successor up to speed. Whether that would happen remained a gametime decision as the sun came up on Inauguration Day, and on a morning that was already proving hectic.

Just after dawn, Biden had stunned his own Justice Department by issuing broad pardons to a slew of people Trump had vowed to punish. That included members of the January 6 Select Committee, former COVID czar Anthony Fauci, and former chairman of the Joint Chiefs Mark Milley, whom Trump suggested was a traitor who should be executed.

Top leaders at the FBI and in the Justice Department were also on high alert that morning for a possible terror attack on the country or another attempt on Trump's life. Undercover agents had for months been keeping close tabs on a Michigan man who'd discussed attacking a U.S. military base. Other threat chatter had been extremely high for weeks too, and they knew transitions were among the most vulnerable times for the government.

Before long, word came from Driscoll and Kissane that they had been told to start making their way from New York to D.C. There was now no doubt that Abbate would have to act quickly. He called Principal Associate Deputy Emil Bove and planned to walk across the street to DOJ to announce his departure in person, but Pennsylvania Avenue was fenced off for the inaugural parade and Bove was soon leaving anyway for inaugural events. Abbate gave Bove the news in a phone call: He planned to retire, effective no later than 12:00 p.m. Bove had previously given Abbate no indication of his transition plans in recent weeks, in either a lengthy meeting they had together or when Abbate asked incoming administration officials directly. But Bove now owned up to the plan to remove him that day. Still, Bove asked Abbate to stay at the Hoover Building until the end of the day to help settle Driscoll and Kissane. Abbate agreed. Abbate quickly got the handful of DOJ leadership still holding down the Justice Department on a conference call, and explained that he knew Kissane and Driscoll were being asked to replace him.

At 11:05 a.m., less than an hour before Donald Trump was sworn in as president, Abbate sent an email to all the senior leadership of the Bureau alerting them he was officially retiring and leaving that day. In response to Trump's clear intent to shake up the Bureau, he was the second person to relinquish the position of FBI director in less than thirty-six hours.

In his three-paragraph note, Abbate didn't mention the forced nature of the turnover, but instead telegraphed a no-drama message. He reminded the team he had already stayed on past his mandatory retirement age—"to help ensure continuity and the best transition for the FBI." Now that Trump's new team was "inbound," he said, it was time to go.

Abbate glanced at a television as Trump started his inaugural address, which he had moved inside the Capitol Rotunda due to a forecast of bitter cold. Trump's message was that he vowed to rebalance the scales of justice.

"Never again will the immense power of the state be weaponized to persecute political opponents—something I know something about," Trump said to some appreciative laughter in the audience. "We will not allow that to happen. It will not happen again. Under my leadership, we will restore fair, equal, and impartial justice under the constitutional rule of law."

In the afternoon, Driscoll arrived first and Abbate showed him to the deputy director's office. An hour or so later, Kissane arrived and Abbate showed him the director's office. The two started telling top Bureau officials of the bizarre and disconcerting vetting questions they'd faced.

Then an even more surreal moment unfolded. Milhoan, the Bureau's top spokeswoman, had been waiting for an announcement from the White House before issuing a press statement about the new leaders. Then, the White House posted the names, but in reverse order, with Driscoll as the director and Kissane as the deputy. FBI officials called over to Bove. The White House messed up, several later recounted Bove saying, but switching the names could be embarrassing: "You guys just have to adjust."

So they did. Kissane got up from the director's office and walked down the hall; Driscoll did the same, moving to the director's office. Before leaving the Hoover Building as an FBI chief one last time, Abbate pulled both New York agents into the director's office.

Abbate said he didn't have a good feeling about the changes that were coming under the new regime.

"You guys are likely going to be asked to do things or make decisions that will challenge you, ethically and morally," Abbate said. "Be prepared for that."

The forty-seventh president and his designees at DOJ got busy that Monday afternoon, as Trump rapidly worked to turn the Justice Department into his spear for revenge. Step one was Executive Order 14147, entitled "Ending the Weaponization of the Federal Government."

The name of the order bore an Orwellian quality. Most of the steps that Trump took or pressed his lieutenants to take under the order were aimed at punishing those at the Justice Department who had investigated him or those he considered political enemies. Within the hour, he issued an order revoking the security clearances of nearly fifty intelligence officials who in 2020 had signed a letter raising doubts about the authenticity of embarrassing emails reportedly from the laptop of Joe Biden's son.

Trump then commuted the sentences of and issued pardons to nearly sixteen hundred January 6 rioters who breached the U.S. Capitol, including defendants who had plotted the break-in and others who had assaulted police. Trump's advisers had sought to soften the ground for weeks beforehand, preparing the public for the fact that he would carry out campaign promises to free many of those who had been convicted of nonviolent crimes. But not even some of Trump's most ardent supporters had expected he would release from prison all of those convicted of the most heinous violence. They underestimated how far Trump would go. Every single rioter. Those convicted of ramming police with flagpoles and fire extinguishers. Those who sprayed officers' faces with bear spray and aerosol grease. Those who crushed police in door frames and smashed their knuckles. Those who dragged, disarmed, and knocked officers unconscious. Trump ordered every one of them set free. Even the leaders of the Proud Boys and Oath Keepers, Enrique Tarrio and Stewart Rhodes, convicted of seditious conspiracy and sentenced to roughly two decades each in prison, were let go.

Adding insult to the hundreds of federal prosecutors and agents who had tirelessly investigated those crimes, Trump also inserted Ed Martin, a right-wing ideologue, as the acting chief federal prosecutor in D.C. He had helped organize Stop the Steal events around January 6 and had himself been near the Capitol on the day of the attack. On paper, Martin had the thinnest qualifications of anyone appointed to serve in that post in fifty years, as he was the first in that time to have neither worked as a prosecutor or judge, horrifying the prosecutors he would soon lead. He did have some relevant experience for the immediate task Trump had assigned to him of dismissing rioter cases. Martin had represented a handful of January 6 defendants and had long railed against the government prosecutions.

Whether due to his rush to please the president or his lack of experience with a lawyer's ethical duties, Martin ended up creating his own conflict of interest within twenty-four hours of taking the job. In one of his first official acts, he instructed his new team to quickly deliver on Trump's order and draft motions to dismiss all its January 6 cases. But the next day, Martin would sign off on dropping the case of his own client, spurring a bipartisan legal watchdog group and Senate Democrats to file ethics complaints with the Missouri and D.C. bars.

Over at Main Justice that Monday afternoon, Bove no longer had to meet with and fire the acting FBI director. But he had a heap of orders from Trump and the White House, which he attacked from midday until late that evening. He reassigned FBI task forces protecting Americans from terror plots to instead work on immigration enforcement. He helped notify five top DOJ career supervisors they were being reassigned. Together they had a century of experience overseeing the department's criminal, public corruption, and national security work, as well as managing sensitive international matters.

Among the five was George Toscas, the deputy assistant attorney general over national security. He felt sadness and shock as he read the notification that he was being reassigned to a new office, far from the kind of national security work to which he'd dedicated decades of public service: the Sanctuary Cities Enforcement Working Group. Toscas, revered by Republican and Democratic political appointees for his devotion to ferreting out spies and terror plots, called Matt Olsen, who had been his boss up until noon that day, to share the bad news. Toscas didn't have to say it. DOJ and national security were his life. He had just a few months before receiving his full retirement.

Toscas had worried since the election that Trump would likely want to punish him somehow; he had been the top career official at DOJ overseeing the Mar-a-Lago records investigation. And still, the speed with which Trump had reached into DOJ to remove him from his critical position shielding the nation was still a shock.

"I can't believe this is happening," Toscas told Olsen.

Another icon that the Trump DOJ team removed from his office that day was Bruce Swartz, a thirty-year veteran and the department's deputy counselor for international affairs. He had negotiated with foreign governments on behalf of five presidents on some of the most sensitive legal cases, including the extradition of Mexican cartel leader El Chapo

Guzmán. Much of his work remained a secret decades later. He was given fifteen days to decide whether to accept a demotion or go.

Many were in shock that Trump would sideline a DOJ legend.

"Now I know we're in trouble," one lawyer in the Criminal Division whispered to another as the Swartz news circulated.

Swartz, seventy-one, was furious for his younger colleagues, but less mystified. He confided to close colleagues that he felt sure it was personal for Trump. In Swartz's case, he had advised Robert Mueller in his special counsel probe and advocated for international subpoenas to probe whether the Egyptian president had provided Trump with a $10 million bribe in 2016. Swartz told his coworkers that he didn't need to keep working, but he was happy to sue if it could help others fight their unjustified and capricious removals.

Back over at the FBI's seventh-floor headquarters, the White House having accidentally transposed the two top leaders' names generated some moments of levity on an otherwise tense day.

A fellow agent and good friend of Driscoll's told him that was impressive: "Congrats. Two promotions in one day."

It gave "Drizz," as he was known by fellow agents, a self-deprecating punch line in the strange days to come.

"I guess I'm the accidental director," he joked.

Driscoll sent an all-staff message to agents and FBI personnel explaining he and Kissane were their new leaders for now, and thanking Abbate for his many years of service.

That afternoon, Driscoll and Kissane then led their first "sivits"—the FBI parlance for an SVTC, or a secure video teleconference—with leadership across the country, and this first address to the lieutenants provided both comfort and comic relief. The seasoned supervisors in the field were used to the perfectly polished presentations of Wray and Abbate; Driscoll and Kissane were new to this and didn't have a week to prepare or a string of assistants to help outline their talking points. The two men sometimes awkwardly shifted from topic to topic, each deferential to the other one, telling each other it was their turn to talk. But the field bosses remarked to each other that Driscoll's and Kissane's presence put them at ease nonetheless. Though the two had very limited headquarters experience, they were dedicated agents who had been top supervisors in field offices and had impressed colleagues whom they overlapped with in the New York office, through which so many agents had passed.

Driscoll and Kissane, however, had reason from the jump to be wary.

The two acting leaders confided to their inner circle that they were confused and concerned by the presence of a landing team of sorts, five or six agents, most of them retired several years back, who were Patel allies and called themselves the Director's Advisory Team (DAT). Several who interacted with them compared notes: They talked as if they ran the place. They sought access to internal case files. They told agents rather casually that they were on special assignment for Patel to help stamp out past weaponization of the Bureau against conservatives, and to identify bad eggs to fire.

Of course, it was against federal ethics rules and norms for Patel, an unconfirmed presidential nominee, to play any active role in agency decisions.

A few DAT members surprised staff by walking around the seventh floor discussing which offices they planned to move into when top Bureau officials were fired. One DAT member, Thomas Ferguson, had retired in 2019 but more recently worked for Senate Judiciary Committee Chairman Jim Jordan. He had been looking through January 6 case files. Together, it sparked a worry that a team of political "enforcers" had been installed in a Bureau made up entirely of apolitical career agents.

One DAT member, Greg Mentzer, had retired from the Bureau in 2018 and had been working on contract as a firearms instructor. He soon listed his new work location on his LinkedIn profile as "Director's office, FBI." In the middle of the first week of the presidency, word traveled in the office that he had told other agents that Patel had asked him to help get information on which field office leaders and agents he and the Trump administration needed to fire.

"Kash wants change," Mentzer said to one colleague, asking for names of people who were "problems."

Mentzer also shared with other seventh-floor personnel that he was going to be searching through the FBI's internal databases for information about the agents who worked on January 6 riot cases and the two DOJ investigations of Trump, again to help Patel root out anyone perceived as a politicized anti-Trump agent.

"Because I just don't know how you could violate a person's civil rights like this," Mentzer said.

Seasoned agents were taken aback by Mentzer's comments, which he would later deny making. Many in the FBI agreed with conservative critics of some of the DOJ's investigative priorities and choices during the Biden administration. Many did not support DOJ's insistence on arresting and prosecuting hundreds of January 6 protesters for what ended up being misdemeanor-level trespassing at the Capitol, when they had engaged in no violence. And some longtime agents were still angry that the FBI didn't first get the former president's permission before searching his property. He had been a president, after all. But they knew that those were judgment calls that were entirely legal. The January 6 prosecutions and the Mar-a-Lago search had ample probable cause and legal justification. Mentzer had been a case agent, they groused, so why didn't he understand how carefully the FBI followed those rules?

Word spread on the seventh floor that the DAT group—what some described as "people associated with Jim Jordan"—were trying to compile a list of January 6 agents to fire. Some who still worked there sent out an SOS to a tiny group of departed colleagues, including former director Wray and a handful of former Justice Department officials.

"It's really bad," one FBI official reported in his SOS on Friday, January 24. "They are coming in and want to potentially fire thousands of agents."

In Trump's Justice Department, the roles of investigators and convicted criminals had all but entirely flipped that week. Hours after the inauguration on Monday, Patel's advisers were inside headquarters and reviewing with suspicion the files of five thousand agents and staff who had done their jobs in tracking down violent protesters and plotters of the Capitol attack. By noon on that Tuesday, January 21, the first wave of January 6 rioters, whom agents had spent years investigating, interrogating, and arresting, had been released from prisons across the country. Just three miles away from FBI headquarters, a handful of defendants emerged Tuesday from the D.C. jail in Southeast Washington to cheers from family and members of the far-right militia group Proud Boys. It was a hero's welcome for the self-proclaimed "patriots."

"We are back—the patriots. We don't have to crawl in the back corners of Facebook and Instagram, being censored," pardoned defendant Jake Lang said as he was freed from the D.C. jail. "We've got X, we've got Trump, we've got Musk. We've got the dream team!"

By Thursday, January 23, nerves on the seventh floor at the FBI were frayed. Aides to Driscoll and Kissane told coworkers and former allies outside the building that Patel's advisory team was going to peer through Sentinel, the Bureau's sensitive database of all its investigative cases. They planned to hunt for agents' names with or without the leadership's help.

"They want to go through it themselves," one explained to his colleagues.

That circle of formers and friends who had received the SOS calls split up a long list of calls to make. They had to plead with a slew of Republican lawmakers, including Senate Intelligence Committee members, to do something, please, before thousands of agents were fired and the nation's premier law enforcement agency didn't have the manpower to combat crime or intercept terrorist plots. They alerted Democratic lawmakers on the Senate Judiciary Committee, who would within days be holding confirmation hearings for Trump's nominees for attorney general and FBI director, Bondi and Patel. And over the next several days, they reached out to reporters they knew at major outlets to detail the mass sacking being threatened inside Bureau headquarters.

The start of the new week, January 27, brought two consecutive "Monday massacres" that would first target some of DOJs best prosecutors, then the FBI's top leaders.

Trump had begun his Monday morning telling senior aides he wanted all the prosecutors who investigated him fired. Sergio Gor, Trump's White House head of personnel, then sent a memo instructing the Justice Department to carry out the firings. By Monday afternoon, terse, identical emails arrived in the inboxes of more than a dozen prosecutors who had worked in Special Counsel Jack Smith's office but remained as DOJ prosecutors.

"Given your significant role in prosecuting the president, I do not believe that the leadership of the department can trust you to assist in implementing the president's agenda faithfully," read the letter, which was signed by Acting Attorney General James McHenry.

Cooney and Gaston, former special counsel prosecutors, walked together from their desks to tell their boss, Denise Cheung, the head of the Criminal Division at the U.S. Attorney's Office in D.C., that they'd been fired. The pair had worked closely together for several years in the D.C. office before joining Smith's team and had returned when Smith's office was shuttered ten days before the inauguration. They had prepared mentally for Trump to punish them somehow, Cooney and Gaston told her, but the tough-as-nails investigators were now visibly angry.

"They can't do that," Cheung said. But the department already had.

When the prosecutors left, tears began to run down Cheung's face.

Smith himself and several others in the office had already resigned or retired from Justice before the inauguration—including Bratt, Edelstein, and Raskin. But Trump wanted to sweep out everyone, including Ray Hulser, the thirty-four-year prosecutor and former head of public corruption investigations whom Smith had recruited to help him lead the office; Tad Duree, a younger prosecutor, who investigated Trump's fake elector plot; and Brett Reynolds, who had handled several sensitive interviews in the documents case.

Like a few others who were fired, Hulser had been traveling when his termination notice arrived. Under the eye of a security guard, he was given fifteen minutes a few days later to come pack his things and depart his office forever.

He loaded his cardboard boxes into his car in the underground garage and began to drive out. A security guard Hulser had gotten to know stepped out of his booth to say goodbye and to offer his support at the shabby way he had to leave.

"This is some bullshit," he told Hulser.

Hulser smiled at this graciousness.

"Thank you, sir," he said.

In the second week of Trump's presidency, after Trump directed the firing and removal of top DOJ leaders, his lieutenants at the White House and DOJ dramatically turned up the heat at the FBI. If Patel had been the not-so-secret hand seeking to clean house at the Bureau, Bove was far more direct.

That week, Bove told Driscoll and Kissane that he wanted a list of names of agents from the Washington Field Office who had participated in the January 6 investigation and also agents involved in the Mar-a-Lago classified documents case.

"We need to do a DOJ review," Bove told them, and said it was possible some agents would need to be fired.

Driscoll said he didn't understand why DOJ needed to review these agents and didn't want to provide such a list. He pointed to the multiple divisions of the Bureau that investigated agents for possible violations of policy or misconduct. Plus, they had an inspector general. Why did Bove need to conduct a DOJ review? he asked.

On the evening of Tuesday, January 28, Bove took several calls from Trump's deputy chief of staff, Stephen Miller, who had assumed the role of exacting the president's revenge and delivering the fearsome new headlines to please both Trump and his supporters. Miller said he had talked with Patel, who was anxious to see more "targeted" officials at the FBI removed from their jobs, to match how swiftly DOJ was firing prosecutors. Patel essentially wanted the FBI firings to happen faster. Miller had pressed Bove to get it done, saying he agreed, according to later reports of Bove's account.

At around 9:30 a.m. on Wednesday, January 29, Driscoll and Kissane were attending the standing morning briefing at the attorney general's conference room. When it ended, Bove asked the two to stay behind for a private "skinny-down" conversation, the kind FBI leaders normally had to discuss sensitive investigations. Bove described Patel's wish that key FBI personnel who authorized probes of January 6 and Trump be fired, and Miller's similar orders received the night before. Some scribbled notes during Bove's presentation that captured the gist: "KP wants movement at FBI, reciprocal actions for DOJ."

Driscoll and Kissane realized as they listened to Bove that he planned to clean out most of the seventh-floor leadership, the executive assistant directors who oversaw all the Bureau's core divisions. They feared there was little they could do to stop him. They were all part of the senior executive service, and the president had issued an executive order allowing him to fire them if he assessed they couldn't implement his agenda. Driscoll and Kissane lobbied Bove to at least keep Michael Nordwall, who headed up criminal investigations, and Bobby Wells, the head of national security. They said they needed a few experienced hands who had run things at headquarters, where neither of them had served until that month.

Kissane said something along the lines of: "It would be really helpful to have these guys here."

Bove said he'd consider this.

Driscoll and Kissane returned to the Hoover Building and asked an office assistant to email all the executive assistant directors, known as EADs, to join them for a meeting at 3:00 p.m.

Most of the executive assistant directors arrived in person; Driscoll opened the meeting. He said that the Justice Department and the White House were making noises that they wanted to fire the senior-most leaders at the FBI who had served under Wray. Kissane warned that some of them were likely "in the crosshairs" and faced the threat of being forced out of their jobs, in part because they were "Wray's people."

"They want the EADs gone," Driscoll said.

Driscoll and Kissane looked physically uncomfortable, and made clear this was not their wish.

"We're just the messengers," Driscoll said.

"What's the timing on this?" one assistant director asked.

"Do we have time to retire?" asked another.

For most, it felt like the world was spinning. They were career agents, not political followers of one administration or another. Yes, Wray had promoted them to their current positions, but they didn't view themselves as allied with Wray. They served the FBI. They would never mention their political views at work, but this was a Republican-leaning group. One director thought to himself: "Hell, several of us voted for Trump."

Once again, officials on the FBI's seventh floor reached out to their trusted friends outside the Hoover Building for help. Hearing again about a threat of mass firings, and one targeting a key swath of experienced national security leaders, some of the former colleagues reached out to Democrats on the Senate Judiciary Committee. The information made its way to a list of questions Democrats were preparing to ask Patel in his confirmation hearing.

On the morning of Thursday, January 30, Senate Judiciary Committee Chairman Chuck Grassley gaveled Patel's confirmation hearing into session at 9:30 a.m.

Just ninety minutes later, at 11:00 a.m., the FBI's executive assistant directors were again sitting together, summoned to their second conference room meeting with Driscoll and Kissane in two days. But this session immediately felt even more urgent, and Driscoll and Kissane wore dour expressions. The two leaders spelled it out: DOJ officials had told them that they were going to fire most or all of the FBI's executive assistant directors if they didn't leave by Monday.

"You have until Monday to retire or you're going to be fired," Driscoll said.

The group had been prepped for this, and still it nauseated them.

When they had time to think and talk alone that Thursday, the executive assistant directors debated their options. By dint of having worked more than twenty years, they were all eligible for retirement. They could fight what seemed on its face like an illegal termination without cause, but they faced big risks. Resisting might unleash Trump's full fury, as Andrew McCabe had suffered when Trump tried to deny him his pension days before he was eligible for retirement. They might have to go without both pay and pension while they fought the firing in the courts.

"Who knows how long this will drag on," one assistant director said.

They didn't want to gamble with their pensions and health-care coverage for them and their families. And in the end, who wanted to fight to work for bosses like this?

But the alternate reality playing out in Patel's hearing gave the FBI leaders a sick feeling in their stomachs.

At about 11:45 a.m., Sen. Richard Blumenthal, a Democrat from Connecticut, started his turn asking questions by thanking Patel for visiting his office on Monday and remarking on the irony that at the time of his visit, DOJ was firing the special counsel's prosecutors simply because they did their jobs.

"You've committed that the FBI will not be politicized. So here's your first test," Blumenthal said. "Will you commit that you will not tolerate the firing of the FBI agents who worked with the Special Counsel's Office on these investigations?"

"Senator, I appreciate the time to visit with you," Patel began.

But Blumenthal cut him off: "It is a yes or no answer and it is your first test."

"Senator, every FBI employee will be held to the absolutely same standard. No one will be terminated for case assignments," Patel said.

That wasn't enough, Blumenthal said.

"I'm not going to accept that answer, because if you can't commit that those FBI agents will be protected from political retribution, we can't accept you as FBI director," the senator said.

As Blumenthal lamented Patel's parsing, the nominee declared: "All FBI employees will be protected against political retribution."

At about 12:45 p.m., after the confirmation hearing resumed from a midday recess, Sen. Cory Booker, Democrat from New Jersey, asked Patel about indications that FBI agents or other staff might be on the chopping block that very day.

"You're under oath," Booker said sternly. "Are you aware of any plans or discussions to punish in any way, including terminations, FBI agents or personnel associated with Trump investigations?"

"Senator, I just want to be clear I had nothing to do with the Department of Justice—" Patel began, but was again cut off.

"That's a yes or no question," Booker said, then repeated it.

"I am not," Patel said flatly.

They watched as Patel claimed—counter to what Bove had told the FBI's two acting leaders—that he had no knowledge of politically motivated firings at the FBI. They listened as he insisted he would never seek to punish or terminate FBI staff for political reasons. They heard him soon after tell Booker he had no knowledge that a small band of former agents—whom Patel was personally close to and who were described as the Director's Advisory Team in office memos—had been installed as political appointees inside the FBI.

"News to me, Senator," Patel said.

Several of the Bureau leaders now being forced out suspected the presumed future FBI director had just lied to Congress. Patel would later repeat that he had no knowledge of personnel actions at the Bureau.

Early that evening Bove and Driscoll and Kissane spoke again about the DOJ leader's full-court press to remove several senior leaders of the FBI. Bove said he was willing to let them keep Wells and Nordwall.

He tried to gain something for his side of the ledger. He again asked for the list of names of agents who worked the January 6 case in the FBI's Washington Field Office. Driscoll said he wasn't comfortable providing that. He cited the agency's long-standing practice of withholding agents' identities and redacting their names from public court filings, so that bad guys couldn't target the investigators or their families. He didn't say aloud one of the primary fears about handing over agent names: It could risk his colleagues' lives if their names ended up in the hands of a president who had sought to villainize individual FBI agents by name on social media.

This wasn't a theoretical risk. Trump had turned other agents' lives upside down in his last presidency.

"I can't believe you're fighting me," Bove said, sounding insulted.

"This is people's careers and they didn't do anything wrong," Driscoll said.

Bove at one point asked for a far more limited set: How about they start with the names of every FBI agent who had been part of the search of Trump's bedroom in Mar-a-Lago?

"I just need a list to cut," Bove said, frustration rising in his voice. "I just need five or six names because Stephen Miller is breathing down my neck."

Bove was acting and talking like a man under significant pressure to deliver some scalps to the White House. But Driscoll wasn't budging. And an increasingly angry Bove wasn't giving up either.

By Friday, Bove had had it. The time for negotiating was over.

He sent a shot-across-the-bow memo titled "Terminations" to Driscoll on January 31, in which he demanded that Driscoll fire seven specific senior leaders unless they had resigned or retired by Monday, February 3, at 5:30 p.m. He named five executive assistant directors. They included Timothy Dunham, who oversaw human resources; Jackie Maguire, the head of science and technology; and Ryan Young, head of intelligence. And there seemed to be an extra punch for the lack of cooperation on agents' names: Nordwall and Wells were added back in as guys to fire.

Additionally, Bove declared that Driscoll would have to fire David Sundberg, the head of the Washington Field Office.

Also listed for termination were Dena Perkins, an acting chief in the Security Division who had already retired, and Jeff Veltri, a previous Security Division supervisor who was now the special agent in charge of the Bureau's Miami Field Office. Allies of Patel's, FBI agents who called themselves "the Suspendables," had blamed Perkins and Veltri for revoking some of their security clearances and ultimately ending their FBI careers. The Suspendables had claimed some of them were targeted for resisting COVID rules or espousing conservative religious views. But in congressional testimony, FBI officials had testified to Congress that these agents were suspended for a pattern of misconduct and security concerns. One agent allied with Patel was found to have threatened a firearms instructor on a rifle range by firing a gun in the path of the instructor. The Bureau suspended two other agents after an investigation into leaks of sensitive case information found digital proof they inappropriately accessed those case files. Like so many MAGA-world claims of the FBI being weaponized against conservatives, the evidence to back up their claims of unjustified, politicized suspensions was contradicted.

In his letter, Bove spelled out a now-familiar justification for this purge of the FBI's top brass.

"I do not believe that the current leadership of the Justice Department can trust these FBI employees to assist in implementing the president's agenda faithfully," Bove added about the FBI executives.

This line infuriated the executive assistant directors and scores of agents who later read it. Their job was never to implement the president's agenda.

"That's sick. That's B.S.," said one EAD. "We adhere to the rule of law. Our oath is not to any politician or individual."

In his memo, Bove also demanded that Driscoll finally turn over by noon on Tuesday, February 4, a list of names of all agents and supervisors involved in the January 6 riot investigation. Bove didn't mention that as a prosecutor in the Southern District of New York, he had actively supervised many of those cases and actually urged Main Justice's National Security Division to help lead the investigation.

After getting the list, Bove said, "The Office of the Deputy Attorney General will commence a review process to determine whether any additional personnel actions are necessary."

Driscoll consulted with aides and lawyers in the General Counsel's Office. The acting director proposed that he send Bove just one name: his own. After all, two weeks after January 6, Driscoll had participated in the arrest of Samuel Fisher, a QAnon conspiracy follower in Manhattan who had a stockpile of ammunition and other weapons. Fisher had pleaded guilty to illegal gun possession and to joining rioters who entered the Capitol that day.

But the lawyers urged Driscoll not to poke the bear. Bove's order to produce names for DOJ was likely legal. Driscoll could get fired and replaced, and the lawyers told Driscoll they wanted him to keep up his fight to protect the agents.

Driscoll worried about Bureau staff hearing partial rumors about the housecleaning of the EADs. He decided the best thing to do was to widely share the bad news. He wrote an email to all FBI staff at around 6:00 p.m., essentially cc'ing a staff of thirty-eight thousand on Bove's "Terminations" memo. Now they all knew from his own words how a DOJ official ordered Drizz to fire senior executives by name and produce the names of nearly five thousand FBI agents and staff who had worked on the January 6 case by noon that coming Tuesday.

"We understand this request encompasses thousands of employees across the country who have supported these investigations," Driscoll wrote to the staff. "I am one of those employees, as is Acting Deputy Director Kissane."

Driscoll didn't get into the details of how forcefully he and Kissane had been resisting giving up a list of people for Trump's DOJ to fire.

"As we've said since the moment we agreed to take on these roles, we are going to follow the law, follow FBI policy, and do what's in the best interest of the workforce and the American people—always."

By Friday afternoon, all the EADs had packed up their awards and personal papers. They met with Kissane and Driscoll in the director's office for bourbon—the favorite spirit of many agents—and a toast to the Bureau they loved. A few recalled their hardest and proudest moments in the field, as case agents on 9/11, gathering evidence at the Pentagon and the Towers. Then the senior executives left the Hoover Building together, 150 years of combined FBI experience walking out the door forever.

Over at the U.S. Attorney's Office that Friday, Criminal Chief Denise Cheung was working furiously and facing a deadline that night to deliver a "memo" to her new chief prosecutor, Ed Martin. The previous Monday, January 27, Martin had launched an internal review, this one focused on prosecutors in the office who had used obstruction charges against January 6 rioters. He had ordered Cheung to conduct it. Now, Cheung had a fifteen-page draft in front of her, a factual summary laying out why prosecutors charged many rioters who entered the Capitol with obstruction of a government proceeding—interfering with Congress's certification of the election—and listing the dozen or so judges who had upheld their decision. She was in her office with a deputy proofreading the memo and the twenty-some attachments, making sure all the facts and dates were accurate. Then the pair saw waves of their staff streaming hurriedly through the hallway to their supervisors' offices.

The anguished-faced attorneys began peppering their supervisors with frightened questions about an email Martin had sent to the entire office just minutes earlier. His note urged staff to follow office policy for retaining documents given "decisions that have been made" to remove some prosecutors from the staff. The group gathered in the hall urgently wanted to know: Were *they* on the list of people who had been fired?

Their supervisors said they'd find out, and called over to the Main Justice unit that manages U.S. Attorney's Offices. They spent the rest of Friday night calling each member of the staff of the Capitol Siege Section to let them know either if they had been terminated, or if they had survived the most recent mass firing.

Trump's Justice Department that weekend scored some good publicity with its supporters by appearing to root out "biased" January 6 prosecutors. Actually, Bove's lieutenants had obtained a list of Capitol Siege Section attorneys and chose to terminate the prosecutors most recently hired, who had fewer legal rights to fight it. It meant the administration fired many who were the most willing among the staff to be transferred to new assignments and help prosecute D.C. gun crimes, a priority for the president's agenda. These younger but go-getter prosecutors would have happily switched to the violent crimes team to get more experience. Three months later, the department was still working to find and hire replacements.

Late Friday night and Saturday morning, Chris Mattei and Margaret Donovan, two former federal prosecutors in the U.S. Attorney's Office in Connecticut, were freaking out and texting each other as they read the news reports about federal prosecutors and FBI agents being fired and threatened. They now worked in private practice; Mattei had made a name for himself in convicting Connecticut Governor John Rowland for campaign fraud. The pair wanted to offer their help to stop what threatened to be the largest FBI purge in history.

On Saturday, Mattei began firing off emails to everyone he could think of who might know about any legal effort being mounted to stall this dangerous defenestration. He pinged former Acting Assistant Attorney General Mary McCord, whom he knew from her work at Georgetown Law preparing for possible militia violence leading up to the 2020 election. She connected him with Norm Eisen, a former ethics czar under President Obama and a board member of the Democracy Defenders Fund, a nonprofit fighting Trump's autocratic moves, who planned to help represent individual FBI agents fearful of being publicly named or fired.

While Mattei and Donovan were trying to offer their help, the FBI

Agents Association was trying to find lawyers like them. Through a former FBI agent in Connecticut, Donovan got them an introduction to the leadership of the Agents Association, a group they had never heard of before that weekend. And to Mattei's and Donovan's surprise, the Agents Association decided they wanted the pair to represent them.

"Are you sure you want us?" Mattei asked. "We'll do whatever we can to help. But we don't have any experience in this. We're a small plaintiffs' firm."

Association president Natalie Bara, an agent who worked drug crimes out of Newark, said she actually did want them. She and association leaders were glad that top-flight lawyers like Eisen, veteran federal employment lawyer Mark Zaid, and others had brought their experience to the fight and would represent individual FBI agents. But, Bara said, she wanted the association to be represented by lawyers who wouldn't be discounted or derided as anti-Trump. Protecting agents' careers and safety was her group's priority, and she didn't want to make apolitical agents a bigger target by giving any ammunition to suggest they were in league with a political side.

Mattei and Donovan were glad to join the team. They had a deep respect for their new clients and considered Zaid and Eisen phenomenal legal partners.

Now they had to put their heads together and file suit for a temporary restraining order. They had to stop Trump's Justice Department from gutting the FBI.

That weekend, under Bove's direction, FBI managers received orders to either fill out surveys answering a list of questions about what actions their individual employees took in the January 6 probe, or have employees complete the survey themselves. Had they executed a search warrant, issued subpoenas for information, or surveilled or arrested a suspect?

Managers and employees had a deadline to return the information: Monday at 3:00 p.m.

That weekend, a team of Washington Field Office FBI agents were helping collect evidence from the freezing Potomac River in the wake of the horrific midair collision of an Army helicopter and a regional passenger jet on January 29. The crash had sent both aircraft into the river and killed all sixty-seven aboard. One agent involved in recovery told her supervisor she was surprised at this paperwork order.

"I just got done pulling body parts out of the Potomac and now I've got to fill out this survey," the agent said.

When Bove's deadline arrived at noon on Tuesday, Driscoll had arranged to send him a list of agents—but instead of names, he provided employee ID numbers. Bove was furious. The same day, the FBI Agents Association filed its suit to stop the release of agents' names.

"This feels like a resistance," Bove said.

"Because it is," Driscoll answered.

[34]

Sign, Quit, or Get Fired

On Friday, January 31, Bove hosted a contentious meeting in his conference room. It was part of an effort by the former defense attorney to get rid of the bribery case against New York Mayor Eric Adams—something Donald Trump wanted. But Trump also wanted something in return.

More than a month before his inauguration, in mid-December, Trump had told reporters he felt Adams had been "treated pretty unfairly" by the Justice Department, an echo of his own complaint about the department's investigation of him. When asked, the president-elect said he would consider pardoning Adams of the charges, which at first blush didn't look that bad to him.

"Now, I haven't seen the gravity of it all, but it seems, you know, like being upgraded in an airplane many years ago?" Trump said, rolling his eyes about one of the accusations. "I know probably everybody here's been upgraded. . . . And that would mean you'll spend the rest of your life in prison? I don't know."

The details were a bit more disturbing; prosecutors said Adams accepted illegal gifts worth more than $100,000, including upgrades, plane tickets, and luxury hotel stays from wealthy Turkish citizens over a decade while serving in local government. In exchange for this largesse, they said, Adams performed favors, such as pressuring city fire officials to let a Turkish consulate open before all fire safety concerns were met.

But Trump did know with great clarity how Adams was the rare Democrat who leaned Trump's way in resisting illegal immigration. In 2023, Adams had publicly complained that the flood of migrants seeking asylum could soon put New York City into a multimillion-dollar budget deficit. Adams crossed swords with many in his party by loudly complaining the Biden administration had failed to help his city manage this "unsustainable" burden on the city's emergency shelters and other services. Few knew that Adams was then under a long-running criminal investigation. In September 2024, city residents read with disbelief the headlines announcing the mayor was indicted for having accepted bribes over several years.

After Trump's election in November, Adams worked to buddy up to the incoming president, ultimately scoring an in-person meeting with him at Mar-a-Lago on January 17, days before his inauguration. The week Trump was sworn in, Adams's lawyer wrote to Trump's White House counsel asking for the pretrial pardon Trump had indicated he might grant. The president then passed word to DOJ that he would like to liberate Adams from this corruption case.

On Monday, January 27, Bove called Acting U.S. Attorney Danielle Sassoon, thirty-eight, a friend of Bove's who had been sworn in to lead the Southern District of New York's prosecutors' office a week earlier, with his support. Sassoon was a talented attorney, a Harvard and Yale grad and a Federalist Society member who had clerked for conservative Supreme Court Justice Antonin Scalia and Judge J. Harvie Wilkinson III of the Fourth Circuit Court of Appeals. She and Bove had worked together in the SDNY office, where she had started as a violent and organized crimes prosecutor in 2016, and Bove had supervised national security and drug trafficking cases. He told her he wanted her prosecutors to dismiss the Adams case, explaining that it was interfering with the mayor's ability to run the city. If freed from this prosecution, Bove explained, Adams could help with a top priority for the Trump administration—combating illegal immigration.

Sassoon told Bove that dismissing the bribery charges was a bad idea. Her team was planning to enter a superseding indictment, she said, based on new evidence that Adams had tried to destroy evidence and told others to do so. She asked that Bove please consider waiting until Todd Blanche was confirmed as deputy attorney general and had a chance to review the case.

"We're on the same page," Bove told her of Blanche, his co-counsel in defending Donald Trump. Blanche also sought to de-weaponize the department, so waiting wouldn't make any difference, Bove said. He told her to think about it.

Bove ratcheted up the pressure by summoning Sassoon and her prosecutors to an in-person meeting in D.C. on that Friday, January 31, to further discuss a dismissal. He gave Sassoon and her team forty minutes to outline the chronology of the case, and to explain their reasoning for continuing to pursue the charges. He invited Adams's lawyers, Alex Spiro and Bill Burck, to the same meeting, where they argued the charges interfered with Adams's ability to govern and had been politically driven by Sassoon's Biden-appointed predecessor. Without having to fight for his innocence at trial, Adams would be free to lead the city and enforce its laws, the lawyers said. Sassoon felt they were repeatedly suggesting Adams would be free to help Trump with immigration enforcement.

While Sassoon and Adams's lawyers were collegial and friendly to each other, the meeting had a lopsided feel. Bove had already spoken privately with Adams's lawyers, urging them to make the precise interference claim that they were now leaning in to, one that Trump had made about the way the Mueller probe had interfered in his first presidency. Burck had worked with Bove in the Southern District years earlier and had recently been hired to represent Trump's interests as the Trump Organization's ethics adviser on foreign deals.

Sassoon found this all deeply disturbing. First she demanded to know: Why the rush to dismiss this case? Forty minutes was not long enough to address all the ethical problems and dubious legal grounds raised by dropping the case now. They also had such compelling evidence Adams had committed these crimes, and more. She felt Spiro and Burck were proposing a quid pro quo, but did not lodge that claim in the meeting.

Bove told Sassoon and her team to think of this like a prison swap in which America provided Russia with one of its prisoners in exchange for the freedom of an American whom Russia had detained. Sassoon considered this analogy was equally problematic. The Justice Department didn't trade leniency based on the profile of the defendant and the favors they could extend to the government.

One of Sassoon's team members had been taking notes on the discussion; Bove ended the meeting after scolding that notetaker and demanding he hand over his notes, saying there had been a lot of leaks in this case.

After ten days, Bove was tired of talking to Sassoon and getting nowhere. On February 10, he formally ordered her to dismiss the Adams case in a memo. News of his memo leaked that day. Lawyers up and down the Eastern Seaboard texted and called one another to speculate on what the new acting U.S. attorney would do.

"She'll be run out of the city if she dismisses that case!" one lawyer warned in one exchange.

The Southern District was quiet, with no immediate response to leadership at Main Justice. Behind the scenes, Sassoon had begun privately drafting her resignation letter that Monday but didn't finalize it. Then Tuesday came and went, with no response to Bove.

On Wednesday, February 12, Sassoon sent newly confirmed Attorney General Pam Bondi an eight-page letter that laid out why she felt that Bove had ordered an improper quid pro quo she could not ethically rubber-stamp. Written as if addressing a judge, the letter carried the power of a well-told story and an appellate brief. Sassoon laid out a direct, unflinching narrative of the pressure Bove placed on her to cross an ethical line, but added legal case citations to back up her points. Sassoon said that Bove's order to dismiss the case—which a grand jury had found probable cause to charge—was ultimately "inconsistent with my ability and duty to prosecute federal crimes without fear or favor and to advance good-faith arguments before the courts." The last part referred to a prosecutor's duty of candor to the court; she couldn't honestly say they had a good or honorable reason to ditch this prosecution.

Sassoon used Bondi's own words, appealing to the new AG by quoting her February 5 memo to all DOJ staff when she was confirmed.

"In your words, 'the Department of Justice will not tolerate abuses of the criminal justice process, coercive behavior, or other forms of misconduct,'" Sassoon wrote. "Dismissal of the indictment for no other reason than to influence Adams's mayoral decision-making would be all three."

She called this leniency in exchange for Adams's help on Trump's immigration policy "a bargain that a prosecutor should not make."

She warned Bondi that the judge presiding over the case would surely investigate what led to the dismissal and find the reasoning lacking—another blow to DOJ's reputation. Sassoon asked the AG to meet with her to discuss the case.

"In the event you are unwilling to meet or to reconsider the directive in light of the problems raised by Mr. Bove's memo, I am prepared to offer my resignation," Sassoon concluded.

Her letter quickly leaked, marking another dizzying round in the fight over Adams's prosecution.

But Sassoon's carefully made points landed like a sack of garbage at Main Justice. Bondi was willing to accept Sassoon's resignation. But they decided perhaps they should put her on leave pending an internal investigation.

By the next day, learning she would get neither a meeting nor a reconsideration, Sassoon sent in her resignation.

That Thursday, on February 13, Bove transferred the Adams bribery case closer to home and more directly under his control, to the Public Integrity Section, or PIN, as it was known at Main Justice.

Bove was mildly embarrassed and highly irritated. He had bet wrong that Sassoon, his friend and former colleague, would do as he wanted. He had begun to complain that if he kept pushing the Southern District now, every single prosecutor in the powerhouse Manhattan office might resign.

Just as the "Sovereign District" of New York prided itself for its independence, so too did PIN. Like so many divisions at DOJ, it had been formed in response to a crisis, Nixon's effort to use the department to cover up the Watergate scandal. Attorneys in this powerful unit had a broad mandate to investigate "criminal abuses of the public trust by government officials" in all three branches of the government and at all levels, local, state, and federal. Attorneys who spent time in PIN usually carried the experience with them for their careers, like a badge of honor.

Starting in midmorning, Bove began reaching out to top supervisors over PIN to tell them it now fell to them to dismiss the Adams case immediately. One by one, the tall trees of the public corruption team fell, rather than agree.

The first to go was Kevin Driscoll, who had been the highest-ranking person over the Criminal Division that supervised the Public Integrity Section. He tried to convince Bove that forcing public corruption prosecutors to sign off on this request was a mistake.

"Don't make someone at PIN sign it," he said. "You will kill the section's independence and reputation for years."

But he got nowhere and resigned rather than force the team to sign the motion. John Keller, who was now the acting chief of the section since Corey Amundson had been removed as head of the office on Inauguration Day, also refused and resigned.

Sometime before noon, Keller called his three deputy chiefs into his office to let them know the bad news. All three, Jennifer Clarke, Rob Heberle, and Marco Palmieri, looked at each other with eyes wide. Keller hoped their resignations would make the front office back off. After a beat, the deputy chiefs lamented it had come to this, praised Keller for his honorable stand, and began to discuss their position if Bove kept coming.

Heberle, who oversaw the Election Crimes Branch, spoke up first.

"You have to make your own decision, but I'm not going to sign this," he said. "I'll resign too."

Palmieri and Clarke immediately agreed. Their good conscience wouldn't let them dismiss a bribery prosecution without any justifiable ethical or legal basis.

Keller then asked the rest of the staff to join him in their conference room. The bearded Keller, a pillar in the section due to his deep knowledge of public corruption law, explained that he had refused an order for PIN to dismiss the Adams case and now, after fourteen years at DOJ, he had to leave.

"Kevin resigned and I had no choice but to do the same," Keller said. "We hope it ends there."

When staffers in the section first heard Keller—the second chief of Public Integrity resigning in the course of three weeks—explain, they were so flabbergasted at first that they just stared at him. He and Amundson had been a good team. Keller had served in the section the longest, and had been a line attorney in the trenches with several of those he now supervised. He biked to work and didn't seem embarrassed to walk into the office in his bike shorts. He was the manager who stayed late with them at the annual holiday party. Attorneys knew that he'd have an instant answer if they had an emergency question during trial.

Ryan Crosswell, a ten-year prosecutor and member of the PIN section, hadn't yet gotten over the sickening feeling about the Trump team driving out their first chief of Public Integrity, Amundson, his mentor. Crosswell, who had first served in the military and rose to become a lieutenant colonel in the Marine Corps, had later worked as a line prosecutor for Amundson in the U.S. Attorney's Office in Louisiana. When Crosswell transferred to the federal prosecutors' office in San Diego, he still called up his old boss for advice from time to time.

"Here are my facts at trial," Crosswell would start. "What do you think?"

After Amundson rose up in the DOJ ranks to become the chief of PIN in 2019, he recruited Crosswell to join the section.

And so Crosswell took it particularly hard when Trump officials removed Amundson from his job. A week later, when Amundson told someone privately that he had heard that leadership was going to try to fire him for cause, he relayed to the larger staff that he wanted to control the way he left and would retire instead. Crosswell was fuming at the unnecessary carnage and cruelty the incoming Trump administration was imposing on truly apolitical public servants, picking them off as if for sport. After hearing the news about Amundson, Crosswell returned to his office, anger rising rather than cooling, and threw his closed coffee thermos at his desk. The velocity of the toss knocked the lid off and sent a spray of hot brown liquid all over his desk and the floor.

Now, late that Thursday afternoon, the bad news about Driscoll and Keller resigning prompted fresh anger, but also another response: It was time for alcohol.

The fifteen or so members of the section who were in the office that day set off for informal goodbye drinks with Keller, an "unhappy hour" of sorts, with the first wave leaving the office after 2:00 or 2:30 p.m. They walked to their regular spot, Astro Beer Hall, a dark bar with lava lamps, fried chicken, and dozens of beers on tap. Its main selling point, however, was its location: a block from their downtown D.C. office at 1301 New York Avenue, or "1301" for short.

Sometime around 3:30—after most people were about to order their second round—the trial attorneys noticed that the three remaining supervisors of their section were putting on their coats and getting ready to leave. Deputy Chief Palmieri, late to the gathering as he finished up some work, had just ordered his first beer when he saw an email on his phone and showed it to fellow deputy chiefs Heberle and Clarke. It summoned all three of them to an on-camera meeting in a few minutes with the acting deputy attorney general.

Back at 1301, the three supervisors gathered on a Teams meeting with Bove and Antoinette "Toni" Bacon, the new acting chief of the Criminal Division. Bove explained he needed them or two other people at PIN to agree that night to sign the motion to dismiss the Adams case.

"It's been a really hard day for me too," he said. "I had to accept the resignation of a close personal friend."

Bove's attempt to be human struck the trio as both disingenuous and tone-deaf. If Sassoon was a good friend, why had Bove forced her to choose between her ethics and a political errand? He held the power to avoid all this, yet he was continuing to force others to make that same horrid choice.

"Can you give us some time to review the facts and the law?" one of the deputies asked. It would be reasonable for PIN to evaluate the corruption case, then give Bove their opinion.

No, Bove said.

Another PIN deputy asked if Bove and Bacon had considered having the top DOJ leadership sign the motion to dismiss instead.

"That's been discussed," Bacon said curtly. And it was not an option.

The call ended with the three Public Integrity chiefs asking the top Trump appointees to give them some time to think. But after a short discussion alone, Heberle, Clarke, and Palmieri each began drafting their resignation letters. Palmieri, the breadwinner for his family, knew he had to resign, even though it meant giving up his salary and a mission he loved. In this fraught and uncertain moment, his thoughts kept returning to his young children. He could figure out the money later, but this decision was forever. He wanted his kids to later understand how he handled this ethical quandary, and he hoped it would gird them if they faced a painful decision in life. A couple of the section attorneys had returned to the office; they got boxes and helped the deputy chiefs pack their pictures and personal effects.

In waves, the deputies returned to their waiting staff at Astro's, and explained Bove's demand and their resignations. Some of the trial attorneys began crying as they heard. Other customers in the bar stared over curiously at this group with the forlorn and shocked expressions, some of whom were pressing their hands over their mouths.

But after the shock, the mood at Astro's shifted to that of a supportive, even loving, wake. PIN alums J. P. Cooney, Molly Gaston, and Ray Hulser had gotten texts from office friends and shown up at the bar as comrades in arms. Former chief Amundson came too. Trial attorneys were hugging their deputy chiefs, praising them for their bravery.

Walking back to his downtown apartment from the bar later that night, Crosswell texted his parents and his two sisters to see if they could talk in a few minutes. Then, once the prosecutor got inside his door, all five connected for a FaceTime video call. He told them things weren't looking so good at the office, and he wanted to prepare them.

"I don't know if I'm going to have a job tomorrow," he said.

Friday was Valentine's Day. At about 9:15 a.m., Bove's assistant sent all the trial attorneys in PIN—more than two dozen in all—an email notice for a mandatory all-hands Teams meeting with him at 9:45. It was extremely short notice, which didn't bode well. Several people had dressed in suits and ties, though they weren't scheduled to be in court, perhaps out of respect for the office of the deputy attorney general. But to some, they appeared dressed for a grim funeral.

They were a vulnerable group without any defense. All but one of their supervisors had resigned in the last twenty-four hours; the only other one was unavailable. She'd gone into labor at a nearby hospital on Thursday.

In an office dealing with the kinds of politically sensitive and contentious cases that PIN managed, the section's supervisors were not just managers, but generals in a pitched battle. They had their attorneys' backs when high-profile political leaders attacked them publicly for their work or unfairly accused them of being politically motivated. The team had their hands tied in this kind of knife fight, in which politicians pounded them in cable television interviews and posts on X. The lawyers could never fight back and defend themselves, and could only speak through their pleadings and in court.

Practically, the PIN managers also had to review and approve nearly every step in an investigation and prosecution case, down to which witnesses to interview and when, and when to travel to them. As Crosswell walked from his downtown apartment to Main Justice that Friday morning, he was on the phone with an office administrator trying to figure out how he was going to make his upcoming trip to New Mexico to prepare witnesses for the trial of Solomon Peña. The unit had indicted Peña, a failed Republican candidate, on criminal charges accusing him of hiring people to shoot at the homes of local Democratic leaders after he lost an election for the New Mexico House of Representatives. Crosswell had inherited the case from a departing PIN attorney and now had to get ready for a March trial.

"Who is approving my travel?" Crosswell asked. The administrative assistant said they would figure it out.

As he continued walking to work, Crosswell had a bad feeling:

"Could this be my last day at DOJ?" he thought.

At the appointed hour of 9:45 a.m., trial attorneys logged on to their computers—most from their offices but several from home or from remote places where they were on assignment—and braced themselves for what exactly the new acting deputy attorney general was going to say. Most had never met Bove and only seen him in news reports describing his central role in trying to fire both federal prosecutors and FBI agents who had worked on investigations of Donald Trump or the January 6 riot.

Now the man being pilloried in online memes as the Nosferatu of Donald Trump's Justice Department was a somber face in one of the many boxes on their computer screens. Adding to the awkwardness, instead of just being a face on a screen, Bove was pictured at the end of an enormous table in a regal, wood-paneled conference room, a lord alone in his manor.

He began the meeting explaining that he was reaching out to them to "steady the ship" through some "turbulent times."

"Yesterday was a hard day for all of us," he said. "I know PIN lost some people. Danielle Sassoon was a personal friend of mine. Yesterday was hard for me too."

Then he stressed that as prosecutors they had to uphold the Constitution.

"That means implementing the agenda that the president was elected to implement," he said.

Some prosecutors found their brows furrowing. That was absolutely not what upholding the Constitution meant.

Bove continued to emphasize the zealous advocacy they all needed to show in advocating for the president, and the need to follow the chain of command to avoid what happened to Sassoon and other PIN supervisors.

"But these types of issues—chain of command, accountability, to the one democratically elected official in the executive branch—they're really important and there's no room for divergence," Bove said.

"I asked us to get together today," he said, to both share his thoughts on what had unfolded, and to ask that "you guys among yourselves figure out who is going to file this motion."

"I need two people to put in a straightforward motion in SDNY," he said, suggesting that those who stepped forward might win promotions. "Those people, today, will emerge as leaders of PIN."

"Let's please just figure this out," Bove said. "I don't care . . . who is willing to file this motion so we can get past this."

He gave them a deadline: one hour. He urged them to report back to him or his office.

Bove signed off from the session, leaving Toni Bacon, who had been on the conference call as well. She reiterated what Bove had said, urging prosecutors to find someone to step forward.

"Please, someone sign this," she said. "We want this to end."

The trial attorneys who were in the office decided they should gather together in person in PIN's large conference room. Those who were remote agreed to dial into the discussion by phone. The group of two dozen prosecutors quickly narrowed down their awful options to three: sign the motion, quit, or get fired. They reached consensus quickly: No one wanted to take Door Number One.

The group began to coalesce around Door Number Two: They should all resign, because the Trump administration would almost certainly shutter the Public Integrity Section or neuter its mission anyway. They could at least walk out knowing they hadn't caved to an unethical order.

Part of their choice was born of the rush to decide. No one in the room really knew for sure whether being fired would harm their ability to get clearances or future jobs. Resigning was less risky, they thought.

But then one prosecutor argued a group resignation was a mistake, and they should all refuse to sign the Adams motion and force Bove's hand. Why make it easy for Trump's new Justice team to evacuate their entire section? the prosecutor asked. That would leave their important cases to wither away and die, and possibly make way for Team Trump to replace them all with obedient ideologues.

Other PIN members noted the signs that Trump appointees were happy to eviscerate or eliminate PIN. Instead of continuing to threaten and fire more Manhattan prosecutors at SDNY, Bove had transferred the case to PIN. He had ultimately pressured five PIN supervisors to sign or resign, a bloodbath that decapitated the office. If they proceeded to resign en masse, the prosecutor said, "it will be a headline for a week and that's about it." But the cost of their resignations to their ongoing cases would be incalculable. At the time, PIN was moving steadily forward in a prosecution of Texas Rep. Cuellar and his wife after indicting them on charges of taking $600,000 in bribes from an Azerbaijan oil company and a Mexico-based bank. PIN attorneys were also slated to soon go to trial in a high-profile military corruption case, in which the government charged Robert P. Burke, a now-retired Navy admiral, with a bribery scheme to steer a sole-source government contract to a New York company in exchange for a lucrative job and stock options after he retired.

"This will guarantee the destruction of our work," the prosecutor said. "Let him fire us."

The attorneys were at very different stages of their lives.

Some were coming closer to the end of their careers, able to see their pension and lifetime health insurance over the near horizon. A few were midcareer, with lots of financial pressures but slightly more agility to leave for a private sector or law firm job. Several young attorneys, Ivy Leaguers and best-of-class law school grads who had just started with the office, had once been filled with excitement to be part of the Department of Justice's noble mission, and were now incensed.

As they debated what was better—being fired or resigning—the attorneys realized they didn't know for certain what would happen to their retirement pay in the two scenarios. Nobody had thought much about the trigger for their retirement benefits until this moment. A person was dispatched to leave the room to check.

Soon prosecutor Ed Sullivan—who had been one of the longest-serving in the office—spoke up. He was in his early sixties, nearing retirement, but some in the room didn't know him well, as he didn't join in a lot of group activities and hadn't had any recent high-profile cases. He said he was worried about everyone getting fired that night and the damage that would inflict on more than two dozen lives.

"I could sign it," he said. "That would give you all some time to find jobs."

Many in the room took a beat to consider this. They viewed Sullivan as a generous soul for making that offer. It would protect those attorneys who relied on this government paycheck to pay their bills—who had kids in school, mortgages to pay, pensions not yet in reach—and might have difficulty quickly finding another job.

Sullivan had been one of the prosecutors in the infamous Sen. Ted Stevens case in 2008, though he was relegated partway through the prosecution to a back-office role rather than handling arguments in court. He noted that his reputation had already taken a huge hit. Signing the dismissal motion for Adams would ding his reputation less than it would the others'.

"This will be easier for me," he said.

The group didn't have a lot of time. Bove had given them an hour.

They debated whether they needed a second volunteer to sign or if Sullivan would be enough. One more attorney said he would agree to sign if it came to that.

Finally, they agreed to Sullivan's idea: He would sign. Then he would see if one PIN signature was enough for Bove.

Sullivan called Bacon's office to let her know he would sign the motion. Much to everyone's relief, Sullivan reported back that the Office of the Deputy Attorney General was satisfied with one sacrificial lamb.

Crosswell felt Sullivan had been a hero for the group. Crosswell personally didn't have a family or a mortgage to worry about, but he felt keenly for those facing the choice between their ethics and their family's protection.

He walked back to his office and began drafting his resignation letter. He appreciated what Sullivan had done, but he just couldn't stay.

"I can't forgive this. I can't work for these people," he told a colleague.

Despite the rushed deadline, Bove's plan to rid the Trump administration of the Adams bribery case took all day to iron out—with several unreported bumps along the way.

Sullivan and several teammates began reviewing the draft pleading—known as a Rule 48 motion—that Bove's office had put together for him to sign. But the team strongly objected to its lengthy and mea culpa message. The draft went on for several sentences explaining how the SDNY prosecutors had erred and their charges were wrongheaded. That created two problems: Neither Sullivan nor anyone at PIN knew enough about the details of the Adams case to make such a judgment, and nobody wanted Sullivan to improperly fault his brethren to the north, whose work they all assumed was legitimate.

As Sullivan and his colleagues proposed changes to the draft, the PIN team was also besieged by the outside world. News of their internal drama was breaking after Barbara McQuade, a well-known former U.S. attorney and Trump critic, had heard from her DOJ sources about the PIN team being "locked in a room" and ordered to dismiss the Adams case. She tweeted just after 11:00 a.m. what she was learning. PIN prosecutors soon saw their phones lighting up with emails, calls, and texts from friends, colleagues—and some reporters. They even heard that SDNY prosecutors would be furious if anyone at PIN signed.

At roughly the same time, the resignation letter of one of the lead SDNY prosecutors in the Adams case leaked and became must-read fodder online. Hagan Scotten, a lawyer with military service and conservative credentials, had written Bove a battle cry against his move to politicize their case. He insisted that "any assistant U.S. attorney would know" that enticing a public official to do Trump's bidding by whitewashing the evidence of his bribes violated the nation's laws and DOJ principles.

"If no lawyer within earshot of the president is willing to give him this advice, then I expect you will eventually find someone who is enough of a fool, or enough of a coward, to sign your motion," Scotten wrote. "But it was never going to be me."

Outside the public corruption unit at 1301, many lawyers and DOJers cheered Scotten for mincing no words. But inside, the words stung. They were all about to be indirectly accused of foolishness and cowardice in endorsing the dismissal. In a series of hallway discussions, several trial attorneys argued they should talk Sullivan out of signing. The unit would look stronger and more principled if they forced Bove to fire them all.

At that point, Bove relayed word he would consider some draft changes that Sullivan and his team requested. The draft would instead emphasize that DOJ leadership and the attorney general had concluded the case was wrongheaded.

At about 3:30 p.m., amid the redrafting, several attorneys walked over to Sullivan's office and urged him to change course and refuse to sign. It was becoming clear, they said, that even one PIN lawyer signing on gave the new Trump DOJ an easy victory and stomped on their collective principles. Sullivan told them he understood their opinion, but he was going to sign.

By 6:00 p.m., after several tense hours, the motion was filed. The prosecutors rushed to check the electronic court record and saw the signatures at the bottom of the pleading: Sullivan, Bacon, and Bove.

Several PIN lawyers were stunned. Five supervisors had been forced out of their jobs, facing orders to compromise their ethical duty as prosecutors. Two dozen more had faced the end of their careers, the danger of losing their income, and a dagger to their reputations. But Bove had ended up signing the motion after all.

One prosecutor sighed:

"They didn't even need us."

Bove would keep one promise, though. In a path littered with resignations of conscience, Sullivan soon was promoted to be chief of the depleted Public Integrity Section.

[35]

"At the Directive
of Donald Trump"

On the morning of Monday, February 24, staffers walking along the second floor at the Department of Justice alerted building security to a mysterious group that had taken over some offices located near the Great Hall, a formal auditorium reserved for major announcements and important ceremonies. The men, all white and mostly middle-aged, worked with the lights turned off and had stacked boxes of audio equipment on the desks and floor, but they refused to say who they were or what they were doing.

The concerned staffers got an email from a building logistics officer the next morning that gave the beginning of an explanation: "There is a high security event happening in the building."

The nature of the "event" became clearer over that Tuesday when a small team of Secret Service agents arrived in the building to conduct an "advance," the methodical security plan typically put together a few days ahead of a public event with the president. They were mapping out the strategy for keeping Trump safe when he planned to make an as-yet-unannounced visit to the building that Friday, February 28.

On Wednesday, two days before, maintenance crews began assembling an elaborate new stage at the front of the Great Hall, hauling in special risers, preassembled walkways, and thousands of yards' worth of panels of bright blue velvet curtains. This two-story hall was one of the most hallowed in the building, a place where attorneys general gathered staff together for significant announcements and to present awards to staffers for brave, ethical, or distinguished service. But it had been judged not grand enough by Trump's White House aides.

"SUPER weird," one Justice staffer, who noticed the preparations, texted a colleague. The Great Hall already had a stage, as well as blue curtains and loads of ceremonial decor.

That night, after most DOJ employees had gone home, administrative staff learned that the White House had called off Trump's visit. No reason was given. But department attorneys noticed that Trump's Friday schedule had gotten unusually full: He was now hosting Ukrainian President Volodymyr Zelensky for an Oval Office visit.

Behind the scenes, Pam Bondi, who had been confirmed as attorney general just three weeks earlier, and Kash Patel, the new FBI director, had been working with the White House on a theatrical flourish for Trump's expected visit. They hoped it would send a clear message that a new sheriff was in charge.

They planned to present their new leader with a welcome gift: the boxes of papers and other personal items that the FBI had seized in 2022 from Trump's home in Mar-a-Lago after investigators concluded he was concealing classified government records there.

The White House got to work rescheduling the visit for two weeks later. But Trump told his deputies he didn't want to wait for his gift. A week after Patel was sworn in as director, the FBI delivered the boxes to Joint Base Andrews, so Trump could fly with them aboard Air Force One that Friday for his weekend trip to Mar-a-Lago. White House aides filmed staffers carrying fifteen cardboard boxes onto the president's plane and shared the video on social media.

"The Department of Justice has just returned the boxes that Deranged Jack Smith made such a big deal about," Trump announced a little after 6:00 p.m. on Truth Social. "They are being brought down to Florida and will someday be part of the Trump Presidential Library.

"Justice finally won out."

Answering reporters' questions about the boxes aboard the flight, Trump's onetime defense attorney and now White House counselor Alina Habba said they were being returned to the place they belonged—Trump's property—and criticized the special counsel's investigation and the invasion of Trump's home.

"Jack Smith is no longer," she said. "We are in the Oval Office."

Meanwhile, Trump's White House aides locked in on a new date for his DOJ visit: Friday, March 14. A whole weeklong hoopla of wedding-like event planning cranked up again inside the Main Justice building. Crews resumed building the new Broadway-style stage and hanging the expanse of velvet curtains. The mystery audio men returned to test and fine-tune the recording equipment so the event could be live streamed to the public.

Acting leaders of the DOJ's Criminal Division—the section that investigates violent criminals, money-stealing fraudsters, and corrupt officials—alerted their staff whose offices were near the Great Hall to prepare to work somewhere else that Friday because they wouldn't be allowed to get to their desks. Their offices, along a hallway between the courtyard and the Great Hall, would be on the red-carpet route for the VIP guests to enter the building and attend President Trump's speech.

Justice Department supervisors noticed something else highly unusual in the preparations that week: Bondi's office had not sent out word for DOJ employees to attend. Leadership usually asked managers to reserve time on their staff's calendars for major ceremonies or speeches in the Great Hall.

But this visit had nothing to do with the new president meeting or

inspiring Justice Department career staff, and everything to do with political comeuppance. The forty-seventh president, a man who had campaigned on seeking retribution against the department, wanted to make
a victory lap, a show of claiming full and total control over the levers of
justice that had so vexed him.

Since his first run for president in 2016, the department had investigated Trump for more than a dozen different crimes.

But Justice had failed to get the case before a jury, and the theatrical
set rising in the Great Hall hearkened to the new reality. Several staffers
saw unmistakable symbolism. Trump's staging scrubbed from view some
of the building's iconic pieces of artwork and decor that had been specifically designed nearly a century ago to celebrate the righteousness of a
nation governed by impartial and equally applied laws, rather than the
whims of royals. For Trump's visit, crews installed fancy new curtains
that covered the two twelve-foot-high, cast-aluminum Art Deco statues
that normally flanked the dais: the female statue *Spirit of Justice* and the
male *Majesty of Law*.

The standard portraits of the president, vice president, and attorney
general no longer hung as a cluster together over the entranceway leading
to the hall. In a show of her loyalty to Trump, Bondi had ripped down the
portraits of Biden, Harris, and Garland that had been left hanging in a
National Security Division office and removed the division's acting chief
from his post for the oversight. Now, as in the countries where dictators
and strongmen ruled, one single portrait, that of Trump, adorned the
wall. He controlled this department, and he would decide what was just
and what was not.

In Justice Department offices across the country, many staffers
watched to see what their new attorney general and new president had to
say, sometimes alone in their offices but often gathered near televisions
together. In one such cluster in the Bond Building, a Justice Department
office building on New York Avenue, a mixed group of attorneys and support staff found themselves laughing and then nearly crying as they tuned
in to the live stream at 3:00 p.m. Some chuckled out loud as they recognized

each new song in the odd mixture that played before the event started. Surely, one said to another, this ragtag mix of tunes—songs from *The Phantom of the Opera* and *Cats*, Reba McEntire's cover of "Jolene" and Bonnie Tyler's "Holding Out for a Hero"—wasn't being piped into the Great Hall. So they checked. Every channel had the same musical backdrop—Trump's team was intentionally blaring his standard campaign set list through the Justice Department. The uninvited staffers could see on television those arriving for the event.

Several Republican state attorneys general, Trump appointees, and uniformed immigration agents dotted the room. VIPs took their seats in the first two rows, including Trump's defense team–turned–Justice Department enforcers: Deputy Attorney General Todd Blanche and Principal Associate Deputy Attorney General Emil Bove. Patel also rated a front-row seat, as did Michael Flynn. Even Walt Nauta, the president's valet and coconspirator who had helped Trump hide boxes of records at Mar-a-Lago, poked his head through the curtains from backstage to check the room at one point.

Just after 3:30 p.m., nearly a half hour late, Bondi emerged from behind the curtain in an off-white suit, beaming and welcoming the audience to what she called a new and improved Justice Department.

She praised Trump as the "greatest president in the history of our country," and said that thanks to his direction, they would get the drugs and gangs "off our streets and get the illegal aliens out of our country."

Then, as if it were the most normal thing to say, Bondi blurted out a line of fealty to Trump that felt foreign and crushing to many who had spent their lives working at Justice.

"We are so proud to work at the directive of Donald Trump."

Several at the watch party at the Bond Building physically recoiled.

"What the fuck?" said one Justice official, a military veteran who was nearing the end of his career.

Despite Bondi's tendency to toss fawning comments in Trump's direction, the group was still shocked. The most important test that nearly every attorney general had stared down since Watergate was a point of inevitable conflict with the president's political goals and a duty to reassert the department's fidelity to the law above all else. Employees who take the oath to work at Justice swear allegiance to one thing: defending the Constitution and applying the law equally.

Dedicating the Main Justice building in honor of Robert F. Kennedy nearly a quarter century earlier, President George W. Bush had come close to capturing the mission many at DOJ felt: "This great building, and all who work here, serve the public in the cause of justice." Biden had similarly sought to reaffirm Justice's independence four years earlier, when introducing Garland: "You are not the president's . . . lawyer. Your loyalty is not to me—it's to the law, the Constitution, the people of this nation."

Bondi's boast that the DOJ now worked at the directive of the president was something the staffers had never heard said in the building. As the gravity of Bondi's comment sunk in, several felt a physical discomfort. They saw her bowing down to the occupant of the Oval Office and surrendering the DOJ's historic independence.

"Well, I guess we know where Bondi stands," said a newer DOJ hire. Trump next emerged from behind the curtain, thanked Bondi, and quickly launched into comparing his crowd size in the Great Hall to that of any other VIP speaker.

"This is a storied hall if there ever was one, and based on the crowd, I think we broke the all-time record," he said.

He thanked the members of his new DOJ team, called them "great people" who were already hard at work going after cartels and violent criminals. He raved about a new senior DOJ counselor for his prowess on Fox News: "Boy, I've been watching him on television. . . . He is really a tough one."

He extended unusually glowing remarks to Blanche and Bove.

"These guys never wilted. They were not shy. They fought. They weren't afraid and they were brilliant," he said, bowing his head in their direction. "And thank you both very much." As he had always yearned for in his first term, Trump now literally had "his" attorneys running the Justice Department.

After his attaboys for his new DOJ team, Trump turned to the part of his speech loaded on the teleprompter. The carefully chosen words served as a screed against his perceived injustices at the hands of the department and foreshadowed how he planned to remake it in response.

"We're turning the page on four long years of corruption, weaponization, and surrender to violent criminals, and we're restoring fair, equal, and impartial justice under the constitutional rule of law," Trump said, insisting the Biden administration had "weaponized" its law enforcement agency against him.

"First we must be honest about the lies and abuses that have occurred within these walls. Unfortunately, in recent years, a corrupt group of hacks and radicals within the ranks of the American government obliterated the trust and goodwill built up over generations," Trump said. "They weaponized the vast powers of our intelligence and law enforcement agencies to try and thwart the will of the American people."

Trump called Special Counsel Jack Smith "deranged" and other government lawyers who had opposed him "scum," so much so that he had ordered the firing of all those from his team who still had jobs at the department. The judges who oversaw the cases in which he was criminally indicted were "the most corrupt judges," Trump said. "It's not even imaginable how corrupt they were."

In the preceding days, the purge had targeted others, with his lieutenants firing the DOJ's top ethics advisers, removing a top layer of the FBI's most experienced leaders, then sidelining and defanging entire teams created to catch and stop corrupt public officials, money launderers, and American businessmen who paid bribes to get contracts. Without a hint of irony, Trump said Americans were lucky that he was now in charge.

He also took the colloquial title of the attorney general for himself. He was now "the chief law enforcement officer in our country," he proclaimed.

Trump grinned at Bondi, Blanche, Bove, and his other Justice Department appointees in the front rows as he told them they had a shot at making November 5, 2024—his election day—the most important date in U.S. history.

"If you do your job great, it'll go down as the most important day, one of them at least, in the history of our country," the president said. "You know, July Fourth was pretty—1776, it was pretty important too. But let's see if we can top it."

As Trump ended his remarks and prepared to leave, his campaign soundtrack fired back up to play one of his all-time favorites: The Village People's "Y.M.C.A." Campaign aides had long ago co-opted the party anthem for gay men, playing the disco tune hundreds of times at MAGA rallies, but surely this was its debut in the Great Hall.

The watch party of DOJ's Criminal Division employees had listened to Trump's speech at the Bond Building in a kind of stunned silence. A few, frowning and disgusted by what they were hearing the president say, abandoned ship mid-speech. Those remaining to the end quietly left the office one by one, saying meek goodbyes as they headed home for the weekend.

Shortly after the speech ended, American Civil Liberties Union Executive Director Anthony Romero issued a statement calling it a "sad day" for the country. Trump had stood at a DOJ podium and attacked even private lawyers who had advocated in court for clients or the public in challenging Trump's policies. He warned of a larger Trump plot to silence criticism and questions.

"It's increasingly clear that we're entering a modern McCarthy moment. When the government is targeting a former ambassador, a legal permanent resident, law firms, and even universities and treating them like enemies of the state, it is a dark day for American democracy," Romero said.

By the end of the day, Trump would leave for his weekend at Mar-a-Lago and a $1 million–a-seat candlelight fundraiser for his MAGA Super PAC. But before departing the White House, the president made clear he had reset the board at Justice. His aim was no longer to simply upend the federal investigations that had threatened to put him in prison or to let out of jail all those who had rioted in his name at the Capitol. Trump and his top advisers had bigger aims at this moment. They would seek to remake the playing field where he had so often lost. Trump would rewrite the rules and then act alone, not only as the sword of Justice but also as judge and executioner.

Two actions Trump took that night would take months for the world to fully recognize as the first daggers driven into the country's promise of a fair and impartial legal system. Trump signed the ninetieth executive order of his new presidency, E.O. 14237, which was soon derided as one of the most narrow and vengeful acts of presidential power in American history. It singled out the work of two private attorneys at Paul, Weiss—including one's pro bono work to hold rioters to account for January 6—as a pretense for the government to punish one of the nation's top twenty-five law firms. The order required the federal government to strip security clearances from attorneys, cancel government contracts, and deny all the firm's lawyers access to government buildings, even courthouses, to represent their clients. The firm had crossed Trump— the order said it had been "undermining the judicial process"—in two key ways. The firm had hired "unethical attorney Mark Pomerantz," who had previously worked at the Manhattan District Attorney's Office, "solely to manufacture a prosecution against me."

This claim ignored the fact that a New York City jury had that year convicted Trump of thirty-four felonies for a series of frauds in that case. Second, the firm employed a former top prosecutor for Special Counsel Robert Mueller's probe who later helped the firm launch a pro bono civil rights lawsuit against groups engaged in violence on January 6, including Oath Keepers and Proud Boys. The order didn't name the firm's partner, Jeannie Rhee, but she had also led Team R, the special counsel unit that had uncovered Russian intelligence efforts to damage Hillary Clinton's campaign and help Trump win the White House in 2016.

Though few noticed, Trump had also hinted in his speech at the second action he had planned for that night. In the Great Hall, Trump singled out his administration's efforts to jail members of Tren de Aragua, a criminal Venezuelan gang that Republicans had seized on during the campaign—albeit based on some dubious accounts—as a growing threat to the country.

"We'll be reading a lot of stories tomorrow about what we've done with them," Trump said. "You'll be very impressed, and you feel a lot safer, because they are a vicious group."

That Friday night, more than 230 men who had been living in the United States under varying immigration status were being held at a detention facility in Texas. They had been rounded up and detained across the country by U.S. immigration agents, often with no explanation. Among them was Kilmar Abrego Garcia, who had left his wife and five-year-old child to run errands on March 12 in the Maryland suburbs of Washington, D.C., and never returned. Garcia's wife is a U.S. citizen, and he had come to the country illegally from his native El Salvador but had been granted a withholding order by a U.S. immigration judge in 2019, preventing him from being deported because he could face deadly gang violence. But amid crackdowns ordered by Trump, he had been detained by newly aggressive immigration agents who erroneously told him his status had changed. Garcia's misfortune could be traced back to a single line in a defunct Maryland gang registry. Six years earlier, Garcia had been spotted in a Home Depot parking lot looking for construction work. According to a filing written by a police officer who was shortly thereafter suspended for alleged misconduct, an unnamed informant said Garcia and others were gang members. The officer wrote that Garcia was seen wearing a Chicago Bulls cap, which the officer wrote in his report was "indicative of the Hispanic gang culture."

Garcia and his fellow prisoners were told Friday night to prepare to board a plane to be deported the next day.

Just after 1:00 a.m. on Saturday, March 15, lawyers at the ACLU and Democracy Forward rushed to finish and file a legal complaint to sue the Trump administration in federal court in D.C. and block the deportation flights out of the Texas detention center. On behalf of five Venezuelan men, the civil rights advocates said their clients were at "imminent risk of removal" from the country and sought a restraining order, calling the deportations illegal.

Trump had invoked the Alien Enemies Act of 1798, a wartime power deployed only three times during America's history—the War of 1812, World War I, and World War II. He claimed the the presence of members of the Venezuelan gang represented an invasion directed by a foreign power, and its invaders could be summarily ejected from the country without notice.

The legal claim was a gargantuan stretch. There was scant evidence that the Tren de Aragua gang was an agent of a foreign power, the country of Venezuela. U.S. immigration agents had also made hasty conclusions that the men were gang members, based on as little as some of them having tattoos. Federal agents had in a few cases also disregarded their status as legal residents. A little after 9:30 a.m., the chief judge of the federal court, James Boasberg, issued a temporary order barring the deportation of the five men named in the suit and then set an emergency videoconference hearing for 5:00 p.m. But when Boasberg asked basic questions—were planes set to leave, had any left yet—the administration's lawyer, Deputy Assistant Attorney General Drew Ensign, said he didn't know.

"Are any removals under this Proclamation planned . . . in the next twenty-four or forty-eight hours?" Boasberg asked. Again Ensign said he wasn't sure. Boasberg told the Justice official to find out and paused the hearing at 5:20 p.m. to give him time to get answers.

But during the short break, at around 5:25 p.m. and 5:45 p.m., two airplanes loaded with the detained Venezuelan men took off from the airport in Harlingen, Texas, where the men had been queued on the tarmac. The planes were headed for Central America.

After the hearing resumed at 6:00 p.m., Boasberg granted a temporary restraining order and, without knowing if the planes were en route to El Salvador, demanded that the men be kept on U.S. soil or returned to the United States to give him time to study whether the Trump administration's use of the wartime powers was legal.

"Any plane containing these folks that is going to take off or is in the air needs to be returned to the United States, however that is accomplished," Boasberg said a little before 7:00 p.m. "This is something that you need to make sure is complied with immediately."

The two planes landed for a pit stop in Honduras just after 7:00. But no one in the Trump administration instructed the pilots to return to the States. The planes continued flying on to El Salvador, their final destination, where the Trump administration had paid the regime of President Nayib Bukele millions of dollars to take them in. Under Bukele's authoritarian government, police accepted the men with a flourish, and filmed the U.S. prisoners as they were shaved, stripped, and frog-marched in shackles into a notoriously dangerous prison for gang offenders called CECOT. After less than two months in office, the Trump administration had thumbed its nose at the direct order of a federal judge—the opening salvo in what some feared was a constitutional crisis.

A onetime law school roommate of Supreme Court Justice Brett Kavanaugh, Boasberg had at times over the years drawn praise from the right, allowing conservative groups access to Hillary Clinton's emails from her private server and, following January 6, handing down comparatively moderate sentences to rioters. But he drew a hard line at Trump's Justice Department's disregard for his order to turn around the planes. He temporarily blocked the administration from using the eighteenth-century law to deport alleged gang members, calling it "awfully frightening."

Trump responded by taking aim, warning he could next turn the power of the presidency against the federal judiciary and determine if anyone would be left on the bench to challenge him. He called for impeaching Boasberg, intimating the robed judge should know he wasn't in the same league as the president.

"This Radical Left Lunatic of a Judge, a troublemaker and agitator who was sadly appointed by Barack Hussein Obama, was not elected

President—He didn't WIN the popular VOTE (by a lot!), he didn't WIN ALL SEVEN SWING STATES," Trump posted on Truth Social, claiming a mandate from voters to get rid of illegal immigrants however he could. "This judge, like many of the Crooked Judges' I am forced to appear before, should be IMPEACHED!!!"

Republicans in Congress took up Trump's charge the same day, moving so quickly that Chief Justice John Roberts issued a rebuke, trying to quell all the impeachment talk by day's end. For more than two centuries, America did not settle court disputes by impeaching judges, Roberts wrote. "Impeachment is not an appropriate response to disagreement concerning a judicial decision."

Over the next two weeks, attorneys for the Justice Department continued to refuse to bring Garcia back, even as a career Justice Department attorney, Erez Reuveni, acknowledged under questioning by a federal judge in Maryland that he should never have been deported. That judge, Paula Xinis, ordered the administration to "facilitate and effectuate" Garcia's return.

The Justice Department responded by putting Reuveni on leave, and the next day it brought out Trump's heavyweight defense attorney to elevate the fight. John Sauer, who had successfully argued Trump's immunity claim before the Supreme Court the previous year, returned to the high court, now as U.S. solicitor general, arguing that since Garcia was now in El Salvador, the order to "effectuate" anything with a foreign power was an invasion of Trump's authority to act on behalf of the United States. "The Constitution vests the President with control over foreign negotiations so that the United States speaks with one voice, not so that the President's central Article II prerogatives can give way to district-court diplomacy," Sauer argued. True, responded the Court, but the administration should "facilitate" Garcia's return and prepare to tell the courts how it was working to do so.

Bukele traveled from El Salvador for an April 14 meeting with Trump. As reporters asked questions, an autocrat's Kabuki theater played out in the Oval Office: Would El Salvador return Garcia? "How can I . . . ?"

Bukele replied. "Like, I smuggle him into the United States, or what do I do?" Trump, who had readily embraced the title of Leader of the Free World in his first term, shrugged. The man who had claimed the greatest political comeback in the greatest country on earth acted as if there were, conveniently, nothing he could do.

But Trump let down the façade. He made clear the arrangement was more than OK. In fact, he suggested, American citizens could be sent to the country's brutal prisons next—a measure that might get around any question of using the Alien Enemies Act. As the Garcia episode had revealed, once someone was outside the U.S., they were in extrajudicial territory, beyond the reach of any remaining constraints Trump had to contend with in America's justice system. "The homegrowns are next, the homegrowns. You've got to build about five more places," Trump told Bukele.

On April 17, the Fourth Circuit Appeals Court weighed in and Judge J. Harvie Wilkinson III, a conservative appointed by President Ronald Reagan and considered by George W. Bush for the Supreme Court, blasted Trump's Justice Department, while also acknowledging the new reality: Garcia was gone and the court had little authority to stop Trump from denying justice.

"This should be shocking not only to judges, but to the intuitive sense of liberty that Americans far removed from courthouses still hold dear," Wilkinson wrote. "The government asserts that Abrego Garcia is a terrorist and a member of MS-13. Perhaps, but perhaps not. Regardless, he is still entitled to due process." Wilkinson made a final appeal to the president.

"The government has conceded that Abrego Garcia was wrongly or 'mistakenly' deported. Why then should it not make what was wrong, right?"

What was now *right* to the Justice Department, however, was to defend forcefully whatever Trump said. In the circular logic of Sauer's argument, Trump's voice was the United States' voice.

It was an idea Bondi seemed to toy with in statements backing the dismissal of Reuveni. "Every Department of Justice attorney is required to zealously advocate on behalf of the United States," she said of Reuveni's punishment. "Any attorney who fails to abide by this direction will face consequences."

Similar anxiety was gripping private sector attorneys across the country. Paul, Weiss chairman Brad Karp had quickly become a Neville Chamberlain figure for many in the legal community. He chose to meet with Trump in the Oval Office and offered to appease him with $40 million in free legal work for causes Trump supported in exchange for dropping his executive order. Karp's and his partners' panic about losing clients quickly splintered the nation's legal community. With Karp's capitulation, Trump saw an opportunity. He launched a broad shakedown of the legal profession, ordering his attorney general to investigate some of the nation's largest firms and their lawyers for possible misconduct or abuse of the legal system. Eight major firms soon followed Paul, Weiss, bending to Trump's will and weakening a core anchor of America's justice system. Combined, the firms promised up to $1 billion in free legal work for causes of Trump's choosing and, more importantly, froze thousands of the nation's top attorneys from taking cases opposing him or his administration. A federal judge soon cited Shakespeare's *Henry VI* to describe Trump's power move: "Let's kill the lawyers *I don't like*."

Trump was just getting started on his enemies list. He issued an executive order launching investigations into the government work conducted by two former Homeland Security officials who had been critical of him in his first term, Christopher Krebs and Miles Taylor. Taylor had penned an anonymous op-ed saying Trump acted erratically and had to be reined in. Krebs oversaw cybersecurity defenses and had maintained the 2020 election had been sound, with no evidence of widespread abuse or fraud. By Trump's order, Krebs was declared guilty of having "denied that the 2020 election was rigged and stolen." With every new executive order from the White House and memo from DOJ headquarters implementing it, Justice withered. In one swoop, more than one hundred career Civil Rights Division attorneys chose to leave the department in late

April when a Republican activist tapped to lead the section announced big changes. The division forged in the Civil Rights movement to ensure fair treatment for minorities would be more interested in the opposite, turning its attention to instead combating "illegal D.E.I."—diversity, equity, and inclusion—programs. Across the street at FBI headquarters, some assistants and office staff who had worked for past FBI executives were banished from the director's seventh-floor suite, and the Bureau turned its polygraph machines on its own ranks, seeking to identify and oust any agent caught talking to a reporter.

Nearing the one-hundred-day mark of his administration, Trump on April 22 sat for an interview with *Time*'s Eric Cortellessa to tout his accomplishments. At the end of the meeting, which included Trump showing off some paintings that he'd chosen to display at the White House, Cortellessa asked one final question.

"You put all these new portraits. One of them includes John Adams. John Adams said we're a government ruled by laws, not by men. Do you agree with that?"

Trump seemed taken aback. "John Adams said that?" he asked. "We're a government ruled by laws, not by men?"

"Well, I think we're a government ruled by law, but you know, somebody has to administer the law," Trump said. So "I wouldn't agree with it one hundred percent. We're a government where men are involved in the process of law, and ideally, you're going to have honest men like me."

ACKNOWLEDGMENTS

We must first thank those who made this book possible, the public servants who shared their brush with history over the last ten years to document the broader story of an institution they loved and watched suffer. Many served their country and the rule of law when America needed their unwavering dedication the most. They did so in the face of daunting threats, sometimes forced to choose between their oath to the Constitution and their beloved careers in public service. Many nonetheless once again risked incurring the wrath of powerful leaders by sharing their unvarnished accounts so future generations could know. Though we cannot name them, we are grateful to so many for helping us document the events that have buffeted the Justice Department and are reshaping our country.

This project would not have gotten off the ground without the stalwart support of our editors and colleagues at *The Washington Post*. We thank our lucky stars that we have spent so much of our combined careers there, working with journalists who have scrupulously sought to uncover and report the facts. We specifically thank our colleagues on the National and Investigative desks who either shouldered a heavier load while we took temporary leave or gave us pitch-perfect advice and encouragement: Dan Balz, Sarah Blaskey, Shawn Boburg, Amy Brittain, Shane Harris, Derek Hawkins, John Hudson, Michael Kranish, Marianne LeVine, Ann Marimow, Nick Miroff, Hannah Natanson, Jonathan O'Connell, Tyler Pager, Ashley Parker, Beth Reinhard, Jeremy Roebuck, Maria Sacchetti, Isaac Stanley-Becker, Perry Stein, Jon Swaine, Matt Viser, and Craig Whitlock. We are grateful for many *Post* editors who consistently championed unearthing the deeper truths that the powerful would rather stay hidden and encouraged us to do just that in book form: Emma Brown, Matea Gold, Dave Fallis, Jeff Leen, Eric Rich, Phil Rucker, Liz Seymour, and Peter Wallsten, as well as *Post* executive editors Matt Murray and former executive editor Sally Buzbee.

We wouldn't be here without a legend in the publishing industry who sagely guided us in this work: Ann Godoff, our editor and the president and editor in chief of Penguin Press. She infused our narrative, urging us to show the intimate, quotidian ways the Justice Department is a living, breathing institution fueled by the shared values and sense of mission of its prosecutors and agents. She helped us chronicle a war for the soul of the department then underway and capture the fight battle by battle. Meeting Ann's high standard is its own priceless reward. We were blessed that our book was in her hands and in those of her fantastic team at Penguin, including copresident Scott Moyers, Casey Denis, Will Heyward, and Sarah Hutson. Thanks also to editorial assistant Victoria Laboz, copyeditor Jane Cavolina, and proofreader Janet Byrne.

We are forever indebted to our agent Elyse Cheney, a true standout in her field. It's our great fortune to work with an advocate so devoted to her authors and relentless in ensuring their work stands the test of time. Thanks also to Grace Johnson at The Cheney Agency.

So many people played critical roles in this book and deserve applause. We thank Julie Tate for her fact-checking rigor and generosity, and Alice Crites and Aaron Schaffer for their indefatigable research at the *Post* that helped us assemble key building blocks. We are indebted to News Logistics chief Liz Whyte and Sam Martin for their help at all hours. A special thanks to "the King," Marvin Joseph, for our portraits.

We also thank the lawyers—whom we are glad to call ours in this work—for their careful reviews and counsel: Yuki Hirose at Penguin Random House; Liz McNamara at Davis Wright Tremaine; Jim McLaughlin and Jay Kennedy at *The Washington Post*.

In the course of reporting this book, we have also greatly admired the dedication required to cover the Justice Department daily. We applaud the reporters who have kept the public informed, chronicling its upheaval day in and day out over the last decade.

AARON C. DAVIS:

I want to thank my wonderful wife, Nicole; our son, Alex, and daughter, Emilia, for enriching my life and also for all their patience, understanding, and encouragement over the last two years of this book journey. I am the luckiest man to count them as my family. As the importance of documenting this pivotal time for our country seemed to grow more urgent, the reporting and writing frequently pulled me away from our precious time together.

I thank my father, Jeff Davis, for instilling in me the work ethic to keep going until the job is done, and my late mother, Bonnie Davis, for teaching me to always look for the best in people. We found that so many people sought to, and acted commendably in these years, and we always tried to capture that. I also am thankful for my indefatigable sister, Laura, as well as my grandparents, in-laws, and so many close friends who helped with logistics and sometimes just a welcomed moment of levity on this long journey.

I am extremely thankful to have had Carol Leonnig as my coauthor on this project. Carol is one of the most tenacious reporters I have ever known. As many newspaper editors have noticed, she has an incredible knack for getting people to talk. But after working together closely, I know it is more than that. She takes time to see people and their actions for who and what they are, and people respond in kind. They come to trust her with their most closely held secrets, knowing she will take great care in telling their stories—and always with active verbs.

From *USA Today* to *Florida Today* to *The Mercury News* and the Associated Press, I have been fortunate over my career to have had many mentors and colleagues who inspired me to become a better reporter. I'm indebted to Susan Goldberg, Peter Eisler, Tom McNamara, John Tuohy, Tom Breen, Bert Robinson, Alvie Lindsay, Mike Zapler, Tom Verdin, and Brian Carovillano. Over seventeen years at the *Post*, I have had too many great editors and colleagues to count, but I especially thank Mike Semel, Steven Ginsberg, Matea Gold, and the editor I've thankfully reported to for more years in my career than any other, Eric Rich.

Looking back at where the reporting began for this book after January 6, I will always be thankful for the amazing team I got to work with on "The Attack" series. Hannah Allam, Devlin Barrett, Karoun Demirjian, Josh Dawsey, Amy Gardner, Shane Harris, Rosalind S. Helderman, Paul Kane, Dan Lamothe, Carol Leonnig, Ellen Nakashima, Ashley Parker, Beth Reinhard, Philip Rucker, and Craig Timberg.

CAROL LEONNIG:

I want to first thank the three people who bring such joy to my life and form its center: my wonderful husband, John Reeder, and my dear daughters, Elise and Molly. They tend to suffer the most when I embark on a tough assignment or a book project. They tolerate my shortcomings amid a pressing deadline, the questionable meals I serve, and the clacking keyboard noise I generate in the house at unpleasant hours. Yet they support me the most, with pep talks, attagirl hugs, and love.

Thanks to my mother, Dolly Leonnig and my late father, Henry Leonnig. She assured me I could do anything I set out to do. He instilled in me a pride in hard work but also was the first person to show me what it meant to love and revere the law. Thank you to my sister, Brooke, and brother, Henry, for all their love and good counsel.

I'm so very grateful to have found a book partner in Aaron C. Davis. He is full of humility despite his boundless talents in reporting, writing, and strategizing. He thought deeply about how to approach this sensitive topic, steering us to greater insights and away from rocky shoals. Working with him was always a treat, even on the most challenging days. I marvel at the skills and unflagging energy he brought to this project—and lent to me. The intensity of our subject made this the hardest book I've done by one measure, but Aaron's enduring calm and kindness made it easier, and possible.

There is no way to fully convey my gratitude to my *Washington Post* family. Please know that it's been my great honor to work alongside you; you've made me the journalist I am, and it would require a separate book to list you all. Special thanks to several who lent their ear and friendship during this work: Emma Brown, Amy Gardner, John Hudson, Greg Jaffe, Sally Jenkins, Caroline Kitchener, Manuel Roig-Franzia, Eric Rich, Ian Shapira, Mike Semel, Pooh Shapiro, Jeff Stein, Lena Sun, Craig Timberg, and Joby Warrick. Thanks also to a far-flung group in journalism who have been enduring guides, friends and role models: Peter Baker, Marty Baron, Jo Becker, Jamie Gangel, Steven Ginsberg, Susan Glasser, Matea Gold, Don Graham, Katherine Graham, Tammy Haddad, Mark Leibovich, David Maraniss, Kevin Merida, Dana Priest, Kara Swisher, Peter Wallsten, Paige Williams, and Bob Woodward.

Thanks to MSNBC's raft of talented hosts, producers, and others who elevate my journalism and broaden the public's understanding of the consequence of these events, including: Mika Brzezinski, Chris Jansing, Rebecca Kutler, Rachel Maddow, Scott Matthews, Sudeep Reddy, Jesse Rodriguez, Stephanie Ruhle, Joe Scarborough, Katy Tur, Nicolle Wallace, and Alex Witt.

I'm blessed with dear friends who don't live and breathe journalism but value what I do and keep me centered. Looking at you guys with love: Kristin and Peter, Michelle and Steve, Liz and Phil, Caity and Michael, Amy and Hassan, Lisa and Frank, Cynthia and Jon, Kathryn and Michael, Jodi and Eldad, Annie and Hunter, Stephanie and Seth, Maria and Dave, Barbara and Art. Love and thanks, too, to my Bryn Mawr squad; my crazy-smart friends at our book club, led by Elizabeth Shreve; and the Cambridge crew: Kelly and Peter, Bernadette and Kevin, Tracie and Steve, Doug and Carol, Karen and Fred. Thank you for reading!

Notes

INTRODUCTION

xviii in a 1935 opinion: CourtListener, "Berger v. United States: Supreme Court of the United States," March 7, 1935," https://www.courtlistener.com/opinion/102436/berger-v-united-states/.

xxiii "weaponized law enforcement": Joan E. Greve, "Trump Rails Against Federal Charges and Accuses Biden of 'Weaponizing' Justice Department," *Guardian*, June 24, 2023, https://www.theguardian.com/us-news/2023/jun/25/trump-rails-against-federal-charges-and-accuses-biden-of-weaponizing-justice-department.

xxiii Republican support for his return: Linley Sanders and Jill Colvin, "Trump Enjoys Strong Support among Republicans. The General Election Could Be a Different Story," Associated Press, August 16, 2023, https://www.apnews.com/article/trump-election-2024-indictments-ddfd50492dc576c0c2ca2d1afe0e4639.

CHAPTER ONE

7 "committed many crimes!": Donald Trump, "Comey drafted the Crooked Hillary exoneration long before he talked to her," Twitter, April 16, 2018, 8:25 a.m., https://twitter.com/realDonaldTrump/status/985856662866202624.

8 So fraught is the decision: *Justice Manual*, "Title 9: Criminal, 9-27.000—Principles of Federal Prosecution," U.S. Department of Justice, updated February 2024, https//www.justice.gov/jm/jm-9-27000-principles-federal-prosecution.

8 established that McCabe had instructed: "A Report of Investigation of Certain Allegations Relating to Former FBI Deputy Director Andrew McCabe," U.S. Department of Justice, Office of the Inspector General, February 2018, https://s3.documentcloud.org/documents/4437277/DOJ-OIG-McCabe-Report.pdf.

8 the impression that he didn't know: Karoun Demirjian and Matt Zapotosky, "Inspector General Referred Findings on McCabe to U.S. Attorney for consideration of criminal charges," *Washington Post*, April 19, 2018, https://www.washingtonpost.com/world/national-security/inspector-general-referred-findings-on-mccabe-to-us-attorney-for-consideration-of-criminal-charges/2018/04/19/a200cabc-43f3-11e8-8569-26fda6b404c7_story.html.

9 "Universities will someday study": Donald Trump, Twitter, November 15, 2018, 9:49 a.m., https://twitter.com/realDonaldTrump/status/1063081553075625984.

9 **Page, the lawyer and former counselor to McCabe:** "Two Ex-FBI Officials Who Traded Anti-Trump Texts Close to Settlement over Alleged Privacy Violations," NBC News, May 29, 2024, https://www.nbcnews.com/politics/justice-department/two-ex-fbi-officials -traded-anti-trump-texts-close-settlement-alleged-rcna154444.

10 **He repeatedly called on Congress:** Toulose Olorunnipa, "'Investigate the investigators' Is the New Trump Rallying Cry to Counter Mueller Report," *Washington Post,* May 4, 2019, https:// www.washingtonpost.com/politics/investigate-the-investigators-is-new-trump-rallying-cry -to-counter-mueller-report/2019/05/04/9319b520-6db6-11e9-be3a-33217240a539_story.html.

10 **Trump's pressure campaign:** Donald Trump, Twitter, June 15, 2018, 6:35 a.m., https://twitter .com/realDonaldTrump/status/1007572229935202304.

10 **Anyone who had known Cooney:** Michael Marshall, "Cooney and Schochet Take Moot Court Finals," UVA Law, April 27, 2004, https://www.law.virginia.edu/news/200404/cooney -and-schochet-take-moot-court-finals.

11 **"What every prosecutor":** Robert H. Jackson, "The Federal Prosecutor," U.S. Department of Justice, https://www.justice.gov/sites/default/files/ag/legacy/2011/09/16/04-01-1940.pdf.

CHAPTER TWO

13 **Was this the work:** Katelyn Polantz et al., "Mystery Mueller Mayhem at a Washington Court," CNN, December 15, 2018, https://www.cnn.com/2018/12/14/politics/mueller-grand -jury-mysterious-friday/index.html.

14 **Unbeknownst to the public:** Aaron C. Davis and Carol D. Leonnig, "$10M Cash Withdrawal Drove Secret Probe into Whether Trump Took Money from Egypt," *Washington Post,* August 2, 2024, https://www.washingtonpost.com/investigations/2024/08/02/trump-campaign-egypt -investigation/.

14 **something big was up:** Polantz et al., "Mystery Mueller Mayhem at a Washington Court."

15 **was a natural choice:** William Finnegan, "Taking Down Terrorists in Court," *New Yorker,* May 8, 2017, https://www.newyorker.com/magazine/2017/05/15/taking-down-terrorists-in -court.

15 **One was code-named:** Andrew Weissmann, *Where Law Ends: Inside the Mueller Investiga- tion* (Random House, 2020).

16 **Trump unexpectedly turned up:** Ishaan Tharoor, "Trump Met His Favorite Middle East Strongman. What Happened Next Will Not Surprise You," *Washington Post,* September 20, 2016, https://www.washingtonpost.com/news/worldviews/wp/2016/09/20/trump-met-his -favorite-middle-east-strongman-what-happened-next-will-not-surprise-you/.

16 **according to campaign finance reports:** Nicholas Confessore and Rachel Shorey, "Donald Trump Starts Summer Push with Crippling Money Deficit, *New York Times,* June 20, 2016, https://www.nytimes.com/2016/06/21/us/politics/donald-trump-money-campaign.html.

17 **Trump welcomed the Egyptian leader:** David Nakamura, "Trump Welcomes Egypt's Sissi to White House in Reversal of U.S. Policy," *Washington Post,* April 3, 2017, https://www.wash ingtonpost.com/politics/trump-welcomes-egypts-sissi-to-white-house-in-reversal-of -us-policy/2017/04/03/36b5e312-188b-11e7-bcc2-7d1a0973e7b2_story.html.

17 **In 2018, Bannon told Mueller's team:** FOIPA Request No.: 1432673-000 provided to Jason Leopold, U.S. Department of Justice, Federal Bureau of Investigation, August 2, 2021, https:// s3.documentcloud.org/documents/21031633/leopold-fbi-302s-foia-mueller-investigation -16th-interim-release.pdf.

18 **Trump seemed convinced:** Monica Langley and Rebecca Ballhaus, "Donald Trump Adds $10 Million of His Own Money for Advertising," *Wall Street Journal,* October 28, 2016, https://www.wsj.com/articles/donald-trump-adds-10-million-of-his-own-money-for-advertising -1477669187.

19 **McGahn told investigators:** Michael S. Schmidt and Maggie Haberman, "White House Counsel, Don McGahn, Has Cooperated Extensively in Mueller Inquiry," *New York Times,* August 18, 2018, https://www.nytimes.com/2018/08/18/us/politics/don-mcgahn-mueller-investi gation.html?hp&action=click&pgtype=Homepage&clickSource=story-heading&module= first-column-region&region=top-news&WT.nav=top-news.

19 **Attorneys for the bank:** Katelyn Polantz, "Law Firm That Represented Russian Interests Part of Mystery Mueller Subpoena Case," CNN, January 9, 2019, https://www.cnn.com/2019/01 /09/politics/russian-interests-law-firm-mueller/index.html.

20 **"Any Grand Jury investigation":** Redacted Transcript from December 14, 2018, in the "In re Grand Jury Subpoena, No. 18-3071" case, (Mueller Mystery Company), https://www .scribd.com/document/428280507/In-re-Grand-Jury-Subpoena-No-18-3071-Redacted -Transcript.

CHAPTER THREE

22 **backed away from the threat:** Aaron Zebley, *Interference: The Inside Story of Trump, Russia, and the Mueller Investigation* (Simon & Schuster, 2024), 158.

22 **"If we do not subpoena":** Andrew Weissmann, *Where Law Ends: Inside the Mueller Investigation* (Random House, 2020), 273.

22 **Mueller late that year:** Zebley, *Interference,* pp. 147–60.

23 **the Supreme Court concluded:** Robert Barnes, Devlin Barrett, and Carol D. Leonnig, "Supreme Court Rules Against Mystery Corporation from 'Country A' Fighting Subpoena in Mueller Investigation," *Washington Post,* January 8, 2019, https://www.washingtonpost.com /politics/courts_law/supreme-court-rules-against-mystery-corporation-from-country -a-fighting-subpoena-in-mueller-investigation/2019/01/08/a39b61ac-0d1a-11e9-84fc -d58c33d6c8c7_story.html.

23 **they took turns:** *United States of America v. Roger Jason Stone, Jr.,* U.S. District Court for the District of Columbia, January 24, 2019, https://www.justice.gov/file/1124706/download.

23 **By sunset, the grand jury:** Devlin Barrett et al., "Longtime Trump Adviser Roger Stone Indicted by Special Counsel in Russa Investigation," *Washington Post,* January 25, 2019, https:// www.washingtonpost.com/politics/longtime-trump-adviser-roger-stone-indicted-by -special-counsel-in-russia-investigation/2019/01/25/93a4d8fa-2093-11e9-8e21-59a09ff1e2a1 _story.html.

24 **The next day, federal agents:** Andrew M. Harris and Bob Van Voris, "FBI Seized Roger Stone's Cellphones, Computers, Hard Drives," *Bloomberg,* January 31, 2019, https://www .bloomberg.com/news/articles/2019-01-31/roger-stone-s-cellphones-computers-hard -drives-grabbed-by-fbi.

24 **On the obstruction side:** Carol D. Leonnig, "Barr Puts Trump's Actions in Best Light Despite 'Substantial Evidence' of Obstruction Cited by Mueller," *Washington Post,* May 1, 2019, https://www.washingtonpost.com/politics/barr-puts-trumps-actions-in-best-light-despite -substantial-evidence-of-obstruction-cited-by-mueller/2019/05/01/dacb0046-6c2a-11e9 -a66d-a82d3f3d96d5_story.html.

24 **On Thursday, February 14, 2019:** Department of Justice, "William P. Barr Confirmed as 85th Attorney General of the United States," February 14, 2019, https://www.justice.gov/opa/pr /william-p-barr-confirmed-85th-attorney-general-united-states.

26 **"No. We have determined":** Zebley, *Interference*, 202.

26 **A few weeks later:** Philip Rucker and Carol Leonnig, *A Very Stable Genius: Donald J. Trump's Testing of America* (Penguin Press, 2020).

27 **After the meeting Rosenstein shared his concern:** Bill Barr, *One Damn Thing After Another: Memoirs of an Attorney General* (William Morrow, 2022), 240–42.

28 **"It would be possible for somebody else":** Rucker and Leonnig, *A Very Stable Genius*.

28 **Zebley heard Barr ask:** Zebley, *Interference*, 203.

29 **"We uttered almost in unison":** Senate Select Committee on Intelligence, "Russian Active Measures Campaigns and Interference in the 2016 U.S. Election," August 18, 2020, https://www .intelligence.senate.gov/sites/default/files/documents/Report_Volume2.pdf, 34.

29 **Three days later:** Matt Zapotosky and Devlin Barrett, "Mueller Did Not Find the Trump Campaign Conspired with Russia, Attorney General Says," *Washington Post*, March 24, 2019, https://www.washingtonpost.com/world/national-security/republicans-and-democrats -brace-for-renewed-battles-over-mueller-report/2019/03/23/56d9f214-4db3-11e9-b79a -961983b7e0cd_story.html.

30 **He was sure the CNN reporters:** Weissmann, *Where Law Ends*, xiii.

31 **That Monday morning:** Nicholas Fandos, Michael S. Schmidt, and Mark Mazzetti, "Some on Mueller's Team Say Report Was More Damaging Than Barr Revealed," *New York Times*, April 3, 2019, https://www.nytimes.com/2019/04/03/us/politics/william-barr-mueller-report.html.

31 **O'Callaghan didn't commit:** Ellen Nakashima, Carol D. Leonnig, and Rosalind S. Helderman, "Limited Information Barr Has Shared About Russia Investigation Frustrated Some on Mueller's Team," *Washington Post*, April 4, 2019, https://www.washingtonpost.com/world /national-security/limited-information-barr-has-shared-about-russia-investigation -frustrated-some-on-muellers-team/2019/04/03/c98e8a02-567a-11e9-814f-e2f46684196e _story.html.

31 **Zebley called O'Callaghan again:** Devlin Barrett and Matt Zapotosky, "Mueller Complained That Barr's Letter Did Not Capture 'Context' of Trump Probe," *Washington Post*, April 30, 2019, https://www.washingtonpost.com/world/national-security/mueller-complained-that -barrs-letter-did-not-capture-context-of-trump-probe/2019/04/30/d3c8fdb6-6b7b-11e9 -a66d-a82d3f3d96d5_story.html.

CHAPTER FOUR

33 **"What are we doing here":** Transcript of Hearing Before the Honorable Beryl A. Howell, U.S. District Court Chief Judge, U.S. District Court for the District of Columbia, February 15, 2019, https://www.dcd.uscourts.gov/sites/dcd/files/Part3_18gj41.pdf.

CHAPTER FIVE

39 **his Bureau career started:** "Andrew McCabe, Deputy Director," U.S. Senate Select Committee on Intelligence, June 7, 2017, https://www.intelligence.senate.gov/sites/default/files/documents /bio-amccabe-060717.pdf.

42 In the late summer: David Shortell, "Justice Department Rejects Andrew McCabe's Appeal to Avoid Prosecution," CNN, September 12, 2019, https://www.cnn.com/2019/09/12/politics /andrew-mccabe-justice-department/index.html.

42 McCabe hung up and was soon: Dylan Byers, "Licht's Non-Zucker Playbook Emerges," Puck, May 4, 2022, https://puck.news/lichts-non-zucker-playbook-emerges/.

47 It was a threshold so low: "Sol Watchler," in *The Judges of the New York Court of Appeals: A Biographical History*, ed. Hon. Albert M. Rosenblatt (Fordham University Press, 2007), https://history.nycourts.gov/biography/sol-wachtler/.

CHAPTER SIX

49 President Trump would nominate Liu: "President Donald J. Trump Announces Intent to Nominate and Appoint Individuals to Key Administration Posts," White House press release, December 10, 2019, https://trumpwhitehouse.archives.gov/presidential-actions/president -donald-j-trump-announces-intent-nominate-appoint-individuals-key-administration -posts-25/.

49 Flynn had admitted: Carol D. Leonnig et al. "Michael Flynn Pleads Guilty to Lying to FBI on Contacts with Russian Ambassador," *Washington Post*, December 1, 2017, https://www .washingtonpost.com/politics/michael-flynn-charged-with-making-false-statement-to-the -fbi/2017/12/01/e03a6c48-d6a2-11e7-9461-ba77d604373d_story.html.

50 thirty-three-page sentencing memorandum: *United States v. Michael T. Flynn*, "United States' Supplemental Memorandum in Aid of Sentencing," U.S. District Court, January 7, 2020, https://int.nyt.com/data/documenthelper/6643-flynn-prosecutors-memo/db25a65301e 8bf9a8683/optimized/full.pdf.

50 The two emphasized the gravity: Spencer S. Hsu and Rachel Weiner, "Michael Flynn Deserves up to Six Months in Prison," *Washington Post*, January 7, 2020, https://www.washing tonpost.com/local/legal-issues/michael-flynn-deserves-up-to-six-months-in-prison -us-justice-department-says-in-reversal-for-former-trump-national-security-adviser/2020 /01/07/e87fcf4a-0c94-11ea-8397-a955cd542d00_story.html.

52 But the news had already leaked: Michael Balsamo, "AP Exclusive: Barr Names New U.S. Attorney in DC," Associated Press, January 30, 2020, https://apnews.com/940f5fb382a31399 544429a700e56385.

CHAPTER SEVEN

55 On February 5, 2020: "Roger Stone Found Guilty of Obstruction, False Statements, and Witness Tampering," U.S. Attorney's Office, District of Columbia, November 15, 2019, https:// www.justice.gov/usao-dc/pr/roger-stone-found-guilty-obstruction-false-statements-and -witness-tampering.

56 A jury had convicted him: "Roger Stone Found Guilty of Obstruction."

56 They planned to recommend: Sharon LaFraniere, "Prosecutors Recommend Roger Stone Receive Up to 9 Years in Prison," *New York Times*, February 10, 2020, https://www.nytimes.com /2020/02/10/us/roger-stone-prison-sentence.html.

56 He threatened Randy Credico: *United States v. Roger Jason Stone Jr.*, U.S. District Court for the District of Columbia, January 24, 2019, https://www.justice.gov/archives/sco/file/1124706 /download.

57 **The nine-year sentence was at the low end:** "Roger Stone Found Guilty of Obstruction."

57 **Shea complained later that day:** "An Investigation of Allegations Concerning the Department of Justice's Handling of the Government's Sentencing Recommendation in *United States v. Roger Stone*," Office of the Inspector General, Department of Justice, July 2024, https://oig .justice.gov/sites/default/files/reports/24-081.pdf.

57 **Cooney privately told Evangelista:** "An Investigation of Allegations Concerning the Department of Justice's Handling of the Government's Sentencing Recommendation."

57 **it came as a relief:** Carol Leonnig and Philip Rucker, *I Alone Can Fix It: Donald J. Trump's Catastrophic Final Year* (Penguin Press, 2021), 56.

58 **In a meeting that Friday afternoon:** "An Investigation of Allegations Concerning the Department of Justice's Handling of the Government's Sentencing Recommendation."

58 **"This is not the hill to die on":** "An Investigation of Allegations Concerning the Department of Justice's Handling of the Government's Sentencing Recommendation."

59 **"We are going to treat Roger Stone":** "An Investigation of Allegations Concerning the Department of Justice's Handling of the Government's Sentencing Recommendation."

59 **Three of the four prosecutors:** "An Investigation of Allegations Concerning the Department of Justice's Handling of the Government's Sentencing Recommendation."

60 **Shea only heard Barr's instruction:** Dan Friedman, "A Key Witness Against Roger Stone Says William Barr Twisted His Words," *Mother Jones*, June 26, 2020, https://www.motherjones .com/politics/2020/06/randy-credico-roger-stone-bill-barr-donald-trump/.

61 **Shea let Barr's office know:** William P. Barr, *One Damn Thing After Another: Memoirs of an Attorney General* (William Morrow, 2022).

61 **"we're going to have to fix it":** "An Investigation of Allegations Concerning the Department of Justice's Handling of the Government's Sentencing Recommendation."

61 **"This is a horrible and very unfair situation":** Donald Trump, Twitter, February 11, 2020, 1:48 a.m., https://twitter.com/realDonaldTrump/status/1227122206783811585?s=20.

62 **The screen showed a Fox News breaking-news alert:** Jake Gibson, "DOJ Expected to Scale Back Roger Stone's 'Extreme' Sentencing Recommendation: Official," Fox News, February 11, 2020, https://www.foxnews.com/politics/doj-expected-to-scale-back-roger-stones -extreme-sentencing-recommendation-official.

CHAPTER EIGHT

63 **Cooney instantly replied:** Zoe Tillman and Jason Leopold, "New Emails Detail the Behind-the-Scenes Drama After the Justice Department Recommended a Lesser Sentence for Roger Stone," *BuzzFeed News*, August 4, 2020, https://www.buzzfeednews.com/article/zoetillman /emails-justice-department-overruled-prosecutors-roger-stone; Justice Department FOIA Request Number: EOUSA-2020-001548, provided to Jason Leopold, U.S. Department of Justice, August 3, 2020, https://www.documentcloud.org/documents/7013177-Leopold-1st-INTERIM -EOUSA-Stone-Zelinsky.html.

64 **An outraged Zelinsky:** "Assistant U.S. Attorney Aaron Zelinsky, Opening Statement," House Judiciary Committee testimony, C-SPAN, June 24, 2020, https://www.c-span .org/video/?c4888898/assistant-us-attorney-aaron-zelinsky-opening-statement.

65 **She also soon received:** Spencer S. Hsu, Josh Dawsey and Devlin Barrett, "Trump Withdraws Treasury Nomination of Former U.S. Attorney for D.C. Jessie K. Liu After Criticism of Her Oversight of Mueller Prosecutions," *Washington Post*, February 11, 2020, https:// www.washingtonpost.com/local/legal-issues/trump-withdraws-treasury-nomination

-of-former-us-attorney-for-dc-jessie-k-liu-after-criticism-of-her-oversight-of-mueller
-prosecutions/2020/02/11/d700dc3c-4d3a-11ea-9b5c-eac5b16dafaa_story.html.

CHAPTER NINE

66 **he had defended the prison time:** Spencer S. Hsu, "Prosecutors Appear To Back Away from Prison Recommendation for Michael Flynn," *Washington Post*, January 29, 2020, https://www .washingtonpost.com/local/legal-issues/prosecutors-appear-to-back-away-from-prison -recommendation-for-michael-flynn/2020/01/29/f861f3e0-42c5-11ea-b5fc-eefa848cde99 _story.html.

67 **Judge Emmet G. Sullivan agreed:** *United States v. Michael T. Flynn*, U.S. District Court for the District of Columbia, December 16, 2019, https://casetext.com/case/united-states-v -flynn-64.

67 **Van Grack's trepidation:** Charlie Savage, Adam Goldman, and Matt Apuzzo, "Barr Installs Outside Prosecutor to Review Case Against Michael Flynn, Ex-Trump Adviser," *New York Times*, February 14, 2020, https://www.nytimes.com/2020/02/14/us/politics/michael-flynn -prosecutors-barr.html.

67 **Van Grack and Ballantine:** Rachel Weiner, "Michael Flynn's Claims of Misconduct Are Baseless, Prosecutors Say," *Washington Post*, February 12, 2020, https://www .washingtonpost.com/local/legal-issues/michael-flynns-claims-of-misconduct-are-baseless -prosecutors-say/2020/02/12/5b9bb77e-4dc6-11ea-9b5c-eac5b16dafaa_story.html.

68 **among the government's voluntary disclosures:** *United States v. Michael T. Flynn*, U.S. District Court for the District of Columbia, April 30, 2020, https://storage.courtlistener.com /recap/gov.uscourts.dcd.191592/gov.uscourts.dcd.191592.189.1.pdf.

68 **But Sidney Powell hailed it:** Aruna Viswanatha, "Mike Flynn's Lawyers Say Newly Unsealed Documents Show FBI Tried to Set Him Up," *Wall Street Journal*, April 30, 2020, https://www .wsj.com/articles/mike-flynns-lawyers-say-newly-unsealed-documents-show-fbi -tried-to-set-him-up-11588219544.

68 **"The Government is not persuaded":** *United States v. Michael T. Flynn*, U.S. District Court for the District of Columbia, May 7, 2020, https://int.nyt.com/data/documenthelper/6936 -michael-flynn-motion-to-dismiss/fa06f5e13a0ec71843b6/optimized/full.pdf.

69 **"I hope a lot of people":** Adam Goldman and Katie Benner, "U.S. Drops Michael Flynn Case, in Move Backed by Trump," *New York Times*, June 10, 2020, https://www.nytimes.com/2020 /05/07/us/politics/michael-flynn-case-dropped.html.

69 **nearly two thousand alumni:** "DOJ Alumni Statement on Flynn Case," Medium, May 11, 2020, https://Medium.Com/@Dojalumni/Doj-Alumni-Statement-On-Flynn-Case-7c38a9a9 45b9.

69 **They also called on Congress:** Matt Zapotosky, "More Than 1,900 Former Justice Dept. Employees Again Call for Barr's Resignation," *Washington Post*, May 11, 2020, https://www.wash ingtonpost.com/national-security/attorney-general-william-barr-michael-flynn/2020/05/11 /d798302e-92da-11ea-82b4-c8db161ff6e5_story.html.

70 **"History is written by the winners":** "Department of Justice Drops Charges Against Michael Flynn," *CBS This Morning*, May 7, 2020, https://www.facebook.com/watch/?v=2475123959 458036.

70 **Barr had first taken a liking:** Nick Madigan and Frances Robles, "Chinese Businesswoman Found Guilty of Trespassing at Mar-a-Lago," *New York Times*, September 11, 2019, https:// www.nytimes.com/2019/09/11/us/yujing-zhang-verdict-maralago.html.

70 **Sherwin reinforced Barr's favorable impression:** "Attorney General William P. Barr Announces the Findings of the Criminal Investigation into the December 2019 Shooting at Pensacola Naval Air Station," U.S. Department of Justice, press release, January 13, 2020, https://www.justice.gov/opa/speech/attorney-general-william-p-barr-announces-findings-criminal-investigation-december-2019.

71 **Barr opted for Sherwin:** Spencer S. Hsu and Keith L. Alexander, "Barr-Installed Top DOJ Aide, Prosecutor of Trump's Mar-a-Lago Trespasser, to Serve as Acting U.S. Attorney in Washington," *Washington Post*, May 18, 2020, https://www.washingtonpost.com/local/legal-issues/barr-installs-top-doj-aide-prosecutor-of-trumps-mar-a-lago-trespasser-over-us-prosecutors-in-washington/2020/05/18/3d2085e4-9471-11ea-82b4-c8db161ff6e5_story.html.

71 **In describing Sherwin:** Hsu and Alexander, "Barr-Installed Top DOJ Aide, Prosecutor of Trump's Mar-a-Lago Trespasser, to Serve as Acting U.S. Attorney in Washington."

71 **"When I fired Comey":** Sadie Gurman, "Trump's Attacks Put New FBI Director in Tough Spot," Associated Press, December 6, 2017, https://apnews.com/article/397e36cbbb004cf39add03933b69f46a.

71 **He warned that firing:** Leonnig and Rucker, *I Alone Can Fix It*, 132.

72 **Barr warned Trump's chief of staff:** Leonnig and Rucker, *I Alone Can Fix It*, 137.

CHAPTER TEN

73 **His office had announced:** "Former U.S. Congressman Charged and Philadelphia Political Operative Pleads Guilty to Election Fraud Charges," U.S. Department of Justice, press release, June 6, 2022, https://www.justice.gov/usao-edpa/pr/former-us-congressman-and-philadelphia-political-operative-pleads-guilty-election-fraud.

74 **The Election Crimes Branch had been created:** "5 Persons in Louisiana Indicted on Charge of Vote-Buying in 1978," *New York Times*, February 17, 1979, https://www.nytimes.com/1979/02/17/archives/5-persons-in-louisiana-indicted-on-charge-of-votebuying-in-1978.html.

74 **Trump refused to say:** "'Fox News Sunday' Interview with President Trump," Fox News, July 19, 2020, https://www.foxnews.com/politics/transcript-fox-news-sunday-interview-with-president-trump.

75 **he blasted universal mail-in voting:** Donald Trump, Twitter, June 30, 2020, 8:36 a.m., https://twitter.com/realDonaldTrump/status/1288818160389558273?s=20.

75 **In August, he continued:** "The 9 Most Notable Comments Trump Has Made About Accepting the Election Results," *Politico*, September 24, 2020, https://www.politico.com/news/2020/09/24/trump-casts-doubt-2020-election-integrity-421280.

75 **FBI agents based in Scranton:** Philip Bump, "Google's cache," Twitter, September 24, 2020, 4:13 p.m., https://twitter.com/pbump/status/1309224451096154119.

76 **But investigators quickly concluded:** "A Report of Investigation Into the Department's Release of Public Statements Concerning a Luzerne County, Pennsylvania, Election Fraud Investigation in September 2020," U.S. Department of Justice, Office of the Inspector General, July 2024, https://oig.justice.gov/sites/default/files/reports/24-082.pdf.

76 **Trump had won the district:** Luzerne County 2016 Election Results, last updated December 2, 2016, https://results.enr.clarityelections.com/PA/Luzerne/64171/184324/Web01/en/summary.html.

76 **no sign of a nefarious plot:** "A Report of Investigation," U.S. Department of Justice.

77 **In addition to encouraging Freed:** "A Report of Investigation," U.S. Department of Justice.

77 **When reporters who had gathered:** "09/24/20: Press Secretary Kayleigh McEnany Holds a Press Briefing," White House Press Archive, YouTube, September 24, 2020, https://www .youtube.com/watch?v=zUPsO-zE89g.

77 **U.S. Attorney Freed released a press statement:** Philip Bump, "Google's cache."

77 **"The preliminary findings of this inquiry":** "Letter to Luzerne County Bureau of Elections," U.S. Department of Justice, press release, September 24, 2020, https://www.justice.gov/usao -mdpa/pr/letter-luzerne-county-bureau-elections.

78 **"We want to make sure":** "U.S. Attorney David J. Freed Reveals Early Findings of Investigation into Discarded Mail-in Ballots," States Attorney, October 8, 2020, https://www.states attorney.org/2020/10/08/u-s-attorney-david-j-freed-reveals-early-findings-of-investigation -into-discarded-mail-in-ballots/.

78 **Government investigators would later find:** "A Report of Investigation," U.S. Department of Justice.

79 **The Trump campaign made false claims:** Ryan Briggs, "Federal Judge Dismisses Trump's Attempt to Stop Vote Counting in Philadelphia," WHYY, November 5, 2020, https://whyy .org/articles/trump-asks-federal-court-to-stop-vote-counting-in-phiadelphia/.

79 **A little after noon:** Stephen Collinson and Maeve Reston, "Biden Wins Pennsylvania, Becoming the 46th President of the United States," CNN, November 7, 2020, https://www.cnn .com/2020/11/06/politics/presidential-election-biden-trump-2020/index.html.

79 **"We all know why":** Lauren Egan and Shannon Pettypiece, "Trump Says Election 'Far from Over' as He Vows to Fight Results," NBC News, November 7, 2020, https://www.nbcnews.com /politics/2020-election/trump-says-election-far-over-he-vows-fight-results-n1246934.

79 **Trump's campaign filed lawsuits:** *Trump for President v. Boockvar et al.*, November 9, 2020, https://www.aclupa.org/en/cases/trump-president-v-boockvar-et-al.

80 **Barr told Donoghue:** *Select Committee to Investigate the January 6th Attack on the U.S. Capitol*, U.S. House of Representatives, 117th Cong., 2nd Session (October 1, 2021), https://www .govinfo.gov/content/pkg/GPO-J6-TRANSCRIPT-CTRL0000034600/pdf/GPO-J6 -TRANSCRIPT-CTRL0000034600.pdf.

80 **In his note to prosecutors:** Memorandum for United States Attorneys, Office of the Attorney General, November 9, 2020, https://int.nyt.com/data/documenttools/barr-memo-elections -fraud/9bf5cac375012c4c/full.pdf.

80 **It was named after:** "Longest-Serving Federal Prosecutor Honored for Six Decades of Service," U.S. Department of Justice, press release, September 24, 2020, https://www.justice .gov/archives/opa/blog/longest-serving-federal-prosecutor-honored-six-decades-service.

CHAPTER ELEVEN

81 **the Oath Keepers:** Josh Gerstein, "Oath Keepers Trial Hears from Members Troubled by Rhetoric Before Jan. 6," *Politico*, October 6, 2022, https://www.politico.com/news/2022/10/06 /oath-keepers-trial-jan-6-00060852.

81 **He had been promoting the idea:** Denise Lu and Eleanor Lutz, "How Oath Keepers Are Accused of Plotting to Storm the Capitol," *New York Times*, January 19, 2022, https://www.ny times.com/interactive/2022/01/19/us/oath-keepers-capitol-riot.html.

82 **Such calls are routed:** "A Look Inside the FBI's National Threat Operations Center," FBI, November 7, 2019, https://www.fbi.gov/news/stories/inside-the-national-threat-operations -center-110719.

82 **No agent followed up:** Emily Zantow, "Defense for Oath Keepers Seizes on Tip to FBI Ahead of Jan. 6," Courthouse News Service, October 11, 2022, https://www.courthousenews.com /defense-for-oath-keepers-seizes-on-tip-to-fbi-ahead-of-jan-6/.

82 **"Death Threats: Militia groups":** Aaron C. Davis, "Death Threats: Militia Groups": "Red Flags," *Washington Post,* October 31, 2001, https://www.washingtonpost.com/politics/interactive /2021/warnings-jan-6-insurrection/.

82 **When asked about whether he would:** Kyle Cheney, "Proud Boys Sedition Trial Shows Group Keying Off Trump Comments," *Politico,* February 9, 2023, https://www.politico.com/news /2023/02/09/proud-boys-sedition-trial-trump-00082067.

83 **"There are still avenues":** Celine Castronuovo, "Flynn Delivers First Public Remarks Since Trump Pardon at DC Rallies," The Hill, December 12, 2020, https://thehill.com/homenews /administration/529956-flynn-delivers-first-public-remarks-since-trump-pardon-at-dc -rallies/.

83 **estimated seven hundred Proud Boys:** Emily Davies et al., "Multiple People Stabbed After Thousands Gather for Pro-Trump Demonstrations in Washington," *Washington Post,* December 12, 2020, https://www.washingtonpost.com/local/trump-dc-rally-maga/2020/12/11 /8b5af818-3bdb-11eb-bc68-96af0daae728_story.html.

84 **"This was a learning experience":** Cheney, "Proud Boys Sedition Trial Shows Group Keying Off Trump Comments."

84 **"Please be in DC":** "Red Flags," *Washington Post.*

84 **Trump had run out of legal challenges:** Elise Viebeck et al., "Electoral College Affirms Biden's Victory on a Relatively Calm Day of a Chaotic Election," *Washington Post,* December 14, 2020, https://www.washingtonpost.com/politics/electoral-college-affirms-bidens-victory-on -a-relatively-calm-day-of-a-chaotic-election/2020/12/14/0994b232-3e48-11eb-9453-fc36ba0 51781_story.html.

85 **She described it as:** Jonathan Swan and Zachary Basu, "Bonus Episode: Inside the Craziest Meeting of the Trump Presidency," *Axios,* February 21, 2021, https://www.axios.com/2021 /02/02/trump-oval-office-meeting-sidney-powell.

85 **"Statistically impossible to have lost":** Tom Dreisbach, "How Trump's 'Will Be Wild!' Tweet Drew Rioters to the Capitol on Jan. 6," NPR, July 13, 2022, https://www.npr.org/2022/07/13 /1111341161/how-trumps-will-be-wild-tweet-drew-rioters-to-the-capitol-on-jan-6.

86 **resigned in April 2017:** Carrie Johnson, "Leader of Justice Department National Security Division on the Way Out," NPR, April 20, 2017, https://www.npr.org/2017/04/20/524905899 /leader-of-justice-department-national-security-division-on-the-way-out.

86 **They referred her to:** "Brian T. Gilhooly Named as Special Agent in Charge of the Mission Services Branch of the Los Angeles Field Office," FBI, press release, June 21, 2021, https://www .fbi.gov/news/press-releases/brian-t-gilhooly-named-as-special-agent-in-charge-of-the -mission-services-branch-of-the-los-angeles-field-office.

86 **One extremist wrote:** *Final Report of the Select Committee to Investigate January 6th Attack on the United States Capitol,* 117th Congress, 2nd Session (December 22, 2022), doc 371, https:// www.govinfo.gov/content/pkg/GPO-J6-REPORT/html-submitted/index.html#es_fn371.

87 **In a new string of exchanges:** *Final Report of the Select Committee to Investigate January 6th Attack on the United States Capitol.*

87 **members encouraged one another:** *Final Report of the Select Committee to Investigate January 6th Attack on the United States Capitol.*

87 **"Then bring the guns we shall":** *Final Report of the Select Committee to Investigate January 6th Attack on the United States Capitol.*

87 **It was one of more than fifty threats:** Matt Zapotosky, "Conservative Platform Parler Says It Warned FBI of 'Specific Threats of Violence' Ahead of Capitol Riot," *Washington Post*, March 25, 2021, https://www.washingtonpost.com/national-security/parler-fbi-capitol-riot/2021/03 /25/addba25a-8dae-11eb-a6bd-0eb91c03305a_story.html.

87 **On December 26:** *Planned in Plain Sight: A Review of the Intelligence Failures in Advance of January 6th, 2021*, Homeland Security & Governmental Affairs, HSGAC Majority Report, June 2023, https://www.hsgac.senate.gov/wp-content/uploads/230627_HSGAC-Majority -Report_Jan-6-Intel.pdf, 27.

87 **"They think they will have":** Carol D. Leonnig, "Secret Service Knew of Capitol Threat More Than a Week Before Jan. 6," *Washington Post*, October 13, 2022, https://www.washingtonpost .com/nation/2022/10/13/secret-service-jan6-messages-house-committee/.

87 **"I think they will have large numbers":** *Planned in Plain Sight*, 29.

87 **The Bureau had a central collection:** Federal Bureau of Investigation, "Privacy Impact Assessment," September 19, 2022, https://www.fbi.gov/file-repository/pia-eguardian-system -091922.pdf/view.

88 **The FBI began tagging:** *Planned in Plain Sight*, 30.

88 **the FBI Washington Field Office emailed:** Email from Federal Bureau of Investigation Washington Field Office staff to Federal Bureau of Investigation Critical Incident Response Group staff, December 29, 2020.

88 **On New Year's Day:** Scott MacFarlane, Rick Yarborough, and Steve Jones, "DC Tunnel History Site Flagged Suspicious Activity Before Capitol Insurrection," NBC 4 Washington, April 17, 2021, https://www.nbcwashington.com/investigations/dc-tunnel-history-site -flagged-suspicious-activity-before-capitol-insurrection/2775341/.

CHAPTER TWELVE

89 **Jeff Rosen had been the acting attorney general:** "WATCH: Rosen Says Trump Was Dissatisfied with DOJ for Not Investigating False Election Fraud Claims," *PBS Newshour*, YouTube, June 23, 2022, https://www.youtube.com/watch?v=n8FHE2EQIvU.

89 **Trump was so spitting mad:** William M. Arkin, "'You Must Really Hate Trump,' a Furious Donald Trump Said to Bill Barr," *Newsweek*, December 1, 2021, https://www.newsweek.com /you-must-really-hate-trump-furious-donald-trump-said-bill-barr-1652450.

89 **The president slapped his hand:** William P. Barr, *One Damn Thing After Another: Memoirs of an Attorney General* (William Morrow, 2022).

90 **"Just say the election was corrupt":** *Subverting Justice: How the Former President and His Allies Pressured DOJ to Overturn the 2020 Election*, Senate Judiciary Committee, October 7, 2021, https://www.judiciary.senate.gov/imo/media/doc/Interim%20Staff%20Report%20FINAL .pdf, 16.

90 **Donoghue couldn't believe:** Michael Kranish and Rosalind S. Helderman, "Echoes of Watergate: Trump's Appointees Reveal His Push to Topple Justice Dept," *Washington Post*, June 23, 2022, https://www.washingtonpost.com/national-security/2022/06/23/jan6-doj-clark-rosen -donoghue-testimony/.

90 **The two senior Justice leaders:** *Subverting Justice*.

90 **"We don't see that":** Michael Kranish, "New Details Emerge of Oval Office Confrontation Three Days Before Jan. 6," *Washington Post*, June 14, 2022, https://www.washingtonpost.com /politics/2022/06/14/inside-explosive-oval-office-confrontation-three-days-before-jan-6/.

91 **any discussion with the president:** *Justice Manual,* "Title 9: Criminal, 1-8.000—Congressional and White house Relations," U.S. Department of Justice, updated February 2024, https://www.justice.gov/jm/jm-1-8000-congressional-relations#:~:text=In%20order%20to%20insulate%20them,Deputy%20Counsel%20to%20the%20President%20(%1-8.600).

91 **In 2018, Trump had chosen him:** "Attorney General Jeff Sessions Welcomes Jeffrey Clark as Assistant Attorney General for the Environment and Natural Resources Division," U.S. Department of Justice, press release, October 11, 2018, https://www.justice.gov/opa/pr/attorney-general-jeff-sessions-welcomes-jeffrey-clark-assistant-attorney-general-environment.

91 **Rosen and Donoghue, slack-jawed:** *Subverting Justice,* 23.

92 **But the pair decided:** *Subverting Justice,* 24.

92 **"[T]hese allegations about ballots":** *Select Committee to Investigate the January 6th Attack on the U.S. Capitol,* U.S. House of Representatives, October 1, 2021, https://www.govinfo.gov/content/pkg/GPO-J6-TRANSCRIPT-CTRL0000034600/pdf/GPO-J6-TRANSCRIPT-CTRL 0000034600.pdf, 43.

92 **He said he planned:** *Subverting Justice,* 35.

93 **"Are we going to find out in a tweet?":** *Subverting Justice,* 36.

93 **That meant a total of ten:** *Subverting Justice,* 37.

93 **"One thing we know is you":** *Subverting Justice,* 38.

93 **Clark inaccurately claimed:** *Select Committee to Investigate the January 6th Attack on the U.S. Capitol,* interview of Richard Peter Donoghue, October 1, 2021, https://www.govinfo.gov/content/pkg/GPO-J6-REPORT/html-submitted/index.html, 124.

94 **"I appreciate your willingness to do it":** Kranish, "New Details Emerge of Oval Office Confrontation Three Days Before Jan. 6."

94 **grateful, one word reaction:** *Subverting Justice,* 39.

96 **"No one knows what is going to happen":** Sara Wiatrak and Jordan Libowitz, "FBI: 'Significant Possibility of Violence' on January 6th," CREW, May 23, 2023, https://www.citizensforethics.org/reports-investigations/crew-investigations/fbi-significant-possibility-of-violence-on-january-6th/.

97 **"These men are coming for violence":** Email from Federal Bureau of Investigation Washington Field Office staff to Jennifer Moore, Matthew Alcoke, and Steven D'Antuono, Federal Bureau of Investigation Washington Field Office, January 3, 2021, https://www.hsgac.senate.gov/wp-content/uploads/230627_HSGAC-Majority-Report_Jan-6-Intel.pdf.

97 **So far there were sixteen Guardian:** *Select Committee to Investigate the January 6th Attack on the U.S. Capitol,* interview of Jennifer Moore, July 26, 2022, https://www.documentcloud.org/documents/23586792-moore-house-j6-committe-deposition-transcript#document/p126/a2202009.

97 **The intelligence summary that day:** January 3, 2021 Email from Federal Bureau of Investigation Washington Field Office.

97 **"FBI WFO does not have":** *Planned in Plain Sight: A Review of the Intelligence Failures in Advance of January 6th, 2021,* Homeland Security & Governmental Affairs, HSGAC Majority Report, June 2023, https://www.hsgac.senate.gov/wp-content/uploads/230627_HSGAC-Majority-Report_Jan-6-Intel.pdf, 34.

98 **None of the dozens of warnings:** *Capitol Attack: Federal Agencies Identified Some Threats, but Did Not Fully Process and Share Information Prior to January 6, 2021,* (U.S. Government Accountability Office), February 2023, https://www.gao.gov/assets/gao-23-106625.pdf, 29.

98 **"$350,000 dollar reward for the head":** *Planned in Plain Sight,* 35.

99 **the message referred to the forum:** *Planned in Plain Sight,* 239.

100 **the night so far lacked any:** *A Review of the Federal Bureau of Investigation's Handling of Its Confidential Human Sources and Intelligence Collection Efforts in the Lead-Up to the January 6, 2021, Electoral Certification*, Department of Justice, Office of the Inspector General, December 2024, https://oig.justice.gov/sites/default/files/reports/25-011.pdf, 45.

CHAPTER THIRTEEN

103 **Miller pressed Rosen:** *Select Committee to Investigate the January 6th Attack on the U.S. Capitol*, interview of Jeffrey A. Rosen, U.S. House of Representatives, https://perma.cc/EC45 -3HFX, 141.

105 **"There's a large crowd":** *Washington Post* staff, "The Attack: The Jan. 6 Siege of the U.S. Capitol Was Neither a Spontaneous Act Nor an Isolated Event," *Washington Post,* October 31, 2021, https://www.washingtonpost.com/politics/interactive/2021/warnings-jan-6-insurrection/.

105 **"Alert at 1022":** Mark Marbut, email, January 6, 2021, https://www.govinfo.gov/content/pkg /GPO-J6-DOC-CTRL0000092958/pdf/GPO-J6-DOC-CTRL0000092958.pdf.

106 **"Make sure PPD knows:** "AR-15 Style Rifle, Other Weapons and Radio Equipment Spotted During Capitol Riot, Jan. 6 Hearing," YouTube, June 28, 2022, https://www.youtube.com/watch ?v=ykJyPXVlco0.

106 **Another Metropolitan Police Department officer:** "AR-15 Style Rifle, Other Weapons and Radio Equipment Spotted during Capitol Riot."

107 **Hutchinson would say:** *Select Committee to Investigate the January 6th Attack on the U.S. Capitol*, interview of Cassidy Hutchinson, U.S. House of Representatives, https://perma.cc / Q2E8- MLD7, 11–12.

107 **agents manning the magnetometers:** "United States Secret Service—Coordinated Response to a Request for Information from the Select Committee to Investigate the January 6th Attack on the United States Capitol," November 18, 2021, https://www.govinfo.gov/content/pkg /GPO-J6-DOC-CTRL0000086772/pdf/GPO-J6-DOC-CTRL0000086772.pdf.

107 **A couple of minutes before noon:** "Transcript of Trump's Speech at Rally Before U.S. Capitol Riot," Associated Press, January 13, 2021, https://apnews.com/article/election-2020-joe-biden -donald-trump-capitol-siege-media-e79eb5164613d6718e9f4502eb471f27.

108 **Then he relayed the news:** Carol D. Leonnig, "Secret Service Knew of Capitol Threat More Than a Week Before Jan. 6," *Washington Post,* October 13, 2022, https://www.washington post.com/nation/2022/10/13/secret-service-jan6-messages-house-committee/.

108 **The speech marked the end of the first quarter:** *Select Committee to Investigate the January 6th Attack on the U.S. Capitol*, interview of Jeffrey Rosen, October 13, 2021, https://www .scribd.com/document/617913661/Jeffrey-Rosen-Transcript, 171.

108 **Kamala Harris was inside:** Betsy Woodruff Swan, Christopher Cadelago, and Kyle Cheney, "Harris Was Inside DNC on Jan. 6 When Pipe Bomb Was Discovered Outside," *Politico,* January 6, 2022, https://www.politico.com/news/2022/01/06/harris-was-inside-dnc-on-jan-6 -when-pipe-bomb-was-discovered-outside-526695.

110 **One yelled to the police:** "See GOP Lawmakers Confront Rioters in Never-Before-Seen Jan. 6 Video," MSNBC, January 6, 2024, https://www.msnbc.com/msnbc/watch/see-gop -lawmakers-confront-rioters-in-never-before-seen-jan-6-video-201475653802.

113 **seeming to put a target:** Rosalind S. Helderman and Josh Dawsey, "Mounting Evidence Suggests Trump Knew of Danger to Pence When He Attacked Him as Lacking 'Courage' amid Capitol Siege," *Washington Post,* February 11, 2021, https://www.washingtonpost.com/politics /trump-tweet-pence-capitol/2021/02/11/cc7d9f7e-6c7f-11eb-9f80-3d7646ce1bc0_story.html.

114 **was hiding in an office:** Melissa Quinn, "Pence's Secret Service Detail at Capitol on Jan. 6 Were 'Starting to Fear for Their Own Lives' as Violence Escalated, Witness Tells Select Committee," CBS News, July 22, 2022, https://www.cbsnews.com/news/pence-secret-service-jan -6-capitol-fear-lives/.

114 **Trump tweeted his takeaway:** "Donald Trump—Flagged Tweets," Factbase, January 6, 2021, https://factba.se/topic/flagged-tweets.

116 **"From former Attorney General Bill Barr":** Kerri Kupec, Twitter, January 6, 2020, 3:55 p.m., https://x.com/kerri_kupec/status/1346923256989802498.

116 **"The violence at our Nation's Capitol":** "Acting Attorney General Jeffrey A. Rosen Regarding the Overrunning of the U.S. Capitol Building," Department of Justice, January 6, 2021, https:// www.justice.gov/opa/pr/acting-attorney-general-jeffrey-rosen-regarding-overrunning-us -capitol-building.

CHAPTER FOURTEEN

120 **"We are looking at all actors":** Devlin Barrett, "Trump's Remarks Before Capitol Riot May Be Investigated, Says Acting U.S. Attorney in D.C.," *Washington Post,* January 7, 2021, https:// www.washingtonpost.com/national-security/federal-investigation-capitol-riot-trump/2021 /01/07/178d71ac-512c-11eb-83e3-322644d82356_story.html.

120 **"I'm going to stand by my earlier statement":** U.S. Department of Justice, FOIA request provided to Jason Leopold, Just Security, November 16, 2021, https://www.justsecurity.org /wp-content/uploads/2022/06/january-6-clearinghouse-doj-foia-capitol-riots-emails -planning-and-response.pdf, 45.

120 **The websites of *The Washington Post* and *The New York Times*:** Barrett, "Trump's Remarks Before Capitol Riot May Be Investigated, Says Acting U.S. Attorney in D.C."; Katie Benner, "Justice Dept. Open to Pursuing Charges Against Trump in Inciting Riot," *New York Times,* January 7, 2021, https://www.nytimes.com/2021/01/07/us/politics/justice-department-trump -capitol.html.

121 **As it happened:** Tyler Pager, Josh Gerstein, and Kyle Cheney, "Biden to Tap Merrick Garland for Attorney General," *Politico,* January 6, 2021, https://www.politico.com/news/2021/01/06 /biden-to-tap-merrick-garland-for-attorney-general-455410.

121 **Jones had risked his reelection:** Mike Memoli, "Longtime Friendship with Joe Biden Pays Off for Jones in Senate Election," NBC News, December 13, 2017, https://www.nbcnews.com /storyline/2017-elections/longtime-friendship-joe-biden-pays-jones-senate-election-n829151.

123 **Monaco's working relationship with Biden:** *Violence Against Women: The Response to Rape,* Senate Report prepared by the Majority Staff of the Senate Judiciary Committee, May 1993, https://web.archive.org/web/20130928123238/http://mith.umd.edu/WomensStudies/ GenderIssues/Violence+Women/ResponsetoRape/introduction.

123 **A couple of days after New Year's:** David M. Herszenhorn, "Biden's Brussels Pick Isn't Just One of the President's Men," *Politico,* August 4, 2021, https://www.politico.eu/article/joe -biden-eu-us-ambassador-pick-mark-gitenstein/.

125 **About twenty-six hours later:** "President-Elect Biden Nominates Merrick Garland for Attorney General," NPR News, January 7, 2021, https://www.facebook.com/NPR/videos/16272893 2266135.

125 **"I want to be clear":** Thomas Franck, "Biden Introduces Attorney General Pick Merrick Garland as He Promises DOJ Independence," CNBC, January 7, 2021.

126 **"Are you out of your effing mind":** "Herschmann Tells Eastman to Get a Great 'Criminal Defense Lawyer,'" *Washington Post*, June 16, 2022, https://www.washingtonpost.com/video /politics/herschmann-tells-eastman-to-get-a-great-criminal-defense-lawyer/2022/06/16 /e512c232-49ab-464a-9fae-e5aee017b473_video.html.

127 **Eastman seemed to absorb the message:** "Pro-Trump Lawyer Sought Pardon After Pushing Plan to Overturn Election," *Washington Post*, June 16, 2022, https://www.washingtonpost .com/national-security/2022/06/16/jan-6-committee-hearings-live-june-16/.

127 **The rioters were fast:** Aaron C. Davis and Carol D. Leonnig, "FBI Resisted Opening Probe into Trump's Role in Jan. 6 for More Than a Year," *Washington Post*, June 20, 2023, https:// www.washingtonpost.com/investigations/2023/06/19/fbi-resisted-opening-probe-into -trumps-role-jan-6-more-than-year/.

128 **Using cell phone tower data:** *United States of America v. David Charles Rhine*, U.S. District Court for the District of Columbia, Motion to Suppress Evidence Flowing from the Geofence Warrant, October 17, 2022, https://www.documentcloud.org/documents/23166814-221017 -rhine-motion-to-suppress.

129 **Barnett had recounted his actions:** Bart Jensen, "Capitol Hill Riot: Judge Gives 54-Month Sentence to Jan. 6 Rioter Who Put Feet Up on Desk in Nancy Pelosi's Office," *USA Today*, May 25, 2023, https://www.usatoday.com/story/news/politics/2023/05/24/jan-6-richard -barnett-pelosi-desk-sentencing/70231549007/.

129 **She had won awards:** *Semiannual Report to Congress*, Office of Inspector General, Department of the Treasury, October 1, 2013–March 31, 2014, https://oig.treasury.gov/system/files /Audit_Reports_and_Testimonies/OIGCA14009.pdf.

132 **before the fraudulent submissions:** "Republican Electors Cast Procedural Vote," PA GOP, December 14, 2020, https://www.documentcloud.org/documents/20423829-pa-gop-electors; Republican Party of Arizona, "The Signing," Twitter, December 14, 2020, https://x.com /AZGOP/status/1338600278459727872?s=20.

133 **An hour later:** Kaitlan Collins and Kevin Liptak, "Trump Tweets He Is Skipping Biden's Inauguration," CNN, January 8, 2021, https://www.cnn.com/2021/01/08/politics/donald-trump -next-steps/index.html.

133 **The tweet, as it turned out:** "Permanent Suspension of @realDonaldTrump," *Twitter Blog*, January 8, 2021, https://blog.twitter.com/en_us/topics/company/2020/suspension.

134 **The House of Representatives voted 232–197:** Nicholas Fandos, "Trump Impeached for Inciting Insurrection," *New York Times*, January 13, 2021, https://www.nytimes.com/2021/01 /13/us/politics/trump-impeached.html.

134 **The single article of impeachment:** H.R. Res 24, Impeaching Donald John Trump, President of the United States, for High Crimes and Misdemeanors, 117th Cong., 1st Sess. (2021), https://www.congress.gov/117/bills/hres24/BILLS-117hres24ih.pdf.

134 **In a briefing for Biden's team:** Missy Ryan, Dan Lamothe, and Paul Sonne, "Threats of 'Armed Protests' in Multiple Cities Challenge National Guard Support for Inauguration," *Washington Post*, January 12, 2021, https://www.washingtonpost.com/national-security /military-biden-inauguration-violence-threats/2021/01/12/0a45cac8-5503-11eb-89bc -7f51ceb6bd57_story.html.

134 **The Pentagon decided it was prudent:** Owen Liebermann, Caroline Kelly, Evan Perez, and Geneva Sands, "Pentagon Authorizes 25,000 National Guard Members for Inauguration," CNN, January 15, 2021, https://www.cnn.com/2021/01/15/politics/pentagon-national-guard -inauguration/index.html.

CHAPTER FIFTEEN

136 Biden signed executive orders: White House Flickr account, January 20, 2021, https://www .flickr.com/photos/whitehouse46/50911775278.

136 Scores of agents and prosecutors: Jordan Fischer, "FBI Now Offering $75,000 Reward for Info on Capitol Riot Pipe Bomb Suspect," WUSA, January 21, 2021, https://www.wusa9.com /article/news/national/capitol-riots/fbi-offering-75000-dollars-for-info-on-capitol-riot-pipe -bomb-suspect/65-92f944da-88f6-491e-99ad-6d8e9f68c18e.

137 rolled back a November 9: Matt Zapotosky and Devlin Barrett, "Barr Clears Justice Dept. to Investigate Alleged Voting Irregularities as Trump Makes Unfounded Fraud Claims," *Washington Post*, November 9, 2020, https://www.washingtonpost.com/national-security /trump-voting-fraud-william-barr-justice-department/2020/11/09/d57dbe98-22e6-11eb -8672-c281c7a2c96e_story.html.

138 The highest-profile of those: Tom Dreisbach, "New Videos Show Alleged Assault on Officer Brian Sicknick During Capitol Riot," NPR, April 28, 2021, https://www.npr.org/2021/04/28 /991654947/new-videos-show-alleged-assault-on-officer-brian-sicknick-during-capitol -riot; Marshall Cohen and Katelyn Polantz, "US Capitol Rioters Charged in Sicknick Case Were Armed with Bear Spray but Only Used Pepper Spray, Prosecutors Say," CNN, April 27, 2021, https://www.cnn.com/2021/04/27/politics/sicknick-capitol-bear-spray-pepper/index .html.

139 They were dressed in paramilitary vests: Tess Owen, "Roger Stone Used Oath Keepers as Security on the Eve of the Capitol Riot," *Vice*, January 26, 2021, https://www.vice.com/en/article /7k9mpd/roger-stone-used-the-oath-keepers-as-security-on-the-eve-of-the-capitol-riot.

139 In the first week of February: Matthew Mosk, Olivia Rubin, Ali Dukakis, and Fergal Gallagher, "Video Surfaces Showing Trump Ally Roger Stone Flanked by Oath Keepers on Morning of Jan. 6," ABC News, February 5, 2021, https://abcnews.go.com/US/video-surfaces-showing -trump-ally-roger-stone-flanked/story?id=75706765.

139 A week later: Christiaan Triebert, Ben Decker, Derek Watkins, Arielle Ray, and Stella Cooper, "First They Guarded Roger Stone. Then They Joined the Capitol Attack," *New York Times*, February 14, 2021, https://www.nytimes.com/interactive/2021/02/14/us/roger-stone-capitol -riot.html.

139 Prosecutors working the cases: Spencer S. Hsu and Devlin Barrett, "U.S. Investigating Possible Ties Between Roger Stone, Alex Jones and Capitol Rioters," *Washington Post*, February 20, 2021, https://www.washingtonpost.com/local/legal-issues/stone-jones-capitol-riot -investigation-radicalization/2021/02/19/97d6e6ee-6cad-11eb-9ead-673168d5b874_story .html.

140 Mitch McConnell said: "Read McConnell's Remarks on the Senate floor Following Trump's Acquittal," CNN, February 13, 2021, https://edition.cnn.com/2021/02/13/politics/mcconnell -remarks-trump-acquittal.

CHAPTER SIXTEEN

143 On February 22, 2021: *Confirmation Hearing on the Nomination of Hon. Merrick Brian Garland to Be Attorney General of the United States*, Committee on the Judiciary United States Senate, February 22 and 23, 2021, https://www.judiciary.senate.gov/imo/media/doc/2021 -02-22-23_-_final_publication.pdf.

144 **"Your law enforcement experience":** *Confirmation Hearing on the Nomination of Hon. Merrick Brian Garland to Be Attorney General of the United States,* 22.

144 **"We all need something to believe in":** *Confirmation Hearing on the Nomination of Hon. Merrick Brian Garland to Be Attorney General of the United States,* 92.

145 **In the very days leading up:** Christine Stapleton and Antonio Fins, "Amid Republican Civil War, Trump Holds Court—And His Grip on GOP at Mar-a-Lago," *Palm Beach Post,* March 15, 2021, https://www.yahoo.com/news/amid-republican-civil-war-trump-122329476.html.

148 **The Justice Department had last brought the charge:** "Nine Members of a Militia Group Charged with Seditious Conspiracy and Related Charges," U.S. Department of Justice, press release, March 29, 2010, https://www.justice.gov/opa/pr/nine-members-militia-group-charged-seditious-conspiracy-and-related-charges; Nick Bunkley, "U.S. Judge in Michigan Acquits Militia Members of Sedition," *New York Times,* March 27, 2012, https://www.nytimes.com/2012/03/28/us/hutaree-militia-members-acquitted-of-sedition.html.

150 **Later that night,** *The New York Times:* Katie Benner, "Justice Dept. Said to Be Weighing Sedition Charges Against Oath Keepers," *New York Times,* March 22, 2021, https://www.nytimes.com/2021/03/22/us/politics/sedition-oath-keepers-capitol-riot.html.

150 **would likely have the final say:** Benner, "Justice Dept. Said to Be Weighing Sedition Charges Against Oath Keepers."

151 **Two weeks after that:** Spencer S. Hsu, "Evidence in Capitol Attack Investigation Trending Toward Sedition Charges, Departing Chief Says," *Washington Post,* March 21, 2021, https://www.washingtonpost.com/local/legal-issues/seditious-conpiracy-charges-capitol-riot/2021/03/21/406da056-8aa2-11eb-a730-1b4ed9656258_story.html.

151 **the department's ethics office concluded:** "Investigation of Alleged Participation in an Unauthorized Media Interview, Office of Professional Responsibility," U.S. Department of Justice, December 13, 2022, https://www.justice.gov/opr/2022-investigative-summary-4.

152 **That attention only intensified:** "Deputy Attorney General and Associate Attorney General Confirmation Hearing," C-SPAN, March 9, 2021, https://www.c-span.org/video/?509635-1/deputy-attorney-general-associate-attorney-general-confirmation-hearing.

155 **In March and April, senior department officials:** "Pre-Decisional & Deliberative/Attorney-Client or Legal Work Product Georgia Proof of Concept," U.S. Department of Justice, December 28, 2020, https://int.nyt.com/data/documenttools/jeffrey-clark-draft-letter/9a9ffa97a521729b/full.pdf.

159 **On May 13, 2021:** Scott Wartman, "Thomas Massie Signs Letter Warning of 'Hyper-Politicization' of Prosecutions in Wake of Jan. 6 Capitol Attack," *Cincinnati Enquirer,* May 17, 2021, https://www.cincinnati.com/story/news/politics/2021/05/17/capitol-riot-rep-thomas-massie-warns-prosecutorial-overreach/5125289001/.

CHAPTER SEVENTEEN

161 **Trump was rewriting the events:** Colby Itkowitz, "Trump Falsely Claims Jan. 6 Rioters Were 'Hugging and Kissing' Police," *Washington Post,* March 26, 2021, https://www.washingtonpost.com/politics/trump-riot-capitol-police/2021/03/26/0ba7e844-8e40-11eb-9423-04079921c915_story.html.

161 **Trump's most ardent supporters:** Dinesh D'Souza, "Biden Is Putting Jan 6 Defendants in Solitary Confinement," YouTube, April 9, 2021, https://www.youtube.com/watch?v=8HWFg1zjh78&t=6s.

161 **Less than a week after Biden's inauguration:** Steve Peoples and Jill Colvin, "GOP Signals Unwillingness to Part with Trump After Riot," Associated Press, January 27, 2021, https://apnews.com/article/gop-donald-trump-edeed40444c700ccc53ed4ffc4e89f4d.

162 **The final Senate tally:** Roll Call Vote, 117th Cong., 1st Sess., U.S. Senate, (February 13, 2021), https://www.senate.gov/legislative/LIS/roll_call_votes/vote1171/vote_117_1_00059.htm.

162 **Online, his supporters further muddied:** Michael M. Grynbaum et al., "How Pro-Trump Forces Pushed a Lie About Antifa at the Capitol Riot," *New York Times*, March 1, 2021, https://www.nytimes.com/2021/03/01/us/politics/antifa-conspiracy-capitol-riot.html.

162 **"The polls show that everybody":** Jason Lemon, "Donald Trump Says '100 Percent' He's 'Thinking About Running' for President in 2024," *Newsweek*, April 29, 2021, https://www.newsweek.com/donald-trump-says-100-percent-hes-thinking-about-running-president-2024-1587411.

162 **53 percent of Republicans:** "53% of Republicans View Trump as True U.S. President—Reuters/Ipsos," Reuters, May 24, 2021, https://www.reuters.com/world/us/53-republicans-view-trump-true-us-president-reutersipsos-2021-05-24/.

163 **The announcement followed:** Amy Gardner, "'I Just Want to Find 11,780 Votes': In Extraordinary Hour-Long Call, Trump Pressures Georgia Secretary of State to Recalculate the Vote in His Favor," *Washington Post,* January 3, 2021, https://www.washingtonpost.com/politics/trump-raffensperger-call-georgia-vote/2021/01/03/d45acb92-4dc4-11eb-bda4-615aaefd0555_story.html.

163 **"The people of Georgia":** Amy Gardner, "Recording Reveals Details of Trump Call to Georgia's Chief Elections Investigator," *Washington Post,* March 11, 2021, https://www.washingtonpost.com/politics/trump-call-georgia-investigator/2021/03/11/c532ea2e-827a-11eb-ac37-4383f7709abe_story.html.

163 **American Oversight saw a clear tether:** "American Oversight Obtains Seven Phony Certificates of Pro-Trump Electors," American Oversight, March 2, 2021, https://www.americanoversight.org/american-oversight-obtains-seven-phony-certificates-of-pro-trump-electors; https://www.americanoversight.org/american-oversight-obtains-seven-phony-certificates-of-pro-trump-electors.

164 **Pelosi's push for an independent:** Nicholas Fandos, "Democrats Failed to Get Enough Votes for an Independent Inquiry into the Jan. 6 Riot," *New York Times,* May 28, 2021, https://www.nytimes.com/2021/05/28/us/politics/capitol-riot-commission.html.

168 **"I assure the American people":** Spencer S. Hsu, "500 Arrested in Jan. 6 Capitol Riot, Including First Charged with Assault on Media Member, Garland Announces," *Washington Post,* June 24, 2021, https://www.washingtonpost.com/local/legal-issues/500-arrested-in-jan-6-capitol-riot-including-first-charged-with-assault-on-media-member-garland-announces/2021/06/24/cc972198-d529-11eb-ae54-515e2f63d37d_story.html.

CHAPTER EIGHTEEN

171 **After a 9/11-style:** Philip Bump, "Senate Republicans Kill the Jan. 6 Commission by a Negative-19 Vote Margin," *Washington Post,* May 28, 2021, https://www.washingtonpost.com/politics/2021/05/28/senate-republicans-kill-jan-6-commission-by-negative-19-vote-margin/.

171 **She invited Republican leaders:** Marianna Sotomayor et al., "Bipartisan House Probe of Jan. 6 Insurrection Falls Apart After Pelosi Blocks Two GOP Members," *Washington Post,*

July 21, 2021, https://www.washingtonpost.com/politics/pelosi-mccarthy-jan6-committee/2021 /07/21/21722d44-ea41-11eb-84a2-d93bc0b50294_story.html.

179 **Returning to the White House:** "Remarks by President Biden at the Dedication of the Dodd Center for Human Rights," The White House, October 15, 2021, https://www.whitehouse.gov /briefing-room/statements-releases/2021/10/15/remarks-by-president-biden-at-the-dedication -of-the-dodd-center-for-human-rights/.

180 **"I hope that the committee":** Donald Judd and Rachel Janfaza, "Biden Says DOJ Should Prosecute Those Who Defy January 6 Committee Subpoenas," CNN, October 15, 2021, https://www.cnn.com/2021/10/15/politics/biden-doj-prosecute-january-6-subpoenas/index .html.

180 **Compared to the way:** Michael M. Grynbaum et al., "Trump's Urging That Comey Jail Reporters Denounced as an 'Act of Intimidation," *New York Times,* May 17, 2017, https://www .nytimes.com/2017/05/17/business/media/trumps-urging-that-comey-jail-reporters -denounced-as-an-act-of-intimidation.html.

180 **later pressed his attorney general:** Bill Bostock, "Trump Said James Comey Could Get 'Years In Jail' After He Admitted 'Sloppiness' in the FBI's Attempts to Spy on a Trump Aide," *Business Insider,* December 16, 2019, https://www.businessinsider.com/trump-suggests-comey -jail-time-after-horrowitz-fbi-report-2019-12.

181 **"The Department of Justice will make":** Amy B. Wang, "Biden Says Justice Department Should Prosecute Those Who Refuse Jan. 6 Committee's Subpoenas," *Washington Post,* October 15, 2021, https://www.washingtonpost.com/politics/2021/10/15/biden-says-justice -department-should-prosecute-those-who-refuse-jan-6-committees-subpoenas/.

181 **A week later, on October 21:** Claudia Grisales, "The House Votes to Hold Steve Bannon in Contempt for Defying a Subpoena," NPR, October 21, 2021, https://www.npr.org/2021/10/21 /1048051026/u-s-house-approves-criminal-contempt-referral-for-steve-bannon.

182 **His agency was still not actively investigating:** Carrie Johnson, "Garland Deflects Lawmakers' Questions on Trump as He Tries to Sidestep Politics," NPR, October 21, 2021, https://www .npr.org/2021/10/21/1048010555/garland-deflects-lawmakers-questions-on-trump -as-he-tries-to-sidestep-politics.

CHAPTER NINETEEN

185 **Windom had racked up impressive wins:** Dan Morse, "Two Men Accused of Plotting 'Race War' Plead Guilty to Immigration-Related Gun Charges," *Washington Post,* June 10, 2021, https://www.washingtonpost.com/local/public-safety/base-guilty-plea-terrorism/2021/06 /10/e10c29d0-c97a-11eb-81b1-34796c7393af_story.html.

185 **Windom had secured:** Shane Harris and Devlin Barrett, "FBI Arrests 3 Alleged Members of White-Supremacist Group 'The Base' Ahead of Virginia Gun Rally," *Washington Post,* January 16, 2020, https://www.washingtonpost.com/national-security/fbi-arrests-alleged-members -of-white-supremacist-group-the-base/2020/01/16/ae8c01d4-386b-11ea-bf30-ad313e4ec754 _story.html.

186 **Eastman had actually referred:** Jacqueline Alemany et al., "Ahead of Jan. 6, Willard Hotel in Downtown D.C. Was a Trump Team 'Command Center' for Effort to Deny Biden the Presidency," *Washington Post,* October 23, 2021, https://www.washingtonpost.com/investigations /willard-trump-eastman-giuliani-bannon/2021/10/23/c45bd2d4-3281-11ec-9241-aad8e 48f01ff_story.html.

CHAPTER TWENTY

193 **The FBI should always use extreme caution:** Rosalind S. Helderman and Tom Hamburger, "At the Center of Mueller's Inquiry, a Campaign That Appeared to Welcome Russia's Help," *Washington Post*, March 22, 2019, https://www.washingtonpost.com/politics/at-the-center -of-muellers-inquiry-a-campaign-that-appeared-to-welcome-russias-help/2019/03/22 /9e8d279e-259e-11e9-90cd-dedb0c92dc17_story.html.

CHAPTER TWENTY-ONE

197 **She then read aloud:** "Rep. Liz Cheney Read Text Messages She Said Mark Meadows Got During the Jan. 6 Siege," NPR, December 13, 2021, https://www.npr.org/2021/12/13/10639 55835/rep-liz-cheney-read-text-messages-she-said-mark-meadows-got-during-the-jan-6-sie.
199 **The last time Justice had won:** Joseph P. Fried, "The Terror Conspiracy: The Overview; Sheik and 9 Followers Guilty of a Conspiracy of Terrorism," *New York Times*, October 2, 1995, https://www.nytimes.com/1995/10/02/nyregion/terror-conspiracy-overview-sheik-9 -followers-guilty-conspiracy-terrorism.html.

CHAPTER TWENTY-TWO

203 **Rachel Maddow complained:** "Transcript: The Rachel Maddow Show, 1/10/22," MSNBC, January 10, 2022, https://www.msnbc.com/transcripts/transcript-rachel-maddow-show-1-10 -22-n1287484.
204 **The indictment laid out:** Spencer S. Hsu and Devlin Barrett, "Oath Keepers Founder Stewart Rhodes Charged with Seditious Conspiracy in Jan. 6 Capitol Riot," *Washington Post*, January 13, 2022, https://www.washingtonpost.com/national-security/stewart-rhodes-arrested-jan-6 /2022/01/13/558ecc42-7414-11ec-8b0a-bcfab800c430_story.html.
204 **An article in the nonpartisan** *Lawfare*: Scott R. Anderson et al., "Seditious Conspiracy: What to Make of the Latest Oath Keepers Indictment," *Lawfare*, January 14, 2022, https://www .lawfaremedia.org/article/seditious-conspiracy-what-make-latest-oath-keepers-indictment.
205 **"And we hope that Main Justice":** "Transcript: The Rachel Maddow Show, 1/13/22," MSNBC, January 13, 2022, https://www.msnbc.com/transcripts/transcript-rachel-maddow-show-11-13 -22-n1287504.
206 **Siemon, of course, wasn't looking:** Nicholas Wu and Kyle Cheney, "Ron Johnson Tried to Hand Fake Elector Info to Mike Pence on Jan. 6, Panel Reveals," *Politico*, June 21, 2022, https:// www.politico.com/news/2022/06/21/jan-6-panel-trump-overturn-2020-election-00040816.
209 **Perez, a respected Justice correspondent:** "Federal Prosecutors Investigating Fake Trump Elector Certifications," CNN, January 25, 2022, https://www.cnn.com/videos/politics/2022 /01/25/fake-electors-monaco-lead-prez-vpx.cnn.

CHAPTER TWENTY-THREE

215 **such a development was not going to stay secret:** Jacqueline Alemany et al., "National Archives Had to Retrieve Trump White House Records from Mar-a-Lago," *Washington*

Post, February 7, 2022, https://www.washingtonpost.com/politics/2022/02/07/trump-records -mar-a-lago/.

219 **"Gosh it seems everyone"**: John Cusack, Twitter, February 9, 2022, 3:40 p.m., https://x.com /johncusack/status/1491512458275696641.

219 **"Every day garland"**: John Cusack, Twitter, February 9, 2022, 5:13 p.m., https://x.com /johncusack/status/1491535829923250183.

CHAPTER TWENTY-FOUR

221 **"This full investigation is predicated"**: "Grassley, Johnson Make Public Whistleblower Records Revealing DOJ and FBI Plot to Pin Trump in Jack Smith Elector Case," Office of Senator Chuck Grassley, January 30, 2025, https://www.grassley.senate.gov/news/news-releases /grassley-johnson-make-public-whistleblower-records-revealing-doj-and-fbi-plot-to-pin -trump-in-jack-smith-elector-case.

221 **It included copies of the fraudulent certificates**: "Grassley, Johnson Make Public Whistleblower Records Revealing DOJ and FBI Plot to Pin Trump in Jack Smith Elector Case."

222 **But inside the FBI**: Julian Sanchez, "The Crossfire Hurricane Report's Inconvenient Findings," Just Security, December 11, 2019, https://www.justsecurity.org/67691/the-crossfire -hurricane-reports-inconvenient-findings/.

224 **the Gold Team were about to hit pay dirt**: Michael S. Schmidt and Maggie Haberman, "The Lawyer Behind the Memo on How Trump Could Stay in Office," *New York Times*, October 2, 2021, https://www.nytimes.com/2021/10/02/us/politics/john-eastman-trump-memo .html.

224 **The team also noticed a Southern California institution**: *John C. Eastman v. Bennie G. Thompson*, U.S. District Court for the Central District of California, January 20, 2022, https:// www.cacd.uscourts.gov/sites/default/files/Dkt%201%2C%20Eastman%20Complaint.pdf.

225 **It was his email address**: Dawn Bonker, "President Struppa's Message on Supreme Court Case," Chapman University, December 10, 2020, https://news.chapman.edu/2020/12 /10/president-struppas-message-on-supreme-court-case/.

227 **"Based on the evidence"**: *John C. Eastman v. Bennie G. Thompson*, United States District Court for the Central District of California, March 28, 2022, https://storage.courtlistener .com/recap/gov.uscourts.cacd.841840/gov.uscourts.cacd.841840.260.0.pdf.

228 **"More than a year after the attack"**: *John C. Eastman v. Bennie G. Thompson*, March 28, 2022.

230 **It asked the committee**: Glenn Thrush and Luke Broadwater, "Justice Dept. Is Said to Request Transcripts from Jan. 6 Committee," *New York Times*, May 17, 2022, https://www.nytimes .com/2022/05/17/us/politics/jan-6-committee-transcripts.html.

CHAPTER TWENTY-FIVE

233 **"Much of this material"**: Matt Zapotosky et al., "National Archives Asks Justice Dept. to Investigate Trump's Handling of White House Records," *Washington Post*, February 9, 2022, https://www.washingtonpost.com/politics/2022/02/09/trump-archives-justice-department/.

233 **pressing for a full accounting**: *United States of America v. Donald J. Trump et al.*, U.S. District Court Southern District of Florida, July 27, 2023, https://www.washingtonpost.com /documents/d9b51c7a-b7a7-44b2-a146-c675b3170adf.pdf?itid=lk_inline_manual_3.

234 **just how much top-secret material:** 9:23-cr-80101-AMC Southern District of Florida. Exhibit 21, filed 4/22/2024, https://www.courtlistener.com/docket/67490070/united-states-v -trump/, 96.

235 **While the FBI was awaiting clearance:** *United States of America v. Donald J. Trump et al.*

236 **"I have concluded that there is no reason":** Debra Steidel Wall, letter to Evan Corcoran, National Archives, May 10, 2022, https://www.archives.gov/files/foia/wall-letter-to-evan -corcoran-re-trump-boxes-05.10.2022.pdf.

236 **transmitted to Corcoran:** "Subpoena to Testify before a Grand Jury," U.S. District Court for the District of Columbia, May 11, 2022, https://www.justsecurity.org/wp-content/uploads /2022/10/just-security-mar-a-lago-grand-jury-subpoena.pdf.

238 **"The FBI will go to great lengths":** "FBI Employee Indicted for Illegally Removing National Security Documents, Taking Material to Her Home," U.S. Department of Justice, press release, May 21, 2021, https://www.justice.gov/opa/pr/fbi-employee-indicted-illegally -removing-national-security-documents-taking-material-her-home.

238 **agents asked about records:** May 19, 2022, FBI WFO memo re "Update from interview today—PLASMIC ECHO," https://static.foxnews.com/foxnews.com/content/uploads/2024 /04/FBI-Plasmic-Echo-Trump-Classified-Documents-Case.pdf.

239 **Michael provided a general timeline:** May 19, 2022, FBI WFO memo.

242 **Little privately shared with Corcoran:** Katherine Faulders and Mike Levine, "Trump Was Warned That FBI Could Raid Mar-a-Lago Months Ahead of Time, Lawyer's Notes Show," ABC News, September 6, 2023, https://abcnews.go.com/US/trump-warned-fbi-raid-mar-lago -team-feared/story?id=102932105.

242 **"Once this is signed":** Katherine Faulders, Mike Levine, and Alexander Mallin, "Attorney Warned Trump 'It's Going to Be a Crime' if He Didn't Comply with Subpoena for Classified Docs: Source," ABC News, November 29, 2023, https://abcnews.go.com/US/attorney-warned -trump-crime-comply-subpoena-classified-docs/story?id=105228569.

244 **Nauta told the former First Lady:** *United States of America v. Donald J. Trump et al.*

245 **attesting that a diligent search:** *United States of America v. Donald J. Trump et al.*

246 **Just a few hours before Trump greeted:** *United States of America v. Donald J. Trump et al.*

CHAPTER TWENTY-SIX

249 **But their first-person descriptions:** Sarah Ellison, Jacqueline Alemany, and Josh Dawsey, "The Subtle Stagecraft Behind the Jan. 6 Hearings," *Washington Post*, June 23, 2022, https:// www.washingtonpost.com/media/2022/06/23/jan6-hearings-story-narrative-stagecraft -james-goldston/.

250 **A tranche of episodes:** Annie Karni, "The Committee Hired a TV Executive to Produce the Hearings for Maximum Impact," *New York Times*, June 9, 2022, https://www.nytimes .com/2022/06/09/us/the-committee-hired-a-tv-executive-to-produce-the-hearings-for -maximum-impact.html.

250 **A supporter with a megaphone:** "Jan. 6 Committee Shows Timeline of How Close Pence Came to Encountering Rioters," NBC News, YouTube, June 16, 2022, https://www.youtube .com/watch?v=N3pnnx3Mc1w.

250 **U.S. Capitol Police Officer:** Caroline Edwards, "I was Slipping in People's Blood: Capitol Police Officer Recalls Graphic Scene from Jan. 6," CNN, June 10, 2022, https://www.cnn.com /videos/politics/2022/06/10/caroline-edwards-capitol-police-officer-graphic-testimony -2022-january-6-hearings-vpx.cnn.

251 Goldston's team ended: Mike DeBonis, "Jan. 6 Committee Uses Video, Testimony to Tell Tale of the Insurrection," *Washington Post*, June 9, 2022, https://www.washingtonpost .com/national-security/2022/06/09/jan-6-committee-uses-video-testimony-tell-tale -insurrection/.

251 The committee's opening day: Ellison, Alemany, and Dawsey, "The Subtle Stagecraft Behind the Jan. 6 Hearings."

251 Trump launched a tirade: An archive of Trump's posts can be found at Trump's Truth, https://trumpstruth.org/search?query=&start_date=2022-06-09&end_date=2022-06-10& sort=relevance&per_page=25.

252 "I made it clear": Devlin Barrett, "As Hearing's Star Witness, Barr Says Trump Was 'Detached from Reality,'" *Washington Post*, June 13, 2022, https://www.washingtonpost.com/national -security/2022/06/13/bill-barr-trump-january-6/.

252 "I am watching": Barrett, "As Hearing's Star Witness, Barr Says Trump Was 'Detached from Reality.'"

253 It is "critical": Ryan J. Reilly, "Justice Department Says Jan. 6 Committee Interview Transcripts 'Critical' to Criminal Investigation," NBC News, June 16, 2022, https://www.nbcnews .com/politics/justice-department/justice-department-says-jan-6-committee-interview -transcripts-critical-rcna33995.

254 On Tuesday, June 21: "Fourth Hearing on Investigation of January 6 Attack on the U.S. Capitol," House Select Committee, C-SPAN, June 21, 2022, https://www.c-span.org/video/?521075 -1/fourth-hearing-investigation-january-6-attack-us-capitol.

254 That evening, Graves's office: Kyle Cheney, "DOJ Endorses Delay in Proud Boys Trial, Citing Jan. 6 Committee's Ongoing Work," *Politico*, June 21, 2022, https://www.politico.com/news /2022/06/21/proud-boys-trial-jan6-delay-00041284.

255 They arrived at the homes: Spencer S. Hsu et al., "Jan. 6 Probe Expands with Fresh Subpoenas in Multiple States," *Washington Post*, June 22, 2022, https://www.washingtonpost.com /national-security/2022/06/22/jan6-fbi-electors-subpoenas/.

255 Early that same morning: Spencer S. Hsu et al., "Home of Jeffrey Clark, Trump DOJ Official, Searched by Federal Agents," *Washington Post*, June 23, 2022, https://www.washingtonpost .com/national-security/2022/06/23/jeffrey-clark-house-search/.

255 Clark appeared on Tucker Carlson's: "Tucker Carlson with Jeff Clark, Trump's Assistant AG Recently Raided by Biden's DOJ—6/23/22," YouTube, June 23, 2022, https://www.youtube .com/watch?v=-TiGJ1OTjiM.

255 In early June, Liz Cheney: *Select Committee to Investigate the January 6th Attack on the U.S. Capitol*, interview of Cassidy Hutchinson, U.S. House of Representatives, https://www .govinfo.gov/content/pkg/GPO-J6-TRANSCRIPT-CTRL0000928888/pdf/GPO-J6 -TRANSCRIPT-CTRL0000928888.pdf, 3.

256 "There is more I want to share": Ken Meyer, "Former Trump Admin Official Alyssa Farah Stuns CNN's *New Day* with Revelation about Cassidy Hutchinson," Mediaite, June 30, 2022, https://www.mediaite.com/tv/former-trump-admin-official-alyssa-farah-stuns-cnns-new -day-with-revelation-about-cassidy-hutchinson/.

256 he had advocated for her: Katelyn Polantz et al., "Exclusive: Trump's Former White House Ethics Lawyer Told Cassidy Hutchinson to Give Misleading Testimony to January 6 Committee, Sources Say," CNN, December 21, 2022, https://www.cnn.com/2022/12/20/politics /trump-ethics-lawyer-passantino-cassidy-hutchinson-misleading-testimony-jan-6.

256 This time it was: "Capitol Buildings and Grounds," Government Printing Office, https://www.govinfo.gov/content/pkg/CDIR-1997-06-04/pdf/CDIR-1997-06-04-CAPITOL .pdf, 11.

256 **Only Cheney and George:** *Select Committee to Investigate the January 6th Attack on the U.S. Capitol*, Hutchinson interview.

257 **"present recently obtained evidence":** Jacqueline Alemany and Josh Dawsey, "Jan. 6 Committee Announces Surprise Tuesday Hearing, Offers Few Details," *Washington Post*, June 27, 2022, https://www.washingtonpost.com/national-security/2022/06/27/jan-6-committee -announces-surprise-tuesday-hearing-offers-few-details/.

258 **That evening, Liz Horning:** *Select Committee to Investigate the January 6th Attack on the U.S. Capitol*, Hutchinson interview, 12.

CHAPTER TWENTY-SEVEN

264 **He called a meeting:** Email calendar invite for August 1, 2022, "Search Warrant Discussion," Case 9:23-cr-80101-AMC Motion entered 4/22/2024, Exhibit 1, 170.

268 **"You are way out of line":** David Rohde, "Inside the Bitter Personal Battle Between Top FBI and DOJ Officials Over Mar-a-Lago," NBC News, September 3, 2024, https://www.nbcnews .com/politics/bitter-personal-battle-top-fbi-doj-officials-mar-lago-rcna169067.

268 **then made things worse:** Callie Patteson, "Trump and His Family Watched FBI Raid on Security Footage, Lawyer Claims," *New York Post*, August 12, 2022, https://nypost.com/2022 /08/12/trump-family-watched-fbi-raid-on-security-footage-lawyer/.

268 **he issued a lengthy statement:** "Trump: 'Mar-a-Lago Home Under Siege, Raided by FBI,'" Associated Press, August 8, 2022, https://www.cbsnews.com/miami/news/trump-says-mar-a -lago-home-under-siege-raided-by-fbi/.

268 **It accused Democrats:** Kaitlan Collins et al., "FBI Executes Search Warrant at Trump's Mar-a-Lago in Document Investigation," August 9, 2022, https://www.cnn.com/2022/08/08 /politics/mar-a-lago-search-warrant-fbi-donald-trump/index.html.

269 **"It is prosecutorial misconduct":** Donald J. Trump, Truth Social post, August 8, 2022, 6:51 p.m., https://truthsocial.com/@realDonaldTrump/posts/108789700493889917.

272 **In western Pennsylvania:** "Man Arrested for Making Threats of Violence Against FBI," U.S. Department of Justice, press release, August 15, 2022, https://www.justice.gov/opa/pr/man -arrested-making-threats-violence-against-fbi.

272 **Beginning after the Mar-a-Lago search:** Alex Horton et al., "Gunman in FBI Attack Was Navy Veteran Who Once Handled Classified Info," *Washington Post*, August 12, 2022, https:// www.washingtonpost.com/nation/2022/08/12/fbi-cincinnati-ricky-shiffer/.

273 **"As I'm sure you can appreciate":** "FBI Director Christopher Wray Addresses Search of Trump's Mar-A-Lago Home," 9News, YouTube, https://www.youtube.com/watch?v=Uats AO5Pc3k.

274 **"Law enforcement is a shield":** Perry Stein, Carol D. Leonnig, Rosalind S. Helderman, and John Wagner, "Trump Seeks Special Master to Review Seized Mar-a-Lago Materials," *Washington Post*, August 22, 2022, https://www.washingtonpost.com/national-security/2022/08 /22/fbi-search-trump-affidavit/.

274 **parts of the FBI affidavit:** Amber Phillips and Aaron Black, "Read the Partially Redacted Mar-a-Lago Search Affidavit, Annotated," *Washington Post*, August 26, 2022, https://www .washingtonpost.com/politics/interactive/2022/full-mar-a-lago-search-affidavit-annotated/.

277 **Within another ten days:** "Affidavit in Support of an Application Under Rule 41 for a Warrant to Search and Seize," U.S. District Court, Southern District of Florida, September 12, 2022, https://www.justsecurity.org/wp-content/uploads/2022/09/just-security-fbi-mar-a-lago -afidavit-with-fewer-redactions-less-redacted.pdf.

CHAPTER TWENTY-EIGHT

280 **communications on Rudy Giuliani's phone:** Kara Scannell, "Feds End Ukraine-Related Foreign Lobbying Investigation into Rudy Giuliani Without Filing Charges," CNN, November 14, 2022, https://www.cnn.com/2022/11/14/politics/rudy-giuliani-investigation-ends.

280 **"I know what I'm going to do":** Shane Goldmacher, "Democratic Group Says Trump Is Breaking Campaign Law by Not Declaring for 2024," *New York Times*, March 14, 2022, https://www.nytimes.com/2022/03/14/us/politics/trump-campaign-fec-violation.html.

281 **Garland's boss also showed no signs:** Mark Leibovich, "So Much for Biden the Bridge President," *The Atlantic*, September 21, 2023, https://www.theatlantic.com/politics/archive/2023/09/biden-reelection-transition-president/675395/.

281 **Title 28, Part 600:** "Part 600—General Powers of Special Counsel," Code of Federal Regulations, National Archives, https://www.ecfr.gov/current/title-28/chapter-VI/part-600.

282 **Smith rebuffed criticism:** Charlie Savage, "Justice Dept. Is Criticized as Corruption Cases Close," *New York Times*, December 20, 2010, https://www.nytimes.com/2010/12/21/us/politics/21justice.html?searchResultPosition=1.

285 **the team stress-tested:** Carol D. Leonnig et al., "Trump Loyalist Kash Patel Questioned Before Mar-a-Lago Grand Jury," *Washington Post*, November 3, 2022, https://www.washingtonpost.com/national-security/2022/11/03/kash-patel-grand-jury-trump/.

290 **Sources said the attorney general:** "Appointment of Special Counsel," U.S. Department of Justice, press release, November 18, 2022, https://www.justice.gov/archives/opa/pr/appointment-special-counsel-0.

CHAPTER TWENTY-NINE

294 **The special counsel's requests:** Amy Gardner et al., "Justice Dept. Subpoenas Ariz., Mich, Wis. Officials in Trump Jan. 6 Probe," *Washington Post*, December 6, 2022, https://www.washingtonpost.com/politics/2022/12/06/jack-smith-trump-communications-subpoenas/.

297 **Trump claiming after the Mar-a-Lago search:** Donald J. Trump, Truth Social, August 12, 2022, 2:19 p.m., https://truthsocial.com/@realDonaldTrump/posts/108811278444540886.

308 **Several said they had signed:** Sudiksha Kochi, "Republicans Are Trying to Take the Trump Fake Electors Narrative and Tie It to the Democrats," *USA Today*, September 10, 2023, https://www.usatoday.com/story/news/politics/2023/09/10/how-trump-and-his-allies-fake-electors-bid-compares-to-a-1960-case/70703750007/.

308 **a Republican in Pennsylvania:** *Final Report on the Special Counsel's Investigations and Prosecutions*, Office of Special Counsel, Department of Justice, January 7, 2025, https://www.justice.gov/storage/Report-of-Special-Counsel-Smith-Volume-1-January-2025.pdf, 14.

309 **"Did anyone ever inform you":** *Final Report on the Special Counsel's Investigations and Prosecutions*, 14.

309 **Smith's team also learned:** *United States of America v. Donald J. Trump*, U.S. District Court for the District of Columbia, August 1, 2023, https://www.justice.gov/storage/US_v_Trump_23_cr_257.pdf.

309 **Trump continued to communicate:** *United States of America v. Donald J. Trump*.

309 **Smith's team discovered that on December 13:** *United States of America v. Donald J. Trump*.

309 **On the evening of December 14:** *United States of America v. Donald J. Trump*.

310 **Smith had early on asked:** *Select Committee to Investigate the January 6th Attack on the U.S. Capitol*, interview of Cassidy Hutchinson, U.S. House of Representatives, June 20, 2022,

https://www.govinfo.gov/content/pkg/GPO-J6-TRANSCRIPT-CTRL0000928884/pdf/GPO
-J6-TRANSCRIPT-CTRL0000928884.pdf.

310 **some of his supporters:** *Select Committee to Investigate the January 6th Attack on the U.S.
Capitol*, Hutchinson interview.

310 **She testified that she overheard:** Jonathan Allen, "'They're Not Here to Hurt Me': Former
Aide Says Trump Knew Jan. 6 Crowd Was Armed," NBC News, June 28, 2022, https://www
.nbcnews.com/politics/congress/jan-6-panel-looks-trump-white-house-cassidy
-hutchinson-testimony-rcna35550.

313 **They hailed from the same generation:** Benjamin Weiser, "Top Terror Prosecutor Settles into
a Familiar Role," *New York Times,* January 12, 2010, https://www.nytimes.com/2010/01/13
/nyregion/13prosecutor.html.

CHAPTER THIRTY

316 **He hadn't been there:** Charlie Savage, "'Deeply Problematic': Experts Question Judge's Inter-
vention in Trump Inquiry," *New York Times,* September 5, 2022, https://www.nytimes.com
/2022/09/05/us/trump-special-master-aileen-cannon.html.

318 **CNN reporters surprised many others:** Kaitlan Collins et al., "Federal Prosecutors Using a Second Grand Jury in Florida as Part of Trump Classified Documents Probe," CNN,
June 6, 2023, https://www.cnn.com/2023/06/06/politics/florida-grand-jury-mar-a-lago-trump
-documents/index.html.

319 **"The corrupt Biden Administration":** Donald J. Trump, Truth Social post, June 8, 2023, 7:21
p.m., https://truthsocial.com/@realDonaldTrump/posts/110511161240386878.

319 **"I AM AN INNOCENT MAN!":** "Statement by Donald J. Trump, 45th President of the United States," June 8, 2023, https://www.donaldjtrump.com/news/87eafc38-d56b-4400-967e
-6d33e8f89a59.

320 **Trump had earlier published a video:** "Donald Trump Vlog: Statement on Indictment—
June 8, 2023," Roll Call, https://rollcall.com/factbase//trump/transcript/donald-trump-vlog
-indictment-statement-palm-beach-florida-june-8-2023/.

321 **He reposted a story:** "Donald Trump Vlog: Statement on Indictment—June 8, 2023."

321 **From the cocoon of the motorcade:** Daniel Baldwin, Twitter, June 13, 2023, 1:48 pm, https://
x.com/baldwin_daniel_/status/1668677077531238402/photo/1.

321 **After whisking him inside, U.S. Marshals:** Shayna Jacobs et al., "Trump Arraigned, Pleads
Not Guilty To 37 Classified Documents Charges," *Washington Post,* June 13, 2023, https://
www.washingtonpost.com/national-security/2023/06/13/trump-court-miami-indictment/.

322 **At a Cuban coffee shop:** Jacobs et al., "Trump Arraigned, Pleads Not Guilty to 37 Classified
Documents Charges." Video is available at https://www.facebook.com/watch/?v=132398918
1809051.

322 **had pushed a "fake narrative":** Robert Draper, "Far Right Pushes a Through-the-Looking-
Glass Narrative on Jan. 6," *New York Times,* June 23, 2023, https://www.nytimes.com/2023
/06/23/us/politics/jan-6-trump.html.

322 **Sitting beside Clark was Ed Martin:** "House Republican Hearing on Investigations and Prosecutions for January 6 Attack on the U.S. Capitol," C-SPAN, June 16, 2023, https://www
.c-span.org/program/public-affairs-event/house-republican-hearing-on-investigations-and
-prosecutions-for-january-6-attack-on-the-us-capitol/628876.

325 **In a moment with family members:** Katherine Faulders et al., "Bombshell Immunity Filing

Details Trump's Alleged 'Increasingly Desperate' Bid to Overturn 2020 Election," ABC News, October 2, 2024, https://abcnews.go.com/US/bombshell-special-counsel-filing-includes-new-allegations-trumps/story?id=114409494.

326 **"Can you believe I lost":** Ashley Parker, "Jan. 6 Hearing Shows Trump Knew He Lost," *Washington Post*, October 14, 2022, https://www.washingtonpost.com/national-security/2022/10/14/trump-knew-he-lost-jan-6/.

326 **he planted an early flag:** *United States of America v. Donald J. Trump*, U.S. District Court for the District of Columbia, August 1, 2023, https://www.justice.gov/storage/US_v_Trump_23_cr_257.pdf.

CHAPTER THIRTY-ONE

327 **Donald Trump stood in a federal courtroom:** Tom Jackman et al., "Trump Pleads Not Guilty to Charges That He Plotted to Overturn Election," *Washington Post,* August 3, 2023, https://www.washingtonpost.com/dc-md-va/2023/08/03/trump-court-appearance-dc-indictment/.

328 **"I seem to check a lot of boxes":** "Judge Tanya Chutkan 'Developed a Think Skin' to Overcome Race-Based Comments, United States Courts, February 24, 2022, https://www.uscourts.gov/data-news/judiciary-news/2022/02/24/judge-tanya-chutkan-developed-a-thick-skin-overcome-race-based-comments.

328 **She would need it with Trump:** *United States of America v. Donald J. Trump*, U.S. District Court for the District of Columbia, Trump Gag Order Motion, September 15, 2023, https://www.documentcloud.org/documents/23979181-trumpgagmot0912523/.

329 **the day after his arraignment:** Kyle Cheney and Josh Gerstein, "Feds Alert Judge to Trump's "If You Go After Me, I'm Coming After You!' Post," *Politico*, August 4, 2023, https://www.politico.com/news/2023/08/04/feds-alert-judge-to-trumps-if-you-go-after-me-im-coming-after-you-post-00109944.

329 **"If Trump doesn't get elected":** "Alvin Woman Admits to Death Threats Against Public officials," U.S. Attorney's Office, Southern District of Texas, press release, November 13, 2024, https://www.justice.gov/usao-sdtx/pr/alvin-woman-admits-death-threats-against-public-officials.

329 **Trump didn't soften his attacks:** Kyle Cheney, "Trump Jabs at Judge in Election Case, Testing Warning Against 'Inflammatory' Statements," *Politico*, August 14, 2023, https://www.politico.com/news/2023/08/14/trump-inflammatory-comments-judge-chutkan-00111041.

329 **In a late August hearing:** *United States of America v. Donald J. Trump*, Transcript of Status Hearing before the Honorable Tanya S. Chutkan, U.S. District Court for the District of Columbia, August 28, 2023, https://storage.courtlistener.com/recap/gov.uscourts.dcd.258148/gov.uscourts.dcd.258148.38.0.pdf, 4.

329 **"The public has an interest":** *United States of America v. Donald J. Trump.*

330 **"This is not about":** Carrie Johnson and Ryan Lucas, "Judge Imposes Partial Gag Order Against Trump in Election-Interference Case," NPR, October 16, 2023, https://www.npr.org/2023/10/16/1205769475/trump-gag-order.

330 **At the same time:** *United States of America v. Donald J. Trump*, Motion to Dismiss Indictment Based on Presidential Immunity, U.S. District Court for the District of Columbia, October 5, 2023, https://storage.courtlistener.com/recap/gov.uscourts.dcd.258148/gov.uscourts.dcd.258148.74.0_1.pdf, 1.

331 **"We have a judicial process":** "Trump Attorneys Argue Against Constitutionality of Impeachment Trial," CNN, February 9, 2021, https://transcripts.cnn.com/show/se/date/2021-02-09/segment/10.

331 *Slate* **magazine published:** Jermey Stahl, "The Most 'Heads I Win, Tails You Lose' Trump Argument Ever," *Slate*, October 6, 2023, https://slate.com/news-and-politics/2023/10/trump-jan-6-judge-chutkan-legal-fail.html.

332 **"above average intelligence":** Michael D. Shear and Peter Baker, "Comey, in Interview, Calls Trump 'Morally Unfit' and 'Stain' on All Around Him," *New York Times*, April 15, 2018, https://www.nytimes.com/2018/04/15/us/politics/comey-interview-trump.html.

332 **"novel approach to immunity":** *United States of America v. Donald J. Trump*, Government's Response in Opposition to Defendant's Motion to Dismiss on Presidential Immunity, U.S. District Court for the District of Columbia, October 19, 2023, https://storage.courtlistener.com/recap/gov.uscourts.dcd.258149/gov.uscourts.dcd.258149.109.0.pdf, 1.

332 **Chutkan sided with prosecutors:** *United States of America v. Donald J. Trump*, Memorandum Opinion, U.S. District Court for the District of Columbia, December 1, 2023, https://storage.courtlistener.com/recap/gov.uscourts.dcd.258149/gov.uscourts.dcd.258149.171.0.pdf.

332 **Trump's legal team:** Alan Feuer, "Federal Judge Rejects Trump's Immunity Claims in Election Case," *New York Times*, December 1, 2023, https://www.nytimes.com/2023/12/01/us/politics/trump-chutkan-immunity.html.

334 **On January 9 a three-judge panel:** "Federal Court Hears Arguments on Whether Trump Is Immune from Prosecution," PBS, January 9, 2023, https://www.pbs.org/newshour/politics/donald-trump-appears-in-court-as-judges-hear-arguments-on-whether-hes-immune-from-prosecution.

334 **As January turned to February:** Kyle Cheney and Josh Gerstein, "As Judges Mull Presidential Immunity, Trump Reaps the Benefits of Delay," *Politico*, January 31, 2024, https://www.politico.com/news/2024/01/31/trump-trial-immunity-delay-00138688.

334 **the appeals court issued:** *United States of America v. Donald J. Trump*, U.S. Court of Appeals for the District of Columbia, February 6, 2024, https://storage.courtlistener.com/recap/gov.uscourts.cadc.40415/gov.uscourts.cadc.40415.1208593677.0_3.pdf.

334 **Roberts sent a private message:** Jodi Kantor and Adam Liptak, "How Roberts Shaped Trump's Supreme Court Winning Streak," *New York Times*, September 15, 2024, https://www.nytimes.com/2024/09/15/us/justice-roberts-trump-supreme-court.html.

335 **Less than a week later:** *Donald J. Trump v. United States*, Certiorari Granted, February 28, 2024, https://www.supremecourt.gov/orders/courtorders/022824zr3_febh.pdf.

336 **"He was looking forward for years":** "Trump Says Judge Won't Let Him Go to Barron's Graduation Due to Hush Money Trial," YouTube, April 15, 2024, https://www.youtube.com/watch?v=s9v3iaX_pRk.

336 **A couple of days later:** Melissa Goldin, "Trump Says New York Judge Won't Let Him Attend Son's Graduation, No Ruling Has Been Made," Associated Press, April 16, 2024, https://apnews.com/article/fact-check-trump-trial-judge-graduation-barron-393373584079.

337 **Trump's team liked to point:** Adam Liptak, "Trump's Claim That He Can't Be Prosecuted Collides with Precedents," *New York Times*, October 12, 2023, https://www.nytimes.com/2023/10/12/us/politics/trump-immunity-supreme-court.html.

337 **argued a Nixon case:** Ann E. Marimow, "Supreme Court Seems Poised to Allow Trump Jan. 6 Trial, but Not Immediately," *Washington Post*, April 25, 2024, https://www.washingtonpost.com/national-security/2024/04/25/supreme-court-oral-arguments-trump-immunity/.

337 **"closest historical analogue":** *Donald J. Trump v. United States of America*, Brief for the United States, Supreme Court of the United States, April 2024, https://www.supremecourt .gov/DocketPDF/23/23-939/306999/20240408191803801_United%20States%20v .%20Trump%20final%20for%20filing.pdf.

338 **From the first sentence:** *Donald J. Trump v. United States*, Transcript of Oral Arguments before the Supreme Court, April 25, 2024, https://www.supremecourt.gov/oral_arguments /argument_transcripts/2023/23-939_3fb4.pdf.

338 **Dreeben, in his opening:** *Donald J. Trump v. United States*, Transcript of Oral Arguments before the Supreme Court.

338 **The back-and-forth that followed:** *Donald J. Trump v. United States*, Transcript of Oral Arguments before the Supreme Court.

339 **By the end of the hearing:** *Donald J. Trump v. United States*, Transcript of Oral Arguments before the Supreme Court.

340 **"*The nature of Presidential power*":** *Trump v. United States*, Certiorari to the U.S. Court of Appeals for the District of Columbia Circuit, July 1, 2024, https://www.supremecourt.gov /opinions/23pdf/23-939_e2pg.pdf, 1.

340 **The decision, authored by Chief Justice Roberts:** *Trump v. United States*, Certiorari to the U.S. Court of Appeals for the District of Columbia Circuit.

342 **Some Justice Department alums:** "Reactions and Highlights of the Supreme Court Decision on Trump's Immunity," *New York Times,* July 1, 2024, https://www.nytimes.com/live/2024 /07/01/us/trump-immunity-supreme-court.

342 **Justice Sotomayor, writing for the court's three liberals:** *Trump v. United States*, Certiorari to the U.S. Court of Appeals for the District of Columbia Circuit.

344 **Donald Trump came within an inch:** Carol D. Leonnig et al., "Secret Service Was Told Police Could Not Watch Building Used by Trump Rally Shooter," *Washington Post,* July 17, 2024, https://www.washingtonpost.com/nation/2024/07/17/secret-service-trump-rally-shooting -homeland-security-investigation/.

345 **Judge Cannon shocked the Justice Department:** Charlie Savage, "Cannon's Dismissal of Trump Case Rejects Precedents of Higher Courts," *New York Times,* July 15, 2024, https:// www.nytimes.com/2024/07/15/us/politics/cannons-dismissal-of-trump-case-rejects -precedents-of-higher-courts.html.

CHAPTER THIRTY-TWO

346 **Trump took the stage:** "Transcript of Donald J. Trump's Convention Speech," *New York Times,* July 19, 2024, https://www.nytimes.com/2024/07/19/us/politics/trump-rnc-speech -transcript.html.

347 **Harris picked up the baton:** Kamala Harris, "On January 6," Instagram post, October 3, 2024, https://www.instagram.com/p/DAr67y0OBsl/.

347 **"They weaponized the government":** "Donald Trump Holds a Political Rally in Glendale, Arizona," Factbase, August 23, 2024, https://rollcall.com/factbase/trump/transcript /donald-trump-speech-political-rally-glendale-arizona-august-23-2024.

347 **the classified documents team:** *United States of America v. Donald J. Trump*, Waltine Nauta and Carlos De Oliveira, U.S. Court of Appeals for the Eleventh Circuit, August 26, 2024, https://www.washingtonpost.com/documents/f69099d7-a16a-40bf-9944-1cefabc7100d.pdf ?itid=lk_inline_manual_8.

350 **the new filing described:** *United States of America v. Donald J. Trump,* Superseding Indictment, U.S. District Court of the District of Columbia, August 27, 2024, https://s3.document cloud.org/documents/25075805/new-trump-indictment-in-election-subversion-case.pdf, 1.

350 **"The Defendant had no official":** *United States of America v. Donald J. Trump,* Superseding Indictment, 24.

351 **Chutkan, who had at times:** Spencer S. Hsu et al., "Judge: U.S. Can Lay Out Trump Election Interference Evidence This Month," *Washington Post,* September 5, 2024, https://www.wash ingtonpost.com/national-security/2024/09/05/trump-jan6-election-interference-case -hearing/.

351 **Trump's lawyers alleged:** Aila Slisco, "Donald Trump Hits Back at Jack Smith's Evidence Proposal," *Newsweek,* October 1, 2024, https://www.newsweek.com/donald-trump-hits-back -jack-smith-evidence-proposal-1962357.

351 **a little more than a month:** Alan Feuer and Charlie Savage, "Judge Unseals New Evidence in Federal Case Against Trump," *New York Times,* October 2, 2024, https://www.nytimes.com /2024/10/02/us/politics/trump-jan-6-case-jack-smith-evidence.html.

352 **On Truth Social:** Donald J. Trump, Truth Social post, October 3, 2024, 6:02 p.m., https:// www.trumpstruth.org/statuses/26970.

352 **He settled on the phrase:** Kristen Altus, "Former President Trump Calls the 'Enemy from Within' More Dangerous Than Any Foreign Entity," FOX News, October 13, 2024, https:// www.foxnews.com/media/former-president-trump-calls-enemy-within-more-dangerous -any-foreign-entity.

352 **"They are so bad":** Lisa Lerer and Michael Gold, "Trump Escalates Threats to Political Opponents He Deems the 'Enemy,'" *New York Times,* October 15, 2024, https://www.nytimes .com/2024/10/15/us/politics/trump-opponents-enemy-within.html.

352 **In a series of social media posts:** Donald J. Trump, Truth Social post, October 25, 2024, https://truthsocial.com/@realDonaldTrump/posts/113369255491639591.

353 **Two days after the election:** Mark Paoletta, X, November 7, 2024, 2:30 p.m., https://x.com /MarkPaoletta/status/1854607439922184513.

354 **Ohio Rep. Jim Jordan:** "Chairman Jordan and Rep. Loudermilk Demand Jack Smith Preserve Records Related to His Politicized Prosecutions of President Trump," House Judiciary Committee, press release, November 8, 2024, https://judiciary.house.gov/media/press-releases /chairman-jordan-and-rep-loudermilk-demand-jack-smith-preserve-records-related.

354 **For his part, Smith that day:** "Read the Special Counsel Filing," *New York Times,* November 8, 2024, https://www.nytimes.com/interactive/2024/11/08/us/politics/smith-jan-6-filing .html.

354 **"Those employees who engage":** Sarah N. Lynch, "Trump Transition Official Warns Justice Dept Staff Against 'Resistance,'" Reuters, November 11, 2024, https://www.reuters.com /default/trump-transition-official-warns-justice-dept-staff-against-resistance-2024-11-11/.

354 **Trump delivered a rebuke:** Isaac Arnsdorf and Josh Dawsey, "Trump Picks Gaetz and Gabbard for Top Jobs, Daring Senate GOP to Defy Him," *Washington Post,* November 13, 2024, https://www.washingtonpost.com/politics/2024/11/13/trump-matt-gaetz-ag-gabbard/.

355 **Standing in a crowd:** "Trump Campaign News Conference on Pennsylvania Vote Count," C-SPAN, November 5, 2020, https://www.c-span.org/program/campaign-2020 /trump-campaign-news-conference-on-pennsylvania-vote-count/556190.

355 **Bondi vowed that Republicans:** Alexandra Hutzler, "What Pam Bondi, Trump's New AG Pick, Has Said about Investigating DOJ Prosecutors," ABC News, November 22, 2024.

356 **lacked experience as an agent:** Carol Leonnig and Philip Rucker, *I Alone Can Fix It: Donald J. Trump's Catastrophic Final Year* (Penguin Press, 2021).

356 **Their cases, their witnesses:** *United States of America v. Donald J. Trump*, Government's Motion to Dismiss, U.S District Court for the District of Columbia, November 25, 2024, https://www.documentcloud.org/documents/25402447-jack-smith-filing-nov-25/.

358 **eradication of "government tyranny":** Kash Pramod Patel, *Government Gangsters: The Deep State, the Truth, and the Battle for Our Democracy* (Post Hill Press, 2023).

CHAPTER THIRTY-THREE

363 **That included members:** Brian Klaas, "Trump Floats the Idea of Executing Joint Chiefs Chairman Milley," *The Atlantic*, September 2023, https://www.theatlantic.com/ideas/archive/2023/09/trump-milley-execution-incitement-violence/675435/.

364 **"Never again will the immense power":** "The Inaugural Address," White House, January 20, 2025, https://www.whitehouse.gov/remarks/2025/01/the-inaugural-address/.

365 **The forty-seventh president and his designees:** "2025 Donald J. Trump Executive Orders," Federal Register, https://www.federalregister.gov/presidential-documents/executive-orders/donald-trump/2025.

365 **Within the hour, he issued:** Jim Clapper et al., "Public Statement on the Hunter Biden Emails," October 19, 2020, https://www.politico.com/f/?id=00000175-4393-d7aa-af77-579f9b330000.

367 **Martin would sign off:** "Bar Complaint Against Edward Martin," The65Project, February 6, 2025, https://the65project.com/bar-complaint-against-edward-martin/.

369 **Patel had asked him:** Senator Dick Durban, letter to DOJ Inspector General Michael E. Horowitz, U.S. Senate, Committee on the Judiciary, February 11, 2025, https://www.judiciary.senate.gov/imo/media/doc/2025-02-11%20RJD%20Letter%20to%20DOJ%20OIG%20re%20Patel%20Allegations.pdf.

371 **It was a hero's welcome:** Walter Morris et al., "Hero's Welcome: Pardoned Jan. 6 Inmates Released from DC Jail to Cheers," NBC News, January 22, 2025, https://www.nbcwashington.com/news/local/heros-welcome-pardoned-jan-6-inmates-released-from-dc-jail-to-cheers/3822099/.

372 **then sent a memo:** Hugo Lowell, "Trump Personally Ordered Firings of Special Counsel Prosecutors," *Guardian*, February 4, 2025, https://www.theguardian.com/us-news/2025/feb/04/trump-jack-smith-special-counsel-prosecutors-firings.

373 **Like a few others who were fired:** Ray Husler, "I'm a Career Prosecutor. Trump Fired Me, but I Know What I Did for the U.S.," *Washington Post*, February 12, 2025, https://www.washingtonpost.com/opinions/2025/02/12/trump-fired-prosecutors-military-spouses/.

379 **But in congressional testimony:** U.S. House Committee on the Judiciary, interview of Jennifer Leigh Moore, June 2, 2023, https://judiciary.house.gov/sites/evo-subsites/republicans-judiciary.house.gov/files/evo-media-document/2023_06_02_Moore%20Transcript2_Redacted.pdf.

379 **Like so many MAGA-world claims:** Ken Dilanian et al.," Senior FBI Official Forcefully Resisted Trump Administration Firings," NBC News, February 1, 2025, https://www.nbcnews.com/politics/national-security/senior-fbi-official-forcefully-resisted-trump-administration-firings-rcna190301.

CHAPTER THIRTY-FOUR

385 **"Now, I haven't seen the gravity":** Joe Anuta, "Trump Says He Is Open to Pardoning Eric Adams," *Politico*, December 16, 2024, https://www.politico.com/news/2024/12/16/trump -open-to-pardoning-eric-adams-00194522.

386 **city residents read with disbelief:** "New York City Mayor Eric Adams Charged with Bribery and Campaign Finance Offenses," U.S. Attorney's Office, Southern District of New York, press release, September 26, 2024, https://www.justice.gov/usao-sdny/pr/new-york-city -mayor-eric-adams-charged-bribery-and-campaign-finance-offenses.

386 **After Trump's election in November:** Maggie Haberman et al., "How New York's Mayor Wooed Donald Trump," *New York Times*, March 15, 2025, https://www.nytimes.com/2025 /03/15/us/politics/eric-adams-new-york-mayor-trump.html.

388 **They also had such compelling evidence:** "Read Former Acting U.S. Attorney Danielle Sasson's Resignation Letter," *Washington Post*, March 5, 2025, https://www.washingtonpost .com/national-security/2025/03/05/sassoon-resignation-letter-text-sdny-eric-adams/.

389 **Sassoon said that Bove's order:** "Read Former Acting U.S. Attorney Danielle Sassoon's Resignation Letter."

389 **Sassoon used Bondi's own words:** "Restoring the Integrity and Credibility of the Department of Justice," U.S. Department of Justice, February 5, 2025, https://www.justice.gov/ag/media /1388506/dl?inline.

397 **At the time, PIN was moving steadily:** Perry Stein and Marianna Sotomayor, "Rep. Henry Cuellar Accused of Taking Bribes from Azerbaijan, Mexican Bank," *Washington Post*, May 3, 2024, https://www.washingtonpost.com/national-security/2024/05/03/henry-cuellar-indicted -bribery-azerbaijan-mexico/.

397 **PIN attorneys were also slated:** Spencer S. Hsu, "Admiral's Romance with Pentagon Official Could Be Central in Bribery Case," *Washington Post*, July 23, 2024, https://www.washington post.com/dc-md-va/2024/07/23/admiral-burke-navy-bribery-case-nextjump/.

399 **News of their internal drama:** Barb McQuade, X, February 14, 2025, 11:01 a.m., https://x.com /BarbMcQuade/status/1890431228085473411.

400 **"any assistant U.S. attorney would know":** Eric Columbus, X, February 14, 2025, 11:02 a.m., https://x.com/EricColumbus/status/1890431363888648385.

CHAPTER THIRTY-FIVE

403 **He was now hosting:** Hanna Arhirova et al., "Trump Says Zelenskyy Is Coming to the White House to Sign US-Ukraine Critical Minerals Deal," Associated Press, February 28, 2025, https://apnews.com/article/russia-ukraine-war-trump-economic-deal-faf1ff881802c 923370053e539ec26e4.

403 **White House aides filmed:** "Trump Staffers Load Boxes onto Air Force One Containing Materials Taken from Mar-a-Lago," Fox News, February 25, 2025, https://www.foxnews.com /video/6369466565112.

404 **"The Department of Justice has just returned":** Victor Nava, "Trump Celebrates Return of 'Boxes' Seized by Ex-Special Counsel Jack Smith—Plans to Put Them in His Presidential Library," *New York Post*, February 28, 2025, https://nypost.com/2025/02/28/us-news/trump -celebrates-return-of-boxes-seized-by-ex-special-counsel-jack-smith-plans-to-put-them -in-his-presidential-library/.

404 **"Jack Smith is no longer":** Zoe Richards et al., "FBI Returns Records from Mar-a-Lago Search to Trump, White House Says," NBC News, February 28, 2025, https://www.nbcnews.com /politics/white-house/white-house-staffers-seen-transporting-trump-boxes-mar-lago -rcna194316.

406 **She praised Trump:** "AG Pam Bondi Speaks at a Law and Order Event at the Department of Justice," DailyMotion, March 14, 2025, https://www.dailymotion.com/video/x9g46hw.

410 **Trump signed the ninetieth executive order:** "Addressing Risks from Paul Weiss," Presidential Actions, The White House, March 14, 2025, https://www.whitehouse.gov/presidential -actions/2025/03/addressing-risks-from-paul-weiss/.

410 **The firm had crossed Trump:** "Addressing Risks from Paul Weiss."

410 **This claim ignored the fact:** Shayna Jacobs et al., "Donald Trump Found Guilty on All Counts in New York Hush Money Trial," *Washington Post,* May 30, 2024, https://www.wash ingtonpost.com/politics/2024/05/30/trump-guilty-verdict-hush-money-trial/.

410 **The order didn't name the firm's partner:** "Addressing Risks from Paul Weiss."

411 **But amid crackdowns:** Ali Watkins and Alan Feuer, "U.S. Says Deportation of Maryland Man Was an 'Administrative Error,'" *New York Times,* April 1, 2025, https://www.nytimes.com /2025/04/01/us/politics/maryland-man-deportation-error-el-salvador.html.

411 **The officer wrote that Garcia was seen:** Katie Mettler et al., "How a Defunct Gang Registry Helped Deliver Kilmar Abrego García to a Salvadoran Prison," *Washington Post,* April 19, 2025, https://www.washingtonpost.com/immigration/2025/04/19/kilmar-abrego-garcia-ice-police -gang-registry/.

412 **two airplanes loaded:** *J.G.G., et al., v. Donald J. Trump, et al.,* Memorandum Opinion, United States District Court for the District of Columbia, April 16, 2025, https://www.courthousenews .com/wp-content/uploads/2025/04/boasberg-probable-cause-contempt-venezuelan -deportations-opinion.pdf.

413 **"Any plane containing":** *J.G.G., et al., v. Donald J. Trump, et al.*

413 **A onetime law school roommate:** Marshall Cohen and Casey Gannon, "'Principled and Fair': Judge Boasberg Had Nonpartisan Record Before Facing Trump's Fury," CNN, March 22, 2025, https://www.cnn.com/2025/03/22/politics/who-is-judge-james-boasberg/index.html.

413 **He temporarily blocked:** Devin Dwyer et al., "Administration Asks Supreme Court to Lift Judge's Block on Deportations Under Alien Enemies Act," ABC News, March 28, 2025, https:// abcnews.go.com/US/administration-asks-supreme-court-lift-judges-block-deportations /story?id=120260082.

413 **"This Radical Left Lunatic":** Donald J. Trump, Truth Social post, March 18, 2025, 9:05 a.m., https://truthsocial.com/@realDonaldTrump/posts/114183576937425149.

414 **Chief Justice John Roberts:** John Fritze, "Chief Justice Roberts Rebukes Trump and GOP Rhetoric about Impeaching Judges," CNN, March 18, 2025, https://www.cnn.com/2025/03 /18/politics/john-roberts-donald-trump-impeachment/index.html.

414 **Bukele traveled from El Salvador:** "Donald Trump Holds a Bilateral Meeting with Nayib Bukele of El Salvador," Factbase, April 14, 2025, https://rollcall.com/factbase/trump /transcript/donald-trump-remarks-bilat-nayib-bukele-el-salvador-april-14-2025/.

416 **"Every Department of Justice attorney is required":** Glenn Thrush, "Justice Dept. Accuses Top Immigration Lawyer of Failing to Follow Orders," *New York Times,* May 4, 2025, https:// www.nytimes.com/2025/04/05/us/politics/justice-dept-immigration-lawyer-leave.html.

416 **$40 million in free legal work:** Michael. S. Schmidt and Matthew Goldstein, "Head of Paul, Weiss Says Firm Would Not Have Survived Without Deal with Trump," *New York Times,* March 23, 2025, https://www.nytimes.com/2025/03/23/us/politics/paul-weiss-firm-trump .html.

416 Eight major firms soon followed: Michael. S. Schmidt et al., "Law Firms Made Deals with Trump. Now He Wants More from Them," *New York Times*, April 16, 2025, https://www.nytimes.com/2025/04/16/us/politics/law-firms-deals-trump.html.

416 penned an anonymous op-ed: "I Am Part of the Resistance Inside the Trump Administration," *New York Times*, September 5, 2018, https://www.nytimes.com/2018/09/05/opinion/trump-white-house-anonymous-resistance.html.

417 turned its polygraph machines: Ellen Nakashima and Hannah Natanson, "FBI, National Security Agencies Using Polygraphs for 'Leak' Hunts," *Washington Post*, April 28, 2025, https://www.washingtonpost.com/national-security/2025/04/28/leak-polygraph-fbi-justice-odni-dhs/.

417 "we're a government ruled by laws": "Read the Full Transcript of Donald Trump's '100 Days' Interview with TIME," *Time*, April 25, 2025, https://time.com/7280114/donald-trump-2025-interview-transcript/.

Index

Abbate, Paul
  background of, 157
  classified documents case, 234, 267–68, 273
  D'Antuono and, 141, 160, 195–96, 267–68
  election of 2024, 353
  January 6 investigation, 141, 157–58, 160,
    195–96, 229
  Trump presidential transition and Driscoll,
    368, 362–65
ABC News, 249–50, 251
Abrego Garcia, Kilmar, 411–12, 414–16
absentee ballots, 74, 163
Adams, Eric, 385–90, 400
Adams, John, 417
Ahmad, Zainab, 15–16, 17, 19, 20
Air Force One, 316, 403
Alcohol, Tobacco, Firearms and Explosives,
    Bureau of (ATF), 108, 114
Alcoke, Matt, 97–98
Alexander, Ali, 83, 139
Alien Enemies Act of 1798, 412, 415
Alito, Samuel, 199, 339
American Civil Liberties Union (ACLU), 409,
    411–12
American Oversight, 163, 221–22
Amsterdam, 288, 293–96
Amtrak, 134
Amundson, Corey, 390–92
Antifa, 108, 162
Arizona, election of 2020, 131–33, 254–55,
    293, 309
Arizona House of Representatives, 254
Arizona Republican Party, 255
Arizona State Attorney General's Office, 133
Assange, Julian, 56–57

Associated Press, 52
Atkinson, Rush, 185
  background of, 153
  January 6 investigation, 153, 187–88, 192,
    196, 200, 201, 259, 281, 317, 319
Au Bon Pain, 102
Axelrod, Matt, 141–42, 152–55, 156
Azerbaijan, 397

Babbitt, Ashli, 138, 147
Bacon, Antoinette "Toni," 393, 396, 399, 400
Ballantine, Jocelyn, 50–51, 67–69, 199
Bank of Egypt, 14–15, 19–20, 23, 34–35
Bannon, Stephen
  Egypt investigation, 17
  election of 2020, 186
  fake electors plot, 222
  January 6 committee, 179–80, 181–82
  McCabe and, 7
Bara, Natalie, 358–59, 383
Barnett, Richard "Bigo," 129
Barr, William P.
  background of, 25
  Comey's firing, 25
  DOJ politicization, 122, 136, 137, 165
  Durham investigation, 281
  Egypt investigation, 33, 36–38, 54
  election of 2020, voter fraud claims, 75–76,
    78–80, 81, 137, 248–49, 251–52, 258, 303
  Flynn case, 41–42, 67–70, 71
  January 6 riots, 115–16, 119, 145
  January 6 committee, 248–49, 251–52, 258
  Liu and, 33, 36–38, 42, 48–49, 51–53
  McCabe case, 41–42, 47
  Mueller special counsel investigation, 25–34

Barr, William P. (*cont.*)
summary of report (Barr memo), 28–32, 33, 222
Patel and, 72, 355–56
resignation of, 89–90, 176
Sherwin and, 70–71, 145
Stone's sentencing, 55, 57–61, 65
Trump and, 24–25, 69, 71–72, 89–90, 251, 258
Wray and, 71–72
Bartiromo, Maria, 162
Bates, John D., 356
Benson, Dan, 238
Benton County Sheriff's Office, 129
Bernstein, Gregory, 302, 307, 324
Biden, Hunter, 365
Biden, Joe
classified documents case, 234–35, 236, 275, 318
DOJ and
Garland AG considerations, 121–22, 123–25
return to "normal order," 136–42, 407
election of 2020, xx, 79, 84–85, 90, 131, 176, 177, 222, 231, 258, 259, 325–26, 352, 355
election of 2024, dropping out, 347
inauguration of, 127, 133–34, 135–36
January 6 investigations, 137–42, 145–46, 164, 179–81, 183
January 6 riots, xx, 109, 111, 114, 115, 121, 125
president-elect, 81, 82, 83, 121–22, 127, 131, 133–34
presidential pardons of, 363
Trump on mental competence of, xvi
Birge, Andrew, 207
Black Lives Matter, 82–83, 100, 142, 161, 251
Black Lives Matter Plaza, 84
Blanche, Todd, 387
election obstruction case, 321, 330–32, 336, 351
Trump's DOJ visit, 406, 407, 408–9
Trump's mug shot, 321
Blue, Matt, 153
Blue Team, 175
Blumenthal, Richard, 376–77
Boasberg, James "Jeb," 333–34, 412, 413–14
Bobb, Christina, 244–45

Bondi, Pam
background of, 354–55
DOJ nomination, 354–55, 371–72, 403
Reuveni's dismissal, 416
Sassoon and Adams case, 388–89
Trump's DOJ visit, 404–9
Booker, Cory, 377
Bove, Emil
Adams case, 385–90, 400
Capitol Siege Section and, 382, 383, 384
Driscoll and Kissane, 363–64, 365, 373–74, 377, 378–80
immigration policy, 367
Public Integrity Section and, 390–401
Trump's DOJ visit, 406
Bowdich, Dave
Egypt investigation, 37–38
January 6 riots, 103–4, 108, 111–13
McCabe case, 45
Bowers, Rusty, 254
Bowser, Muriel E., 102
Bragg, Alvin, 335–36
Bratt, Jay
classified documents case, 216–19, 235–39, 241, 243–47, 284–87, 294–98, 307, 311–13, 315, 318–20, 319
search of Mar-a-Lago, 261–62, 264–66, 269, 275
Meadows's interview, 296–98
Smith special counsel investigation, 294–98, 301–2, 304, 311–13, 315, 318–20
Breyer, Stephen G., 56, 227
Bromwich, Michael, 40, 41, 42, 46
Bukele, Nayib, 413, 414–15
Burck, Bill, 387–88
Bush, George H. W., 286
Bush, George W., 43, 286, 303, 356, 407, 415
Butler, Pennsylvania, assassination attempt on Trump, 344, 346

Cannon, Aileen
classified documents case, 273–74, 284, 295, 312-13, 316, 317, 319–20, 344–49, 356
Cannon, Alex, 213, 274
Capital One, 19
Capital riots of January 6 of 2021. *See* January 6 riots

Capitol Police
January 6 investigation of death of Sicknick, 138, 147
January 6 riots, 101–3, 108–11, 113, 128–29, 198
background to events, 84, 88, 98
January 6 committee, 250–51
Capitol Rotunda, 110–11, 113, 364
Capitol Visitor Center, 322
Carlin, John, 150
Carlson, Tucker, 251, 255
Carter, David O., 225–28
Carving Room, 65
CBS, 70, 148–52
cell phone data, 127–28, 220, 258, 322
Charlottesville United the Right rally, 172, 173
Chávez, Hugo, 85
Cheney, Liz
election of 2024, 280–81
January 6 committee, 171, 175, 197–98, 226–27, 231
public hearings, 249, 250, 253, 255, 257–58
Trump on, 162, 280–81
Cheung, Denise, 372, 381–82
Chicago Law School, 123
Childs, Michelle, 334
Chutkan, Tanya S.
dismissal, 356
fake electors plot, 340–42
immunity claim, 332–34, 338, 340–42, 348, 351–52
pretrial proceedings, 327–34, 335
superseding indictment, 348, 351–52
CIA (Central Intelligence Agency)
Egypt investigation, 14–15, 19–20, 36–37
election of 2020, 90
Plame case, 303
Cianci, Vincent "Buddy," 193
CIMs (case impression memos), 8, 9
Cipollone, Pat, 85, 92, 93, 94, 258
Civil War, xviii, 78, 169, 308
Clark, Jeffrey
attempt to install as attorney general, 177, 296, 307, 350
background of, 91
election of 2020, voter fraud claims, 91–94, 322, 350

January 6 investigation, 177, 178–79, 255
Republican hearing, 322–23
Smith special counsel investigation, 296, 307, 350
Clarke, Jennifer, 390–93
Clarke, Kristen, 125
classified documents case, 211–19, 232–47, 311–20
criminal investigation, 234, 235, 238, 241, 245–47, 263, 265–66, 271, 276, 277–78, 283–87
June 2022 subpoena, 262–63, 274
May 2022 subpoena, 236, 238–43, 261
NARA and criminal referral, 215–16, 218, 219
release of search warrant affidavit, 274–76, 277
search of Mar-a-Lago, 261–78
search warrant considerations, 235, 237, 240–41, 263, 264
Smith special counsel investigation, 296, 298–99, 300, 304, 305–6, 311–20, 319–20, 343, 344–45, 347–50, 403–4
Florida venue, 315–17
grand jury, 318–19, 349–50
surveillance video, 262–63, 264–65
Trump efforts to delay return, 235–36, 239–40
Trump's efforts to conceal documents, 233–34, 246–47, 264–65
Trump's efforts to declassify, 285–86, 297, 306, 343
Trump v. United States, 320–23
Clinton, Bill, xxii, 23
Clinton Foundation, 8
Clinton, Hillary
election of 2016, xvii, 23, 44, 56, 215, 410
El-Sisi meeting, 16
email controversy, 44, 215, 217, 238, 265, 266–67, 413
McCabe and, 4, 8, 9, 44
Starr's investigation, 23
Trump and classified documents case, 240
CNN, 30, 318
January 6 investigation, 179, 180–81, 208–9
McCabe and, 39–43
Monaco's interview, 208–9
Stone's sentencing, 63–64, 65

Code of Federal Regulation, 281–82
Coley, Anthony, 180–81
Collins, Kaitlan, 179–80
Comey, James B., 180, 332
    election of 2016 and Hillary Clinton, xxi, 44
    firing of, 4, 6, 18, 23–24, 25, 40, 43–44,
        71, 357
    McCabe and, 8–9
conspiracy theories, xviii, xxi, 71, 107, 250,
        251–52, 322, 323
Cooney, J. P., 372, 394
    background of, 56
    classified documents case, 298–99, 319–20
    fake electors plot, 132, 205
    holiday party, 357–58
    January 6 investigation, 138–41, 157, 193, 260
    McCabe case, 8, 9, 10–12, 46–47, 54
    Smith special counsel investigation, 293,
        295, 296, 298–302, 304, 323, 324, 338
    Stone's sentencing, 57–61
Corcoran, Evan
    classified documents case, 235–37, 241–47,
        306, 315
        search of Mar-a-Lago, 264–65, 267,
            271–72
Costa, Robert, 176, 186, 224
COVID-19 pandemic, 67–68, 74, 75, 101, 119,
        146, 201, 297, 343, 379
Crabb, John, 151, 153, 186, 192–93, 195, 199,
        222, 228–29
Credico, Randy, 56–57
Crossfire Hurricane, 140, 217, 222–23, 267,
        273, 297
Crosswell, Ryan, 391–92, 394, 395, 399
Cuellar, Henry, 397
Cullen, Richard, 174–75
"Cult of Jack," 305
Cusack, John, 219
cybersecurity, 5, 353, 416

Daniels, Stormy, 335–36
D'Antuono, Steven
    background of, 95
    classified documents case, search of
        Mar-a-Lago, 261–62, 264–68
    fake electors plot, 209–10, 221
    January 6 investigation, 127–28, 141,
        154–55, 160, 187, 192–96

January 6 riots, 103–5, 110, 111–13
    background to events, 95–100, 103
D.C. Circuit Court of Appeals, 122, 168,
        199–200
"deep state," xxi, 355
Delta Force, 360
Demers, John, 94, 135
Democratic Congressional Campaign
        Committee, 173
Democratic National Committee, 23, 108–9,
        155, 187
Dennehy, Jim, 359, 362–63
De Oliveira, Carlos, 244
Detroit News, 203
Digital Forensic Research Lab, 86–87
Director of National Intelligence (DNI), 75,
        214, 351
Dodd, Chris, 179
Dog Park, 300, 323, 344
DOJ. See Justice Department, U.S.
Dominion Voting Systems, 90
Donald J. Trump Presidential Library, 233,
        403–4
Donoghue, Rich
    election of 2020, voter fraud claims, 78–80,
        90–94, 177
    January 6 riots, 111–13, 115
    January 6 committee, 191
Donovan, Margaret, 382–83
Dreeben, Michael, 337, 338–39, 342
Driscoll, Brian, 360–65, 368–69, 373–79,
        380–81, 384
Driscoll, Kevin, 390, 392
DuCharme, Seth, 50–51
Dunham, Timothy, 378
Duree, Timothy "Tad," 307, 308, 310, 372–73
Durham, John, 281, 298

Eastman, John, and fake electors plot, 126–27,
        176, 179, 186
    FBI investigation, 222, 224–28
    Smith special counsel investigation, 294,
        309, 310
Edelstein, Julie
    classified documents case, 237, 284–85, 286,
        305, 306, 312
        search of Mar-a-Lago, 262, 270, 276
    Meadows's interview, 296–98

Smith special counsel investigation, 294–98, 301–2, 305, 306, 312

Edwards, Caroline, 250–51

Egypt, 13–20, 33–38
  CIA source information, 14–15, 19–20, 36–37
  DOJ and, 33–38, 52–54
  Mueller special counsel and Team 10, 16–20, 23, 24, 33–34, 368
  Supreme Court and, 14, 20, 21, 23

Ehrlichman, John, 308

Eisenhower, Dwight D., xxvii, 69

Eisen, Norm, 382, 383

election obstruction case, 323–44
  dismissal of, 356
  immunity dispute, 331–35, 337–44, 349–50, 351
  original indictment and arraignment, 323–26
  pretrial proceedings, 327–35
  superseding indictment, 347–52

election of 1960, 308

election of 2016, xix, xxi, 4, 76
  Comey and Hillary Clinton, xxi, 44
  Egypt investigation, 13–20, 368
  Russian interference in. See Russian interference in election of 2016
  WikiLeaks and, 23, 56–57

election of 2020, xx
  fake electors plot. See fake electors plot
  McLellan and National Archives, 129–33, 207–8
  Pilger and Election Crimes Branch, 73–80
  voter fraud claims, 73–86, 90–94, 126–27, 176

election of 2024, xxii–xxiii, 279–81, 346–47, 352
  Biden drops out, 347
  DOJ and 60-day rule, 279–80
  Republican National Convention, 346–47
  Smith special counsel investigation and, 310, 329, 333
  Trump's announcement, 288–89

Eleventh Circuit Court of Appeals, 284, 295, 349, 356

El Salvador, 412–15

El-Sisi, Abdel Fatah, 14–17, 19, 34, 53

Engel, Bobby, 257

Engel, Steve, 92, 93

Ensign, Drew, 412

Epshteyn, Boris, 222, 294

Espionage Act of 1917, 215, 284, 315, 316

Evangelista, Alessio, 57

Executive Order 14147 (Ending the Weaponization of the Federal Government), 365–66

Executive Order 14237, 410

Facebook, 336, 371

fake electors plot, xviii, 176–79, 203–10, 220–31
  FBI and, 178–79, 220–31, 254–55
  George and DOJ, 176–79, 223–24, 226–27
  McLellan and, 129–33, 206–9, 214–15
  National Archives and, 129–33, 205–8, 220–22, 230
  Nessel and Michigan, 203–7
  Smith special counsel investigation, 293–94, 296, 307–11, 324
  Windom and DOJ, 207–10, 220–31, 254–55

Fauci, Anthony, 363

FBI (Federal Bureau of Investigation). See also specific persons
  classified documents case, 232–47, 318
    search of Mar-a-Lago, 261–78
  Comey's firing, 4
  Counterterrorism Division, 86, 98, 100
  Critical Incident Response Group, 88, 360
  Crossfire Hurricane, 140, 217, 222–23, 267, 273, 297
  Detroit Field Office, 95, 157, 267
  Driscoll and Kissane, 360–65, 368–69, 373–79, 380–81, 384
  Egypt investigation, 17, 18, 35–36, 37–38
  election of 2020, 75–76, 84, 85–88
  fake electors plot, 175, 178–79, 220–31, 254–55
  Flynn case, 66–69
  Guardian program, 87–88, 97, 99–100
  Hostage Rescue Team, 104, 112, 113, 360, 361
  Interview Report Form FD-302, 191–92
  January 6 investigation, 127–29, 136–42, 157–60, 186–88, 192–96, 359
  January 6 riots, 101–16
    aftermath of, 119–20
    background to events, 84–88, 95–100

January 6 riots (*cont.*)
  McCabe case, 4–12, 21–22, 39–42
    grand jury, 5, 7, 9–10
    Wall Street Journal article, 8–9
  National Threat Operations Center, 82, 87
  national tip hotline, 73, 82, 84, 98, 128
  Patel's nomination, 355–57
  Trump and immigration, 367–68
  Wray steps down, 356–57, 361
FBI Agents Association, 358–59, 382–83, 384
Federalist Society, 91, 386
federal prosecution of Trump. *See* election
  obstruction case
Ferguson, Thomas, 369
Ferriero, David, 212, 297
Fifth Circuit Court of Appeals, 33
First Amendment, 86, 97
Fleet, Jamie, 172, 173, 257
Floyd, George, 142, 251
Flynn, Michael
  Egypt investigation, 17
  election of 2020, 83–84, 85–86
  5K letter, 49–51
  sentencing of, 41–42, 66–70
  Turkey lobbying, 49–51
  withdrawal of case, 68–69
FOJs (Friends of Jack), 305
Ford, Gerald, 337
Fourth Circuit Court of Appeals, xix, 386, 415
Fox News, 62, 63, 407
  election obstruction case, 349, 352–53, 355
  election of 2020, 74–75, 77
  January 6 riots, 161, 162
  January 6 committee, 197–98, 251, 255
  search of Mar-a-Lago, 268
Frankenstein Brief, 226–27
Freed, David, 76–77, 78
Freedom Plaza, 98–99

Gaetz, Matt, 322, 354–55
Gardner, Amy, 163
Garland, Merrick
  background of, 122–23
  Biden's attorney general considerations,
    121–26
  classified documents case, 223, 234, 235,
    239–40, 316–17, 319–20
    search of Mar-a-Lago, 270–71, 275–76, 277

  confirmation hearings, 142–46
  DOJ independence and restoring trust,
    xvii–xviii, 164–69
  election obstruction case, 324–25, 339–43
  election of 2020 and Georgia, 167–68
  election of 2024 and 60-day rule, 279–80
  fake electors plot, 203–4, 209, 210, 223,
    229–30
  January 6 investigation, 143–44, 146–49,
    150–51, 154–55, 156, 159–60, 166–70,
    179–81, 183, 185–86, 196, 199–200,
    202, 223, 252–53
  January 6 riots, 124–25
  Principles of Federal Prosecution, 122,
    164, 326
  Sherwin and, 146–49, 150–51, 159
  Smith special counsel investigation
    appointment of, 287–90
    conspiracy charge, 323–26
    guidelines for appointment, 281–82
    meeting, 282–83, 285
  Trump presidential transition and, 353
  Wray and, 146
Garman, Jamie, 230, 303
Garten, Alan, 262–63
Gaston, Molly, 10–11, 12, 65, 338, 372, 394
General Intelligence Service (Egypt), 34
George, Dan, 174–79, 210, 223–24, 226–27, 256
Georgia
  election of 2020, 163, 167–68, 224, 254–55,
    309, 340
    criminal investigation, 163, 167–68, 241
    fake electors plot, 130, 131, 177, 224,
     254–55
    voter fraud claims, xix, 90–94, 126, 177
    runoff elections of 2021, 121, 124
Giuliani, Rudolph W.
  election of 2020, voter fraud claims, 90,
    254, 303
  fake electors plot, 176, 179, 309, 310
  January 6 riots, 186
  Smith special counsel investigation, 280,
    294, 309, 310
Goldston, James, 249–50, 251
Gold Team, 175, 178–79, 223–27
Google, 128
Gore, Al, 286
Gorelick, Jamie, 122

Gor, Sergio, 372
Gorsuch, Neil, 339
Gosar, Paul, 322
Government Gangsters (Patel), 355, 358
Graham, Lindsey, 303
Grassley, Chuck, 375
Graves, Matthew M.
  background of, 184
  fake electors plot, 220–21, 231
  January 6 investigation, 183–88, 192, 196,
    198–202, 209–10, 220, 253–54, 259–60
Griffin, Alyssa Farah, 255–56
Guardian, 87–88, 97, 99–100
Gupta, Vanita, 125, 202
Guzmán, Joaquín "El Chapo," 367–68

Habba, Alina, 404
Hannity, Sean, 198
Harbach, David, 298, 304, 305, 311–12,
  319–20
Harris, Kamala
  election of 2024, 347, 352
  Garland AG considerations, 123–24
  January 6 riots, 108–9
Harris, Marc, 175, 176, 178, 225
Harris Teeter, 300
Harvard University, 5, 33, 123, 386
Hawaii, 308
Heaphy, Tim
  background of, 172–73
  January 6 committee, 172–79, 189–92, 231
  public hearings, 253, 257–59
Heberle, Rob, 390–93
Henderson, Karen, 334
Herschmann, Eric, 85, 93, 126–27, 212–13
Hill, The, 63
Hirshhorn Sculpture Garden, 189
Holder, Eric, 148, 166, 342
Homeland Security, U.S. Department of, 75,
  96, 115, 272–73, 416
"Honors Program," xvii–xviii, xxiii, 215, 216
Horning, Liz, 258
House Ethics Committee, 354
House Judiciary Committee, 354
House Oversight Committee, 215–16
House Select Committee on January 6. *See*
  January 6 committee
Hovakimian, Patrick, 93, 94

Howell, Beryl A., 70, 129, 306
  Egypt investigation, 19–20, 33–35
Hsu, Spencer, 59, 62
Hulser, Ray
  classified documents case, 298–99, 304–5,
    311, 315
  election obstruction case, 324, 338
  Smith special counsel investigation, 296,
    298–99, 300, 304–5, 311, 315, 324, 338
  Trump DOJ and, 372–73, 394
Human Rights Division, 283
Hutchinson, Cassidy, 107
  January 6 committee testimony, 255–59, 310

immigration, xx, 367–68, 411–16
Ingraham, Laura, 161, 197
International Criminal Court, 282
Iran, 298, 306
Iraq war, 303

Jackson, Amy Berman, 57
Jackson, Jesse L., Jr., 184
Jackson, Ketanji Brown, 124
Jackson, Robert H., 10–11
Jacobs, Greg, 224
January 6 commission, proposal for,
  162–63, 164
January 6 investigations, xv, xvi–xvii, xviii,
  136–42, 145–60, 166–70, 179–81,
  280–81, 296. *See also* January 6
  committee; Smith, Jack, special
  counsel investigation
  of FBI, 127–29, 136–42, 157–60, 186–88,
    192–96, 359
January 6 riots, xv, xvi, 101–16, 296
  aftermath of, 115–16, 119–21, 127–34
  authors' reporting on, xx–xxi
  background to events, 81–88, 95–100
  morning of, 102–4
  one-year anniversary of, 202
  Pence and certification of election, 109,
    111–15
  pipe bombs planted, 108–9, 136, 147,
    155, 187
  the riots, 109–15, 161
  Trump's pardon of rioters, 366–67, 371
January 6 committee, 171–82, 197–98, 363
  Bannon subpoena, 179–80, 181–82

January 6 committee (*cont.*)
   Biden's presidential pardons, 363
   congressional hearings, 248–60, 310
      Hutchinson's testimony, 255–59
   DOJ and, 191–92, 230–31
   fake electors plot, 203, 207, 225–28, 230–31,
      254–55, 293–94
   formation and objective, 171–72
   George and, 174–79, 210, 223–24,
      226–27, 255
   Heaphy and, 172–79, 189–92, 231, 253,
      257–59
   Meadows and, 197–98, 249, 255, 258–60
   Smith special counsel and, 299
   Windom and, 252–53
Jed, Adam, 20, 55–56, 58, 59, 64
Jensen, Jeff, 67
Johnson, Ron, 161, 183
Joint Chiefs of Staff, 103, 306, 363
Jones, Alex, 139
Jones, Doug, 121–22
Jones, Jason, 228–29, 264, 266, 267
Jordan, Jim, 171, 354, 369, 370
Justice Department, U.S. (DOJ). *See also*
    specific persons
   Biden and return to "normal order,"
      136–42, 408
   Bondi's nomination, 354–55, 371–72,
      403, 406
   Civil Division, 33, 91, 110, 125, 164
   Civil Rights Division, 125, 416–17
   classified documents case, 216–19, 232–47
   Counterintelligence and Export Control
      Section, 214, 216, 295–96
   Egypt investigation, 13–20, 33–38, 52–54
   Election Crimes Branch, 73–80, 391
   election of 2020, 73–80, 85–88
   fake electors plot, 176–79, 203–10, 214–15,
      254–55
   firing of Capitol Siege Section, 381–84
   Fraud and Public Corruption Section, 5–8,
      53, 56, 58, 184, 214
   Garland and independence, 164–69
   Honors Program, xvii–xvii, xxiii, 216
   Human Rights Division, 283
   immigration policy, xvi, 367–68, 411–16
   January 6 investigation, 136–42, 145–56,
      179–81, 183–88

January 6 riots, 119–20
National Security Division, 33, 50, 148, 153,
      157, 184, 206, 216, 235, 274, 280, 283,
      289–90, 296, 314–16, 379, 380, 405
Office of Legal Counsel, 26, 93
political independence of, xvii–xviii, 6,
      32, 405
Principles of Federal Prosecution, 8, 122,
      164, 326
prosecutors-in-training, xvii–xviii
Public Integrity Section (PIN), 11, 56, 74,
      167–68, 207, 282, 296, 298, 305, 334,
      390–401
60-day rule, 279–80
Stone's sentencing, 55–65
Team R, 15–16, 23–24, 26, 28–32, 410
Trump and. *See* Trump, Donald, DOJ and
Trump's presidential transition,
      353–55
Just Security, 139

Kagan, Elena, 339
Karp, Brad, 416
Katz, Rita, 86–87
Kavanaugh, Brett, 199, 339, 356, 413
Kavanaugh, Chris, 173, 174, 185–86, 187
Keller, John, 390–91, 392
Kelly, John, 44
Kennedy, John F., 172
Kennedy, Robert F., 407
Kent, David, 3–12, 21–22, 41–42
Kerik, Bernard, 186
Kilmeade, Brian, 197–98
Kim Jong-un, 212
Kingsbury, Kendra, 237, 284
King & Spalding, 43
Kinzinger, Adam, 171
Kislyak, Sergey, 66, 68
Kissane, Rob, 361–65, 368–69, 373–78,
      380–81
Klain, Ron, 122, 124–25, 134, 164
Klapper, Matt, 201
"Knowledge of the Falsity," 326, 350–51
Kohler, Alan
   classified documents case, 218–19, 234,
      237–38, 240–41
   search of Mar-a-Lago, 262–71, 273,
      274–77

Kohl, Ken, 153
Kravis, Jonathan
  background of, 56
  resignation of, 64–65
  Stone's sentencing, 53, 55–65
Krebs, Christopher, 416–17
Ku Klux Klan (KKK), 308
Kupec, Kerri, 115–16
Kushner, Jared, 16, 17

Laster, John, 213–14
Lauro, John F., 330–32, 351
Lawfare, 204
Leavitt, Karoline, 356
Lee, Mike, 358
Lenzner, Jonathan, 59, 61, 64, 196, 229
Letter, Doug, 225–26
Levin, Mark, 349
Levi, Edward, 126
Levi, Will, 111–12
Lewinsky, Monica, 23
line attorneys, 5, 35, 37, 165, 307, 324, 391
Little, Jennifer, 241–42
Liu, Jessie
  background of, 33–34
  Egypt investigation, 33–38
  Flynn and, 41–42, 50
  forced departure of, 48–49, 51–53
Los Angeles, immigration raids in, xx
Lucier, Casey, 174–78, 225, 226, 227
Luzerne County, Pennsylvania, 75–79
lynching, 200
Lyons, Derek, 224

McCabe, Andrew
  background of, 39–40
  CNN and, 39–43
  FBI case, 4–12, 21–22
    grand jury, 5, 7, 9–10
    righteous case, 11–12
  forced retirement of, 46–47, 376
  indictment of, 41, 42–44, 47
  September 11 attacks, 40
  Team M, 15–16, 22–23, 30
  Wray and, 43–46
McCarthy, Andrew, 409
McCarthy, Kevin, 115; 134
McConnell, Mitch, 111–12, 115, 122, 140

McCord, Mary, 85–88, 98–100, 382
McCullough, Terry, 172, 173, 257
McDaniel, Ronna, 309
McEnany, Kayleigh, 77
McGahn, Donald F., II, 19
McGuireWoods, 174, 286, 296–97
McHenry, James, 372
Maddow, Rachel, 203, 204–5
Maguire, Jackie, 378
mail-in voting, 74–75, 77–80
Make America Great Again (MAGA), 83,
  98–99, 102, 251, 409–10
Maloney, Carolyn B., 216
Maloney, Sean Patrick, 173
Manafort, Paul, 15–16, 22–23, 30
Mar-a-Lago, 70, 145, 386, 409–10
  classified documents case, 212–13, 215–16,
    223, 232–47, 306–7, 315–16, 367, 370
  FBI search of, 261–78, 357
Marando, Michael, 55–56, 58, 63–64, 65
Marshals, U.S., 13, 14, 33, 99, 114, 321, 329,
  333, 338
Martin, Ed, 322–23, 366–67, 381–82
Massie, Thomas, 159
Mattei, Chris, 382–83
Meadows, Mark
  classified documents case, 212–13, 280,
    286–87
  election of 2020, voter fraud claims, 89,
    92, 93
  January 6 riots, 107
  January 6 committee, 197–98, 249, 255, 258,
    259–60
  Smith special counsel interview, 296–98,
    302–4, 305
Mehta, Amit, 149–51
Mentzer, Greg, 369–70
Merchan, Juan M., 336
Metrick, Jason, 130–31, 205–7
Metropolitan Police Department, 106–7
Michael, Molly, 238–39, 246, 261–62, 265
Michigan, 363
  election of 2020, fake electors plot, 130, 133,
    203–9, 255, 293, 309
  Whitmer kidnapping plot, 95, 148
Midyear Exam, 217
Milhoan, Cathy, 268, 269, 365
Miller, Christopher, 103

Miller, Marshall L., 281, 282
Miller, Stephen, 373–74, 378
Milley, Mark, 305–6, 363
mishandling of documents. *See* classified
    documents case
Mitchell, Cleta, 294
Mnuchin, Steve
  Egypt investigation, 16, 17–18
  Liu and, 48–49
Monaco, Lisa
  appointment as deputy attorney general,
    123, 124, 125
  background of, 123
  classified documents case, 214,
    270–71, 290
  CNN interview, 208–9
  fake electors plot, 207, 208–9, 229–30, 231
  January 6 investigation, 142, 152–57, 166,
    167, 169, 170, 180, 184–88, 193–94, 196,
    200, 201, 259, 290
  Smith special counsel investigation, 281–82,
    290, 324
  Trump presidential transition, 353
Moore, Jennifer, 97, 99
MSNBC, 203, 204–5
MS-13, 415
Mueller, Robert S., III
  Monaco and, 123, 153
  Parkinson's disease of, 27
Mueller special counsel investigation
  Barr's meeting, 25–28
  Egypt probe, 16–20, 25, 33–37, 368
  Flynn and, 49–50, 66
  McCabe case and, 4, 9, 22
  organization of, 15–16
  potential obstruction of justice, 16, 24–27,
    30, 330–31
  report, 24, 28–32
    Barr's summary ("Barr memo"), 29–32,
      33–34, 42, 222–23
  Russian interference and Team R, xxi, 4, 9,
    13–14, 15–16, 18, 22, 23–24, 26, 28–29,
    31, 217, 218, 222–23, 238, 267, 281,
    298, 410
  Smith special counsel and, 311, 330–31
  Stone's sentencing, 56–57
  Team M, 15–16, 22–23, 30
  Team 10, 16–20, 23

  Team 600, 16, 26
  Trump's complaints about, xxi, 4, 9,
    320–21, 387
mug shot of Trump, 321–22
Musk, Elon, 371

National Archives
  classified documents case, 211–19, 232–47,
    262, 286–87
  fake electors plot, 129–33, 205–8,
    220–22, 230
National Bank of Egypt, 14–15, 19–20, 23,
    34–35
National Guard, xvi, 101, 114, 119, 135
Nauta, Walt, 243–44, 246, 263, 294, 307, 406
Nehls, Troy, 110–11
Nessel, Dana, 133, 203–7
Newman, David, 153, 214, 315, 316, 317, 319
New Mexico House of Representatives, 395
Newsmax, 159, 251
New York Times, 120, 122–23, 139, 150,
    282, 335
New York University, 139
Nightline (TV show), 249–50, 251
Nike Air Max Speed Turfs, 155
Nixon, Richard, xvii
  Ford's pardon, 337
  Levi and, 126
  resignation of, 7
  Stone and, 56
  Supreme Court and, 341, 349
  Watergate, 26, 390
Nordwall, Mike, 358–59, 374, 377, 378–79
Norris v. Alabama, xviii
Nunes, Devin, 72

Oath Keepers
  January 6 investigation, 138–39, 141, 147,
    149, 169–70, 187–88, 195
  January 6 riots, 155, 186
    background to events, 81–84, 86–87
  seditious conspiracy charges, 204–5
  Trump presidential pardons of, 366
Obama, Barack
  Eisen and, 382
  El-Sisi and Egypt, 17
  Flynn and, 69
  Kravis and, 56

Monaco and, 123
Trump and, 212, 413
O'Callaghan, Ed, 25–26, 28–29, 31, 42
Olsen, Matthew G.
  background of, 183–84
  classified documents case, 235, 236, 238,
    239–40, 253, 283–87, 314–15, 319
    search of Mar-a-Lago, 262, 264, 266–72,
    275–76
  January 6 investigation, 183–88, 198–202,
    216–19
Ornato, Tony, 106–7, 257

Page, Lisa, 8, 9–10
Palmieri, Marco, 390–93
Pan, Florence, 334
Paoletta, Mark, 353–54
Park Police and January 6, 102, 103, 104–5
Parler, 87, 88, 98
Patel, Kash
  Bara and, 358–59, 383
  Barr and, 72, 355–56
  classified documents case, 285–86
  confirmation hearing, 375, 376–77
  Director's Advisory Team (DAT), 369–72
  Driscoll and Kissane, 361, 368, 369, 371–72,
    374–78
  FBI nomination, 355–57, 403
  Government Gangsters, 355, 358
  the Suspendables, 378–81
  Trump's DOJ visit, 403
Paul, Weiss, Rifkind, Wharton & Garrison,
  410, 416
Pearce, James, I. 305–6, 312, 315, 334, 338
Pellettieri, John, 338
Pelley, Scott, 148–49
Pelosi, Nancy
  January 6 commission proposal,
    162–63, 164
  January 6 riots, 111–12, 115, 129
  January 6 committee, 171–73, 257
Pence, Mike
  January 6 and certification of election, 109,
    111, 113–15, 191, 206, 224, 296, 307, 350
  January 6 committee, 174, 191, 250–51
  Smith special counsel investigation, 296,
    307, 340, 350
  So Help Me God, 307

Pennsylvania and election of 2020, 75–79, 81,
  90, 130, 308–9
Pennsylvania Avenue, 98–99, 101, 109, 110
Pensacola Naval Air Station shooting, 70–71
Pentagon Papers, 308
Perez, Evan, 180–81, 209–9
Peril (Woodward and Costa), 176, 186, 224
Perkins, Dena, 379
Perry, Scott, 91
Philadelphia Convention Center, 78–79
Philadelphia Field Office, 75–76
Philbin, Pat, 93, 94, 212–13
Phillips, Channing, 150, 152–58, 160, 169–70
Pieper, Derek, 240, 262
Pilger, Richard, 73–80, 137
Plame, Valerie, 303
Polite, Kenneth A., Jr., 230, 253
Politico, 203
Pomerantz, Mark, 410
Portland, Oregon, 153–54
Postal Inspection Service, U.S., 221
Potomac River midair collision of 2025, 383–84
Powell, Sidney, 66–67, 85–86, 294
Prelogar, Elizabeth, 324–25, 349
President's Daily Briefs (PDFs), 213–14, 283
Presidential Records Act of 1978, 212, 235
presidential records case. *See* classified
    documents case
Principles of Federal Prosecution, 8, 122,
  164, 326
Proud Boys
  January 6 investigation, 139, 147–48, 150,
    158, 169–70, 187–88, 253–54
  January 6 riots, 106, 109
    background to events, 82–84, 87–88,
    97, 168
  Trump presidential pardons of, 366

QAnon, 380
Quarles, Jim, 26–27, 31

Rabbitt, Brian, 49, 51–52, 61
Raffensperger, Brad, 163
Rahman, Omar Abdel, 199
Raimondi, Marc, 110, 115–16, 149–50
Rasheed, Abdullah, 81–84
Raskin, David, 283–90, 306–7, 312–13, 372
Raskin, Jamie, 253

Ratcliffe, John, 343
Reagan National Airport, 320
Reagan, Ronald, 286, 341, 415
Red Massari, 35–36
Reno, Janet, 123, 199
Republican National Committee (RNC), 108,
    155, 187, 309
Republican National Convention (2024),
    346–47
Reuveni, Erez, 414, 415–16
Reynolds, Brett, 306, 373
Rhee, Jeannie, 23–24, 28–32, 410
Rhodes, Stewart
    January 6, background to events, 81–84
    January 6 investigation, 170
    seditious conspiracy, 201, 204–5
    Trump presidential pardon, 366
Roberts, John
    Barr's swearing in, 24–25
    Egyptian bank case, 20, 21
    election obstruction case, 334–35, 340,
        341, 356
    Trump and impeachment of judges, 414
Romero, Anthony, 409
Rosenberg, Chuck, 40
Rosen, Jeffrey
    as acting attorney general, 42, 89
    Barr's resignation, 89–90
    election of 2020, voter fraud claims, 90–94
    fake electors plot, 177–78
    Flynn case, 50–51
    January 6 investigation, 155–56
    January 6 riots, 103, 108–10, 112–16
    January 6 committee, 191, 249
    Liu's departure, 51–53
    McCabe case, 42
Rosenstein, Rod, 15, 25, 26, 27, 31, 42, 190
Rowland, John, 382
Russian interference in election of 2016,
        xvi–xvii, 4, 9, 13–14, 15–16, 18, 22,
        23–24, 26, 28–29, 31, 217, 218, 238, 281,
        298, 410
    Crossfire Hurricane, 140, 217, 222–23, 267,
        273, 297

Sanctuary Cities Enforcement Working
    Group, 367
SAPs (Special Access Programs), 214

Sassoon, Danielle, 386–89, 396
Sauer, John, 338–39, 341, 414, 415
Scalia, Antonin, 386
Schertler, Dave, 42, 46
Schiff, Adam, 175
Schmitt, Rob, 251
Schoen, David, 331
Schumer, Chuck, 115, 146
Schwartz, Melissa, 40
SCIF (Senstive Compartmented Information
    Facility), 26, 236, 270, 298
Scotten, Hagan, 400
SEAL Team 6, 339, 342
Secret Kitchen, 300, 353
Secret Service
    January 6 riots, 102, 104–5, 106–8, 112,
        114, 257
    search of Mar-a-Lago, 264, 268
    Trump assassination attempt, 344–45
    Trump's DOJ visit, 402–4
sedition, 139, 147–48, 150, 151, 169, 184, 188,
        199–202, 226, 338
Senate Intelligence Committee, 371
Senate Judiciary Committee, 143–45, 146,
        152, 177
    Patel's confirmation hearing, 369, 371–72,
        375, 376–77
Senate, U.S. and January 6 riots, 111–12
September 11 attacks (2001), 26, 33, 40, 163,
        184, 218, 283
Sessions, Jeff, 15, 86, 124
Shafer, David, 255
Shea, Tim
    Egypt case, 53–54
    Flynn case, 68–69, 70
    Liu's departure, 51, 52
    Stone's sentencing, 52–53, 57–61
Sherwin, Michael
    background of, 70–71
    January 6 investigation, 119–20, 127–29,
        136–38, 140, 141, 145–52, 159,
        166–67, 198
    "branches" of, 137–38
    identifying suspects, 127–28,
        136–37
    seditious conspiracy charges, 147–51,
        156, 198
    60 Minutes interview, 148–52, 198

January 6 riots, 105–6, 108, 110
Pensacola Naval Air Station shooting, 70–71
Shields, Kamil, 3–12, 21–22, 41–42
Shry, Abigail Jo, 329
Sicknick, Brian, 138, 147
SITE Intelligence Group, 82, 86–88, 99
60 Minutes (TV show), 148–52
Slate (magazine), 331
Smith, Jack
  background of, 282
  bike accident of, 287–88
  Garland's meeting with, 282–83, 285
  Kravis and, 56
Smith, Jack, special counsel investigation, xix,
    293–345, 408
  announcement of investigation, 290
  appointment of, 287–90
  classified documents case (CDI), 296,
    298–99, 300, 304, 305–6, 311–20, 343,
    344–45, 347–49, 403–4
    Florida venue, 315–17
    grand jury, 318–19, 349–50
  conspiracy to commit fraud charge, 323–26
  election interference case (EI), 293, 295, 296,
    300, 301, 304, 307–8, 323, 354–55
  election obstruction case, 323–44
    dismissal, 356
    immunity dispute, 331–35, 337–38, 342,
      349–50, 351
    Knowledge of the Falsity, 326, 350–51
    pretrial proceedings, 327–35
    superseding indictment, 347–52
  Evidence Summary (ES), 324
  fake electors plot, 293–94, 296, 307–11, 324
  firings of, 372
  five investigations of, 296
  holiday party, 357–58
  interview rules, 302
  key operating principles, 300–302
  management style, 300–302, 304–5
  Trump presidential transition and, 356,
    357–58
So Help Me God (Pence), 307
Sotomayor, Sonia, 339, 342, 344
Southern District of New York, 26, 283,
    379–80, 386–90, 397, 400
Speedy Trial Act, 329–30
Spiro, Alex, 387–88

SSMs (special security measures), 298–99
Starr, Ken, 23
State Democracy Defenders Fund, 382
Stemler, Patty, 200–201
Stepien, Bill, 294
Stern, Gary, 211–14
Stevens, Ted, 67, 282, 398
Stone, Roger
  background of, 56
  election of 2016 and WikiLeaks, 23, 56–57
  indictment of, 24
  January 6 investigation, 139, 141
  January 6 riots, 155, 186
  trial and sentencing of, 52–53, 55–65, 65
Stop the Steal, 83–84, 96, 140, 175, 366
Strzok, Peter, 10
"substantial federal interest," 12
Sullivan & Cromwell, 5
Sullivan, Ed, 398–401
Sullivan, Emmet G., 67, 69
Sundberg, David, 379
Sutherland, George, xviii
SVTC (secure video teleconference), 368–69
Swartz, Bruce, 367–68
SWAT (Special Weapons and Tactics), 72, 101,
    103, 110, 111, 112, 360

Tarrio, Enrique, 97, 366
Tatel, David, 20
Taylor, Michelle, 30–31
Taylor, Miles, 416–17
Telegram, 83
Terwilliger, George, 286–87, 296–98, 303–4
TheDonald.win, 82, 87, 99
Thibault, Timothy, 194, 221, 222
Thomas, Clarence, 345, 349
Thompson, Bennie, 172–73, 181–82,
    231–32, 253
TikTok, 97
Till, Emmett, 200
Toscas, George
  background of, 216
  Biden's inauguration, 135
  classified documents case, 216–19, 238, 239,
    240, 284–85, 290, 314–15
  search of Mar-a-Lago, 262, 264–68,
    275–77
  January 6 investigation, 153–54

Toscas George (*cont.*)
   reassignment of, 367
   Smith special counsel investigation, 290,
      314–15
Tren de Aragua, 411, 412
Trump, Barron, 247, 336
Trump, Donald
   Adams case, 385–90
   assassination attempt on, 344, 346
   Barr and, 24–25, 69, 71–72, 251, 258
      resignation, 89–90
   classified documents case, 212–16, 232–47,
      285–86, 343, 344–45
      efforts to declassify, 285–86, 297, 306, 343
      search of Mar-a-Lago, 261–69
      Smith special counsel investigation,
         315–22, 347–49, 403–4
   conspiracy theories, xxii–xxiii, 71, 107,
      249–50, 251–52, 323
   DOJ and, xiii–xiv, xviii–xxiv, 71–72, 372–73,
      395–96, 409–11
      enemies list, 373–74, 416–17
      Executive Order 14147, 365–66
      Executive Order 14237, 410
      firing of Capitol Siege Section, 381–84
      "Monday massacres," 372
      visit to headquarters, 402–9, 410–11
   election obstruction case, 323–44, 352
      mug shot of, 321–22
   election of 2016, xix, xx, 4
      Egypt investigation, 13–20, 23, 24, 33–38,
         54, 368
   election of 2020, xv, 309, 325–26
      voter fraud claims, 73–86, 90–94, 107,
         126–27, 133, 176, 343
   election of 2024, xviii–xix, 162, 242, 274,
      280–81, 311, 346–47, 352–53
      announcement, 288–89
   fake electors plot, xix, 129–33, 163, 176,
      220–31, 254–55, 340–41
   Flynn and, 69, 71
   immigration policy, xvi, 367–68, 411–16
   impeachments, 121, 134, 139–40, 161–62,
      280, 331, 339, 355
   inauguration of 2025, 364
   January 6 investigations, 139, 140–41, 171,
      280–81

   January 6 riots, xix, xx, 102, 104, 105, 106–9,
      112–14, 130, 161–62, 308
      aftermath, 120–21, 161, 163–64
   January 6 Committee, 175–76, 251
   McCabe case, 6–7, 9, 10, 21–22, 45–46
   presidential pardons of, 366–67, 371
   presidential transition of 2020–2021,
      126–27, 228
   presidential transition of 2024–2025,
      353–56
   Smith and. *See* Smith, Jack, special counsel
      investigation
   Stone and, 55–59, 61–62, 155
   Stormy Daniels scandal, 335–36
Trump, Donald, Jr., 161–62, 198
Trump, Ivanka, 249, 258
Trump, Melania, 243–44, 247
Trump National Doral Miami, 320
Trump National Golf Club Bedminster, 243,
   246–47, 297–98, 305, 307, 315
Trump National Golf Club Washington,
   D.C., 79
Trump Presidential Library, 233, 403–4
Trump rallies, 344, 346, 347
Trump Tower, 18
Trump University, 354–55
Trump v. United States, 320–23
Truth Social, 251, 269, 272, 318, 320–21, 329,
   352, 403–4, 413–14
TS/SCI (top secret/sensitive compartmented
   information), 214, 271–72
Turkey, 49–51
Twenty-Fifth Amendment, 121
Twitter, 116, 133, 219, 308, 340

Ukraine, 121, 355, 403
United Nations General Assembly, 16
United States of America v. Donald J. Trump.
   See election obstruction case
University of Connecticut, 179
University of Virginia, 10, 173, 185, 190
US Code 241, 307–8, 323
US Code 371, 221, 323
US Code 1512, 147–48, 198, 200,
   220–21, 323
US Code 1519, 220
USSC 5K1.1, 49–51

VanDevender, Cecil, 338
Van Grack, Brandon, 50–51, 66–69
Vaughn, Amanda, 132–33
Veltri, Jeff, 379
Venezuela, 85, 411–12, 411–15
Vice, 138–39
Vietnam War, 129, 225
Vincent, Miriam, 131
Virginia and election of 2020, 131–32

Wallace, Chris, 74–75
Wall, Debra Seidel, 236
Wall, Jeff, 93
Wall Street Journal, 8–9
War Room (podcast), 222
Washington, George, 3
Washington Post, xiii, 54, 59–60, 62, 120, 163,
    215–16, 328, 356
WashingtonTunnels.com, 88
Watergate, 4–5, 7, 26, 122, 145, 164, 165, 282,
    340, 341, 390, 407
Weissmann, Andrew, 22–23, 30, 31–32
Wells, Bobby, 358–59, 374, 377, 378–79
Whitaker, Matthew G., 46
Whitehouse, Sheldon, 143–45
White House Situation Room, 270
Whitewater, 23, 194, 356
Whitmer, Gretchen, 95
WikiLeaks, 23, 56–57
Wiles, Susie, 280, 298
Wilkinson, J. Harvie, III, xxiii–xxiv, 386, 415
Wilkins, Robert, 328
Willard Hotel, 139, 176, 186, 193–94,
    195–96, 209
Windom, Thomas
    background of, 190
    classified documents case, 261–62
    fake electors plot, 207–10, 220–21, 227, 229,
        254–55
    January 6 investigation, 185–87, 189–93,
        195–96, 252–53, 258–59
    Meadows and, 259–60, 302–4

Smith special counsel and election
    interference, 296, 302–4, 307–8,
        323, 338
Wisconsin, 133, 293, 310
"witch hunt," xxi, 10, 321, 322
witness tampering, 56, 57
    US Code 1512, 147–48, 198, 200,
        220–21, 323
Wolking, Matt, 78
Wood, John, 175
Woodward, Bob, 176, 186, 224
World Trade Center bombing of 1993, 199
Wray, Christopher A.
    Barr and Trump, 71–72
    classified documents case, 233–34,
        240–41
        search of Mar-a-Lago, 263, 264, 268,
            273–76
    Egypt investigation, 37–38
    election of 2020, 76
    fake electors plot, 228–30
    January 6 investigation, 146, 157, 159–60,
        184, 196
    January 6 riots, 120, 134
    McCabe case, 43–46
    Russia election investigation, 222–23
    steps down, 356–57, 361
    Trump presidential transition, 353

Xinis, Paula, 414

Yates, Sally, 121–22, 173
"Y.M.C.A." (song), 409
Young, Ryan, 378

Zaid, Mark, 383
Zebley, Aaron, 18–19, 26–29, 31
Zelensky, Volodymyr, 355, 403
Zelinsky, Aaron, 55–56, 58, 59, 61, 63–64
Zients, Jeff, 123–24
Zoom, 152, 167
Zucker, Jeff, 42–43